# HOW TO GO RAILWAY MODELLING

# HOW TO GO RAILWAY MODELLING

Norman Simmons

PSL Patrick Stephens, Cambridge

1st edition April 1972
2nd edition June 1975
Reprinted September 1976
3rd edition January 1980
Reprinted August 1980
4th edition September 1981

**British Library Cataloguing in Publication Data**

Simmons, Norman
How to go railway modelling—4th ed.
1. Railroads—Models
2. Models and modelmaking
I. Title
625.1'9    TF197

ISBN 0-85059-557-6

Photoset in 9 pt Plantin Roman
by Manuset Limited, Baldock, Herts. Printed in Great Britain on 100 gsm Fineblade coated cartridge, and bound, by The Garden City Press, Letchworth, Herts, for the publishers, Patrick Stephens Limited, Bar Hill, Cambridge, CB3 8EL, England.

# Contents

# Introduction

The continued unprecedented growth of interest in railway modelling, sustained by new ideas, new techniques, new scales and gauges, and an ever-increasing flow of new products from manufacturers and suppliers, has resulted in the hobby becoming more and more complex.

The variety and apparent intricacy of the hobby can be bewildering to a beginner. But he (or she!) need not be put off or make a false start if time is taken to digest the basics within this book. The amazing scope and variety of the hobby is fully examined, with detailed advice on not only how to recognise problems but also how to tackle or avoid them. Readers can then decide for themselves what type of model railway best suits their need, or their pocket, and how they can make a start.

In the eight years since this book was first published, it has gone to four printings, thus exceeding even my best hopes and certainly those of my publisher, and I am more than proud to find that it has now established itself as a classic 'primer' on the hobby. This latest, enlarged third edition has been completely revised, reset and redesigned. The line illustrations have all been re-drawn and virtually all the original photographs replaced.

The popular image of a model railway is a plaything for children. In many ways this is good since it ensures a steady flow of young new recruits to the hobby. Many of today's adult railway modellers, myself included, started with a child's train set. But when you see the highest form of the art, as developed by the leading model railway personalities, you realise that there is more to it than at first meets the eye. Whilst it may not be possible for everyone to reach the same high standard of craftsmanship as set by the hobby's top exponents, the goal is there and is worthy of attainment. Anyone with the slightest glimmer of interest in railways or aptitude as a model maker can find a consuming and worthwhile challenge in railway modelling and is capable of leaving his mark.

Railway modellers are notorious for adapting materials and drawing inspiration from a number of different sources unconnected with the hobby, but to a much larger extent they rely on a healthy supporting trade—commercial manufacturers, suppliers and retailers alike—who provide the basic raw materials and necessary parts for the hobby. The trade is in turn sustained by the modellers. It follows, therefore, that the more railway modellers there are the better it will be for everyone concerned with the hobby. I hope that this book will encourage others to take it up and expand the ranks still further.

I would like to acknowledge the assistance given by Brian Monaghan and a large number of manufacturers who generously supplied photographs with which to illustrate this latest edition. I must thank John Woodman for photographs of his layout (and for the loan of models), and John Edwards, Mike Gearing, Mike Hart, George Welsh, Barlow's Models and Mainline Railways who also loaned models. I am indebted to Dr C.G. Sumner for the authoritative information on the development of 00 and HO gauges which was incorporated in the previous edition and has been repeated here and to Roger Amos for a number of valuable comments which have been incorporated in the chapter on Electrical Equipment.

Finally, I must acknowledge all those railway modellers, who write articles for the monthly magazines and take the trouble to exhibit their models and layouts at exhibitions, for the inspiration and encouragement they have unwittingly given.

Fleet, Hampshire, June 1979. — Norman Simmons

## Chapter 1

# What is railway modelling?

Basically speaking, railway modelling is the art of creating in miniature a working replica of a full-size railway. It is perhaps significant that we refer to the subject as *railway* modelling, not train modelling or engine modelling. Herein lies the essence of the difference between railway modelling and most other forms of model making, since we concern ourselves with the railway as a whole. This means the sum of many things—locomotives, coaches, wagons, track, stations, signalling, civil engineering such as bridges, embankments, cuttings, viaducts and tunnels, and the landscape through which the railway passes. All these facets require space in which to set them out and space in which they can be operated. Unlike, say, aero or ship modelling, where a static model is considered as an entity in itself and occupies no more space than the overall dimension of the model or the glass case in which it is often kept, railway modelling has to have sufficient space for all the many individual items to be properly displayed and integrated. Also, all these individual parts take time and money to acquire. Whereas you can become an aeromodeller with quite a modest outlay on one kit and a few simple tools, it takes quite a deliberately conscious effort to decide if you want to take up railway modelling. It is natural, therefore, that you will want to give the subject some careful thought and consideration before you start and before you commit yourself.

Having decided to take up the hobby it might be helpful to consider three important points before you actually begin.Decide what you can afford in three things, namely space, time and money. These considerations will, in many ways, dictate the kind of model railway you will be able to create. If you have space, time and money in abundance then there need be no end to the size, shape, scale and extent of the layout you set out to build, but if any one of these factors is limited it will more than likely have a restricting effect on the model railway. Too little space to spare will cramp the size and possibly the scale of the layout. Too little spare time will limit the amount of equipment you will be able to build yourself and will increase your dependence on the trade or else affect the extent of the layout. Too little money to spare will obviously cut down the amount of ready-made proprietary equipment you will be able to buy and will mean that you will have to construct as many things as you can yourself with the cheapest basic raw materials.

As a model railway is a cumulative thing which builds up gradually over a period of time it is, in my view, vital to consider these three important points before you start so that you know what you are letting yourself in for at the beginning. There is no point in spending a lot of money on expensive equipment because it looks nice in the shops, only to find that there is not enough room at home in which to operate it. Also, it's no good thinking you are going to build the most elaborate layout when you haven't the space to put it in, or the time to spare to keep it properly maintained. Similarly, you cannot expect to build all your track, rolling stock and accessories if you never have time enough in which to do it. In the rush of enthusiasm at the start of a new hobby it is all too easy to gloss over and overlook these points.

I think it is very important not to be too ambitious and to risk over-reaching yourself at the beginning. A model railway is essentially a working model and a great deal of the satisfaction of creating one is, of course, to be able to operate it when it is built. If you are too ambitious to start with the end may never appear in sight and the struggle against time and the drain on your financial resources may lead to disillusionment and the ultimate abandonment of the project. Learning the hard way like this might lead you to wasteful scrapping of earlier efforts or, at worst, complete alienation with model railways and the search for another hobby. Although I consider it important to start with modest aspirations, you should always keep the future in sight. In choosing a site for the model railway, for instance, pick one that can be extended later on. A simple project can always be incorporated into a larger scheme at a later date, provided you have given thought to this at the start. Examples of this can be found in a branch line layout which can be incorporated into a larger main line scheme; the extension into the garden of a layout built in a garden shed; the continuation of a layout round the walls of a room; or the extension of a track from one baseboard to another. It is very easy to be taken in by the large and complex layouts you see at exhibitions when you first become interested in model railways, but it is important not to aim too high to begin with and to start with more modest, more easily attainable aims.

Railway modelling is literally a hobby for all ages. It is also one that can be enjoyed by both sexes, although it must be admitted it is more often the pastime of men and boys. Some marvellous work has, however, been done by ladies, some of it self-inspired and self-created but more usually as a contribution to a husband's layout rather than a project that has been started and finished alone. There is more than one exception to this though, and some fine models have been made by ladies. I know of no examples of layouts built by brothers and sisters or mothers and sons (although I expect to be proved wrong), but of course one of the most common relationships in railway modelling is the joint efforts of a father and son. Model railways are an acknowledged favourite pastime for children and, if aided and encouraged by parents, can foster a unique and lasting father/son relationship. I know few other hobbies which can offer so much in bridging the generation gap, always provided that there is the germ of appreciation to begin with. A keen father forcing interest in railway modelling on to a disinterested son can, of course, have the opposite of a beneficial effect, but I fancy that these cases are in the minority. Even if the son later chooses other interests which he finds more absorbing and turns his back on a model railway, leaving the father to carry on alone, I feel sure the first combined efforts, the working side by side and the pooling of ideas, will have helped to create a bond between them.

Railway modelling is an ideal pastime to take up during retirement. The big bugbear of lack of time becomes less of a problem with no business affairs to attend to. Provided that your eyesight and manual dexterity remain reasonably intact the limitations of a fixed retirement income can be compensated for by the time factor, which will allow more opportunity for hand construction and a consequent saving in money. An older person with a store of memories can very often be the envy of younger people when it comes to building historical models. Recollections of day-to-day events are very often of things which were not thought important enough to be recorded at the time and so, therefore, cannot afterwards be found in books. It is often amazing how many details of such commonplace things that occured as relatively recently as the 1930s can be clouded by time. The colours of GWR stations and the exact shade of green used by the Southern Railway in this period have been the subject of controversy lately, since precise details of these simple features, because they were so simple, escaped accurate documentation at the time. Anyone with accurate recollections of this period has been listened to with baited breath. We are, of course, all getting older and if we cannot find time now for building the model railway of our dreams it is near to the next best thing to do some quiet research and fact-storing during the odd quiet moments. This can perhaps be put into use when retirement comes along and at long last we can use the time between 9.00 am and 5.00 pm to do some actual modelling.

The hobby can also be very educational in that it develops many latent skills and encourages you to exercise your mind. Planning and building the railway develops the ability to draw, to paint and to create with the hands, as well as promoting craftsmanship, patience, and an understanding of basic handyman techniques. You need not be an artist to be a railway modeller, but in building a model railway you are in a sense creating a three-dimensional picture and developing a means of expression and skill, much as an artist does. Attempting to copy faithfully the prototype (which is the expert's word for the original or real thing) develops your powers of observation and an appreciation of every-day things. A train journey to most people seems to be a tiresome thing which has to be endured in order to get from one place to another. A railway modeller, on the other hand, can find it very absorbing, studying things which he knows he is going to model. Subjects as mundane as fencing, hedges, trees, the layout of signals, station furniture, posters, trackwork, station platforms and the formation of trains can all be taken for granted until you have the job of building them in miniature and then you realise how little you know and just how much detail has simply not been looked at before. The scenic side of railway modelling can help you to develop a tremendous sense of colour; you learn to appreciate the subtle shades that go to make up a grassy meadow or field, trees, foliage, brickwork, concrete, earth, ballast and the surfaces of roads and footpaths. In trying to create these subjects in model form you become more aware of what these things are like in real life.

Also, in attempting to follow the full-size railway in depth, modellers need to undertake a degree of research into the prototype. To do other than this is merely playing trains, which is really only scratching the surface. There is currently a vast field of literature on railway and allied subjects, a great deal in public libraries and much more in bookshops up and down the country. Whilst I know some railway modellers have little knowledge of the prototype, and some surprisingly enough take little interest, I feel that to make the whole thing really worth while you cannot afford to remain too ignorant of the full-size original of any model you are creating.

There are umpteen railway and model railway clubs throughout Britain and in many other countries of the world. Some of the railway clubs specialise in specific branches of the hobby, for example a particular preservation project like the Bluebell Railway Preservation Society; a former railway company like the Great Western Society; a particular geographical or national location like the Irish Railway Record Society; or a type of propulsion like the Electric Railway Society, to mention just a few categories and just one example in each. Clubs catering for the model railway hobby are usually organised nationally, or even internationally, and, although they may have their recognised centres or local groups (particularly true of the preservation societies of course), they rely on news sheets and club magazines for maintaining contact between members. There are some similarly organised model railway clubs but the aim of the majority is to provide a permanent meeting place where club members can co-operate in building one or more club layouts. By their very nature, therefore, most model railway clubs are geographically organised and are largely run to serve the needs of individuals within a given district. Because these are so many, and changes occur so frequently, it is not practical to list them in these pages.

Most of these model railway clubs hold exhibitions from time to time and one way of finding out what railway modelling is all about and how you can go about it is to visit one or more of them. Just one word of warning though, you must remember that in the majority of club exhibitions the staging has been done in members' spare time and with limited resources. Most exhibitions are one- or two-day affairs and the exhibitors, who often receive no more reward than the satisfaction of showing their models to others, may have devoted all their available spare time for weeks beforehand as well as during the show, with the added risk of damage and pilferage to their models. I take my hat off to the many exhibitors who do take the trouble to show off their work to the delight and pleasure of others. Perhaps because of the limited time available (either because the exhibitor's own time is restricted or, as is more often the case, because the hall where the show is being held can only be hired for a limited period and there is thus insufficient time in which to set up the exhibits), some model railway layouts on display seem to have more than their fair share of gremlins. The floor may not be level, resulting in the baseboards being distorted. The power points may not be ideally placed, or some important piece of wiring or paintwork may have got damaged in transit. All of these things can cause trouble which may not reveal itself until the public audience is assembled. The visitor who sees rolling stock derailing or locomotives stalling on pointwork may form the wrong impression. The sight of a soldering iron almost permanently plugged in might give the idea that this is always necessary with a model railway but it needn't be and more often than not it isn't. Also exhibitors have to eat on occasions and a break in operating sessions can sometimes only be avoided if the reins are handed over to other less experienced and maybe junior members, who are perhaps not familiar with the controls or the wiring circuit.

Whether by luck or design I don't know, but some exhibitions are better than others and I cannot over-emphasise the necessity of seeing as many as you can and forming your opinion over a period rather than making a snap, hasty judgement after one visit. Model railway exhibitions are in many ways unique in that I know of few other hobbies which give rise to so many. This perhaps demonstrates the attraction of railway modelling as much as anything, and the wide cross-section of people you see at these exhibitions is surely conclusive proof of the universal appeal of the hobby to both sexes of all ages. Perhaps one of the main attractions is that, all things being equal, railway models are *working* models.

At a model railway exhibition you can usually glean some idea of what the organising club is like and you can judge if it is the sort of club you wish to join and whether it is likely to cater for your main interests. Many other clubs nearby are usually invited to exhibit, and should you be thinking of joining one an exhibition is a good way of getting to know those in your district and it will also help you to make up your mind to join one. As well as the local clubs which cater for local interests there are also national clubs which devote themselves to specialist model fields, such as the N Gauge Society or the Gauge θ guild. There are also many full-size railway clubs, preservation societies, etc, that embrace model railways as part of their interests and models are often used to promote the clubs' aims. I enjoy enormously visiting exhibitions. The amount of effort and enthusiasm that is in evidence is often quite staggering and everyone is co-opted into making the exhibition an entertaining affair for the public, from the local dignitary who is often invited to open the show, to the sisters, girl-friends, wives and mothers who run the refreshment counter.

Railway modelling is usually regarded as a highly individual form of modelling in that the modeller works unseen at home amidst his own family and home surroundings, but if you are in need of companionship, the local model railway club may provide just what you are looking for. As a means of acquiring information, hints and tips, ideas, encouragement and sometimes even assistance, there is no better advice I can give than to seek out and join your local club. If there isn't one nearby then I humbly suggest that an advertisement in the local paper or in one or more of the various hobby magazines is more than likely to find someone else of like mind who is willing to join forces with you in starting a club of your own. New clubs are being formed all the time, as you will discover from becoming a regular reader of the hobby magazines.

The mention of magazines leads me to refer in detail to them. There are five main British magazines, four published monthly: *Model Railways, Model Railway Constructor, Railway Modeller,* and *Model Trains,* and one published bi-monthly, *Continental Modeller*, all devoted entirely to the hobby of railway modelling. Many more are published in other parts of the world. A list of some of the main ones is included in Appendix 2. The longest running British magazine, *Model Railways,* which was originally known as *Model Railway News,* began publication in 1925. I would regard a regular subscription to one if not all of these monthlies as essential if you wish to find out more about the hobby and keep abreast of the many new developments which are forever taking place. The classified advertisements often provide opportunities to purchase secondhand equipment with which you can make a start in the hobby, and the advertisements of the many manufacturers and retailers keep you informed of the steady flow of new products, of which the hobby never seems short. The main feature articles showing the achievements of modellers are a constant source of inspiration and there is usually a wealth of prototype information, photographs and drawings on which you can base your own models. The regular receipt of each new magazine is an event to which I personally have always looked forward for nearly 40 years and still I can find something new and interesting in every new edition. I am sure much of the expansion in the model railway hobby in recent years has been due to the specialist press, and in return they rightly deserve the support of every modeller.

Reference has already been made to the trade, to both manufacturers and retailers, and the importance of a thriving model railway industry cannot be over-emphasised. However much you may aim to avoid the use of commercially produced models and to construct your own model railway as far as possible, there are almost bound to be some items which will have to be bought. The super craftsman may stop at nothing, and even produce his own locomotives and rolling stock. Maybe a few even think nothing of casting and turning their own wheels and building an electric motor, but I am willing to bet that very few individuals have drawn their own rails! Most scratch-build modellers who work from basic raw materials rather than using kits or adapting commercially produced models, incorporate ready-made parts such as wheels, motors, and ready-mixed paint and transfers in their finished models. Even the raw material itself would in some cases be difficult to obtain if it were not for the services of the model railway retailers who alone are prepared to supply the specialist sizes in the relatively small quantities that modellers need.

In the past the manufacturing side of the model railway industry in Britain tended to divide itself into two parts; on one side we had the large scale production firm that catered for the toy market where considerations of cost, robust construction and high production runs were uppermost, and on the other side we had the specialist model railway firm which aimed to satisfy the enthusiast largely through kits and spare parts. Many of the smaller firms will be quite unknown to newcomers, but to enthusiasts these firms have become firmly established household names. A list is included in Appendix 3 and like most other Appendices in the book the list is growing with each edition. It is probably true to say that many more train sets are sold as toys than ever find their way into a purpose-built model railway, but it is also true to say that there has been a shift in emphasis in recent years and, with constant voice through the clubs, magazines and individual comment, the mass-produced products sold as toys are now nearer to scale models than they have ever been. This is particularly marked in the most popular British 4 mm scale 00 gauge where, as well as improving standards of scale and authenticity, all the main manufacturers have become aware of the need for compatibility in couplings, track and wheel standards. The scale-minded model railway enthusiast who opts for 00 gauge is able to choose—from the products of the large-scale manufacturers—a selection of authentic scale models that are ready to run straight from the

**Below** *The Airfix GWR Prairie Tank rightly caused a stir when it came out as the first of a new generation of 00 gauge British outline models. MGW pony wheels have been fitted to this model to improve it still further.*

**Bottom** *The latest Hornby Railways locomotive models have come a long way from the early Tri-ang models from which they were descended. Typical of the later introductions is this fine 00 gauge model of LNER A4 Pacific No 4902 'Seagull'* (Hornby Railways).

box. Notwithstanding the higher standards now being achieved, prices are commendably low and allowing for inflation the latest products offer better value for money than ever before. Because the specialist side of the business aims at a more limited market the production runs have to be smaller and the unit cost for each item is often higher than the mass-produced product. Some of the moulds, machine tools and materials used in commercial model making are very expensive and manufacturers have to consider this aspect carefully before embarking on a new item or range of products. Most of the smaller specialist firms avoid the higher costs by using less expensive techniques such as white metal castings, perhaps the most common, and by offering their products in kits. The other alternative to high tooling costs is to manufacture by hand, and of course today this is even more expensive, which accounts for some quite small but exquisitely detailed hand-built models costing tens and even hundreds of pounds.

The variety of products available today; ready-to-run models, kits, component parts, accessories, electronic control systems, etc, has never been surpassed and great credit is due to the industry for the way it has responded to, and in some cases even created, a demand for more and more new items. There is now, as a result, hardly any basic requirement in the material sense missing from the hobby and we are very fortunate in having such a firm base on which to develop.

However well the hobby may be organised, with clubs, magazines and manufacturers, it would be nowhere without the model railway retailers. I cannot emphasise too strongly how important it is when starting the hobby to pick a good model railway retailer, a shop which is managed and staffed by someone who is prepared to look after you and to guide you through the early unfamiliar days. Provided you do not choose the last Saturday afternoon before Christmas, or some other time when the shop is packed with customers, most retailers worth their salt are prepared to offer advice as well as service and to spend some time with their customers. A list of leading retailers who stock model railway items is included in Appendix 4, and reference to one of the magazines will keep you abreast of any new ones that open up within reasonable distance of your home town or those prepared to deal with you through the post. They are scattered far and wide and seemingly few towns or populated districts are without a model shop of some sort. As with most things in life, there are the good and not so good retailers and you are best advised to shop around, but when you have found a dealer with whom you get on well, stick by him and I am sure you will soon become firm friends. The Model Engineering Trade Association, or META as it is referred to, is a body to which many British manufacturers and some retailers belong, and the META sign is a good indication that you will receive responsible salesmanship and trustworthy advice.

*00 gauge models of a Highland Railway Meat Van, Loco Coal Wagon, and a 'Small Ben' 4-4-0 constructed from Cotswold kits. The wagons have plastic body parts and cast metal underframes and the locomotive is cast metal* (Sutherland Model Casters Ltd).

**Top** *Roco have taken full advantage of the mass of detail to be found in the otherwise compact design of this DB Class 58 2-10-0 goods engine* (Richard Kohnstam Ltd).

**Above** *Pride of place in the Liliput range of Continental HO locomotives must go to this handsome model of the DR Class 05 4-6-4 No 05.003 in works grey finish. Notice the fine valve gear and the detail in the cylinder and crosshead* (Liliput).

The American model rail roading market is, of course, very much bigger than its British equivalent and this is reflected in the truly tremendous range of items available, particularly in the 'ready-to-run' field. Many of the well-known European manufacturers—such as Rivarossi and Liliput—make models specially for the American market and these are also sold in Britain and in other countries. A growing number of enthusiasts outside America are tempted to model American-style lines, probably due to the availability of the very colourful and well-finished American models in both HO and N scales. There are two major American railroad modelling magazines, *Model Railroader* and *Railroad Model Craftsman*, both journals of high repute, and these should be required reading for anyone wishing to model American railroads (or indeed wishing to see what such projects might offer).

In America the major organisation supporting and guiding the hobby is the National Model Railroad Association (NMRA), which is very roughly an equivalent to Britain's META in as much as it has sought to improve standards of models and dealer service. The NMRA also caters for the enthusiast, however, not solely the trade, and it has some overseas branches including one in Britain.

The other major model railway market is the Continent of Europe, and the European manufacturers between them turn out a fantastically large range of models covering, principally, the systems of France, Germany, Italy and Austria (though other nations are catered for in a smaller way). Once again the 'ready-to-run' side of the market is very well looked after, with models available in all the common scales (except 00). Standards are high and the quality, again, tempts a lot of British modellers to turn to Europe for the basis of a layout. In both Britain and America there are a good number of hobby shops which now stock European models.

With model railways moving further and further away from the toy train set image there seems to have developed a greater dividing

*Perhaps the ultimate in model railways; a radio-controlled live steam locomotive. The radio receiver in the box van operates the regulator through a mechanical linkage. The locomotive, an Archangel Models 'Snowdon Ranger', was adapted to radio control by John Edwards and is seen on his 16 mm scale garden railway.*

line between model shops staffed by model makers who are keen on their trade and toy shops which very often rely on girl or lady assistants who are more informed about dolls and teddy bears than they are on the intricacies of an 00 gauge 12 volt DC electric train set. At one time most toy shops of any standing boasted a working train set circling an oval track in their shop window, but nowadays such a sight is rare and the salesmanship does not extend itself to anything more than the display of a few static boxed items in a corner of the window. This seems a pity as there is no doubt that many of us who are now adults, active in the model railway hobby today, started off with a toy train set which we were given every encouragement to possess. I think it is very important that we retain a steady flow of new recruits to the hobby by this time-honoured means and wherever possible I think we should try and make up for the apparent lack of drive on the part of some toy shops by encouraging wherever and whenever we can an interest in toy trains amongst our nephews and nieces as well as sons and daughters.

These then are some of the aspects of the model railway hobby as they appear on the surface today. But foremost are the thousands of individuals who like yourself had to start somewhere at some time and have found railway modelling a creative, absorbing and worthwhile hobby and pastime. With the help of the following chapters I hope it will not seem as bewildering as it may appear at first glance, and that you will not be put off joining in. If you do decide to enter the ranks I am sure you will find yourself very welcome.

## Chapter 2

# Finding room for a model railway

At one time it was commonplace for a toy tin-plate train set to be unpacked from its box, set up on the floor ready for an operating session and then packed away again afterwards, almost as a matter of course. Part of the fun perhaps was creating new methods of laying the rails and dodging the table and chair legs that got in their way. The dark cavernous spaces under armchairs and sofas became tunnels and the rise and fall of the tracks over carpets and rugs gave the locomotives a chance to show off their haulage powers. Any sense of realism that was aimed at leaned heavily on the imagination to bring it to fulfilment. I am sure those early manipulations of standard-length straight and curved rails, points and crossings, gave one a good start over less fortunate children when it came to geometry lessons at school! Certainly much ingenuity and skill was required to ensure perfect geometrical form for the layout, and it was a point of honour not to strain the tracks together when perhaps we knew perfectly well that another $\frac{1}{4}$ straight rail was required. The rails in those days were fairly robust affairs, and they needed to be to withstand clumsy juvenile hands and the occasional misplaced foot of the operator—or, even worse, a heavy footed parent! Such a layout was invariably clockwork and 0 gauge, or even something larger if one goes back still further in time.

It was the coming of electric propulsion and the smaller 00 gauge (more about the various gauges in Chapter 4) that the floor lost favour and we came to talk of table-top layouts. For the first time the relatively small 00 gauge made it possible to consider a table top as a space on which to build a model railway and at the same time the small size of 00 gauge necessitated moving up from the floor because the rails could not be made so strong and play resistant and it also became difficult to handle the small models so low down. With track of any size, too much connecting and disconnecting of the rails weakens and distorts them in time. The rail joints can become a potential source of derailments and also a point at which the electrical conductivity can break down. There is a good reason why full-size railway lines are referred to as the permanent way, and this is how they should be on a model railway if perfect running is the aim. So I think we can say quite definitely that any idea of a temporary track system laid out on the floor or any other position where the rails have to be put down and taken up has to be ruled out. The establishment of this idea, basic though it may be, is to some extent the first important step in making progress from a toy train set to a model railway. There is, of course, a lot more besides!

If not the floor, then where can we go? The usually acceptable answer is somewhere about table-top height. This probably suits some people but I would advise studying your own physical build first before slavishly copying past accepted practices. I am 6 ft 2 in tall, which is generally accepted as being a bit above average, and I find something higher than a table top is more comfortable. This is particularly true if I am standing up at a table, and more often than not I find this position more appropriate when operating a model railway than sitting down, which somehow never seems to be entirely satisfactory. There always seems to be something out of reach when you are sitting down and the constant bobbing up and down can be more tiring than standing up all the time. Table-top height is usually around 2 ft 4 in or 2 ft 5 in, but I find something like a kitchen working top height of around 3 ft is the minimum convenient level and I am happier if the layout can be higher still, say something like 3 ft 6 in. I had a layout at one time which, to clear the furniture it was built on, had to be at a height of approximately 4 ft. I found no snags to this whatsoever, and many advantages, most of all the fact that I liked to get my eyes down to the level of the track on occasions to find a viewpoint more nearly matching that of the real thing. Also, there is far less back-aching stooping when the layout is reasonably high off the ground. To go too far can, of course, be a distinct disadvantage, since if the layout is too high the background becomes hidden by the foreground and visibility is reduced, which makes it rather difficult to check the setting of points to see whether a road is clear. Once again, to draw on full-size practice, remember that signal boxes are perched up high above rail level. To sum up I would say the ideal measurement is somewhere between 3 ft and 4 ft depending on your own height.

The width of a layout is also a factor which can be determined by your own build and physical proportions. At 6 ft 2 in I have a fairly long reach and I am perfectly comfortable stretching across to the centre of a table, but this might be beyond the reach of a smaller person. All these details are, of course, just a matter of common sense but often they do not occur to some people until the layout is well advanced, and then it may be too late to do anything about it. It saves a lot of trouble if these points are considered at the outset before any hard work is done.

Tables are instinctively thought of as being the ideal shape and size for a model railway baseboard. They are quite satisfactory on a number of occasions although they can be inhibiting in respect of the type of layout you can build. In my view there is a much better alternative, namely the layout built on a series of shelves of varying width around the walls of a room, as shown in fig 1. A round-the-wall layout is much more accessible and provides far more scope for an interesting layout. Also, in many cases, it is still possible to carry out the normal functions in the room, for example a bedroom or a bed-sitter can remain a bedroom or a bed-sitter with the layout *in situ* round the walls, whereas a table-top baseboard providing less amount of usable track space would dominate the centre of the room, as shown in fig 2. Normally a baseboard 3 ft or more in width requires access on both sides. This would certainly be true of a continuous run layout built on a table where the running tracks have of necessity to be laid near the edge. If the table is pushed to a wall or into a corner to make more usable space in the room, this will make a large part of the model railway inaccessible. A point worth noting comparing fig 1 with figs 2 and 3 is that the baseboard areas are roughly the same whereas the track footage in fig 1 is double the length of the track footage in figs 2 and 3. The prospects for developing the track layout on the station site in fig 1 are also far greater yet there is much less dominance over the room. If the room is being used for other purposes and space is limited the site for the station need be no more than 2 ft in width. This would be ample for 00 gauge and could be reduced, even halved for N gauge. The shelves round the remaining walls can be as little as 4 in wide for a single track in 00 gauge, 6 in for double track, although something wider would be preferable if the lineside is to be developed with scenery. An additional bonus is that the space under the station site can be used for storage as I will explain later.

Supports suitable for a round-the-wall layout can be of the simple metal bracket type for the narrow shelves or they can be made up from 2 in × 2 in timber, such as shown in fig 4. These would be 'Rawlplugged' to the wall and in effect the wall adds strength and support to the layout. The gap across the entrance to the room can be bridged by a simple hinged lifting bridge or by a removable section of baseboard which can be simply lifted out and put away when the layout is not in use.

I appreciate that in the case of rented homes, it may not always be possible to fix brackets directly to the walls. In such circumstances it will be necessary to provide some form of free-standing bracket or trestle. Alternatively, it may be possible to fix the free-standing type of bracket to the floor instead of to the wall, thus compensating for any lack of rigidity normally provided by fixing to the wall. Failing all this, a good stout piece of furniture such as a chest of drawers is an ideal base on which to fix the main baseboard for a model railway. As I will explain in Chapter 5 when talking about layout planning, with an end-to-end type of layout it is not essential that it should run completely round the room, and the chest of drawers can then form the base for the main terminal station with an extension to one side providing sufficient room over which to operate a service.

There is sometimes a temptation to give too little thought to the possibility of ever having to uproot the layout. If the time comes to make a move it may then be found that the layout cannot be removed from the room without dismantling, or else it has become so firmly fixed in position that it means the track becomes damaged when trying to dislodge

**Fig 1** *Much more model railway can be accommodated around the walls of a room, compared with a table in the centre (see fig 2).* **Fig 2** *The same size room (12 ft × 8 ft) as in fig 1, but with the table in the centre—which occupies all the available space—provides a much smaller working area.* **Fig 3** *A table against the corner of a room provides more usable space or, alternatively, permits the use of a larger table. However, access to the far corner of the layout becomes a problem.*

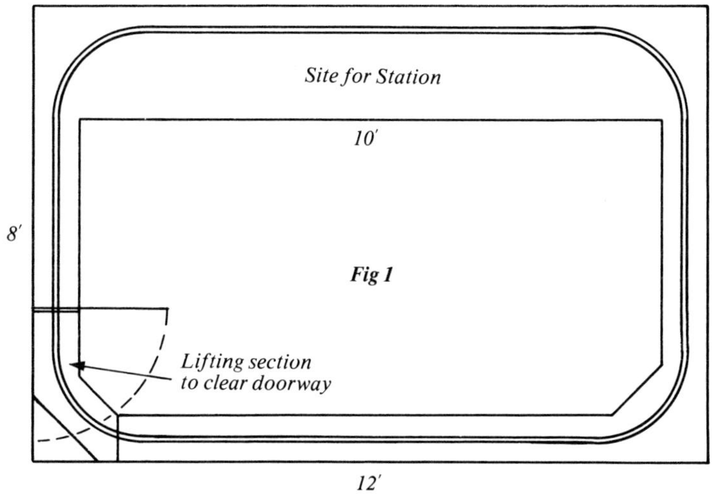


Fig 1

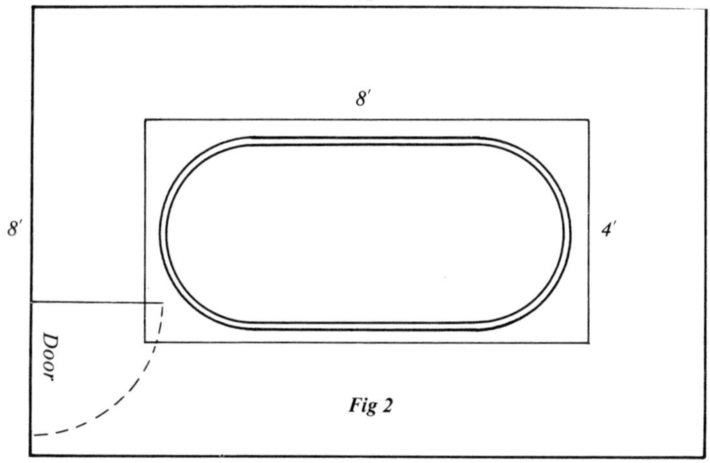


Fig 2

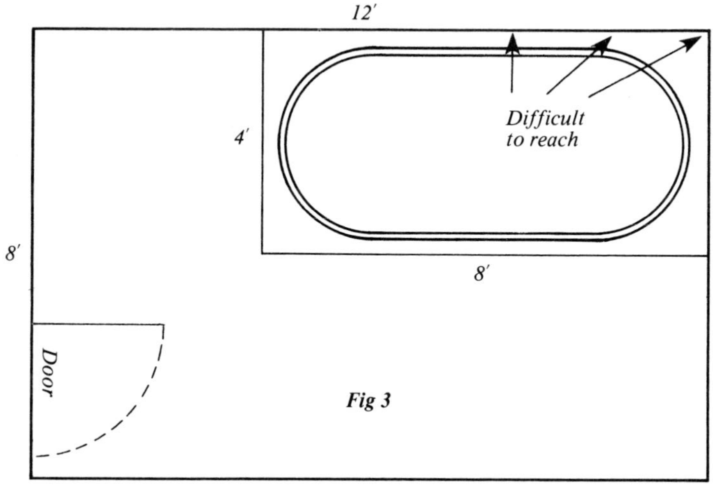


Fig 3

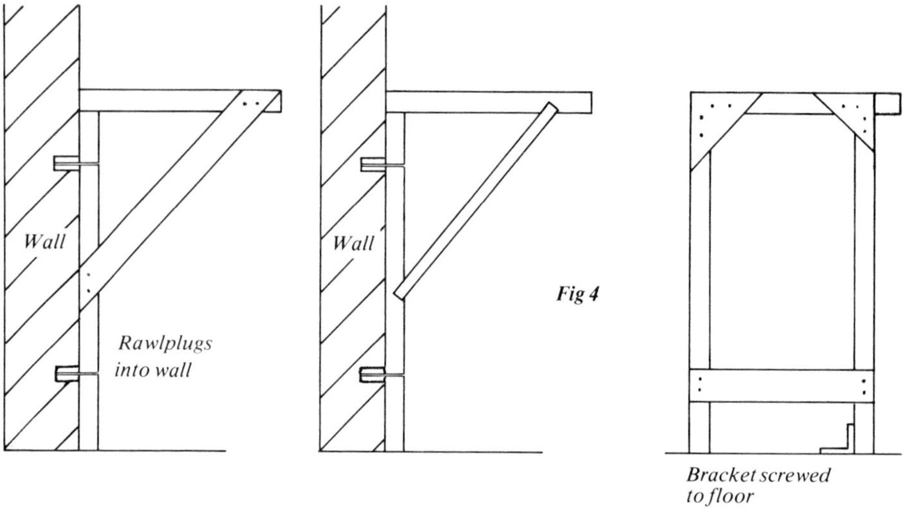


**Fig 4** *Two types of wooden bracket and a trestle support for a 'round the wall' type layout. The trestle can be free-standing, thus avoiding the necessity of screwing into the wall.*

and dismantle the baseboard. Unless you are absolutely sure you are not likely to move, or your circumstances are never going to change, it is as well to make some provision for the easy removal of the layout if and when the time comes. This can be done by ensuring that the baseboard is divided into individual sections, each being reasonably portable. No hard and fast rules can be laid down for the size of these baseboard sections as the maximum dimensions will depend on the entrance to the room, A downstairs room with a pair of French windows opening out on to the lawn will probably have no restrictions at all, but an upstairs room reached up a winding staircase will obviously need some consideration. I mention this knowing that many, if not most, baseboards are assembled in the room in which they are to be used and I once had a devil of a job myself with a baseboard which measured 8 ft × 4 ft in an upstairs room which led off a narrow landing. In these circumstances something less than the height of the door frame, say about 6 ft, would have been better for the maximum length of the baseboard. This would have enabled it to have been turned on to its end and would have made the job of removal much easier.

A permanent layout fixed to the walls of a room can be removed when necessary provided the baseboard is not so long that it becomes difficult to handle. Greasing the screws when they are fixed into place will prevent them rusting and will make them easier to remove; the holes they leave in the wall can simply be filled in with plaster. The layout itself, that is the baseboard containing the track, can, however, be a problem unless the individual baseboard units are made completely self-contained. This means stopping all rails short at the baseboard edge and making all wiring readily accessible where it crosses from one board to another. If this is done thoroughly it will facilitate rapid removal of the layout should you wish to exhibit it at any time, and it would be worth while keeping this idea in mind. The individual baseboard units should in this case be of a size that can be easily transported and you might like to check on the interior dimensions of your car before you make any decision. Something like 4 ft × 2 ft is probably a maximum size for reasonably easy handling. Where you have no ideas of showing your handiwork at exhibitions, the baseboard units need not be entirely self-contained. The rails can be allowed to bridge the gaps between the baseboard units, providing the possibility of a disturbance at some later date is designed into the layout, and steps can be taken relatively simply to lift the rails. For example, make sure that there are no points or crossings straddling the gaps between the units and ensure that there are only straight rails which can, if necessary, be cut simply with a hacksaw blade as shown in fig 5.

There are any number of materials you can use for constructing baseboards and their supports, but timber is generally favoured as being easy to work, durable and of sufficient strength for the purpose. There are many different ways of constructing baseboards too, but my own particular favourite, assuming a layout is built round the walls of a room, is the tried and trusted open framework made of 2 in × 1 in timber with a covering of ½ in insulation board. An example of such a framework built round the walls of a room 10 ft × 7 ft 6 in is shown in fig 6. Here the main area of the layout, which incorporates all the important station, goods yard and engine servicing facilities, is built on a framework 10 ft × 2 ft along one long wall of the room, and narrower framework only 1 ft wide extends the layout along one end and along the other long side of the room. An opening section across the door allows access to the room, at the furthest end of which the layout is carried across the work bench by a piece of chipboard. The chipboard was used at this point because it is more self-supporting than the soft insulating board and did not require supporting underneath with the 2 in × 1 in framework. This gave a lot more clearance above the work bench. A number of modellers prefer to use chipboard rather than insulation board and I would suggest that, when a layout is likely to be moved more often, it is probably preferable since it is much more robust, harder and likely to retain screws and other fixing devices much longer and firmer. Its disadvantages are that it is heavier, more expensive and much more noisy if the rails are laid directly on it.

To make the framework using 2 in × 1 in timber can be very easy if you are content to have simple butt joints, which in many cases are all that are necessary. Alternatively, the job can be made a little stronger and perhaps more professional by using housing joints as shown in fig 7. Housing joints are easy to do with a tenon saw which has a depth gauge built on. The one I use has a metal bar bolted to the blade of the saw, the bolts passing through slots in the blade. The height of the bar can be adjusted by releasing the two wing nuts which hold it in place and, when released, allow the bar to slide up or down. The height of the bar above the teeth of the blade will determine the depth of the saw cut, thus ensuring that every cut is made exactly to the same depth. With a simple gauge such as this it is perfectly possible quickly and accurately to cut a whole row of housing joints along the baseboard frame side members, and to a constant depth. Provided that all the cross members are cut to exactly the same width, this will ensure that the baseboard is kept to an

**Fig 5** *The position of points should be planned either side of the join between the two baseboard sections, as at 'B', and not straddling the join, as in 'A'.*

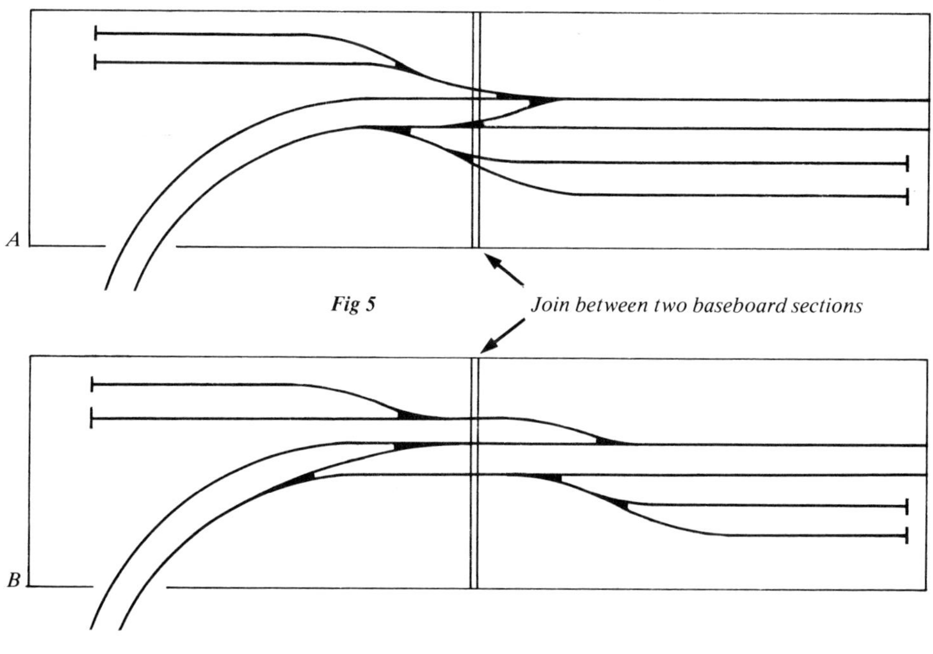

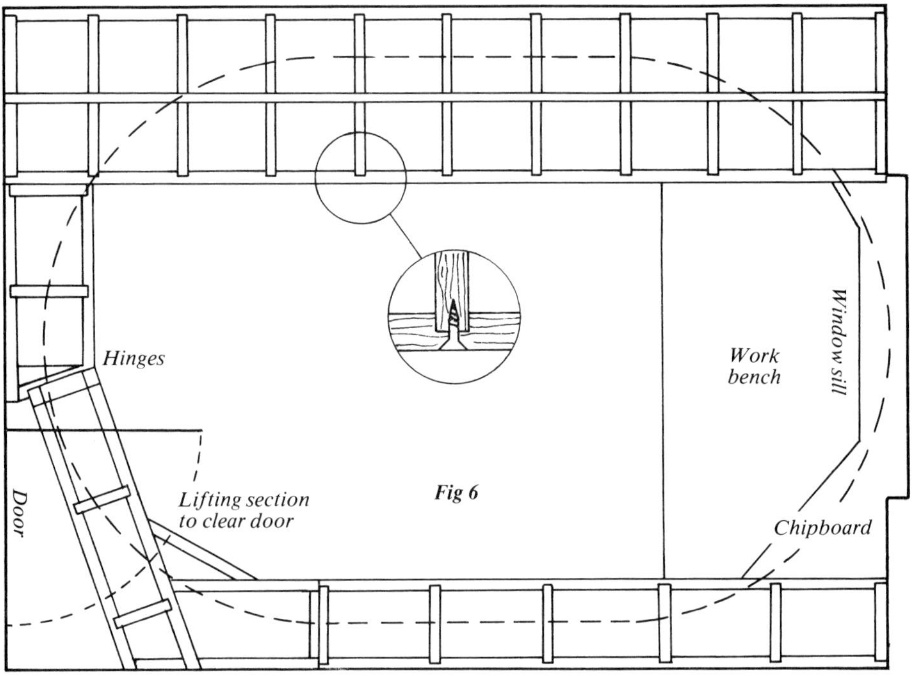


Fig 6

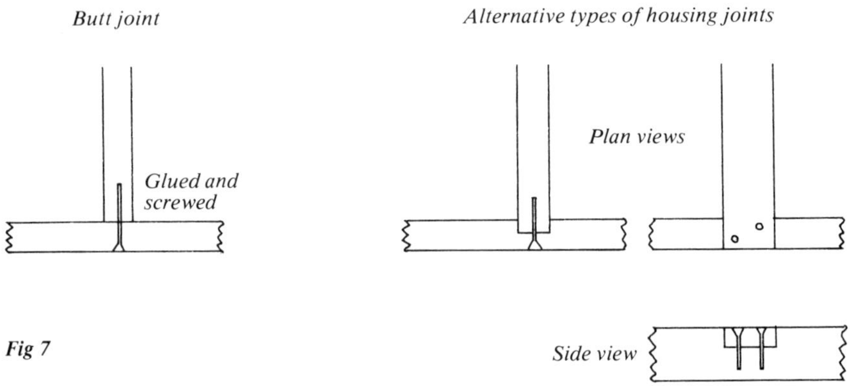


*Fig 7*

**Fig 6** *Suggested 2 in × 1 in open framework baseboard installed round the walls of a room 10 ft × 7 ft 6 in. The track is carried over the workbench by a piece of chipboard to provide greater clearance beneath. Note the use made of the window sill to provide valuable extra space.* **Fig 7** *Simple butt joints (left) are, in many cases, adequate for baseboard framework, but simple housing joints (right) make the frame that bit stronger and more professional-looking.* **Fig 8** *Cross-section and part front view of a baseboard supported along its back edge by 1½ in × 1 in batten Rawl-plugged to the wall. The front edge is supported by vertical 2 in × 1 in timber, bracketed to the floor and bolted to the baseboard framework. The cupboard space formed beneath can be fronted by hardboard sliding doors, as shown.*

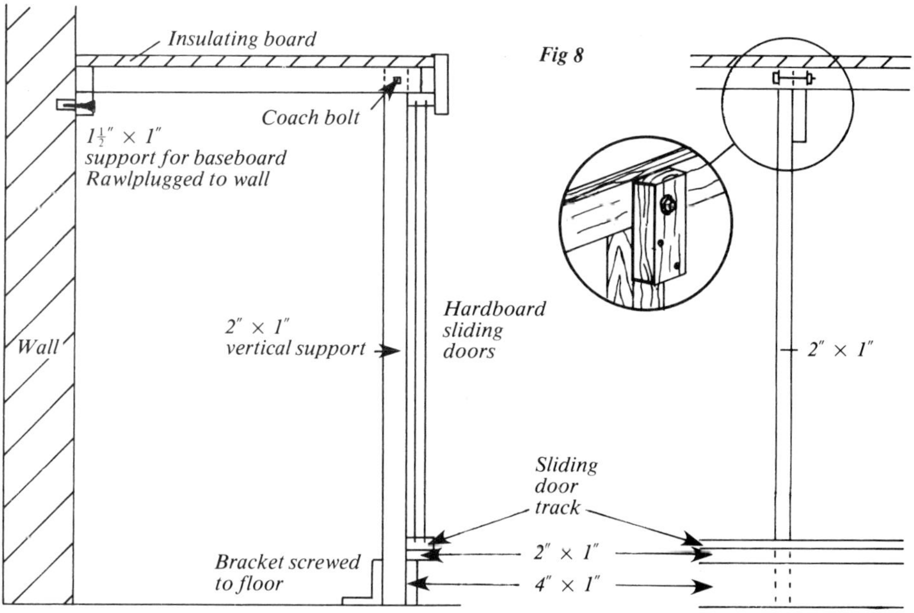


even width. Two 1¼ in no 8 screws are sufficient to hold each joint when using housing joints, but of course something longer will be required, say a 2 in or 2¼ in screw, if you are using ordinary butt joints.

The ½ in insulation board which forms the top of the baseboard should be supported at 1 ft intervals so, on a framework 2 ft wide, support should be provided lengthwise down the centre of the frame. This can be a length of 1 in × 1 in timber inserted in grooves cut in the cross members. I suggest supporting the back edge of the baseboard on a length of 1½ in × 1 in timber screwed to the wall and if possible, depending on the location, with similar supports at each end. If a wall is not available to give support at one or both ends, vertical supports cut from 2 in × 1 in timber are sufficient to provide enough support to the front edge of the frame, as shown in fig 8. The vertical supports can be screwed to the floor with brackets and at the top they can be bolted or screwed to the baseboard frame cross members. The result of such a construction is a perfectly rigid and robust assembly which will withstand any reasonable weight or strain without distortion. The cost need not be all that expensive either. The space under a baseboard such as this can be very useful for storage, and sliding doors or a curtain can be fixed along the front of the unit to make it a reasonably tidy piece of furniture. The sliding doors facing the cupboard under my own layout are simply sheets of hardboard sliding in specially provided track which can be obtained from almost any do-it-yourself store.

One does not need to be a carpenter to be a model railway enthusiast and there is no need to be put off by the idea of having to build a baseboard. The degree of skill required is only very basic and tools need consist of little more than a saw, set square, chisel, mallet, screwdriver and something to make the holes for the screws. Ideally use an electric drill but a hand drill will also do the job and is cheaper but a little slower.

In America there is a popular style of baseboard underframe which was evolved by the magazine *Model Railroader* and goes under the name of 'L-girder construction'. It is both simple and economical. The basis of this type of framing is the L-girders themselves which are made from 1 in × 2 in softwood glued and screwed at right angles along one edge of 1 in × 4 in planks so forming the L-shape. The girders thus formed are used longitudinally like the long sides of the conventional type of underframe, and support legs are attached to these and crossbraced. Joists of 2 in × 1 in wood are then screwed at about 12 in intervals across between the girders, which are always used with the 'L' in an inverted position, presenting a flat edge to take the joists or anything else which needs to be attached. For station yards or flat areas generally, insulation board sheet is just screwed down to the joists in the usual way. Out in the 'country', risers can be screwed to the L-girders as required to take the track bed above or below datum level. To give a valley, for instance, you can attach the second run of L-girders below the first when you get to a corner, a chimney breast, or some other convenient point and the L-girders can be made up of lengths from 3 ft to 6 ft or more as required to suit your layout and any rise or fall in the terrain. For a very 'scenic' type of layout this system gives obvious advantages.

The choice of baseboard surface is a vexed one and there are champions for each different sort. One material that most people agree is not any good for a model railway is hardboard. It is too thin, too liable to warp, will not take pins or screws and is altogether an undesirable material for this job. I must admit, on a well-supported surface and in a position where the layout is seldom disturbed, I strongly favour $\frac{1}{2}$ in thick wood fibre insulation board. One of its biggest virtues is that it lives up to its name and has a sound-deadening property which is an important factor when running model trains, especially where noise might cause disturbance to other people. A model train running on rails laid directly on to a hard surface, such as deal or plywood, can make a deafening sound and, apart from the irritation, which can be particularly bad on a continuous layout where the train goes round and round, it can also take away much of the realism. As well as its sound-deadening properties, insulation board is relatively light, very easy to work, cheap in comparison with other alternatives, takes pins for fixing trackwork etc, and can be gouged out easily to lay in point rodding or to cut out inspection pits or holes in the surface of the baseboard exactly where and when they are required. However, as mentioned previously, insulation board is relatively soft and flexible and does require adequate supporting at around 1 ft intervals.

Should the layout be a portable one, and some ideas on this subject will be discussed later, it may be preferable to use a harder, firmer surface such as chipboard rather than insulation board. It is heavier, a little more expensive and much less sound-absorbing, but it is also less flexible and therefore more suitable for a portable layout which is likely to be lifted on end and subjected to more handling in unaccustomed positions than the permanent layout which sits in one plane throughout its life. Blockboard and plywood can also be used but they are generally more expensive still, especially plywood in the thicker sizes which is required if warping is to be avoided. I have, however, used plywood for a tiny narrow gauge layout, but the whole layout was no bigger than 3 ft × 2 ft, which is not the type of layout we are discussing here. This particular layout was built like a box with a hinged lid. A high level terminus was connected via a ramp to a low level circuit and the plywood forming the base for the high and low levels was $\frac{1}{4}$ in thick. The low level was supported round the sides to make it look like a shallow box and the high level was hinged like a lid. This was a perfectly successful baseboard design and is still seeing service today, but it is a rather specialised type built in the main to demonstrate the small size potential of narrow gauge modelling. I doubt whether it would be appropriate for a larger layout. Sound deadening is not a problem with the small scale narrow gauge models since they are so very light in themselves and travel at comparatively slow speeds that they do not generate the hollow roaring sound that some larger models make on hard surfaces. Sound deadening can be applied in other ways should it be found that insulation board is unsuitable for a particular location, as I will show in the chapter on building the layout. But this apart, insulation board does have so many desirable properties that I can recommend it as a baseboard surface to be used

**Fig 9** *A hinged baseboard section to span a gap across a doorway. Note how the strain is taken off the hinges by the supports at 'A' and 'B'.*

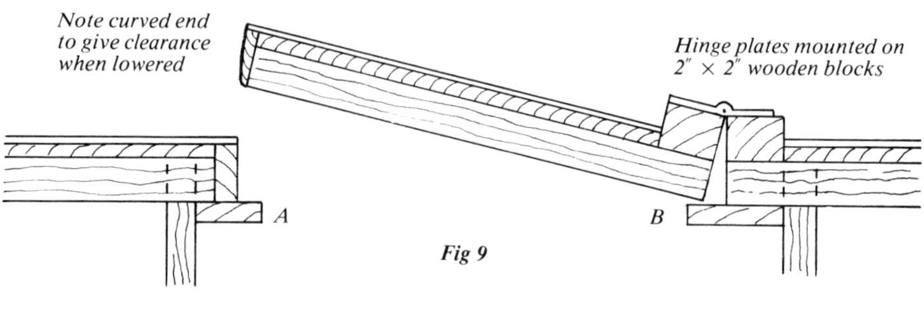


Fig 9

**Fig 10** *Contact wires are soldered to the copper strip on both sides of the track as shown using* a) *dressmaker's snap fastener socket and* b) *dressmaker's snap fastener lug. Solder* a *to one wire and* b *to the other having first passed each wire through the folding section baseboard as shown.*

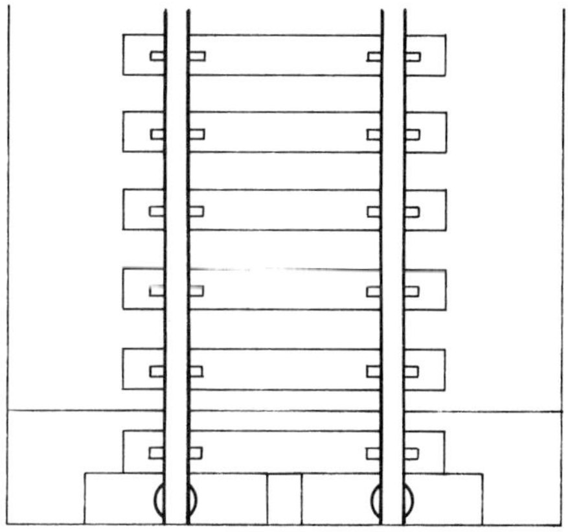


***Fig 10***

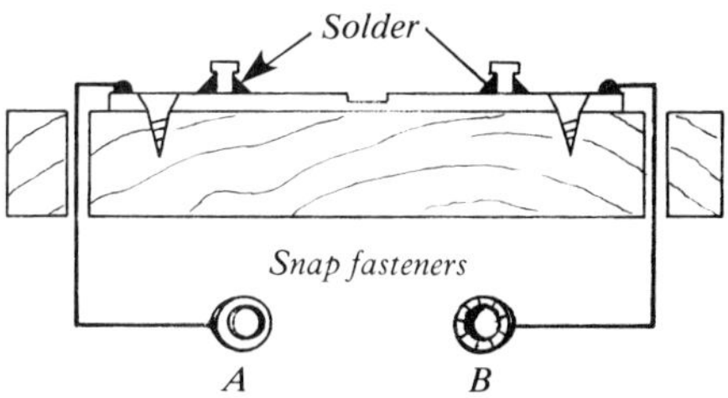


wherever possible, provided the layout is going to be reasonably permanent.

The baseboard framework shown in fig 6 encircles most of the room, but the all-important bridging section across the door is something that needs to be given special attention. It is, of course, possible just to have a section of baseboard which can be dropped into place and lifted out when access to and from the room is required. However, it is much more convenient if this section is pivoted at one end and made to hinge upwards. The important point to remember in a situation such as this is to keep the fulcrum point of the hinge well above the level of the track. Other points to watch for are the ends of the rails. Make sure they are well anchored. (See fig 10.) Fig 9 shows an example of a type of hinged section which can be used and which is easy to make out of timber using techniques no more complex than the baseboard framework already described. The hinges, ordinary 2 in square ones known as backflaps, are screwed, or preferably bolted, right through 1 in thick spacing blocks and into or through the framework itself. The best way to fit the hinges is to place the hinged section into position and support it at both ends with suitable pieces of timber screwed to the underside of the baseboard framework. After the hinges have been screwed and/or bolted in place the support at the hinged end can then be removed. It is preferable to complete all work on the baseboard and the hinged section before laying the track.

Carrying the current across the gap left by the hinged section can be accomplished in a number of different ways. The simplest is to carry a lead down one leg of the baseboard support, along the floor and up the other. The hinged section itself can be wired up to the adjacent baseboard with the wiring loose enough to take care of any movement when the section is raised. The snag with a system such as this is that it is very easy to make a mistake and drive a locomotive off the end of the rails when the hinged section is raised. Some form of rubbing contact can be arranged between the hinged section and the rest of the baseboard which can be made to carry the current across the bridge, but will cut the current off as soon as the bridge is raised. An alternative to the rubbing contact idea would be to have a snap fastener system to carry the current. Separating the snap fasteners to allow the bridge to be raised would break the circuit on one of the running rails which would prevent the locomotive from getting anywhere near the edge. (See fig 11.) This system is also suitable for portable/Exhibition layouts needing a folding section which is not permanently attached to anything other than the baseboard. It is also useful for 0 gauge modellers for coach lighting links between carriages and for many other wiring uses.

I appreciate that not everyone is in the fortunate position of having a whole spare room in their house which can be devoted entirely to a hobby, whether it is railway modelling or anything else. But it must be emphasised that, however desirable it may be to have a model railway room, it is not absolutely essential and there are a number of different solutions to the space problem which can be considered as alternatives. I suppose the first obvious hunting ground if a normally habitable room cannot be spared is to find some other area within

Fig 11

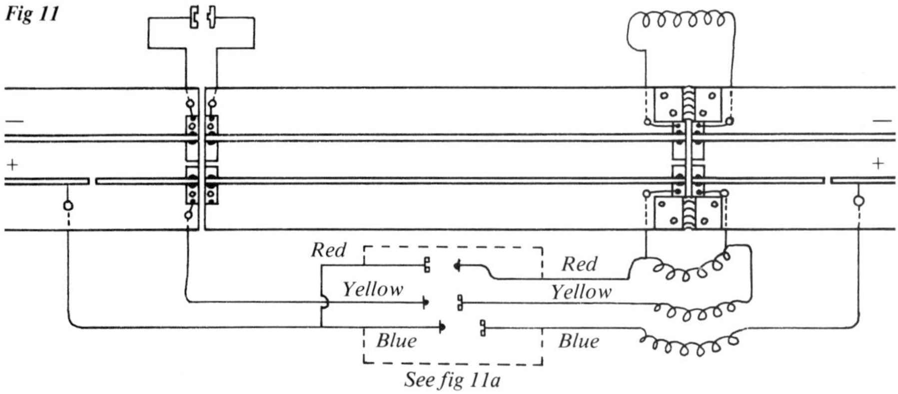


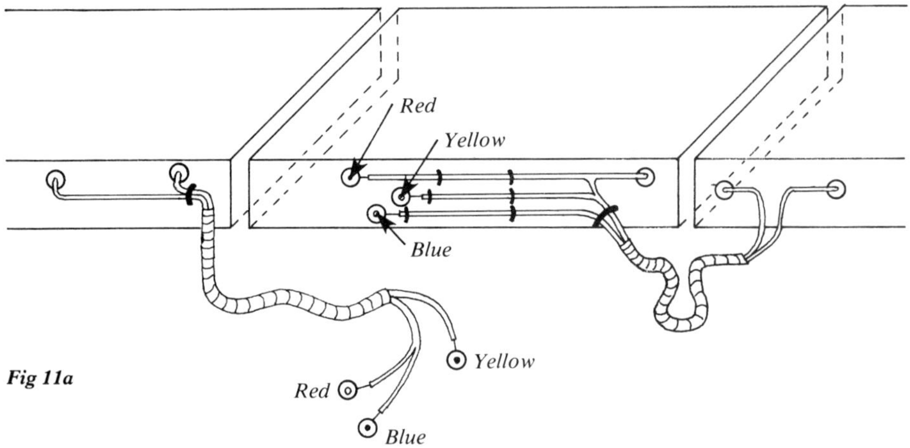


Fig 11a

**Figs 11, 11a** *Care must be taken to ensure there is sufficient wire at the hinged side of the folding section before fixing so that it can be lifted easily. Different coloured wires are used so that the correct connections can be made (blue to blue etc). As the section is self contained it can be used on both permanent and portable layouts.*

the house that is not usually lived in, such as the loft, basement or garage. A basement is probably the best of these three alternatives because it is often a place where there is an even temperature. It is cool in summer and not too cold in winter and, if the property is in a fit condition at all, it should not be damp. But I realise that less houses are built in Great Britain with basements these days and the older houses that were built with them are becoming fewer in number. The next most practical location therefore is the loft.

The loft can be a very worthwhile area to investigate, as the pages of model railway magazines will testify, since a large number of very successful layouts have been constructed in this otherwise unused and neglected space. At first glance the average loft does not look very promising. To begin with it is probably difficult to get into. Once access has been gained it is awkward to move about inside since, in all probability, there are no floor boards and you have to move on tiptoe from joist to joist, at the same time dodging the roof-supporting beams. Most lofts are dark, cavernous, dirty and dusty places and the air smells anything but fresh and sweet. No wonder that many people, on making an investigation of their loft, feel that the odds are too great, and turn their back on the place, close the trap door and forget all about it. But if you are prepared to spend a few pounds on bringing the place up to scratch it is surprising what can be achieved. Make no mistake, it will cost a few pounds, but the outlay will depend on how much of a handyman you are and what tools and materials you have on hand. When making a case for spending a few pounds from the household budget, remember that there are a considerable number of side benefits to be derived from having the loft converted, apart from the obvious one of making a place fit for a model railway to live in. It will enhance the value of the property, assuming it is your own; it will give greater heat insulation to the whole house; and the improved access and habitable space created will be useful for storage and for other domestic purposes.

The first thing to do is to improve access to the loft. The generally accepted method is to install a form of loft ladder and there are a number of different proprietary designs available. When designing ladders for lofts, most of the specialist manufacturers seem to have made provision for nearly every contingency, and it seems that few situations are so difficult as to make the fitting of one or the other of these ladders impossible. I can only speak from experience about one type of loft ladder—a wooden version manufactured by Benson's, Pontefract Avenue Works, Pontefract Lane, York Road, Leeds—which has proved thoroughly satisfactory since it was installed. I hasten to add that I have no connection with this firm other than being a very satisfied customer. When in use, the trap door leading to the loft can be opened and the ladder brought down into position within seconds, and all with the very minimum amount of effort.

Having improved the access to the loft the next step is to fix up some form of lighting, with a switch near the trap door entrance. Fluorescent tubes are recommended as the ideal lighting system, since they reduce the amount of shadows. A power source for the railway can also be considered at this stage.

Then the all-important floor can be laid. Articles appear from time to time in the various do-it-yourself journals and magazines about the subject and it is as well to look at some back numbers and study them thoroughly before embarking on the job, since a number of practical considerations need to be looked into. If in any doubt, professional advice should be sought to ensure that the joists, which will form the base of the floor, are of sufficient strength to take the added weight of the floor and yourself when walking on it. With the access improved, the floor boarded and lighting installed, the loft already begins to take on a cosy, inviting atmosphere. Any further improvements such as insulation, heating, ventilation and decoration, can follow when time permits. Meanwhile a start can be made on the all-important model railway.

As an alternative to a basement or loft, the next likely place to be considered is the garage. Access is usually no problem, although the presence of a car will most likely limit the space available, but the difficulties of heating, combating dampness, extreme temperature variations, dirt and dust are usually greater. I am not much in favour of a garage as an all-the -year-round location for a model railway, not only because of these difficulties but also because the average brick-built garage can be a pretty cheerless place in the winter. Speaking for my own garage it is very difficult to keep clean because of the dirt that falls from the car, the leaves that blow under the door, the shavings that fall from the work bench and the cobwebs produced by the countless spiders that choose to make it their home, to say nothing of the perpetual dust which rises from the concrete floor or falls from the unplastered walls. I don't doubt that these difficulties could be overcome, and the place knocked into shape made draught-proof and damp-proof, kept clean, heated and even decorated. However I do not relish the idea of being separated from the rest of the household and banished to the garage every time I want to enjoy some work on my model railway. You may or may not feel the same.

Perhaps a better solution if you have to seek covered accommodation outside the house is to invest in a garden shed built specially for the purpose of installing a model railway. There are any number of different sizes and varieties available to suit almost any location. With a raised floor and with suitable insulation of the walls they can be made cosy, dry and comfortable inside, even during very cold winter weather and with adequate ventilation they need not be too hot in the summer. It is important to avoid the direct rays of the sun in a building such as this, especially when the sun is at its fiercest, since sunlight can have a very damaging effect on a model railway. The deterioration of plastic models in shop windows after exposure to the heat of the sun is well known but, in addition to the heat effect which produces twisting and bending of the plastic, the sun also fades the colours. This can be particularly bad with printed card parts used for lineside buildings, and can also play havoc with the colours in the various materials used for creating scenic effects, grass, bushes and trees, etc.

Extreme conditions such as high temperatures, the glare of the sun or undue exposure to dampness should be avoided wherever the layout is built, since there are limits to what many of the materials used in railway modelling can withstand. For one thing, it follows from the reduction in scale of the model that tolerances cannot be so great as

*A magnificent concrete viaduct carries a 'Black 5' and seven coach train across the lawn in the natural scenic setting of Don Neale's 0 gauge garden railway* (Brian Monaghan).

they are with the real thing; so it only needs a slight displacement of the model to make it almost unworkable. If the wood used for a baseboard shrinks, twists or expands it will most likely take the track with it. It can be quite distressing to see carefully laid track thrown out of alignment because of the movement of the baseboard, and this can happen all too easily if the conditions under which the model railway is kept, operated or stored are not controlled within reasonably tolerable limits. I have even known track to become distorted after the installation of a central heating system! A previously satisfactory piece of baseboard became affected by the radiator which had to be installed nearby and as a result the baseboard dried out, shrank, and in doing so displaced a length of track. The track, about 2 ft long, was on a curve and was held at each end. It was prevented from moving outwards or inwards, so as the wood shrunk the track tried to lift itself up in the air. No wonder trains started to derail themselves at this point!

Details like this need watching and it is no good building a baseboard, laying the track and forgetting all about it. In particular, you should never lay track in such a position that access becomes difficult at a later date, perhaps because the baseboard is extended, thus making it awkward to reach across to the parts that were first constructed. Inspection, maintenance and cleaning of the track, as well as the recovery of derailed rolling stock, should always be allowed for when designing and building the baseboard. The best remedy for extreme climatic conditions is to be prepared for all eventualities. Use good quality timber, keep the baseboard under constant surveillance all through the year and avoid the obvious trouble spots such as radiators, windows in direct line with the sun, damp patches on walls, water pipes, etc. Wherever possible install your model railway where there will be adequate insulation against heat and cold, ensure that some form of heating is provided which will keep temperatures above freezing in winter, and fix up really adequate ventilation to avoid overheating in those all-too-rare days of summer heatwave.

Notwithstanding what I have just said, the most extreme conditions are to be found outdoors in the garden but, despite the apparent hardships, many model railways in all gauges even down to N have been built outdoors and have survived for many years the ravages of wind and rain as well as extreme temperatures. Railways such as these will not, of course, be the complete scenic models that we build indoors, and all rolling stock will have to be brought indoors after each operating session. Buildings such as stations, bridges and signal boxes will have to be built out of particularly robust materials, heavily protected against the elements if they are to be left permanently installed outdoors. Additional hazards with an outdoor model railway can be weeds, falling leaves, shifting stones and soil washed down by the rain as well as cats, dogs, birds, wild animals and insects which can either sit on the railway line or nibble, gnaw or scratch away at the track-work and the adjoining countryside. But with all these added difficulties there are also some tremendous advantages, particularly the one of space, and the freedom and exhilaration of being able to enjoy your hobby outdoors. If really bad weather prevents you from working on the line or enjoying an operating session outdoors there is enough construction work to keep you occupied indoors on the work bench. In fine weather, which can be any day from January to December, the sheer delight of being able to watch a train snaking its way along apparently endless miles of track is something that must surely make up for all the extra hard work. Constructing and operating a garden railway is not a venture to be approached lightheartedly. It is rather more demanding of time than most other forms of railway modelling since there is much more maintenance work to do. This must be done regularly if Mother Nature is not to take over as she surely will do if not resisted, as anyone who has seen an abandoned full-size railway branch line will testify. The one big advantage is that maintenance sessions on the railway can also be combined with gardening, something that is rather difficult to concentrate on with an indoor model railway, as some neglected gardens belonging to railway modellers will bear witness!

There are, perhaps, two basic sorts of garden layout. On the one hand there is the type that is built on a wooden framework, trestle or baseboard which is kept well clear of the ground, possibly even running round the garden fence about 3 or 4 feet above ground level, or there is the other sort which is built at ground level, either low down on the ground itself or in such a position that the ground is built up to form an embankment either side of the line. The former type is in many respects more like an ordinary model railway built for indoor use, except that the baseboard happens

*The combination of two hobbies; gardening and model railways. A magnificent example of how a model railway can be made to blend into the scenic setting of a rock garden* (Brian Monaghan).

to be outside and everything has to be built to withstand the weather. It is the latter sort, built to run at ground level, which demands the greatest attention, both in the building and in the maintenance, but which at the same time provides the most satisfying result. Here there is a tremendous opportunity to combine your skill as both a gardener and a railway modeller to create a remarkably realistic setting for a layout, using rocks, rock plants, dwarf conifers, bushes, flowers and trees. Despite the out-of-scale nature of some of these plants most of these outdoor garden railways provide a very realistic setting for a model train.

To build such a line you can either lay the track on a suitably drained foundation and build a rock garden around it, or else the route for the line can be carved out of the existing terrain. Either way, the work of getting the correct levels and gradients on which to lay the track has to be planned and carried out very carefully, and the track base must be firm and above all very well drained. Concrete or stone are probably the best foundation materials, and if wood is to be used it should be well preserved and properly treated. The track will have to be regularly inspected to remove displaced stones and leaves, and the ballast should be picked over from time to time to assist in the drainage and to remove any weeds that take root. Some of the modern weedkillers may be effective, but I would recommend carrying out a sample test application first to ensure that the type you are going to use is not likely to have a harmful effect on the track. One thing is certain, steel rail, even treated steel rail, cannot be used successfuly outdoors for any length of time and a non-ferrous metal such as nickel silver should be employed.

Garden railway modelling is really a subject in itself. Several books have been devoted to this aspect of the hobby and articles appear in the monthly magazines from time to time. In the brief mention here it is enough to know that the garden is an accepted place in which to build a model railway. Some excellent ones have been built which show that, whatever problems exist, and it cannot be denied that there are problems, they can be overcome. I have no personal experience of garden railway modelling and cannot speak with authority on the subject, but I can appreciate the advantages of such a location from the examples I have seen, and I feel encouraged to recommend it to anyone who is willing to try.

To come back indoors again, the modeller who cannot find a spare room, or space round the walls of his bedroom or bed-sitter, who hasn't a loft or a basement, who has no room in his garage after he has parked the car, and who does not fancy the garden, still need not despair. Some excellent portable schemes have been tried and tested and have been found to be perfectly acceptable. Some examples are shown in figs 12-16.

**Fig 12** *(left) A baseboard hinged to a wall. When in use, it is swung down and the free end supported by a folding trestle.* **Fig 13** *(right) A rack of baseboard sections, with the permanent section forming the top. Sections to extend the layout stack away behind the curtain when not in use.*

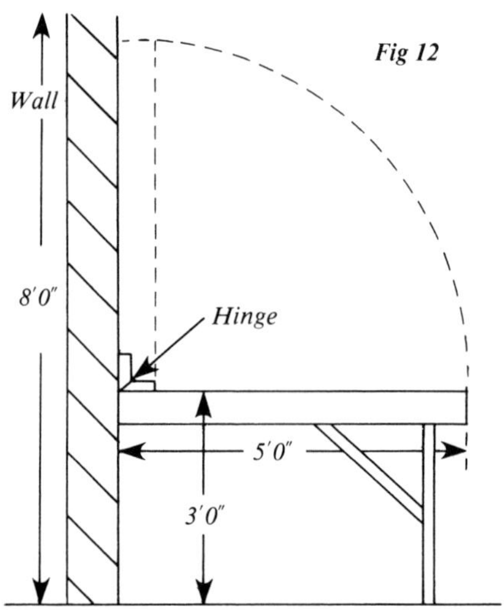


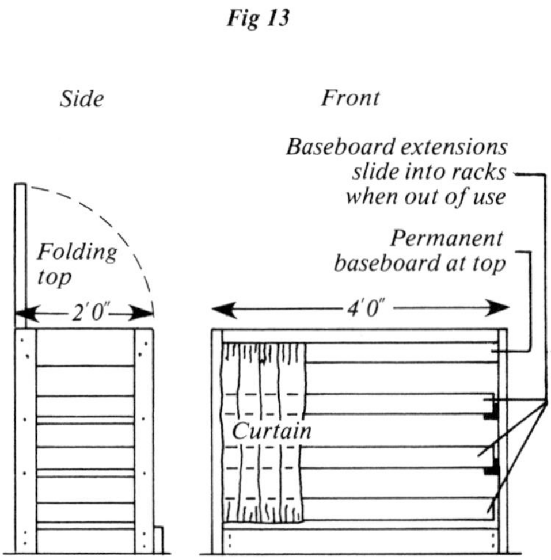

Fig 12 shows a scheme whereby a baseboard is hinged against the wall. When out of use it folds up against the wall and takes up no more space than the depth of the baseboard frame. To allow for any permanent features on the layout, such as buildings and signals, the depth of the frame should be at least 6 in on an 00 gauge layout. To bring the layout into use, the baseboard is simply swung down through 90 degrees and supported at the free end on a trestle. The trestle can be free-standing or it can itself be hinged to the underside of the baseboard. Alternatively, support for the free end of the baseboard can be provided by a chair or some other piece of furniture of the appropriate height. The only restriction on this system is that the height of the ceiling will limit the length of the baseboard, unless two such baseboards are built, each hinged on opposite walls and arranged so that they meet in the middle when they are lowered. Another alternative might be to hinge the long side of the layout along the wall, and in this case the length of the layout can be as long as the wall itself.

Fig 13 shows a simple system whereby a layout is built on a series of baseboards, each of a standard and easily manageable size and which, when out of use, can be stacked away in a specially constructed frame. The frame can be disguised as a piece of furniture, either with curtaining or sliding doors built to obscure the front, and the top can be used to display ornaments in much the same way as a sideboard. When in use the layout would have to be assembled by fitting the separate baseboard sections to trestles, which can also be accommodated in the storage frame.

Illustrated in fig 14 is a simple scheme where a layout consists of two baseboards hinged at one end so that they can be folded together like the covers of a book. When in use, one end of the layout is swung open, thereby doubling the length of the layout. Suitable trestles can be fitted with hinges to the underside of the baseboards, or alternatively the whole unit can be rested on a dining or kitchen table. When folded up, the unit could be slid away out of sight under the bed. A wallpaper pasting table, such as can be obtained from most do-it-yourself shops, is made on the same principle, except that the hinges work the other way so that the tops of the table fold outwards. Also, they usually have a surface of thin plywood or hardboard which is not very suitable for model railway, as explained earlier.

Fig 15 shows a rather similar idea to fig 12, except that the two baseboard sections are hinged along their side instead of at one end. Here it is suggested that one side could be permanently fixed to the wall. The space underneath the baseboard could then be used for storage. The half of the layout which swings down could be supported by trestles when the layout is in use, and out of use it

**Fig 14** *(left) An extending baseboard built on the principle of a decorator's table.* **Fig 15** *(right) A baseboard fixed to a wall and extendable in width by means of a folding section.*

*Fig 14*

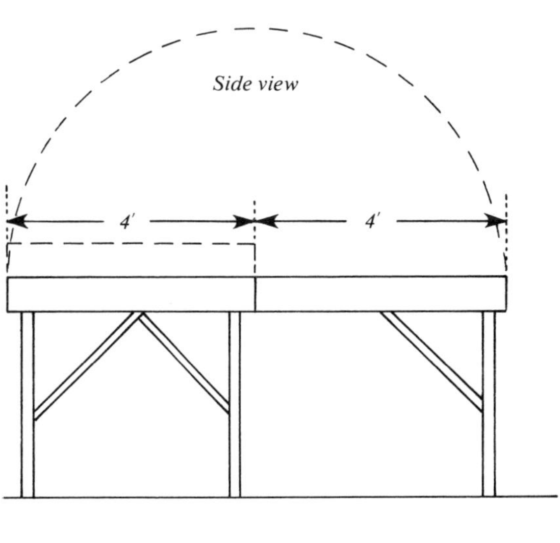


*Fig 15*

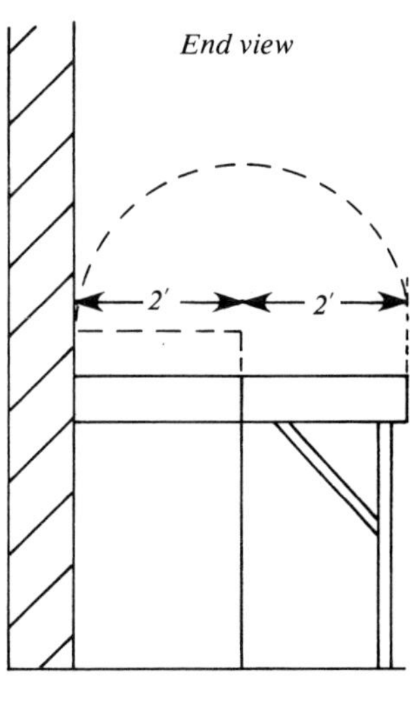

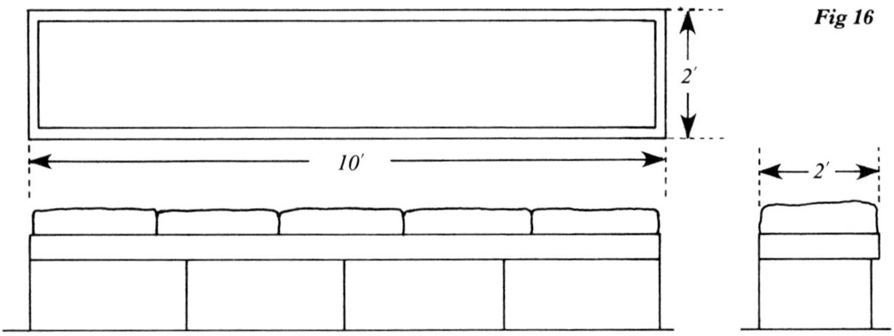


**Fig 16**

**Fig 16** *Removing the seat cushions of this bench seat uncovers a lid which can be lifted to expose a baseboard 10 ft × 2 ft, which is suitable for an N gauge layout.*

could swing back to form a top to the cabinet, very similar to a sideboard.

A simplification of fig 15 is given in fig 16, where the baseboard, a long narrow one, is incorporated into a bench seat which can be made as a permanent feature along a wall or under a window. Removing the cushions uncovers a lid which, when raised, reveals a model railway layout. The snag with this idea is that the space is very restricted and too low down.

Many other ideas are possible and may come to mind. A visit to the Peco Modelrama at the Peco head office in Beer, just two miles west of Seaton in Devon, is well recommended as a source of inspiration. Here you will find examples of working model railway layouts in various gauges from N to O built in settings that simulate typical locations to be found around the house or garden. The simulations are very realistic, in many cases cleverly contrived and illustrate, in practical terms, not only how and what space can be utilised to the best advantage but how it can be done and how attractive the end result can be made to be. If you or your domestic authorities have any uncertainties about how a model railway can be incorporated into your home a visit to the Peco Modelrama will dispel the doubts. For the indoor exhibits it is normally open all the year but for the outdoor amenities it opens from the Spring Bank Holiday to mid-October. Very often the brightest ideas are inspired by the most difficult and unpromising situations. It is probably true to say that a really determined model railway enthusiast will find some room somewhere to create a layout wherever he or she may be. I have even heard of one being built in a submarine! Many articles have appeared in the model railway press showing some of the very small gauge layouts being built in suitcases, on coffee tables, and even in a television cabinet and a violin case! Where there's a will there's a way is a very apt saying, but please remember to keep it a permanent way in the sense that the track is laid down permanently on the baseboard, and, if there is any moving to be done, it is the baseboard that is moved and not the track. One final word on this subject—if you do decide to build a portable or folding type of baseboard, don't forget to remove all your rolling stock from the track and fix all the accessories firmly in place before you put the layout away for the night.

## Chapter 3

# Choosing the type of layout you want

It is perfectly possible to build a model railway without ever first thinking about what type it is going to be, or even what type it is after you have finished. Track can be bought and laid to fill the space available, equipment —including locomotives, carriages and wagons—can be purchased because it catches your eye or it appeals to you, and the whole lot can be made to work and can be operated with tremendous pleasure, just as the fancy takes you. Is there anything wrong in that? It could be argued that if *you* find it satisfactory then this is all that matters, and there is not a lot of point in anyone else worrying about it any further. However, it is a bit like the schoolboy who starts a stamp collection with a bumper pack of pictorials and a tube of glue and proceeds to stick his stamps in the album in no particular order, and with absolutely no thought for the future or even why he is doing it. It may satisfy him at the time, when he knows no better, but the wiser, more mature collector realises that a stamp collection is pointless unless the individual stamps are sorted, properly arranged and displayed in groups or themes.

As with any hobby there are recognised ideal standards, which add purpose to it. Rather than simply accumulating a haphazard collection of unrelated models, it is surely much more satisfactory to decide on a particular period, location and theme for the full-size prototype of your model railway and build up a collection of models and equipment within that framework. Such a model railway with a clearly defined purpose or theme will provide more satisfaction to build and operate and is likely to have more lasting value and appeal than the first sort. It is largely a personal opinion which I know not everyone shares, but it is worth the consideration at the start before you commit yourself to spending time and money which you may later regret.

When talking about types of railway I have in mind their outward physical characteristics based on known examples of actual railways. Instead of just amassing a whole load of equipment and filling in every square inch of space on the baseboard with sidings and running rails, why not base the layout on a particular aspect of full-size railways that interests you most? If you have an overwhelming fascination for the largest express passenger locomotives you will want a main line setting in which to operate them. Ideally, this should have a length of track which will enable the locomotive to accelerate its train to a realistic express speed. If you like the peace, quiet and slower moving pace of a country town you will find a lot of satisfaction in a branch line layout. You may admire the powerful looks of foreign locomotives or, at the opposite end of the scale, the quaint charm of the narrow gauge. All these various types of railways have their different characteristics which can be recreated in model form. Surely, therefore, it is a wise move to get to know something about your chosen prototype before you start to model it.

Surprisingly, not everyone approaches railway modelling this way. To some people the model is the beginning and the end, and as long as one model lines up with another, is reasonably proportioned and looks and works well, it is the limit of their ambitions. I would like to point out that there can be a lot more to the hobby than just that, as very many people have found to their pleasure. The hobby has been growing up over many years and whereas in the early days the measure of a layout was in the amount of equipment, track and rolling stock you managed to cram into a given space, nowadays it is largely judged by the degree of realism and faithfulness to the prototype that it manages to achieve. This is probably due to the higher standard of realism of the individual models themselves. Gone are the days when it was accepted that a manufacturer could produce one model of rather dubious outline and offer it to the public as either 'Flying Scotsman', 'Royal Scot', 'Caerphilly Castle' or 'Lord Nelson', with only the colour of the paintwork and the engine name and number to distinguish one locomotive from another. Now we have come to expect a much higher standard of realism with each individual model offered by commercial manufacturers and home builders. Also, it follows that we should not want to spoil this by displaying and operating such authentic-looking models in anything other than an equally authentic-looking setting.

The best way to achieve a sense of realism and authenticity is to acquire some knowledge of the genuine article. The best way of all is, of course, to have direct contact with, or experience of, actual railways, but not all of us who are interested in making historical models or models of foreign railways are able to achieve this aim. The obvious answer is, of course, to do as much reading about the subject as possible and to study as many photographs and drawings as you can get hold of. Back numbers of the various model railway magazines are probably the best source of information, since the material they contain will be tailored to the requirements of railway modellers, whereas so many other sources of information such as the enthusiast railway books, railway histories and technical books on railways often leave gaps in the sort of detailed information that modellers seek. However, from whatever source, you cannot have too much prototype information and you should aim at building up a library of books, drawings and photographs covering all aspects of your chosen prototype and location. This will stand you in good stead for future construction work, as well as providing you with a background of knowledge which will enable you to create a really authentic model railway.

When establishing a theme and a type of layout which aims at authenticity it is not always necessary to limit your powers of creation to such an extent that you just slavishly copy a particular prototype, past or present. Very often some of the most realistic and attractive looking layouts are really the product of a flight of fancy. Peter Denny's Buckingham Branch layout is a typical example. He has created a most authentic-looking period Great Central Railway layout in a railway location which is completely imaginary. Though the railway system he has modelled never actually existed, at least it might have been possible, and the collection of rolling stock and accessories is authentic for the Edwardian period he has chosen to model. The introduction of a British Railways Britannia Pacific at the head of one of his trains or the parking of a model Leyland National bus in the station yard would, of course, destroy all the atmosphere. Go a stage further and deliberately mix up your periods such as this and introduce a completely unrestricted variety of models and the layout

*'Welsh Pony' and train at Madderport on the late John Ahern's Madder Valley Railway. The premises of Quibble & Cuss, the estate agents, are just to the right of the horse bus standing in Pool Street. This historic model railway is on display at the Pendon Museum, Long Wittenham, Berks* (Pendon Museum).

would degenerate into a meaningless collection.

Sometimes, however, it is possible to get away with a freelance layout, by which is meant a model railway that is not representative of any particular company, period or location. But, strangely enough, it is not as easy as it may look. In fact, if it is to be done satisfactorily, it calls for as much, if not more, artistry and skill than the layout that religiously follows a particular prototype. With a freelance layout you become your own mechanical and civil engineer which is, after all, assuming a rather large mandate. The classic example of a freelance system is the late John Ahern's Madder Valley Railway. On this layout—which, by the way, is now being looked after by the Pendon Museum at Long Wittenham, Abingdon, Berkshire—locomotives and rolling stock based on prototypes drawn from all over the world were successfully operated together without raising anyone's eyebrows. He even mixed locomotives and rolling stock of different gauges which necessitated them being built to different scales, but somehow or other they looked perfectly natural in the setting he created. In fact, John Ahern's work was universally admired and has probably inspired more layouts than any other single source. Despite the outrageously varied collection of locomotives and rolling stock, he succeeded in knitting them all together and creating an atmosphere, a sense of 'oneness', which immediately stamped the model 'Madder Valley', almost as if it was an actual location instead of the product of one man's fertile imagination. This was due in no small measure to his skill as a landscape, scenic and building modeller as his classic works on the subject, 'Miniature Landscape Modelling' and 'Miniature Building Construction', bear witness.

We can, of course, always invent excuses for satisfying our particular fancies when it comes to rolling stock. The favourite situation these days is to run a preservation line where it is possible to argue a case for mixing a very wide variety of rolling stock. The Bluebell Line in Sussex operates full-size locomotives which probably never met in their lives before they became preserved, and it is very easy to visualise other situations and other preservation schemes which might just as easily have come about. But preservation schemes are not the only source of imaginative projects. If, for example, the Channel tunnel had been built 50 years ago when it was first thought of, it might now have been possible to see Continental locomotives as well as rolling stock running on British Rail and vice versa. This chould be an excuse for adding a few of the wonderfully detailed Continental models to a British model railway system.

It is sometimes fascinating to imagine situations that might have been, especially if there is some foundation for the theory. History is full of examples of 'might-have-been's if certain events had happened in a different way. What, for example, might the Great Western Railway look like today if it had never been nationalised in 1948? What might the Lynton and Barnstaple Railway look like if a preservation society had been formed to save it instead of letting it be scrapped by the Southern Railway in 1935? What might a railway system have looked like in the Outer Hebrides if some important industry had developed in one of the islands which necessitated the construction of a line? As well as the purely imaginary situations such as these there are any number of actual schemes for building railways that never came to fruition. Some got as far as the building of earth works and civil engineering structures which never carried any revenue-earning rails, whereas others, maybe, got no further than the publication of a company prospectus. Many such schemes are revealed in the numerous railway history books that are available from bookshops and libraries, and they afford excellent subjects for imagining what things might have been like if they had been built. Creating a fictional history for such a line can become an absorbing sideline which gives scope for imagination as well as the need for research. Perhaps your own home town had an idea for building a railway at one time which came to nothing?

I remember reading once of an ambitious post-World War 2 scheme for building a new station at Bath, in Somerset, which would have combined the Midland and Somerset and Dorset Railway station at Bath Green Park with the GWR at Bath Spa. What a place that would have been with S & D 2-8-0s, Midland Class 2 4-4-0s and Black 5s rubbing shoulders with GWR Castles, Kings and Halls and all the rest of the copper-capped brigade! This particular scheme might be too large a project to build in model form, as it was found to be with the full-size original, but there must be many other local schemes of lesser calibre which you may know about or could find out about in your own home area and which might form the basis of a model railway.

When deciding on the type of model railway you wish to build, there are a number of decisive factors which will govern your choice

**Top** *Lynton & Barnstaple Railway 2-6-2T No 761 'Taw' in Southern Railway livery construction from a Weald Models 009 cast metal kit on a Minitrix chassis* (Weald Models).

**Above** *Here is a locomotive that might have been but never was! A German 2-6-8-0 Mallet which was designed in 1943 for working heavy freight trains but was never built. This imposing Marklin HO model bears the number 53.0001 which was allotted to the prototype* (Marklin).

and which you will have to consider at the outset if you are not to experience disappointment later. For example, obviously there is no point in setting your sights on a main line system if the space you have available is very limited. Main line express passenger trains require a lot more space in which to operate if they are not going to look ridiculous. In particular, they need wider-radius curves and a lengthy stretch of track on which to run if the train lengths are not going to look unreasonably short. Space therefore is a principal factor in determining the type of layout you can build successfully.

The availability of proprietary equipment may also be a point you will need to consider. If your ability to do a lot of the construction work is limited, you may need to fall back on ready-to-run proprietary items. Luckily, today the trade has introduced a wide range of items to satisfy most popular needs, especially in 00 and HO scales. However, despite the wide choice of accessories and construction aids available, it is simply not physically possible to cater for every single need. Boiler fittings are a case in point. Unless you are prepared to turn chimneys, domes and safety valve covers yourself, or have them turned for you at a price, you are possibly going to find it difficult to complete models of some of the older pre-grouping railway company locomotives. The amount of spare time you can afford is another important factor to take into construction. As well as the time needed for construction there is also the question of maintenance to consider. This is something that beginners seldom give thought to until they come face to face with the problem. They find that they are devoting more and more time to cleaning and maintaining track, points and electrical connections and not enough to carrying out operating sessions and further new construction work. The larger and more complex the layout, the more cleaning there is to do and the greater the chance of point blades coming un-soldered, of the electrical wiring coming adrift or of the switches requiring attention.

Another point to consider, assuming you are keen to choose a particular prototype subject as a modelling project, is whether you are going to be satisfied with the limitation you may have set yourself in choosing that particular prototype, bearing in mind that the varieties of different locomotives may have been severely limited. I have in mind, for example, the Southern Railway Lyme Regis branch which would make a very attractive model scenically, but so far as I know there was only one type of locomotive that ran on this branch in latter years. Therefore, I am sure a modeller would begin to feel the limitations of such a modelling project after all the building and construction work had been completed. I think most of us like to see a bit of variety in our motive power and rolling stock, and undoubtedly it adds interest to the hobby. To deny yourself this pleasure would eventually be regretted, I feel sure.

The modern image enthusiast is almost bound to want to build a main line type of layout, since the very essence of modern railways is long haul set trains operating on city-to-city routes. But is the more rigid set format of the modern trains going to limit operating possibilities? In particular, are the liner trains which, so far as the actual rolling stock is concerned, consist of nothing more than bogie flat wagons, going to be as much fun to operate as the old fashioned pick-up goods type where shunting operations can give infinite variety to the format of a train? You may well think 'yes', in which case you will presumably have thought it all out beforehand, but don't spend time and money on building a layout only to find out after it is completed that the operating possibilities are limited.

In talking about modern railways I am thinking primarily of those in the UK, where it is the avowed policy of British Railways to concentrate on main line traffic. BR prefer freight which can be moved in train loads between major rail centres rather than individual wagon loads originating from, or destined to go to, small outlying branches, factory sidings and small town stations, yards or depots. The situation is not quite the same in America and on the Continent, where the quieter backwaters of the railway system, though declining, are still to be found. Here it is possible to indulge in modern practice using up-to-date diesel locomotives hauling modern wagons in short-length freight trains of less than half-a-dozen wagons, each containing individual loads.

Nostalgia can be one of the most persuasive forces in choosing a subject for railway modelling. It is undoubtedly one of the reasons why the hobby is booming so much today. Britain's railways, and in fact railways all over the world, have gone, or are going through, a period of tremendous change which is radically altering their appeal. People still watch them from the lineside, but no doubt for different reasons than they did 20 or 30 years ago. Not many of the people who watched the trains go by then can find the same interest today. To those people 'things ain't what they used to be', and modelling has become a means of creating a three-dimensional moving picture in miniature of something that was known and loved in the past, and is no longer there to be seen as a matter of course today. There is nothing wrong in that. If railway modelling is a hobby and a pastime why shouldn't the person—if he wants to—let it pander to his old-fashioned, outdated ideas and let him enjoy his backward-looking sentiment? Your own private model world is the perfect safety valve for expressing feelings such as these. There are enough occasions in our everyday life when we may have to conform to current trends and ideas and in very many instances we see the need and would not have it otherwise. But the sort of person who gained pleasure in whiling away the hours on a country station platform watching a tank engine shunt wagons in the goods yard, witness the local stopping passenger trains arriving and departing, the expresses roaring through and noting the variety of rolling stock and traffic movements, cannot be expected to experience the same pleasure today, when in all probability the station is closed to traffic, the goods yard rails lifted and the buildings and platform razed to the ground.

However, the old order of doing things is perfectly possible in model form and harms no one. There is no denying, with all the material aids there are today, that it is possible to produce some very realistic and convincing effects guaranteed to evoke thoughts of nostalgia from even the most hard-bitten cynic. The period you may wish to recapture will be governed by all sorts of personal motives, but setting a target date in your mind for the period of the model you intend to create will, if you do the job properly, involve the application of a certain degree of discipline in choosing prototypes to model, their colour schemes and insignia, and even such things as posters and hoardings, if you are going to succeed in creating a completely authentic model which, to you, represents a period in your past.

An authentic-looking model layout can be achieved by paying 100 per cent attention to detail—if you have the time to spare. But it is not by any means essential to work to such infinite limits, and indeed in many cases, particularly when it comes to scale distances, it is quite impossible to do so. As long as the atmosphere is established, the exact number of sleepers, paving stones, telegraph poles and other insignificant trivia does not matter at all. In choosing to build a particular model station, for example, many details such as the correct number and length of sidings, size of platforms and radius of points and curves may not be possible to reproduce within the space available. This is where the eye of an artist comes in. An artist can paint a picture which somehow or other looks more convincing and evokes a greater sense of awareness of the subject than the most technically perfect photograph; yet should this be a portrait, it does not need to show every whisker, every wrinkle or blemish on the skin. The most successful portraits not only succeed in portraying the visual appearance of the sitter, they also tell you something about the subject as a person. The true artist does this with an eye and a feeling for the subject that defies description, but in essence he concentrates the subject matter on to his canvas, emphasising what matters at the expense of the more insignificant detail. In a sense the artist is someone who knows what to leave out rather than what to put in, and I am sure this is true about the successful 'authentic' railway modeller. To evoke the sensation of the original prototype requires some degree of faithful observation and copying, but there are many details that can be legitimately shrunk to fit the space available, and some others that can possibly be left out altogether.

When it comes to deciding what type of layout you want to build, the sky is the limit these days. Never before has there been so much variety to choose from and never before has it been so difficult to decide, and hence to make a start! This question of choice is sometimes a double-edged weapon. Too much of it and the need to make a decision itself becomes a problem. Provided you can overcome the problems of space, availability of proprietary parts and models, and any possible limitations on your budget or your free time, the question of choice does of course become a very personal one. You are obviously going to build the type of layout that interests you most and the reasons for your choice can be manifold. Let us take a look at the different types of layout you can choose from today, and the possible advantages or disadvantages of each one. I will ignore as far as possible the question of scale or gauge at this stage as we will discuss this more fully in the next chapter.

In no particular order of priority, merit or importance, I would suggest the following broad categories for differentiating between the various types of layouts:

## Main line

By this I mean a large layout on which you can run main line express passenger trains of at least five or six coach length at scale express passenger train speeds. Even in the smallest gauges and scales such a layout demands a fair degree of space to accommodate the large-radius curves and length of running rails that are necessary if any degree of realism is to be achieved. The sight of an express train chasing its tail round a tight circle of track looks quite ridiculous and unworthy of the attentions of a serious modeller. Five or six coaches are the very minimum you should aim at, as most main line express passenger trains are usually double this length. Needless to say, any improvement on five or six coaches will add realism to the layout. Station platforms, assuming a station as a necessity, must of course be long enough to accommodate the coaches and, if it is to be a terminus, the locomotive as well. Size and the space available are really the limiting factors when deciding whether you can build a main line layout. One of the desirable features of such a layout is that it gives unlimited scope for operating models of your choice, since there need not be any restriction on the type of locomotives or rolling stock you can legitimately run. You can have the largest express passenger engines, goods engines, small tank engines and as much rolling stock, carriages and wagons as you can find room for.

## Branch line

Perhaps the opposite end of the scale to a main line layout, the branch line has become tremendously popular because of its space-saving possibilities. Even so, most prototype branch lines occupied (the past tense is more often than not necessary, as most of them are now closed) more space than the average modeller could hope to spare, but a large degree of licence can be used to compress station track plans, sidings and lineside

*The high level approach to Pool End terminus on John Woodman's extensive 00 gauge main line layout. To the left just beyond the turntable is the loco depot maintenance workshop and to the right in the far distance the coaling stage can be seen* (Tom Boulter).

features into the minimum space available without detracting too seriously from the overall effect. Above all, most branch line layouts can be operated realistically with short length trains, two or three coaches being quite sufficient in some cases, with engines that are themselves short in length. The generic description 'branch line' has also come to include the small cross-country through route which was also operated by short length trains and small engines, and had an atmosphere similar to the branch line. However, the important difference with the branch line is that it had a terminus at the extreme end of the line. It is the building and operating of such a terminal station that provides so much of the attraction of the branch line layout. The one possible snag is that, generally speaking, you have to exclude the larger, more exciting engines from your stud of locomotives, although there are probably enough exceptions to this rule to justify anyone breaking it if they really feel they must.

## Modern

By modern we generally mean the contemporary post-steam era of today. Perhaps the odd steam locomotive can be allowed to creep in, but broadly speaking—in Britain at any rate—the motive power will be diesel or electric. Such a layout will, if it is to achieve any reasonable degree of realism, demand a fair amount of space as the tendency for modern railway systems is to concentrate on long haul block trains travelling great distances at speed. The same problems that apply to main line layouts will therefore apply to the

modern-style system, in that large radius curves and a reasonably long length of run will be required. The main advantage of modern contemporary layouts is that you can draw inspiration from the real-life locomotives and trains which can be seen working any day of the week. Problems regarding the prototype, such as livery, details of construction, up-to-date modifications, operating methods, etc, can be resolved quite simply by going out to see for yourself. The disadvantages, in addition to the big one of space requirements, appear to me to be that, since most modern trains run as block trains or multiple units, which shuttle back and forth, there does not appear to be so much opportunity for variety of rolling stock, train formations and operating methods as there does with the older type of railway system that had a greater emphasis on individual wagon loads.

## Historical

Using historical in the very broadest sense I mean anything that is not contemporary with today. In Britain this type of layout could be broken down into very clearly defined periods based on events that affected the structure or organisation of our railways. The most obvious periods and events are: post- or pre-nationalisation, pre-grouping, Edwardian, or early Victorian primitive. The post-nationalisation period of the middle to late 1950s perhaps offers the widest choice of prototype material, since during this time most of the locomotives and rolling stock from the four main pre-nationalisation railway companies were still operating together with the standard British Railways designs and there is scope for mixing steam, diesel and electric propulsion together. Despite the many advantages this period offers, it is not so universally popular amongst modellers. Perhaps it is because it is still so recent and hasn't yet fanned the flames of nostalgia.

Possibly the most popular historical period for modelling is the immediate pre-nationalisation era of the late 1930s and 1940s (but ignoring the war years), and the big attraction of this period is undoubtedly the smart liveries used by the four main railway companies—LMS, LNER, GWR and SR. There is a very wide choice of equipment, kits, finished models and accessories covering this period and no practical difficulty in the way of making a successful model. The GWR is acknowledged as being the most popular of the four main groups and there is no shortage of kits, models and prototype information to enable anyone to make an authentic model based on GWR practice, provided you are prepared not to introduce post-nationalisation prototypes or mix post-World War 2 locomotives and liveries on a layout based on practice in the 1930s. This sort of discipline takes some watching. It comes easy enough if you have accurate memories of the periods concerned, but you are at the mercy of other people if you were born after this period. Checking up on past practices can be regarded as part of the fun of an historical layout and it is well worth while to make a thorough job of it for the satisfaction it undoubtedly gives. You may, however, have to prepare yourself for the time when someone tells you that things were never done that way and you have been wasting your time because you have done it all wrong! It's bound to happen so prepare yourself for it so that it doesn't worry you so much when it comes. If you have got all your facts together and you can prove you are right and the other fellow is wrong, so much the better!

Going back into history still further, the next generally accepted demarcation point in British railway history is the grouping of 1923, when the then comparatively large number of independent railway companies, some of them quite small in size, were amalgamated to make the big four. The immediate pre-grouping period was marred by World War 1, but prior to that we of course had the Edwardian period and this is generally accepted as being the heyday of Britain's railways. Railways spread their tentacles all over the country and carried all the freight and passenger traffic that was worth carrying. Competition was beginning to be felt though, mainly from the electric street trams, but this only encouraged the railway companies to devise means of combating the opposition which added yet more variety to an already abundant collection of locomotives and rolling stock. Because of this tremendous variety of equipment and the wide diversity of designs, liveries and colour schemes, the model railway manufacturers can only scratch at the surface, and it is in many cases difficult to build up a comprehensive and at the same time representative collection of rolling stock

**Opposite** *The garden is one solution to the space problem when running scale-length 11 coach trains on a modern image layout. A Class 50 heads towards Birmingham New Street (through the tunnel into the shed at the top of the picture) as a LMR Class 83 takes the electrified route to Wolverhampton on Don Jones's 00 gauge garden layout* (Brian Monaghan).

GREAT CENTRAL

items for one particular company, using commercially produced models and parts. It must therefore be accepted that, for an Edwardian layout, rather more items must be home-made or scratch-built than for models based on a later period in time. Nevertheless, there are exceptions to this rule and a number of manufacturers, including one of the big toy firms, realising the attraction of the Edwardian period, have produced some complete ready-to-run models and a fair selection of kits and accessories. Some companies are better served than others. The Great Western, London & North Western, London Brighton & South Coast, Midland and Caledonian railways are represented by several kits and models at the moment and there are one or two others besides, so there really need not be too much difficulty.

When it comes to scratch-building or assembling kits, perhaps the biggest single problem will be the painting, lining and lettering. Not all pre-grouping colours are available ready-mixed, so careful preparation will be required in a number of cases. Then, when it comes to adding the lining and lettering, the elaborate styles used by most pre-grouping companies will require a fair degree of skill to apply, and there is not the wide range of transfers to help that there is with the post-grouping period. Unless you are particularly skilful as a painter it is very probable that some simplification of the livery details will be required.

Going back to the first days of railways, the early Victorian primitives such as the Liverpool to Manchester Railway present another and different challenge to modellers since, as well as having to construct practically all the equipment yourself, you will also have to do a lot of the research. Just about everything was different in those days—locomotives, coaches and wagons, signalling and even the trackwork which, judging from the early prints we see, appears to have been ballasted with cinders which hid all traces of the sleepers. Some fascinating models have been made of this period, including at least one GWR Broad Gauge layout with some of the very complex mixed gauge track. There is absolutely no shortage of material, although a fair amount of digging will be required to establish facts on many items which we take for granted today. Modelling in this period does call for a lot of hard work, but at least you have the satisfaction of doing something different and of arousing the interests of others should you decide to put the results of your work on exhibition. It might also be considered that you are undertaking a worthwhile piece of historical research.

It almost goes without saying that anyone who is interested in modelling based on historical times, whatever period is chosen, is well advised to join the Historical Model Railway Society, which caters for the needs of such modellers. The historical facts that modellers seek are not necessarily those recorded by historians, and more specialised information is required than can usually be found in most history books on railways. Piecing together such information can be a long business if you work on your own. However, it is often possible to find someone in a society such as this who has already covered the same ground and who will be willing to share his information with you. It really is amazing how absorbing the quest for information can become once the interest has been roused, and the need for such research can offer a new dimension to the hobby.

## Overseas railways

National characteristics can result in different types of railways as practically everyone knows, and an increasing number of railway modellers in Britain are turning to the Continent of Europe or to North America as a source of inspiration for their railway modelling. In many cases this is due to the increasing amount of beautifully detailed model locomotives and rolling stock of foreign manufacture now being imported into the country. The difficulties of importation usually result in slightly higher prices, but some people regard the extra expense as justified in exchange for the high degree of

**Top left** *A 4 mm scale North British Railway brake third finished in the NBR-lined lake livery built by D.C. Lawrence* (Larry Goddard).

**Centre left** *This beautifully finished 4 mm scale Pickersgill 4-4-0 No 97 resplendent in Caledonian livery is a most useful locomotive for Scottish model railway enthusiasts since the class ranged wide over Scotland and lasted intact into BR days. The model was built from a Nu-Cast cast metal kit* (Nu-Cast Model Engineering).

**Left** *This magnificent Great Central 4-6-2T (LNER Class A5) in 4 mm scale was built from a Nu-Cast cast metal kit. The fine detail, lining and lettering, and not least the reflection in the dome, mark the high standard of finish on this model* (Nu-Cast Model Engineering).

workmanship that most of these models exhibit. Another reason for the increasing popularity of overseas railways, particularly those on the Continent, is the growing tendency to take holidays abroad. What better reminder can you have of a past holiday enjoyed or a future holiday yet to come than to have a model of the railways you can see whilst you are there?

So far as the Continent is concerned there is so much equipment available that you can build up a representative collection of rolling stock and accessories for most European countries, especially France, Germany, Italy, Austria and Switzerland. The characteristics of each of these countries' railways differ widely, but perhaps the most popular are the Alpine regions of Bavaria, Austria and Switzerland. The scenic settings possible in model form can be nearly as breathtaking as the originals and they lend themselves well to modelling, since the many tightly curved spirals, tunnels and lines climbing over one another enable a comprehensive layout with immense operating possibilities to be constructed in a very small space. As well as locomotives, rolling stock, overhead electric gear and all the other paraphernalia required to build up a representative Continental railway system in miniature, there is also an unsurpassed range of colourful plastic building and accessory kits designed to a constant scale which enable anyone to build up the authentic scenic setting. Perhaps because there is so much ready-made proprietary equipment obtainable from abroad, very few Continental railway modellers go in for scratch-building and hand-constructed locomotives and rolling stock appear to be the exception rather than the rule. There is, of course, nothing to stop the craftsman making his own models but traditionally Continental modellers usually rely on the excellent ready-to-run models produced by the trade.

Modellers of American-type railways, on the other hand, go in for a lot of kit building as well as ready-made items. American models are also very well supported by manufacturers outside America, who find the American market an attractive prospect for building up a lucrative export trade. As a consequence, there is a vast range of equipment available from manufacturers all over the world, but most of it compatible. Quite a lot of this equipment is available in Britain and there are firms who specialise in American prototype models and their importation. It must be admitted again that, with the difficulties of importing, prices are on the high side, but the quality and uniformly high standard of most

**Below** *This splendid HO model of the Swiss railways Class Ae6/6 electric locomotive is one of the newer additions to the Roco range* (Richard Kohnstam Ltd).

**Above right** *The magnificent LGB Austrian narrow gauge 0-6-2T is shown to advantage in this view. Running on 1 gauge track and built to a scale of 1:22.5 it is electrically operated and fitted with a smoke generator* (LGB).

**Right** *The fascination of American model railroads is well portrayed in this view of John B. Porter's HO system. The Reading Railroad Camel-back 0-4-0 switcher is waiting to position two elaborately lettered boxcars as a Southern Pacific mogul brings a passenger train into Highfield station. The 4-wheel caboose in the bottom left-hand corner is fitted with a Kadee 'buck-eye' coupler* (Brian Monaghan).

2
U 43

Ford
412

*The Bavarian Pacific Class locomotive is understandably popular amongst Continental manufacturers. The classic lines are well captured in this Marklin Mini-Club Z gauge model* (Marklin).

of the products attract a lot of people to this branch of modelling. Another attraction is the scenic possibilities in American-style layouts. They can and usually do reach high levels of ingenuity, with wooden trestle bridges crossing rugged mountains gorges in terrain and between towns which look very reminiscent of the Wild West of the cowboys.

I have little personal experience of American railway modelling, or railroad modelling as we should perhaps refer to it, but the advantages appear to be perfectly obvious in that there is no lack of equipment and no shortage of inspiration so far as subject matter is concerned. The only possible difficulty I foresee is to be able to resist buying one of those Union Pacific 'Big Boy' 4-8-8-4s and, having bought one, finding room in which to operate it. Admittedly most of the commercially made locomotive models of American prototypes are ingeniously designed to enable them to traverse minimum-radius curves, but who wants to spoil the sight of those magnifient beasts by having it practically chasing its own tail? The sheer length of most items of North American rolling stock, locomotives, carriages and freight cars is a bit daunting and for best effect it would appear necessary to choose an American railroad system only if you have the space available. However, this is purely my personal reaction, and there is ample scope for you to build a compact model based on American branch line practice.

In talking broadly of Continental and American-type railways I realise that these, too, can be broken down into categories much as I have done previously with Britain's railways. You can go back in history and pick whatever period interests you the most. There is, for example, a wide interest in old-time American locomotives and rolling stock, and consequently there is a fair amount of equipment available in model form covering this period. Continental models tend to favour the more modern post-war era, but older models are not by any means unknown. In contrast to railways at home, those on the Continent have been expanding their traffic at a high rate in post-war years and this is abundantly clear when travelling abroad, especially in France, Germany and Switzerland. Railway wagons appear everywhere, from individual ones in small factory sidings, many of them having to cross' public roads to reach their destination, to vast well-stocked marshalling yards and freight depots. To many people's eyes the typical Continental model railway looks overcrowded compared with what we are used to in Britain, and there is an apparent tendency to cram in as much equipment on the baseboard as the space available will stand. To some extent this criticism is valid, but at the same time there are many congested railway centres on the Continent that create this impression in real life, and the Continental modeller can find justification for portraying something similar in his own miniature system. The bimonthly magazine, *Continental Modeller,* is recommended reading for the average enthusiast modelling overseas railways. For details, see Appendix 2.

## Track gauge

As well as the geographical and historical distinctions one can choose from, there is yet another area of choice, namely the one of track gauge. By this I mean the gauge of the prototype, not the model, as model gauges are discussed in the next chapter. When referring to prototype railways we generally talk about standard gauge or narrow gauge. Standard gauge is 4 ft $8\frac{1}{2}$ in, which owes its origins to Britain and its adoption throughout the rest of the world to the fact that British engineers took the gauge with them when they built many of the overseas railways. Narrow gauge is anything less than 4 ft 8½ in, and can cover a very wide range. The most popular narrow gauges are probably 2 ft, 3 ft, 1 metre and 3ft 6 in, but there are any number of others particularly in the 2 ft to 3 ft range. They can, of course, go down to as little as 15 in as we know with the Romney Hythe and Dymchurch Railway and the Ravenglass & Eskdale Railway. It follows that any of these narrow gauge prototypes can be modelled and you have the choice of deciding either to adjust the scale of your models to suit a particular recognised model track gauge or you can adjust the model track gauge to suit a particular model scale. We will go into this in more detail in the next chapter. The smaller narrow gauge models have a particular charm of their own as invariably the prototypes were built to fulfil a need for transport in a remote area, or where traffic potential was too small or the terrain too difficult to justify the expense of a standard gauge line. The need for economy usually manifests itself in steeper gradients and sharper curves, both of which lend themselves to modelling where space is restricted. The scenery can also be spectacular too. The need for economical operation often results in those delightful mixed trains consisting of both passenger coaches and goods wagons of ancient and long-lasting vintage, all of which make such delightful subjects for modelling.

There is no lack of suitable prototypes on which to base a narrow gauge model layout, but there is a tendency amongst modellers working on narrow gauge prototypes to mix their prototypes rather more freely than the standard gauge modellers who invariably prefer to follow one particular company. This freelance aspect of narrow gauge railway modelling is generally tolerated and accepted, but why this should be so, more than it is with the standard gauge, is difficult to understand or explain. Possibly it is because many actual narrow gauge systems, even the best regulated ones, have an independent atmosphere of their own. Certainly many of them have a very wide variety of rolling stock and equipment which is often lacking on the larger standard gauge prototypes, and it is quite possible to find a narrow gauge railway on which no two engines or carriages look alike. To add another of your own invention to your own layout is hardly likely to raise many eyebrows.

It is not at all difficult to dream up reasons for building an imaginary narrow gauge system, possibly as a preservation scheme or as a gesture in serving some remote area of country without rail transport. Whatever the reason, you can delight in designing and building your own locomotives, carriages and wagons, evolving your own livery, company crest and 'corporate image' if you want one, and creating a world of your own in minature which can be good fun. Alternatively, you can pick a particular prototype and create a faithful image of it. The latter course will undoubtedly require a degree of scratch-building as, with one or two exceptions, there is only a small nucleus of narrow gauge material available from the trade. The exceptions include the Isle of Man Railway (3 ft gauge), the Festiniog Railway (1 ft 11½ in gauge), the Talyllyn Railway (2 ft 3 in gauge) and an Austrian 760 mm gauge prototype, where both locomotives and carriages are available as complete models or in kit form.

No talk of track gauges would be complete without mentioning the broad gauges, that is gauges larger than the standard gauge of 4 ft

*The Austrian firm of Liliput have a comprehensive range of HO9 locomotives, rolling stock and accessories including this delightful little 0-6-2T and train* (Liliput).

*Waterford & Limerick Railway No 20 'Galtee More' has come off the turntable to run round the train at Castle Rackrent on Richard Chown's 7 mm scale Irish broad gauge layout. The locomotive tender is fitted with a speaker for simulated sound operated by a Pacific Fast Mail sound controller* (Brian Monaghan).

$8\frac{1}{2}$ in. These exist throughout the world, notably the 5 ft gauge in Russia, the 5 ft 3 in gauge in Ireland and part of Australia, and the 5 ft 6 in gauge in Spain, Portugal and parts of India and South America. There was also, of course, Brunel's famous 7 ft $0\frac{1}{4}$ in on the GWR, but this was dropped as long ago as 1892. Strangely enough, most of these broad gauges, with the exception of Brunel's, appear hardly distinguishable from the standard gauge when seen in the flesh and you have to make a conscious attempt to notice any difference when looking at them. This is some justification at least for ignoring the difference when making a model of one or other of them. If you do wish to model one of these broad gauge systems (the Irish railways are very popular amongst modellers and there are some delightful prototypes to be found amongst them to model) the difficulties of working to an exact scale/gauge ratio may make it necessary to compromise. The 7 ft gauge is, of course, quite a different thing. It always was a curiosity and the effect in model form is quite stunning. To choose the old GWR broad gauge would involve a lot of hard work since very little proprietary equipment could be used. But the small number of models I have seen produced to this prototype gauge convince me that here there is a lot of scope for the really inventive modeller who wants to do something rather different from the rest.

## Chapter 4

# How to decide on scale and gauge

The choice of scales and gauges has never been wider. Each has its merits and its place in the order of things, and each is worthy of full consideration before finally making up your mind which one to follow. A necessary feature of railway modelling is that everything on a layout is, or at least should be, built to a constant scale. There is not the freedom that there is in some other modelling hobbies to change scale from one model to another. The only way you can change is either to scrap or perhaps part-exchange your earlier efforts and start all over again, or else build and operate more than one complete layout. The last suggestion is not so outrageous, as more and more people are beginning to find out. The commercially produced items of equipment for the new smaller gauges are becoming so fascinating that some modellers who have long-established layouts in one of the older, larger scales are now building a second small portable layout on which they can indulge their liking for the new small scale products. The two-car family is now being joined by the two-layout railway modeller!

Scales and gauges are sometimes bewildering for the beginner, but they are the first basic rule or standard by which all railway modelling is categorised and judged. It is thus important to have a ready understanding of the descriptions, code names and relative position of each scale so that you have some idea of what your fellow railway modellers are talking about. It is also necessary to grasp the distinction between scale and gauge, since these terms are often used together and regrettably sometimes become misplaced.

As far as the railway modeller is concerned, scale means the ratio between a unit of measurement on a model compared with a unit of measurement on the comparable full-size prototype. For example, a model measuring 10 in, based on a full-size prototype which measures 10 ft, would be built to a scale of 1 in to the ft. (A map which shows every mile as 1 in is drawn to a scale of 1 in to the mile; a 1-in Ordnance Survey map is drawn to the ratio or scale of 1:63,360.)

Another way of regarding scale is to express it as a ratio. The ratio of reduction of a model built to the scale of 1 in to the ft would be 1 to 12, 1:12 or 1/12.

In railway modelling we have, in the past 40 or so years at least, grown up with the idea of expressing scale as so many millimetres to the foot, eg, 2 mm to the ft, 3.5 mm to the ft, 4 mm to the ft and 7 mm to the ft, etc. The common use of millimetres in railway modelling has until recently been a frequent means of first becoming acquainted with the metric scale. There is probably a well-meaning historical basis for this business of mixing millimetres with feet, but I must confess that I do not know the reason. I only know I have grown up with it and have found it easy to use and to think with. This is particularly true with 4 mm scale (4 mm to the ft), since 4 mm is easily divided by 4 to give the equivalent scale dimension for 3, 6 or 9 in. A 4 mm scale model of a locomotive driving wheel 5 ft 9 in in diameter is 23 mm, and it easily becomes second nature to do the calculation $5 \times 4 = 20 + 3 = 23$ as simple mental arithmetic when the occasion arises. The recent introduction of the new British N gauge scale of $2\frac{1}{16}$mm to the foot has, however, complicated the thought processes. For a scale such as this, which does not have such a simple unit of measurement, I think it is essential to use a special conversion rule, such as the 'British N Scale' produced by Peco, showing feet reduced to the correct scale dimension. You simply find out the full-size prototype dimension in feet and measure off the scale measurement from the ruler. Likewise, to find the scale dimension in feet from a model, you measure the model with the ruler and read off the dimension in feet. (See fig 17).

Another useful aid when making a drawing in one scale copied from another drawn to a larger or smaller scale is to construct a ruler showing both the scales you are using, each one drawn along opposite edges of the ruler, with lines connecting relative units of measurement. (See fig 18.) This way it is simple to translate the dimension from one scale to the other without having to go through any

***Fig 17***

***Fig 18***

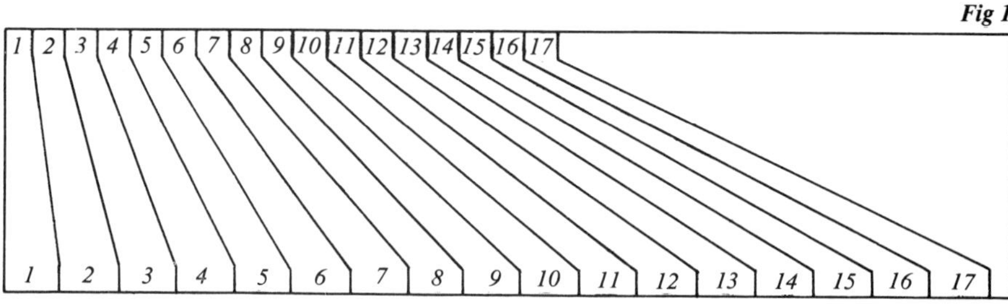


**Fig 17** *This handy N scale rule (reduced in size here) is produced by Peco and is available from stockists.* **Fig 18** *A simple home-made ruler for converting measurements from one scale to another—in this case from 4 mm scale (00 gauge) to 7 mm scale (0 gauge) and vice versa. Each division represents 1 ft.*

complicated mathematical processes. First, from the drawing you are copying, you simply read off the measurement along the side of the ruler having the scale that corresponds to that drawing, then you read off the corresponding unit of measurement on the other side of the ruler and transfer this to the new drawing you are making.

Gauge or track gauge is, as we have discussed in the previous chapter, the distance between the two running rails. There is also another form of gauge, known as the loading gauge, which refers to the maximum permissible width and height for railway rolling stock to enable it to clear bridges, tunnels, station platforms and other obstructions which come close the railway line. The *track* gauge on British, Continental and American standard gauge (4 ft 8½ in) is virtually the same but, because the *loading* gauge is bigger on the Continent and in America, it is possible to run much wider and taller locomotives, carriages and wagons on these railways than is permissible in Britain. (See fig 19.)

In Britain the maximum permitted height and width is normally only 13 ft 6 in and 9 ft 0 in, respectively, less on some lines with particular loading gauge restrictions, and more in a few other cases where the gauge has been built more generously. However, in Europe, rolling stock which is over 10 ft wide can be operated, and in America they can run rolling stock 15 ft high and 10 ft 6 in wide. In South Africa, although the track gauge is only 3 ft 6 in (1 ft 2½ in less than in Britain), the rolling stock can be as wide as 10 ft, which is 1 ft wider than in Britain. It is important to realise the distinction between track gauge and loading gauge and to remember why Continental and American railway rolling stock is so much bigger, wider and taller than in Britain, although the rails are nominally gauged the same distance apart.

You could be forgiven for assuming that if we decide to make an accurate model railway engine to a scale of 4 mm to the ft we would also make the track gauge to the same scale. Assuming a standard gauge locomotive we would expect the track gauge for a 4 mm scale model to be 18.83 mm (ie 4 ft 8½ in at 4 mm to the foot = 4 × 4 = 16, plus 2 = 18, plus 2½/3 or 5/6 = 18.83). If you are prepared to go to the trouble of making the locomotive yourself to a high-precision standard there is absolutely no reason why you should not use a gauge of 18.83 mm. In fact this can be and is being done on an increasing scale and there are a number of commercially available parts and accessories to assist in the process but, as yet, no ready-to-run models. A model railway built to an accurate scale track gauge requires a higher level of painstaking construction work on track and rolling stock and those who are not prepared to devote so much time to this task, as desirable as it may be, or feel they do not possess the necessary skill, have to rely on the trade for a large part of their equipment.

To produce model railway equipment in

large numbers that will sell at reasonably competitive prices commercial manufacturers cannot afford to make all their products to the same high standard of precision as a meticulous worker with time to spare. In addition, to enjoy maximum sales which is essential if prices are to be kept at saleable levels, these firms have to cater for a wide ranging market including inexperienced youngsters as well as the dedicated enthusiasts. As a result, they have to incorporate into their models a certain amount of robustness to withstand relatively rough treatment and the occasional knock and bang. In addition, the rolling stock has to be designed to traverse curves sharper in radius than any that would be found in prototype practice. Therefore moving parts have to be thicker in proportion to their full-size counterparts. Also greater clearance has to be provided between moving parts to give perfectly free movement and to enable bogies to pivot sufficiently to negotiate the sharp-radius curves. The running rail itself has to be slightly wider to give it enough strength and the wheels have to be thicker, with wider and deeper flanges to ensure that they retain their place on the rails. I know these ideas are being successfully challenged by the true scale modellers and I also know that the degree with which manufacturers add thickness and tolerances to their models is being whittled down compared to 35, 20, or even just a few years ago. However, it is probably true to say that, for commercially produced models built down to a price level and capable of going round curves of short radius, it will never be possible for manufacturers to offer exact scale models of British prototypes with the severe limitations of the British loading gauge.

Some working parts, particularly the outside valve gear on locomotives, have to be built differently on the model compared to the full-size engine, and in many cases it becomes difficult in the restricted space available to build a model with the same working actions as the prototype. Bogie sides are another case in point. It is common practice for commercial manufacturers to produce bogies for coaches, vans and bogie wagons out of metal castings or plastic mouldings. To make these with any degree of strength or rigidity they must be proportionally thicker than the full-size bogie if tolerances between wheel and bogie side are not be brought to, commercially speaking, unworkably fine levels. So, for commercial reasons, the track gauge for most British outline model railway equipment is something less than the scale dimension of the full-size track. The reason for this is almost entirely due to the restricted width of the full-size British loading gauge.

The foregoing explains the subject of scales and gauges and the problems that can arise with them. Now let us take a detailed look at the different scales and gauges that are recognised and commonly used in the model railway hobby today, and consider some of the advantages and disadvantages of each. Beginning with Standard Gauge (4 ft $8\frac{1}{2}$ in) systems and starting with the newest and smallest:

## Z gauge

*1:220 or approximately $1\frac{1}{2}$ mm to the foot scale; 6.5 mm gauge.*

The German firm Marklin astonished the model railway world at the 1972 Nuremberg Toy Fair by introducing this entirely new ultra-small gauge marketed under the banner

**Fig 19** *Average British, Continental and American loading gauges.*

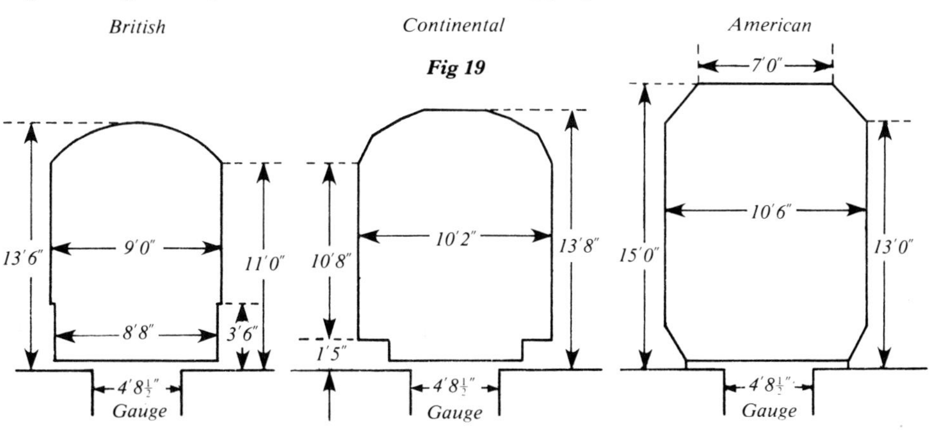

**Top** *The incredible detail incorporated in this Marklin Mini-Club Z gauge Swiss 1C-C1 'Crocodile' makes it difficult to believe that the track gauge is only 6.5 mm and the model itself is only just over 3½ inches long. Notice also the commendable scale appearance of the overhead catenary. The model incorporates a switch to enable it to pick up current either through the pantograph or from the rails* (Marklin).

**Above** *Elmer Products have announced a range of British outline Z gauge models based on Marklin Mini-Club components. Shown here are two HST power cars* (Marklin).

of the Marklin Mini-club System. It is a complete system comprising working model outline steam, diesel and electric locomotives, carriages, wagons, track and a growing range of accessories, so that an authentic model railway can be built up using the products of this one proprietary make. The smallest 0-6-0T locomotive is only $1\frac{7}{8}$ in long, a 4-6-2 Pacific locomotive with 3 working headlights $4\frac{3}{8}$ in long, and a Continental coach $4\frac{7}{8}$ in long. Models of British as well as German and Swiss prototypes are available. If space is very restricted and you are determined to have a layout, Z gauge could be your answer. Understandably prices reflect the high degree of precision needed to make such small models.

## 000

*1:152.4 or 2 mm to the foot scale; 9.5 mm gauge.*

This was the forerunner of the ultra-small scales but has been superseded in the commercial world by N gauge, with which it should not be confused. Because 000 has not been adopted commercially it is now only used by the modeller who was either formerly established in the gauge before the trade entered into the ultra-small scale field or else because he is prepared to undertake a lot of highly detailed work himself. As such it is only likely to remain a scale for the dedicated enthusiast. The 2 mm Scale Association serves the needs of the band of enthusiasts who have accepted the challenge of modelling in this scale. The brilliantly successful work that has been achieved in this very small scale leads one to believe that any and all things are possible in railway modelling.

## N gauge

*1:148 or 2.06 mm/1 ft scale for British prototypes*

*1:160 or 1.91 mm/1 ft scale for Continental prototypes; 9 mm gauge.*

N gauge has a track gauge of 9 mm but has two scales—1:148 for British prototypes and 1:160 for Continental prototypes. This is due in the main to the restrictions of the British full-size loading gauge, as explained earlier. N (for 9 mm) gauge was pioneered on the Continent and in a very short space of time has attracted a flood of new equipment from a number of commercial firms, principally in Germany and Italy. To enable British modellers to enjoy the fruits of some of these developments from overseas, the slightly larger British scale was devised to enable mechanisms and certain equipment built by Continental manufacturers for models designed to the large Continental loading gauge to be incorporated in the restricted loading gauge of British prototype models. Trackwork with a common gauge of 9 mm is, of course, used by both Commercial and British scales.

N gauge is developing rapidly, and a wide variety of models is now available. As I feel so assured that the gauge is firmly established I am confident that the choice of products is bound to increase.

There are a number of positive advantages in this gauge. The principal one is the reduced space required compared to the other larger gauges. It is practically half the size of 00 and HO, which for so long were previously accepted as the smallest practical table-top scales. So far N gauge models have been to a uniformly high standard, and most modellers find the gauge very satisfying to work with. The workmanship, detail and performance are mostly the equal of larger-scale commercially produced models, and in some cases, particularly with regard to performance, appear to be superior to those of larger scales. Perhaps this is due to the degree of precision with which N gauge models have to be made, for they have to be very good to work at all.

One important advantage, which so far N gauge has been able to hold on to, is the universal coupling that has become standard and which means that proprietary equipment of all the different makes can be mixed and operated together. In this respect N gauge has the advantage of being a latecomer, since all the big problems which beset the earlier larger scales and gauges were ironed out by the time N gauge appeared.

I would recommend N gauge to any would-be newcomer to the hobby. It is a practical gauge and so far the wide choice of products are reasonably priced, considering the precision with which they have had to be designed and manufactured. Although the gauge has possibilities for a minimum space layout, the best way to approach N gauge is to continue to think in terms of the space we are accustomed to with 00 and other larger gauges and to expand the layout to fill the space! You can then do all the things that are so desirable, but so difficult in the larger scales, such as use large-radius curves, long station platforms and train lengths (N gauge locomotives are fantastic haulers) and generally introduce a degree of spaciousness and realism which is so often sadly lacking from layouts built to larger

*N Gauge owes much to the early pioneering work of Arnold-N (formerly Arnold Rapido) who introduced their first train set in 1960. Additions to their comprehensive range are constantly being made and shown here are three new locomotives introduced in 1981: DB Class E50 Co-Co and DB Class E16 1-D-1, both electric locomotives, and DB Class 96 ex-Bavarian State Railways 0-8-8-0 Mallet Tank* (Arnold).

**Above** *British N gauge is ably supported by Graham Farish who have added this fine model of BR Class 47 No D1662* Isambard Kingdom Brunel *to their range of 1:148 scale locomotives* (Graham Farish).

**Right** *The full potential of N gauge is demonstrated in this part view of Tim Watson's 'Gouldby for Caldecote'. Caldecote village is the centrepiece of this beautifully executed scenic model. Gouldby station is in the foreground. All this in a space only 11 ft × 5 ft 6 in. The hand-built 'Lickey Banker', seen waiting in the station yard ready to assist a heavy train up the 1 in 37 gradient (top left), shows that scratch-building in N gauge is not impossible* (Brian Monaghan).

scales. The one disadvantage is the difficulty most people are likely to have in scratch-building. It is not impossible, as many examples already produced will prove, but for the average modeller it is certainly not going to be as easy as with 00 and the larger gauges.

## TT

*1:120 or 2.5 mm/1 ft scale for Continental prototypes; or 1:101.6 or 3 mm/1 ft scale for British prototypes, where it is known as TT3; 12 mm gauge.*

I was an active model maker when TT3 was introduced commercially in Britain by Tri-ang, but I was committed to 00 at the time and could find no compelling reason for switching to TT3. I know this is an entirely personal view which is not by any means shared by everybody, but I have tried very hard to find any real advantage with TT3. It seems to me that whatever space-saving advantages there were in TT3 over 00 have now been completely overshadowed by N gauge with perhaps the most important exception of scratch-building. The scale of 3 mm to the ft used with TT3 shows no dramatic reduction on 00 as N gauge does and, although it cannot be denied that there is a reduction and it is possible to build a TT3 layout in a smaller space than 00, the space saving, to my way of thinking, does not compensate for all the commercial complications that must follow with the introduction of a new scale. If a manufacturer in the model railway business wants to keep faith with his established 00 customers, and at the same time satisfy his TT customers, almost everything has to be duplicated, and for what purpose? A slight space saving advantage. To my mind it does not seem worth the effort but, as I know only too well, many people will disagree with me.

PALETHORPES
LMS

To a certain extent it is unfair to compare TT with N gauge today because, at the time TT was introduced, there was no such thing as a commercial N gauge. The advantage of hindsight makes it easier to form a judgement.

TT and TT3 still have a large and faithful following and, although it has been discarded by Tri-ang, TT3 enthusiasts are still supplied with a range of basic parts, including track, wheels and a number of kits, and new products continue to appear from time to time. The firms who carry on supporting TT3 do so remarkably well, but I suspect they do it to cater for the enthusiast already committed to the gauge. Unless anyone has personal connections with someone already using the gauge or because the local district model railway club favours TT, I doubt whether many people consciously choose to start railway modelling in this gauge today. I should imagine one would find N gauge a more attractive proposition. There are some advantages in TT gauge over other gauges, mainly because it is still one in which you can indulge in reasonably detailed scratch-building without using a microscope and with the assistance of a number of necessary parts available from the trade, but as a compromise between N and 00 I doubt whether it is a very great contender today. TT3 also has the ad-advantage of common standard couplings and wheels, etc, all based on the original Tri-ang standards, which were relatively finer than in their 00 models of the time.

## HO

*1:87 or 3.5 mm/1 ft scale; 16.5 mm gauge.*

When the scale of 3.5 mm to the ft and gauge of 16.5 mm were first introduced in Great Britain in the 1920s they were designated 00. It was only in the '30s, when some British modellers began to adopt the alternative scale of 4 mm to the ft, that a need arose to avoid confusion between the two scales. The term HO, a contraction of 'Half-O', was generally adopted as a designation for 3.5 mm scale, and 4 mm scale models were referred to as 00. The advantage of HO is that it has a true scale gauge ratio as it uses a gauge of 16.5 mm which, with a scale of 3.5 mm to the ft is almost exactly the scale equivalent of 4 ft 8½ in. Because of this HO at one time had strong support from modellers. Unfortunately the trade reacted otherwise and most British manufacturers, including Hornby when they introduced their Dublo range in 1938, adopted 00. With the lack of commercial support, HO lost ground and now it is little used by modellers of British outline prototypes. However, the reverse happened on the Continent where, because of the advantage of their larger loading gauge, there was no incentive to depart from the near correct scale/gauge ratio that HO offered. As a result HO is now only found commercially outside Great Britain where it has probably established itself as the world's most popular scale and gauge.

## 00

*1:76 or 4 mm/1 ft scale; 16.5 mm gauge.*

This is the most popular scale and gauge in Britain, but is virtually unheard of elsewhere. The reason for this can again be found in the difference between the British and Continental loading gauge. When 00 was first in-introduced in this country it was with a scale of 3.5 mm to the ft but some modellers and commercial manufacturers considered there was an advantage in using a larger scale allowing a greater clearance outside the wheels for models built within the confines of the British loading gauge. As always with this problem (we have already met it in N and TT gauges) it is the loading gauge width that is the biggest factor. The width of Continental rolling stock is approximately 10 ft which, with a scale of 3.5 mm to the ft, means a model width of 35 mm. The maximum width of British rolling stock is 9 ft which, to the same scale of 3.5 mm to the ft, means a model width of only 31.5 mm. Subtract the width of the track gauge, 16.5 mm, from both these measurements and you will see that, whereas Continental models can have a space either side of the rails of 9.25 mm in which to fit wheels, axleguards, coach bogies, locomotive valve gear, etc, British models can only have a space of 7.5 mm, a reduction of nearly 2 mm either side. In an attempt to alleviate the difficulties of the reduced loading gauge and the limited space it allowed, it was decided to invent a scale of 4 mm to the ft which would give British models the same advantage as the Continentals. The 9ft width of British rolling stock becomes 36 mm in 4 mm scale, which is much nearer the dimension of Continental models.

Some people regard this levelling of the sizes of HO Continental models and 00 British models as an advantage, since they claim that the similarity in size makes it possible to run the two together. Personally, I find this a very big disadvantage as it seems irrational to me to want to run two models of anything together when they are built to different scales. Everyone knows that locomotives and carriages on the Continent look so much bigger than they do in Britain. This is one of the fascinations of foreign railways, and one of the ways in which the senses become alerted when travelling abroad. Yet when a magnificent model such as the French Jouef 141R 2-8-2 is placed alongside a Hornby 'Evening Star' 2-10-0, the 141R 2-8-2 appears overshadowed by the British locomotive and is only marginally longer, quite contrary to what would really happen if the two full-size locomotives were to be lined-up together. The situation is really brought home, so to speak, when a Continental manufacturer produces models of British prototypes. Lima did this when they first entered the British market. They had a fairly extensive range of British outline locomotives and rolling stock, all to HO scale, but they looked faintly ridiculous if they were mixed with any home produced products. No one manufacturer can hope to retain sole allegiance to his products. At some time or another, modellers are going to want to combine the products of one manufacturer with another. Presumably in recognition of this, Lima withdrew their range, retooled (which must have been expensive), and re-introduced the models in 00 4 mm scale. Unfortunately the lesson does not appear to have been learnt since two more Continental manufacturers have since introduced British outline models in HO. As models they are perfect and very desirable despite their comparatively high price. The price does, however, reflect the quality and might not be an overwhelming deterrent but because they look so out of place on a 4 mm scale 00 layout I am sure a lot of British railway modellers are put off buying them. Which seems such a pity considering the amount of research and skilled craftsmanship that must obviously have gone into their production. Perhaps they may have a wider appeal outside the UK which may, of course, have been the intention.

As much as the distinction between HO and 00 may be regretted there is nothing any of us can do about it now, as 00 has become so entrenched in Britain that there is absolutely no possibility of it ever being dropped in favour of HO. There are, however, a number of advantages with 00. The slightly larger scale does give a shade more space in which to scratch-build and in which to fit locomotive mechanisms. Furthermore, the ease with which you can multiply or divide 4 makes it very easy to convert feet and inches into millimetres. For the scale enthusiast who cannot tolerate the sight of standard gauge rolling stock running on narrow gauge track (16.5 mm is really only 4 ft $1\frac{1}{2}$ in in 4 mm scale) there is always the alternative solution of using a wider gauge to make the track gauge fit the scale rather than reduce the scale to fit the track gauge, as we shall see later.

00 is so wonderfully served by the British manufacturers, particularly for scratch-builders and kit builders. There is every imaginable item of equipment—wheels, castings, transfers, etc—available from the trade so that 00 presents the least difficulty and the best variety of equipment of any of the scales and gauges.

You will find some manufacturers refer to 00/HO or HO/00. In some cases the use of this joint reference to the two gauges is correct, since by using the same track gauge, 16.5 mm, most track components are suitable for either HO or 00 models. This is not strictly true though when one considers the sleepers for HO and 00 gauge track. Sleepers (or ties as the Americans prefer to call them) on British 00 gauge track should really be spaced further apart than on Continental or American HO gauge track, but not everyone is sensitive enough to worry unduly about this and they are content to use either HO or 00 gauge track components, hence the expression HO/00. It is not correct to use the phrase HO/00 to denote the scale or size of a model, since HO uses one scale and 00 another. Airfix are fond of this but, to be fair, they use it largely in an area where it could possibly get by and be excused. It certainly does not apply to their Railway System which sticks scrupulously to 4 mm scale but I refer to their use of HO/00 for some building kits and for their many sets of plastic figures. After all, we do have people in all sorts of sizes, tall or short, fat or thin, and it might be arguable that a figure is either a short thin 00 one or a tall fat HO one! It is also sometimes possible to mix HO and 00 buildings and scenic effects together, since who is to argue that a building or tree in HO scale is not really a small 00 building or tree, and vice versa? Slightly smaller HO accessories can also be used to good effect to add a sense of perspective to the background parts of a model railway. Even some TT accessories may be used this way. But in the main I do not recommend mixing HO and 00 items together that have a fixed linear dimension, such as a locomotive or an item of rolling stock, since the difference in the two scales immediately becomes apparent when the two are run close together.

At least one manufacturer, in trying to steer a middle course between HO and 00, has tried to introduce an 'International scale' of approximately 3.8 mm to the ft, using of course the same 16.5 mm gauge as 00 and HO. This has not met with universal approval as the reduction in scale from 00, despite the fact that it is only 0.2 mm per ft, it quite noticeable over, say, the length, width and height of a railway carriage, compared with other similar models built to 4 mm scale.

There is also a small following for American 00, which uses a 19 mm track gauge, but for which there is no commercial support.

## EM and Protofour/Scalefour

*EM 1:76 or 4 mm/1 ft scale; 18.2 mm gauge. Protofour/Scalefour 1:76 or 4 mm/1 ft scale; 18.83 mm gauge.*

I hope followers of these standards will excuse me linking them together, but it is my view, rightly or wrongly, that one evolved from the other and they all share the same ancestry. EM Gauge, for 'Eighteen Millimetre', came about as a result of the growing dissatisfaction with the undersized track gauge used in 00. 18 mm itself was not entirely to scale but in the days in which it was adopted as a standard it was considered near enough and it certainly was a decided step in the right direction. More recently the EM Gauge Society, which has represented this gauge since 1955, introduced revised track and wheel standards which included a revised track gauge of 18.2 mm minimum (0.2 mm wider on 24 in curves) and this has now become the Society's recommended track gauge. Despite the popularity of EM gauge amongst the more enthusiastic and discerning modellers the gauge is not catered for by any of the major producers of model railway equipment and there are no ready-to-run items of rolling stock available. To take up EM gauge, therefore, you will need to do a fair amount of scratch-building or else conversion work on proprietary models, but nevertheless the conversion of 00 gauge models to EM gauge is not very difficult and there is a range of commercial items to make this possible. Track is not now such a problem as at least two firms, Ratio and SMP, produce track with plastic sleeper bases in EM gauge. SMP's is ready assembled and flexible and Ratio's is easily assembled by simply sliding the rails into the chairs moulded on the sleeper bases. There are no ready assembled points available but SMP produce a range of EM point kits, two of which have plastic sleeper bases and there is talk of something similar from Ratio. The overall effect of EM gauge is convincing, and for the more discerning enthusiast the extra time and trouble is well worth while. If you are undecided it is best to see a few EM gauge layouts and make a comparison with 00 gauge yourself, since the advantages are better experienced than described.

The inevitable quest for even better and finer standards occupied the attention of a group of railway modellers who produced a set of standards known as Protofour, sometimes referred to as P4. There is next to no compromise with this system, which is not only a gauge but a set of standards governing track and wheels, and an attention to detail and fine scale standards in areas which have been neglected because of the commercial dictates of the trade. As one would expect, a correct scale gauge ratio has been evolved and the track gauge, which is exactly right for 4 mm scale, is 18.83 mm. Do not be frightened by the two places of decimals. After all, 18.83 mm is only a description of a unit of measurement and once set by an accurate measuring instrument it remains constant. With a selection of tools and gauges set to 18.83 mm it should be no more difficult to build track to this gauge than say to 16.5 mm, 18.2 mm, or whatever else you choose. In addition to the correct gauge, there are standards for the rail section, wheel back-to-back measurements, tyre width, wheel and rail contours and the crossing flangeway and check rail clearances. These may sound rather impressive and mean little to the beginner, but more readily appreciated will be the superb scale three-link couplings which make the normal types used by modellers look like *Queen Mary* anchor chains. There is a Protofour Society from which further information can be obtained, and already a number of items are available from Studio Lith Ltd to assist modellers who want to start using these precise, exacting, but thoroughly practical standards. Protofour is not for the faint-hearted and it requires a degree of precision, accuracy and patient handiwork beyond that required in other gauges such as 00. However, there is growing support for the commendably high standards originally set by Protofour and a number of tools, gauges, wheels and track parts are commercially available which open up the possibility to a wider audience.

Also involved in the furtherance of 18.83 mm gauge is the Scalefour Society and also the EM Gauge Society whose rules were changed to embrace all gauges between 18 mm and 18.83 mm in 1969. There are differences of opinion as to the compatibility of Protofour with the standards set by other societies and whether components from one manufacturer can be mixed with another. The subject is too complex and too controversial to air in these pages and would-be 18.83 modellers can only

*The perfection of Scalefour is well portrayed in this view of the trackwork on the North London Group's 'Heckmondwike' exhibition layout. LMS 3F 0-6-0 No 3284 is about to trundle by on an empty coal train* (Brian Monaghan).

be advised to contact the Societies concerned and form their own conclusions. Ratio's easy to assemble track with plastic sleeper bases is available in 18.83 mm (as well as in 18.2 mm) and is approved by the Scalefour Society down to 3 ft 6 in as a minimum radius.

## S

*1:64, $\frac{3}{16}$ in/1 ft or 4.76 mm/1 ft scale; $\frac{7}{8}$ in or 22.2 mm gauge.*

This gauge is not catered for commercially in Britain, though it is in America. However, a number of 00 items such as wheels, parts for constructing track, mechanisms, etc, can be utilised. The advantage claimed for this gauge is that it enables slightly larger models to be constructed which provide greater scope for detailing, but which will not take up quite so much room as 0 and 1 gauge. Some very fine S gauge models have been built and exhibited from time to time but, largely because of the complete lack of commercial support, S gauge is hardly likely to appeal to a beginner unless he is prepared to construct a lot of parts which in other gauges can normally be purchased ready-made. Wheels are likely to be the biggest problem since, although it is possible to use some 00 wheels, they will be proportionally smaller in S gauge and some of the larger locomotive driving wheels will not be catered for commercially at all. For anyone interested there is the S-Gauge Model Railway Society.

## 0

*1:43.5 or 7 mm/1 ft scale (UK), 1:48 or $\frac{1}{4}$ in/1 ft (USA); 32 mm gauge.*

At one time 0 gauge was the most popular gauge and it was actively supported by the trade, especially by the mass-production manufacturers who catered mainly for the toy market. The trend away from large homes into smaller labour-saving flats and semi-detached houses, and the development of the table-top layout capabilities of 00 and HO between the two World Wars, were largely responsible for its demise. However, although 0 gauge has for so long been deserted by the popular manufacturers, it has in recent years been showing signs of staging a comeback both in Britain and on the Continent. In Britain it is fairly well supported by that part of the trade which produces parts and accessories and hand-built locomotives, but the latter in particular tend to be rather expensive. 0 gauge equipment is generally more expensive than the smaller scales and gauges, but it is probably true to say that, because of its larger size, less equipment is required to fill a given space, so overall it may not necessarily consume that much more money.

One big advantage I feel with 0 gauge, going up the scale and comparing it with other smaller gauges, is that it is the first gauge that results in models having some worthwhile weight and stability built into them. 0 gauge locomotives have to be solidly and robustly constructed and, in using the traditional materials of brass, steel, tinplate and wood, finished models sometimes weigh-in at pounds rather than ounces. Plastic has been used to produce 0 gauge models and, in fact, one of the first uses of plastic in model railways I ever remember was a fine 0 gauge railway carriage which was produced by the Leeds Model Co Ltd before Word War 2. The former Tri-ang 'Big Big Trains', now produced by Novo Toys Ltd, provides a cheap source of models for adaptation to serious 0 gauge use and the Italian firm Lima also include British outline models in their inexpensive range of 0 gauge equipment. Also readily available, but somewhat expensive, are the Pola Maxi and Rivarossi ranges of 0 gauge equipment which, though basically of Continental outline, can be adapted to British styles.

Within 0 gauge we have Course Standard, Unified Standard and Fine Standard. They all use the same track gauge of 32 mm but differ in the dimensions used for wheels, in particular the all-important back to back dimension, check rail clearances, etc. Similar moves are taking place as has already happened in 00 in that attempts are being made to bring the track gauge and standard dimensions nearer to scale. One of the most promising is Scale 7 which has adopted a track gauge of 33 mm which is just .04 mm more than the true 7 mm scale track dimension of 32.96 mm. As with 4 mm scale though, the track gauge is but one dimension and to adopt Scale 7 standards one needs to be particular about a lot more than just the track gauge. Also like 18.83 mm gauge in 4 mm scale, Scale 7 looks really good and is worth considering if you are making a start and are not committed to anything else.

So many things can be done easily in 0 gauge that are either impossible or very difficult in other smaller gauges. Real live steam models are, for instance, perfectly feasible and practical in 0 gauge and trackwork can be built just like the real thing, with cast chairs pinned to wooden sleepers. Traditionally trackwork is invariably built by the modeller, although Peco have the nucleus of a fine range of 0 gauge flexible track and point parts suitable for course, unified or fine standard which can provide an excellent foundation for an 0 gauge layout. If you have the space, a little more cash to spare for your initial outlay and the time to do more scratch-building, I would recommend 0 gauge and 7 mm scale as a very satisfying scale in which to work.

### 1

*1:30.5 or 10 mm/1 ft scale; 45 mm gauge.*

The requirements for more space, cash and time to do your own construction work apply even more to 1 gauge, but the advantages are worth it. As anyone who has seen the Gauge 1 Society's stand at an exhibition will confirm, gauge 1 models really steal the show. The sheer size of the models is a real delight. Locomotives look big and heavy and wagons and coaches roll noisily but swiftly and smoothly over the track and pointwork which really looks like the real thing.

Perhaps the ideal setting for a gauge 1 layout is the garden—a garden shed to house the line's HQ, terminal station and rolling stock (provided the shed can be securely locked as there is a ready market for these models!) and the great outdoors to provide a setting for wide sweeping curves and long galloping straights. Power can be by steam, internally or externally fired (that means by a heat source which can either be inside the firebox or outside under the boiler), electricity or clockwork, or any other means of propulsion you like to devise. I think anyone who gets a taste for 1 gauge, usually from knowing someone who already has such a layout, will probably move heaven and earth to build one of their own, but building a 1 gauge layout is very demanding in every respect. Ready-to-run rolling stock is nearly all second-hand and usually fetches high prices, but the German firm of Marklin have a range of locomotives and goods and passenger vehicles, as well as a number of track parts, which could form the ideal basis of a 1 gauge layout.

**Top right** *The Lima 0 gauge LMS 4F 0-6-0 here shown 'out of the box' can easily be improved by fretting out the spokes, adding wire handrails and fitting a scale chimney. It also lends itself well to a number of conversions. A fine model to start an 0 gauge model railway.*

**Centre right and right** *Marklin Gauge 1 6-wheel coach. The close up shot shows the detailed interior through one of the opening doors.*

L M S
4547

Nichtraucher
DB
Nichtraucher
2

## Narrow gauge

The references to gauges have so far been concerned solely with standard 4 ft 8½ in gauge prototypes. However, it follows that, within a chosen scale, you can build a narrow gauge prototype, and the track gauge would of course be in the same ratio of scale as the model. When building a model of a non-standard gauge prototype you have the choice of either using a gauge which attracts commercial support, thereby making the scale suit the gauge, or of choosing the scale first and fixing the gauge to suit the scale. The former course is preferred whenever possible, since wheels are usually the most difficult item for modellers to fabricate themselves, and by choosing a gauge which is supported by the trade, you are sure to have a ready supply of wheels, mechanisms and working parts. In Britain, real-life narrow gauge systems are flourishing under the post-war fever for preservation schemes, and the popularity of such lines as the Talyllyn, Festiniog, Isle of Man Railway, Welshpool and Llanfair, and British Rail's own Vale of Rheidol no doubt account for the wave of interest in narrow gauge modelling.

Recapping on the previously mentioned standard gauge model systems, you will remember that we have the following established gauges actively supported by the trade, particularly in respect of wheels, mechanisms and track—9 mm (N), 12 mm (TT3), 16.5 mm (HO/00) and 32 mm (0). With a scale of 4 mm/1 ft, the 9 mm gauge of N gauge becomes a scale 2 ft 3 in, which is the exact gauge of the Talylln Railway; the 12 mm of TT3 becomes a scale 3 ft 0 in, which is the exact gauge of the Isle of Man Railway and many fascinating, but now closed, narrow gauge lines that used to operate in Ireland. And as we have also shown, 16.5 mm in 4 mm scale of 4 ft 1½ in, which by any standard ought to be a narrow gauge, but the only company I have heard of that operated a line built to this gauge was the Wigan Coal & Iron Company, and I know nothing of its extent or duration. Apart from this company it will be seen that quite a number of important narrow gauge prototypes can be successfully modelled in 4 mm scale, utilising track and wheel components of other gauges. It is also probably true to say that a fair degree of licence can be allowed with these minor gauges and it can be regarded as permissible to extend the use of 9 mm gauge track to cover prototypes on gauges from 2 ft to 2 ft 6 in, thus allowing many more prototype systems to be modelled in 4 mm scale. The reason for this is mainly the loading gauge used in narrow gauge prototypes. The locomotives and rolling stock are so wide relative to the track gauge that a widening or narrowing of the track gauge of the model can usually be accommodated without difficulty. Also in many cases, particularly with the smaller gauge lines, the bodies are so low down on the wheels and bogies that any alteration made to the underframes of the model to suit practical considerations are largely obscured and can be more easily tolerated and overlooked.

There is a real advantage in trying to stick to a recognised scale as well as gauge when building a model narrow gauge layout, since there are a number of standard gauge items and accessories that can be equally at home on a narrow gauge system. Buildings, road vehicles, miniature people, and what are generally referred to as lineside accessories, are the obvious examples. In this respect, there is a great advantage in choosing a narrow gauge model railway as it is possible to equip such a line built to 4 mm scale with a vast range of items, some designed specifically for 4 mm scale narrow gauge, others that were originally designed and intended for the large standard gauge models, and yet more drawn from the range of track, wheels, mechanisms,

*An OON3 model of an Isle of Man Railcar (ex-County Donegal Railway) made from the Anbrico 4 mm scale cast metal kit* (Anbrico Scale Model).

*Llanhaiadr station, locomotive depot and goods yard on the 009 Llanhaiadr & District Quarry Railway built by the junior members of the Warrington MRC. This layout is built on two 4 ft × 2 ft baseboards. The area of this scene is under 4 ft × 2 ft and shows how much detail can be incorporated in a narrow gauge layout in the minimum of space* (Brian Monaghan).

wagon chassis and other items intended for N gauge—the best of both worlds in fact! Narrow gauge layouts are also ideal for the person who is obliged to construct a minimum space layout, since the trains can traverse sharper radii and climb steeper gradients than their larger standard gauge cousins. Individual items of rolling stock are shorter and train lengths can be kept within quite minimal dimensions, which restricts the size of station platforms, engine sheds, sidings and other associated items. Narrow gauge models can be made to look very attractive scenically, as anyone who has visited the Welsh narrow gauge railways will acknowledge, and from the operating point of view the wide choice of prototype material leaves a lot of scope for modelling. Many people operate a narrow gauge system as a feeder to a standard gauge line, thereby combining the two gauges on one baseboard. This opens up tremendous possibilities for mixed gauge track, joint stations where the two gauges meet and for scenic work involving bridges and viaducts over which the narrow gauge can be made to climb and cross over the standard gauge rails. Alternatively, a narrow gauge layout can be developed on a baseboard of its own, either as a subordinate project to a larger standard gauge system or as the sole railway modelling project.

Narrow gauge railway modelling is widely supported by the trade. Most developments are in the 4 mm or 3.5 mm scale field, where it is referred to as either 00-9 or HO-9, 00 or HO denoting the scale and 9 the gauge of the track in millimetres. Another method of describing narrow gauge scales and gauges is to denote the scale by referring to the normal standard gauge, eg 00, followed by N to denote narrow gauge, and then, followed by a figure denoting the prototype track gauge in feet. Thus 00N3 would describe a 4 mm scale 3 ft narrow gauge line. Therefore 00-9, HO-9 and 00-12 would be referred to as 00N2.25, HON2.5 (approximately!) and 00N3. Special narrow gauge track is commercially available, particularly the Peco 'Crazy Track' which is

GUARD
3

3
3
3
3
3

**These pages** *The Peco Great Little Trains series of 00-16.5 narrow gauge prototype (7 mm scale on 16.5 mm track) includes locomotives, coaches and wagon kits as well as flexible track and a means of converting standard Peco 00 gauge points to narrow gauge. Here shown is the Fletcher Jennings 0-4-2 Saddle Tank from the Talyllyn Railway, a 4-wheel coach converted to a brake end with the addition of the Guard's ducket supplied, a bogie coach assembled from two kits, and some delightfully typical Welsh narrow gauge wagons* (Peco).

flexible and features authentic-looking rough wood grained sleepers arranged in the haphazard fashion so often found on narrow gauge lines. There is no shortage of rolling stock, wagons, coaches and locomotives, and kits of parts are available for converting N gauge locomotives into 00-9 or HO-9 narrow gauge models. There is also a 009 Society. HO3, which uses a 10.5 mm track gauge, is popular in the USA.

The next size up in narrow gauge modelling is the $5\frac{1}{2}$ mm/1 ft scale 12 mm gauge pioneered commercially by GEM using readily available TT gauge track and wheels. A quite comprehensive selection of Talyllyn and Festiniog Railway prototype models were on the market at one time but this range of equipment has now been withdrawn by the manufacturer. GEM also produce a series of 4 mm scale equipment on 12 mm TT gauge track for models of the 3 ft gauge Isle of Man Railway. There is a lot of scope for modelling in 00-12 as, apart from the Isle of Man Railway, there were at one time a large number of 3 ft gauge railways in Ireland which attract a lot of attention from railway enthusiasts and which make excellent subjects for railway modelling.

In 7 mm scale, 9 mm, 12 mm and 16.5 mm gauges would represent scale gauges of 1 ft 3 in, 1 ft 7 in and 2 ft 4 in. 1 ft 3 in is, of course, the gauge of the Ravenglass and Eskdale Railway and the Romney Hythe and Dymchurch Railway, and 2 ft 4 in is very near the Talyllyn 2 ft 3 in gauge. There was one narrow gauge railway built to 2 ft $4\frac{1}{2}$ in gauge which is so near to 16.5 mm gauge in 7 mm scale as to make no difference. This is catered for commercially by Peco who have taken over the production of a range of locomotive and rolling stock kits based on the Glyn Valley Tramway that once roamed its way from Chirk to a village called Glyn-Ceiriog just inside Wales near the Shropshire border. They also produce special narrow gauge flexible track and have devised a method of converting their 00 points to 0-16.5 standards. DJH Kits Ltd also produce a range of locomotive and wagon kits in 0-16.5. Moving up again to the 10 mm scale, 9 mm, 12 mm, 16.5 mm and 32 mm become the equivalent of approximately 11 in, 1 ft $2\frac{1}{2}$ in, 1 ft 8 in and 3 ft 3 in, which have very little practical application for narrow gauge modelling except that the latter gauge is not too far removed from either 3 ft gauge or metre gauge. One other narrow gauge standard that is becoming popular is 16 mm scale using 32 mm 0 gauge track. This, of course, represents a prototype track gauge of 2 ft and is an example of narrow gauge modelling built to an existing gauge rather than to a recognised scale. Live steam is a possibility with this scale and gauge. For anyone interested there is the Association of 16 mm N G Modellers. One German manufacturer, Lehmann, known as LGB, has

**Top and above** *Two impressive models from the Archangel Models range of ready-to-run 16 mm scale gauge 0 narrow gauge live steam locomotives; Vale of Rheidol 2-6-2T 'Prince of Wales' internally fired by methylated spirits and 'Jack' a coal-fired 0-4-2T. I am sure most railway modellers whatever their interests would aspire to owning one or other of these. The coal fired 'Jack' will run with four bogie coaches for up to 10 minutes on two small shovelfuls of anthracite weighing 12 grams* (Archangel Models).

introduced a range of giant narrow gauge models to 1:22.5 scale on 45 mm (1 gauge) track, which is near enough the exact scale equivalent of metre gauge. 1:22.5 scale is something like 14 mm to the foot, which makes you realise the giant stature of these models. They must surely be the ultimate in narrow gauge models, if not in commercial model making of whatever scale or gauge. Metre gauge is a common prototype gauge for narrow gauge railways on the continent of Europe and in other parts of the world, so the potential scope for these models is pretty good. The LGB range is intended for indoor as well as outdoor use, but their tremendous size must surely be best appreciated in a garden setting where they would look delightfully at home wending their way through flower beds and rockeries, and possibly even scale-size garden gnomes!

## Chapter 5

# Planning the layout

Having discussed the types of layout that are possible, where they can be accommodated and what scale and gauge we can use, the next important step is to design the plan of the layout and the formation of the tracks.

The complex layout of points, crossings, sidings and running rails at stations, either in real life or in other people's model railways shown at exhibitions, may at first glance appear bewildering to the beginner. But each item of trackwork should have a purpose and a reason for its existence, and there are a number of guiding rules and principles which determine their use and their position in the scheme of things. The factors which govern the use and positioning of tracks, points and crossings in real life should equally apply to a model. However, with the model there are additional practical considerations which must be allowed for, considerations which are peculiar to the world of railway modelling and the practical compromises we have to set ourselves. There are such things as accessibility for maintenance, cleaning or rerailing derailed rolling stock, the necessity for track to double back on itself, thus requiring excessively sharp radius curves, the sometimes awkward shape and position of our baseboards and the clearances available above, below and at either side of the track. These are some of the factors which trouble modellers greatly but which are of little comparative concern in the case of the full-size railway, where in the majority of instances there is adequate space to provide for all these contingencies.

In other words, we have problems, but of all the difficulties that face railway modellers the designing and planning of a layout gives the greatest delight in solving. Hardly a model railway magazine is complete without a track plan of some sort, and new layout plans often form the subject of regular monthly features. The easy way to design your own layout might be to simply not bother at all, but just to scan through a few magazine back numbers, or some of the excellent plan books that are available, choose a ready-made plan which roughly fits your baseboard area, and build your layout accordingly. Quite seriously though, I do offer this as a practical suggestion as the vast majority of the published plans in books and magazines are the result of years of valuable experience, which you might pay for dearly if you choose to ignore and do without. However, there are some practical points on layout planning which you might like to consider first before you make up your mind whether to choose a ready-made plan or to make up one of your own.

Any successful track layout plan must, if it is to be satisfying to the modeller, fulfil as many of the following conditions as possible:

**1** It must fit the space available.
**2** It must not be too ambitious and must be within the bounds of practicability to construct, complete, maintain, clean and operate.
**3** It must provide ready accessibility to both track and rolling stock.
**4** It must have gradients within easily workable limits.
**5** It must have sufficiently large radius curves to suit the rolling stock you intend to operate.
**6** It must provide sustained operating interest.
**7** It must conform as far as possible to acceptable railway practice.
**8** It must provide sufficient working and siding accommodation for the rolling stock it is proposed to operate.

Point number 1 of course goes without saying, and needs no further amplification. The only comment I can perhaps add is that, in some cases, it is just possible to make the space fit the plan. For instance, layouts can sometimes be extended temporarily in various directions, one obvious example being the extension from a baseboard to a window sill or even through an open window and out into the garden. I once had this problem in a garden shed in which I attempted to construct a model railway. The shed was only 7 ft 6 in × 4 ft 6 in, which really was not big enough for the plan I wanted, so I cut a pair of tunnel holes in the end wall of the shed and ran a semi-circle of track outside, thus effectively extending the space available by a good 2 ft 6 in or more. The outdoor section was removable and the tunnel mouths could be sealed up when not in use to prevent animals and insects from getting into the shed. It was not damaged or disfigured at all, as it was a wooden shed made from weather boarding. Where the line left and re-entered I removed the original weather boarding and substituted a replacement length from which tunnel mouths were cut. When eventually the shed was sold to make way for a larger concrete garage, the original weather boarding was replaced and no one was any the wiser.

I am sure I have emphasised point 2 enough already, but it is something that must be considered. We very often come across those magnificent exhibition layouts at seaside towns and big departmental stores, where a vast network of lines can be seen with seemingly dozens of trains moving in all directions. Such layouts are frequently the source of inspiration for a model railway of your own, but you must remember before you attempt to copy anything like it that these layouts are run professionally. They are attended to throughout the whole working day, which is more often than not far more time than can be spared by the average modeller.

Point number 3, accessibility of track and rolling stock, is one which needs to be borne in mind at all stages of designing *and* building the layout. In the planning stage it may be reasonable to expect ready access to a certain point on the baseboard when it is empty and devoid of any obstructions, but it may be another thing trying to reach that same spot to renew an unsoldered joint or to prise out some displaced chips of ballast from between the check rail or switch blade of a point when an item of scenery or a lineside accessory has been installed nearby. The switch blades of points are probably the biggest single item of trackwork liable to give trouble in use and they should, wherever possible, be placed in an open and accessible position. Points and crossings are also the items of trackwork which are most likely to cause trouble to rolling stock, so it is advisable to resist the temptation as far as possible of laying points in tunnels, where they would be difficult to reach when releasing stalled locomotives or rerailing derailed rolling stock.

Access to rolling stock is particularly important and, although it may be possible to build and operate the perfect layout which, with automatic couplings and all the latest electronic devices can be operated 'untouched by human hand', it is often necessary to assist the odd stubborn locomotive that refuses to budge when the current is switched on. Coupling and uncoupling operations can be done automatically, but with some forms of coupling, eg, the popular three-link type, this is not possible and it may be necessary to provide access to uncouple a locomotive or coach from a train. This may rule out the use of an overall roof for a station or affect the siting of an overbridge at the end of a platform. The more coupling and uncoupling required the greater the need for accessibility, hence the necessity to position stations and goods yards within easy reach and sight of the operator. On the other hand, locomotive sheds can be relegated to the back of the layout, out of the way, since the locomotives moving into and out of them travel as single self-contained units without the necessity for coupling operations.

It is easy enough to understand the necessity to limit the angle of gradients, point number 4, since a gradient that is too steep will simply not allow a locomotive to climb it. Furthermore, it can cause problems to a descending train, since it is likely to rush down out of control if the gradient is too steep. Some modern electronic controllers do however take care of this possibility. Most modern commercially produced model locomotives can, on their own, climb gradients steeper than would be found in real life, but it becomes a different story as soon as a trailing load is added. Some of the older commercially produced model coaches and wagons have a high rolling resistance and literally have to be dragged along by the locomotives. Thankfully, most manufacturers have realised this and have done something about improving the wheel bearings to make things easier for the engines. N gauge rolling stock is generally very good in this respect, aided also by the relatively low weight, and quite long trains of N gauge coaches and wagons can be hauled successfully up steep gradients by N gauge locomotives.

With real railways, gradients are deemed necessary by geographical features and the lay of the land. The steepness or otherwise of the gradient depends on the height and size of the hill to be climbed or the valley to be descended. On a model railway there are not usually any hills since baseboards are not only invariably built flat and level but they are purposely built that way. Gradients can be built into a layout just for the fun of it, but this is rather unusual and, more often than not, a gradient is installed to enable one line to climb up over another. In these cases we need to gain sufficient height to clear the tops of locomotives and rolling stock passing under-

*The reference in this chapter to gradients assumes the normal adhesion worked railway. Rack and pinion mountain railways are something of an exception. Fleischmann produce this HO gauge 0-6-0T nicknamed 'Green Charlie' which works either by adhesion or by rack and pinion. In the latter form it will climb gradients up to 35 per cent, approximately 1 in 3!*

neath, plus the height of the track and the baseboard supporting it. In 00 gauge this usually works out at something like 2½ to 3 in, depending on the thickness of the baseboard supporting the overhead track. If this supporting surface is simply the deck of a bridge it can be quite thin, say about ¼ in or even less—the thickness of a piece of plywood. If, however, you are building a complete high-level baseboard then you will need to allow for whatever thickness you are using, which is likely to be at least ½ in for a piece of chipboard or as much as 2½ in for another open frame baseboard with insulation board covering, as shown in fig 20.

On real railways, gradients are, in Britain at least, expressed as a ratio of the height the track rises, measured over a given distance. Examples are 1 in 150, 1 in 748 or 1 in 1508. In America, gradients are expressed as a percentage. For example, a gradient of 1 in 25 is 4 per cent, 1 in 50 2 per cent, and 1 in 100 1 per cent, etc. I am always very impressed by the precise definition of some of these measurements and the degree of accuracy that they must represent. Anyone who has ever read any steam locomotive performance articles will know how easily a change in grade can affect things. Gradients that were hardly detectable visually, looking outwards from the carriage window, were all too discernible from the sound of the locomotive exhaust. Yet the majority of these gradients are, by model railway standards at least, modest in the extreme. The Settle Carlisle line has a minimum gradient of 1 in 100, the climb out of Kings Cross to Copenhagen Tunnel is 1 in 107, and most of Shap is at 1 in 125. We have got to get to the extreme cases such as the Lickey Incline (1 in 37¾), Dainton (1 in 36 minimum) and the Folkestone Harbour Branch (1 in 30) before we reach anything like acceptable model railway practice. When full-size trains were operated with steam locomotives on these three inclines, additional motive power in the form of a banking or a pilot engine, or sometimes one or more of each, was required to assist the train engine up the gradient. Yet railway modellers frequently expect their locomotives to haul trains up similarly steep gradients unaided! For a model railway gradient it is hard to generalise since there is a vast difference in the 'rollability' of most commercially produced rolling stock, but I would suggest that nothing steeper than 1 in 30 is desirable and 1 in 40 is better still. Now, if we are going to clear a 3 in high obstacle with a gradient of 1 in 40 we are going to need a run of at least 10 ft. 1 in 30 reduces the length of run to 7 ft 6 in, but you can see already that the space problem rears its head as soon as the subject of gradients arises. One method which can sometimes be applied to the situation is to lower one track whilst at

*Fig 20*

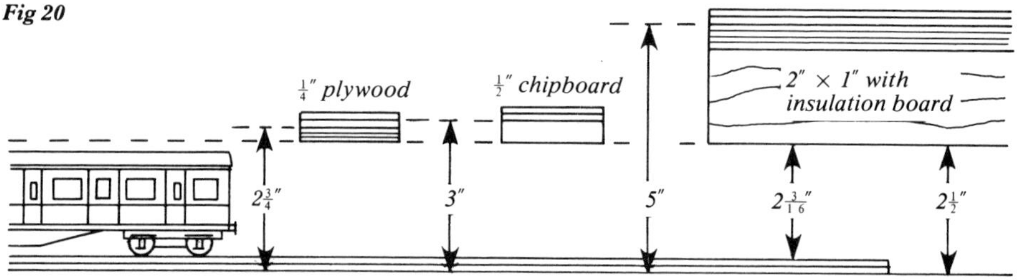


**Fig 20** *Dimensions for high-level baseboards using different materials. Figures are for clearances in 00 gauge. Flexible track on foam ballast strip is itself* $\frac{5}{16}$ *in high in 00 gauge and should be allowed for when planning high-level areas.*

the same time raising the other, thereby halving the length of run required, as shown in fig 21.

It almost goes without saying that gradients should be approached gradually and not like a wedge of cheese. The bottom and top of the gradient, where the changes in grade occur, should be curved and smoothed out gently when viewed from the side so that there is no sudden transition. If necessary, this gradual easing into and out of the gradient can be done within the overall length allowed, thereby effectively steepening the middle part of the grade, since at least it will allow the train to rush the gradient and, by the time the engine has overcome the worse part, the track will start to level out slightly which will enable the train to keep moving. (See fig 22.)

It may not always be possible to restrict gradients to straight track but it is preferable to do this wherever you can, or at least to confine the steepest part of the gradient to the straight stretch, since you impose two sets of forces against the movement of the train if you subject it to climbing a gradient round a curve. Another point to watch is to avoid as far as possible having any curves, pointwork or breaks in the baseboard immediately at the bottom or at the top of a change in grade, and certainly do not have such features as points or crossings on the gradient itself. Leave at least one carriage length clear between the start or finish of a gradient before you introduce any of these features. Gradients *can* cause operating troubles such as stalling and they can be a potential source of derailments, but they *need not* be troublesome if only you respect them and treat them and your rolling stock with respect.

Now, regarding point number 5, it is probably true to say that no one can afford to lay out curves on a model railway in anything like the same way as those on the full-size railway. Even in a garden it is rather rare to come across exactly the kind of curvature you see on the real railway, if only because it is a little unusual for a real train to want to reverse its direction of movement and double back on itself. Ninety degree curves happen on occasions, I will grant you, but 180 degree curves in normal open country must be somewhat of a novelty and 360 degree curves unheard of! Yet on a continuous layout we subject our rolling stock to movements at speeds round curves which would scare the pants off the crew of a real train. I believe the accepted minimum radius curve on British railways which can be traversed without a continuous check rail is something like 10 chains, which is 660 ft, and in 00 gauge works out at approximately 8 ft 8 in. But this is the *minimum* and most curves are much less sharp than this. High-speed main line curves are not normally made sharper than about half-a-mile radius, approximately 34 ft in 00, yet many of the proprietary 00 gauge systems utilise curves as sharp as 15 in!

In some circumstances, where space is limited and where for instance we have a baseboard only 4 ft wide, we do not have much choice in the matter if we wish to construct a continuous layout, since in a width of only 4 ft it is impossible to plan a continuous run with a curvature of more than 2 ft radius. To allow a nominal couple of inches margin round the outside of the track the curve ought to be about 1 ft 10 in radius in fact. But it should be realised that such sharp radius curves rule out any possibility of utilising a baseboard 4 ft wide for fast main line express passenger trains in 00 gauge, if any degree of realism is to be aimed at and achieved. It is possible to disguise such sharp radius curves or even hide them in a tunnel, but it is better to find a little more space and to increase the radius of the curves as much as possible or, if this cannot be done, change over to a smaller scale. Three feet radius is a generally accepted desirable standard for 00 gauge and should be increased in relation to the scale of larger gauges. For N gauge you might be tempted to think that by application of the rule, 3 ft for 00 gauge, something like 18 in radius would be suitable. But rather than diminish the standards for N gauge I do recommend raising the standard and retaining 3 ft as a minimum radius. This will achieve maximum realism.

Peco have recognised the desirability of large radius curves with their range of 00 and N gauge trackwork, for they have very thoughtfully provided a 5 ft radius point in 00 gauge and a 3 ft radius point in N gauge. This is a brilliant piece of commercial planning and one that deserves a lot of support. It is often in points and crossovers that the effects of sharp radius curves are most felt and noticed. The most undesirable effects are the overhang at the front and rear of a vehicle. The longer the vehicle the worse the effect, and the extreme cases occur with the larger Pacific-type locomotives which can be seen on some proprietary layouts with the front buffer beam pointing in one direction and the curvature of the track in another. When a locomotive such as this pushes wagons or coaches round a curve the buffer heads of the locomotive and the wagon or coach are nowhere near aligning. As soon as normal straight track is reached the buffers side-swipe each other, locking themselves behind the buffer heads (buffer locking, we call this) and the lighter of the two vehicles becomes derailed. The troubles with sharp radius curves are in fact doubled when propelling vehicles over a crossover or reverse curve, since the effect of one curvature is added to the other, as seen in fig 23, with the result that even some reasonably short length vehicles can become buffer locked.

In realising that everyone just does not have room to install scale curves on their layout, all model railway manufacturers have attempted to overcome the buffer locking problem by designing their rolling stock, and particularly their couplings, so that the buffers never come together, let alone lock. I appreciate that this is a thoroughly practical and workmanlike method and without it hardly any model trains would be sold today. But for the nostalgic modeller who likes to see his buffers touching and who likes to use loose three-link couplings, the only alternative is to use as large a radius as possible, 3 ft at the very minimum and preferably something larger, or else limit the rolling stock to short wheelbase four-wheeled vehicles or four- or six-coupled locomotives. I must emphasise that the question of radius of curves is entirely related to the type of layout and rolling stock you wish to operate, as it is of course in real life. On a model dockyard layout, coal mine or gas works siding, which only sees short wheelbase four-coupled locomotives and wagons, you could probably get away with 12 in radius curves in 00 and a 4 mm scale tramway layout can be built with even sharper curves, but please do not expect the same standards to

**Fig 21** *Lowering one track whilst at the same time raising the other can halve the length of track required to clear a given rise.* **Fig 22** *The bottom and top of a gradient should be curved and smoothed out gently to avoid sudden transitions in steepness.* **Fig 23** *Buffer locking can become a problem if curves are given too sharp a radius particularly, as here, on a reverse curve.*

*Fig 21*

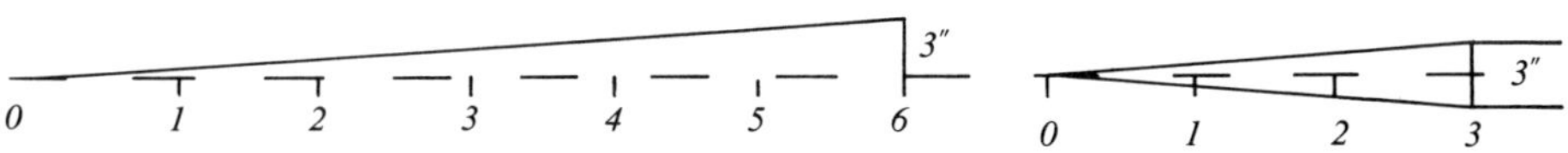


*Fig 22*

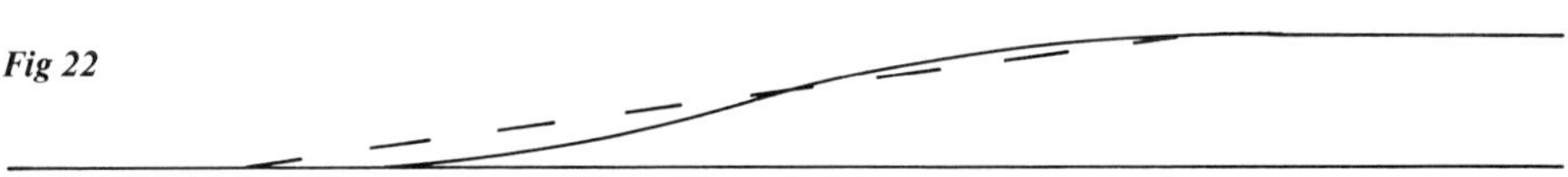

*Fig 23*

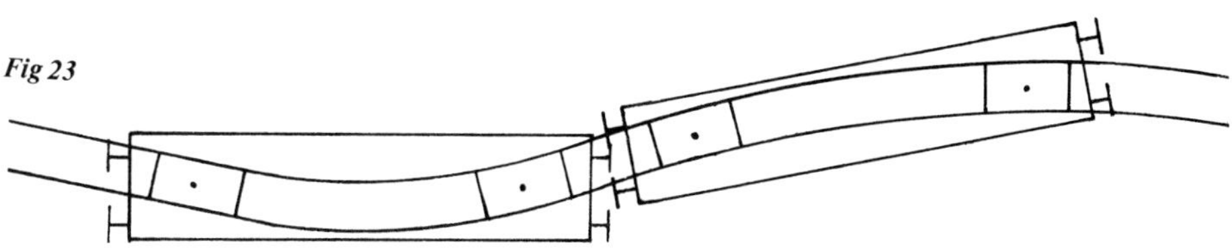

apply to a main line Pacific locomotive hauling an express passenger train, or to a multi-wheeled locomotive pushing long wheelbase loose coupled bogie vehicles over reverse curves. Plan your curves to suit your rolling stock.

One thing I have not mentioned, but perhaps ought to at this stage, is the subject of transition curves. In theory at least, curves should be approached gradually, otherwise an abrupt change from straight track to curved track can have a shock effect on the locomotive and train as it enters the curve. In practice, however, I have found that most model railway rolling stock is fully capable of making the transition without difficulty, even at quite high speeds, but you may—from the appearance point of view if nothing else—make provision for the initial radius of the curve to be a little larger than the main part of the curve, thus avoiding an abrupt change in the track geometry. Similarly, although this has no place in the subject of layout planning, it might be as well to discuss superelevation of curves. This is the practice of canting the track so that the outside rail on a curve is higher than the inside rail. This can be observed on full-size railways on practically every curve and can be detected readily when travelling in a train. It is done to help counteract the effect of the curve itself, in much the same way that roads are cambered, but in model railways it is not required for any practical reason. It does help to add realism, however, and provided there are no points or crossings on the curve to complicate the matter I recommend adding a little superelevation wherever you can. On full-size British railways the rails are generally canted to a maximum of 6 in, which of course is 2 mm in 00. Either cardboard or balsa wood could be used for packing up the outer rail, but be careful to make the transition as progressive and gentle as possible.

Point number 6, to provide sustained operating interest, is very important, but unfortunately cannot always be visualised in advance. You can try and imagine the operating scope of a layout from a plan on a piece of paper, but the proof of the pudding is invariably in the eating. One important point which affects both the operating possibilities of a layout and its basic shape is whether it is to provide a continuous run by means of an unbroken oval or circuit of track or whether it is to be 'end to end'. The continuous run layout lacks the realism of a full-size railway, since no train in real life is made to run over the same length of track, passing the same scenery and lineside settings continuously with only seconds separating each circuit—sometimes derisively referred to as tail-chasing. However, there is a credit side to the continuous layout since it cannot be denied that the sight of a train in motion at a reasonably fast speed, say the equivalent of 60 to 65 mph, is very satisfying and is one of the reasons why some of us take up railway modelling. When observing a model train travelling at such a relatively high speed round a circuit of track you tend to watch the train, not the track or scenery, and it is possible to close your eyes and thoughts to the fact that it is the same length of track each time. By limiting your field of view you only need to watch the engine, the movement of the coupled wheels, valve gear and motion, and the swish of the carriages as they pass by to obtain satisfaction from the sight. A continuous run layout can be disguised to a large extent to cover up the undesirable effects of tail-chasing.

The secret is to achieve a limited field of view and to break up the continuous aspect with tunnels, cuttings or scenery. These will obscure the curves at each end of the layout which are necessary to bring the train round and back again. Another positive step is to try and model the observed section of the continuous run track through a nondescript scenic setting devoid of particular landmarks, which will minimise the effect of passing the same spot on each occasion. It might be particularly desirable, for instance, to avoid bringing the train through the same station on every circuit. A reversing loop which changes the direction of the train can also help. Of course, the best single factor is to make the continuous run as long as possible since the longer the train takes to complete each circuit obviously the less continuous it will appear, but not all of us can take this step. One big advantage with a continuous run layout is that locomotives have a chance to be run-in and this can be quite important with some that have noisy gears and stiff working parts which only become eased after they have been given an airing. Bench runs can help on occasions, but it is my view that there is nothing to beat a run under load round a continuous layout for say half-a-dozen circuits.

The end-to-end type of layout can take a number of forms, from the simple straight line to a complex system of curves, loops, reverse loops, flyovers and what have you. The shorter the layout the slower the speeds that can be obtained, so if you want to see a locomotive get into its stride and watch it moving for any length of time before it has to come to a halt you will need at least a 20 ft run in 4 mm scale. It always seems to me that the end-to-end layout is best operated by two people, each at their respective ends of the layout. One extreme of this idea is to have each end in separate rooms, with a tunnel through the dividing wall. Trains would then be despatched by timetable and signalled properly with a system of bell codes as the only means of communication between each operator. Such degrees of enthusiasm are not, of course, essential and it is perfectly possible to operate a two-man layout within sight and sound of each other and possibly be a good deal friendlier too! One advantage of two operators is that the one despatching a train can, after it has got into its stride, leave the control and subsequent stopping to the second operator who can take over the train at a given point on the track. The first despatch operator can then have the pleasure of watching the train pass out of sight without having to be concerned with its control. When next a train reappears in the reverse direction after a decent time interval, the first operator can gain considerable pleasure from receiving a train, the formation of which is quite unknown to him, since it will have been made up by the second operator from rolling stock he is holding at his end of the line.

The common formation for a line such as this is to have a terminal station at one end and what is known as a 'fiddle yard' at the other. A fiddle yard is just that! It is somewhere where an operator can manipulate or fiddle with the formation of trains from whatever stock he has available. At public exhibitions the fiddle yard is often hidden from view. There are any number of different forms a fiddle yard can take, from the simple bank of storage sidings (fig 24) to the most elaborately engineered turntable affair, such as shown in fig 25, where different trains on different tracks can be lined up with the entrance and exit roads and at the end of an operating session the trains can be reversed and returned to their starting point. The simple kind of storage bank illustrated in fig 24 will have to rely on 'hand shunting' to change the formation of the trains, for instance to uncouple the locomotive, reverse its direction and couple it up at the opposite end. Handling such as this is

**Fig 24** *A simple bank of fiddle yard storage sidings.* **Fig 25** *A more elaborate turntable storage yard, with tracks long enough to hold both engine and coaches.*

*Fig 24*

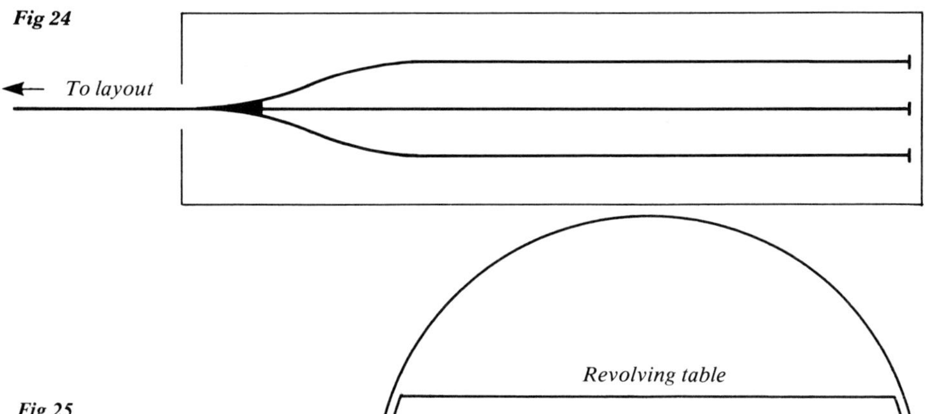


*Fig 25*

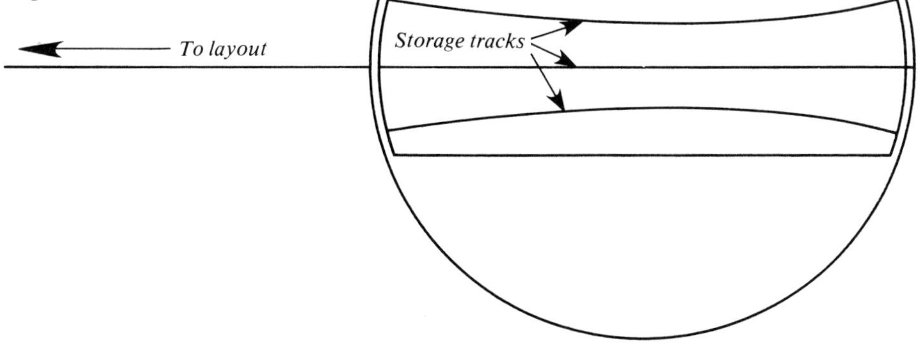

**Fig 26**

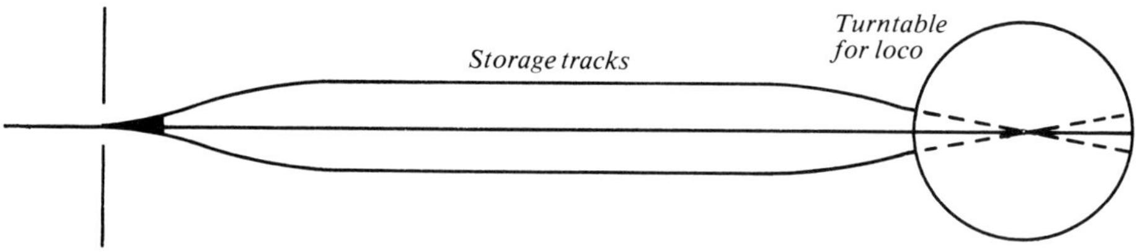


**Fig 27**

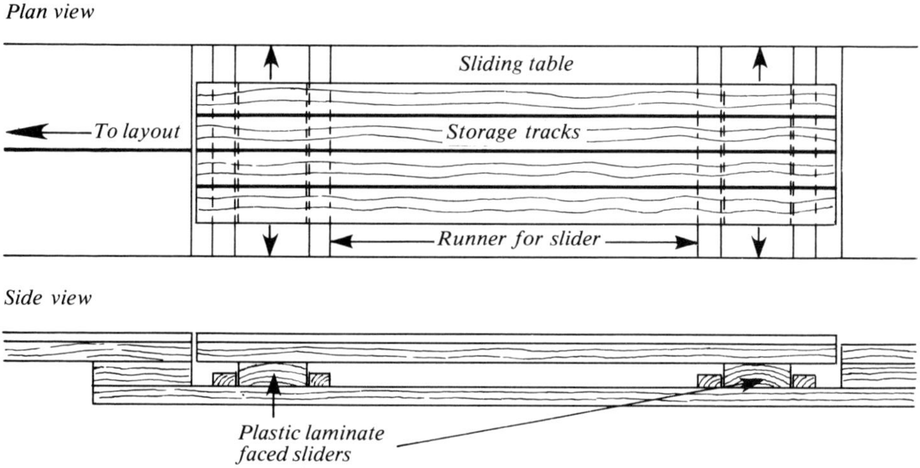


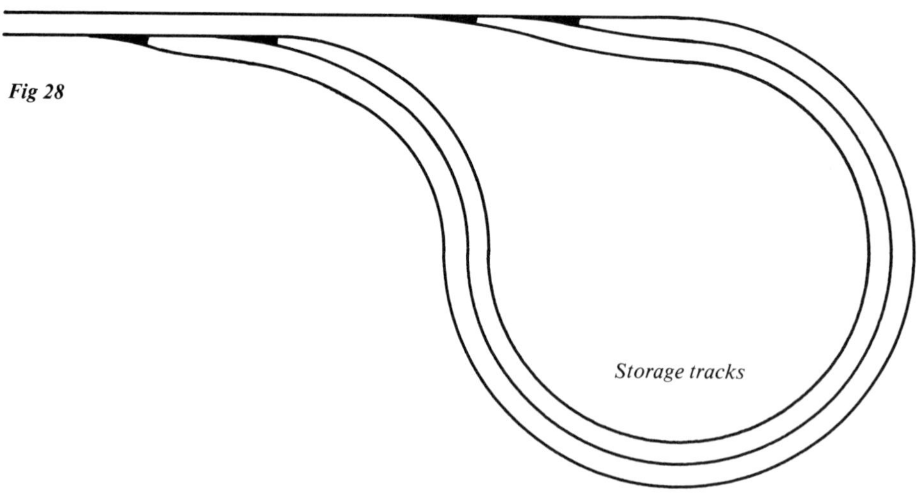


**Fig 28**

permissible in a fiddle yard, whereas of course it would be frowned on out in the open in the public gaze.

Another alternative is to have a turntable at the far end of the bank of sidings so that the locomotive can at least be turned and transferred from one road to another without having to lift it by hand. (See fig 26.) Yet another permutation is to have the bank of sidings on a traverser which will allow any particular track to be lined up with the exit road to enable a particular train to enter or leave the yard. The traverser can be a simple affair, such as shown in fig 27, which relies on Formica or some other form of shiny proprietary laminate to provide the bearing surface for the movable board or table which simply slides back and forth to line up the required track with the entrance or exit road. The length of the traverser will be governed by the length of train you wish it to accommodate. A small country branch line in 4 mm scale can be operated by a train of three or four coaches which, with the engine, would be something like 4 ft long. This same length would accommodate a 10- or 11-wagon freight train, which is quite a realistic and respectable load for a country branch line. Yet another type of fiddle yard can take the form of a series of reversing loops. This will have the advantage of reversing the direction of the train without the need for a turntable or hand movement, but it will take up a lot more space since the overall size of the loops will be at least double the minimum radius of the curves you are using. (See fig 28.)

Possibly one of the most satisfying forms of layout plan is one that combines the advantages of both a continuous and non-continuous run, an out and back scheme with a continuous run in between. Variations on this basic theme are shown in figs 29–34 inclusive.

In fig 29 the train leaves the terminal station at point A, traverses the circuit as many times as required and returns back to A. In fig 30 the train can leave the terminal station from one platform, traverse the circuit as many times as required and return to the other platform of the same station. Fig 31 is very similar to fig 30, but the terminal station is on a different level to the normal continuous run which passes underneath the station throat at point B. The track extension at point C is optional since it is not required to provide a continuation of the main circuit, but it could be useful because a triangular junction outside a terminal station can be of great assistance in the manoeuvring or turning of stock. In fig 32 the train would leave one terminal station at point A, traverse the main circuit and then enter the second terminal station at point B. Fig 33 is in many ways a development of fig 29 in that it relies on a reversing loop to bring the train back into the terminal station. The difference is that the reversing loop is inside the circuit, which enables the train to traverse the circuit after it has reversed direction and before it is made to return to the terminal station.

Another advantage of fig 33 over fig 29 is that a second station, a through station, could be installed on the reverse loop at point B, space permitting, which would provide a number of additional operating opportunities. Fig 34 provides out-and-back facilities using a through station instead of a terminal station. A train can leave from, say, the left of the station and join the circuit at point A, traverse the circuit via the tunnel and the hidden line as many times as required and then return to the station from the right-hand side at point B. In fig 34 the part of the circuit behind the station is hidden from view in a tunnel or possibly, as an alternative, behind scenic effects forming a backcloth to the station. These suggestions do not by any means exhaust all the possibilities but they do give an idea of some of the basic plans for track layouts which you may be able to make use of in whatever space you have available.

I have deliberately avoided going into detail, not even bothering to mention whether the plans are based on single or double track since in many cases this sort of detail can obscure the basic shape of a layout, and it is this that I am concerned with more at this stage. But in ignoring the details, already some basic facts of life begin to emerge. If any of the track plans in figs 29–34 are to be developed into a fully detailed layout plan they are going to consume a fair degree of space. Take the most compact one, which is probably fig 34. If you are working in 00 4 mm scale, the minimum length for the platform forming the station will need to be at least equal to the longest train you intend to operate. You would obviously like to emanate the full-size railway, which sees nothing exceptional in 11, 12, 13 or 14 coach trains, but

**Fig 26** *Storage tracks can usefully be combined with a locomotive turntable.* **Fig 27** *Another permutation is to accommodate the bank of sidings on a traverser, which permits individual storage tracks to be lined-up with the exit road.* **Fig 28** *Another form of fiddle yard, comprising a series of reversing loops.*

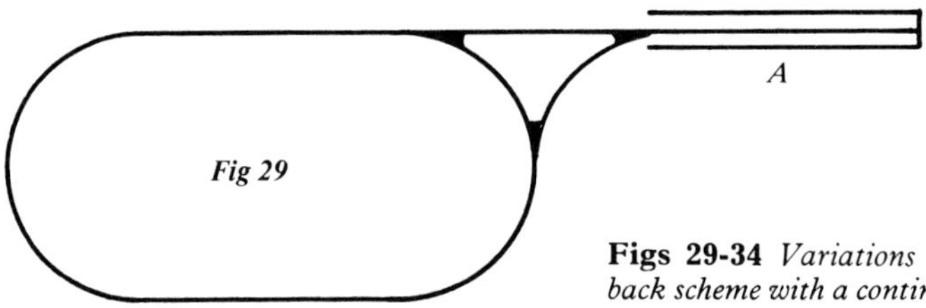


**Figs 29-34** *Variations on the basic out and back scheme with a continuous run in between.*

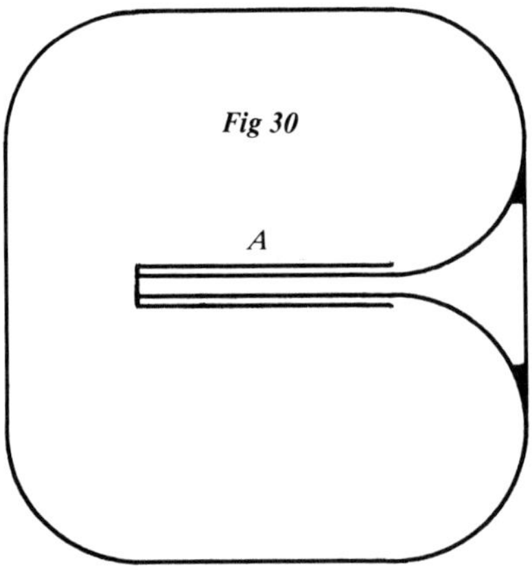


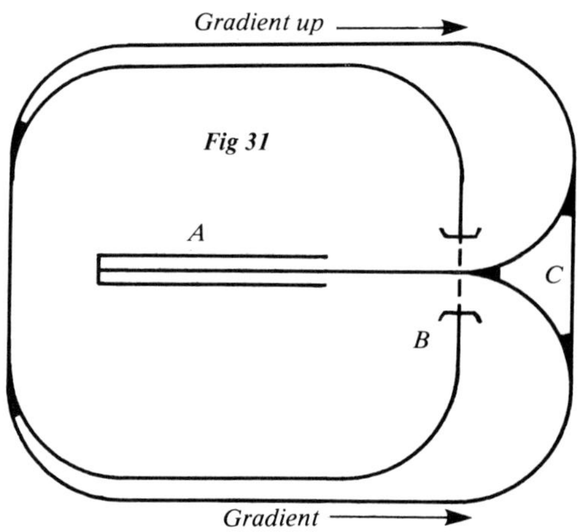


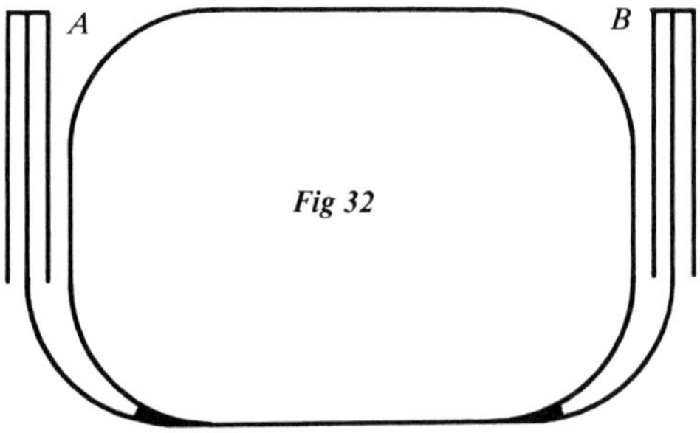


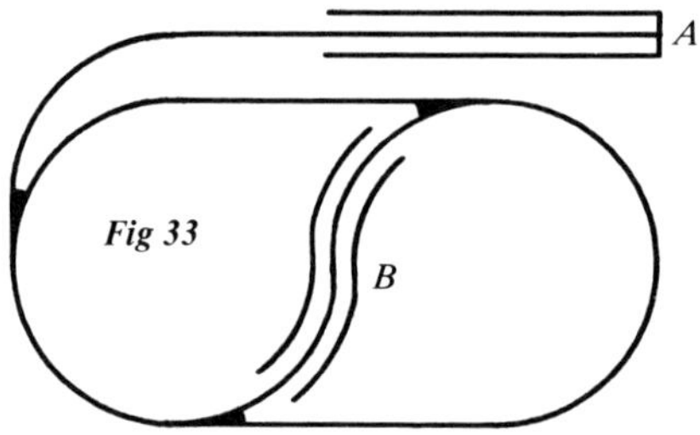


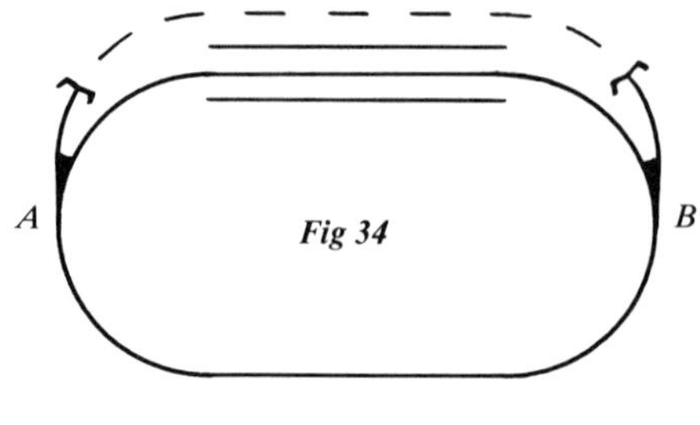

with coaches in 00 4 mm scale working out at approximately $9\frac{1}{2}$ in long, this would mean a platform length of something like 9 to 11 ft! Reducing our train to, say, six coaches, we can halve the platform length to 5 ft, and this is not a bad length to aim at. Now, assuming you start the curves to join points A and B on fig 34 at a point immediately at the ends of the platform, you will need as much space either end of the platform as the minimum radius curve you are using. (See fig 35.) Assuming 2 ft radius curves, which really is something less than the ideal minimum we discussed earlier, you will add 2 ft to either end of the station, 4 ft in all, so already in 00 4 mm scale you have consumed 9 ft of space and have made no provision for the insertion of points or turnouts to lead off from the track passing through the station. To make such provision you want to allow yourself at least another 2 ft at one if not both ends of the station. (See fig 36.) This extra space either end of the platform will enable you to install double track through the station, provide a second platform and put in a goods loop which can lead into the goods yard, south of the station. But it has also added another 4 ft to the length of the station, making a total length of 13 ft, and we still have only a minimum token requirement. Though I spoke of using 2 ft radius curves, in 00 gauge you ought really to be thinking in terms of 3 ft radius curves which would, in fact, add another 2 ft to the simple plan in fig 36.

Perhaps this has demonstrated how simple it is to run away with yourself when it comes to planning a layout for a model railway. It is all too easy to think up a scheme which looks all right until you get down to the detailed planning stage and find that you just cannot get that proverbial quart into the pint pot. However, it is possible sometimes to compromise and do some pruning, and the example we have just been discussing is a case in point. Suppose, for instance, that we bring the goods loop round the other side, to the north of the station. It would then be possible to install the turnouts to the loop on the curve leading into the station instead of using up space on the straights. In turn, this would reduce the necessity for having quite so much space for straight track at either end of the platforms. It might also be permitted to stagger the platforms so that, by moving the south side platform of the station to the left, out of centre, it would be possible to install a point at one end from which to bring a siding along the south side of the station. (See fig 37.) These slight modifications bring the overall length down by 2 ft, which can either be utilised in squeezing the layout into a restricted area or can be used to increase the radius of the curves. Wherever possible the latter is preferable.

The station layout in fig 37 is really very simple, too simple in fact, and makes no provision for public access to the station, station buildings or any of the amenities we expect to find on a full-size railway. When considering such needs we may well have to revise the plan again, and so it goes on! Layout planning is very much a long-term trial and error process, one thing leading to another, and always you have to work within the confines of limited space. To persevere with fig

*Fig 35*

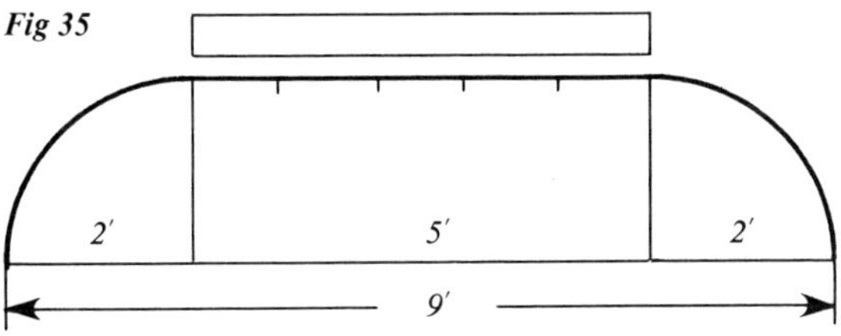


**Figs 35-38** *All measurements given in figs 35-38 are for 00 gauge, and can be halved for N gauge.*

*Fig 36*

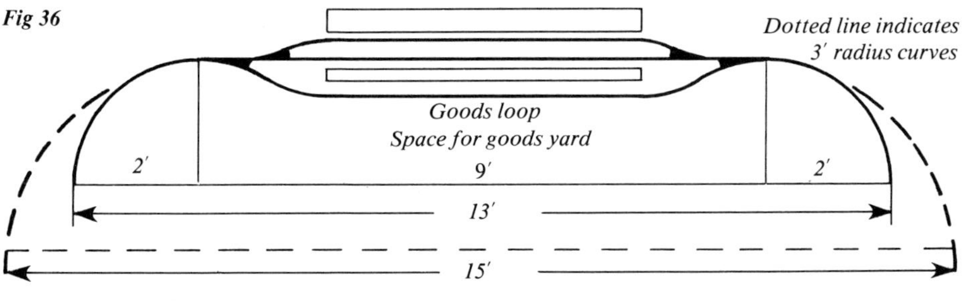

*Fig 37*

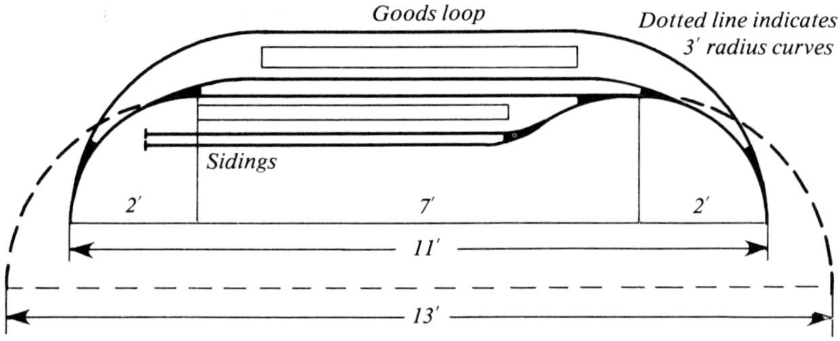


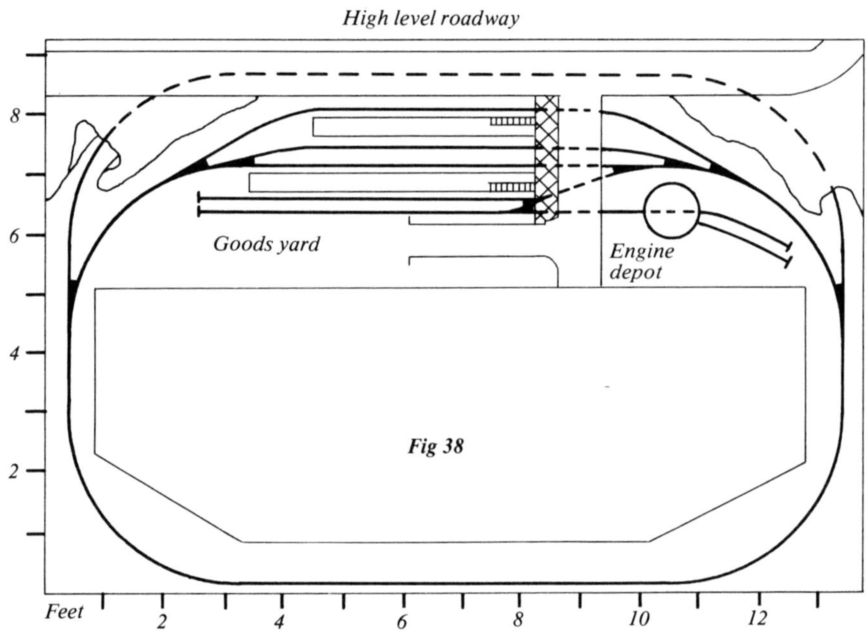


*Fig 38*

37, what have we achieved so far? On the credit side we have a two-road, two-platform station with a goods loop on one side and a siding on the other. On the debit side we have no station buildings, no goods yard, goods shed or public access to the goods yard or station, and no engine depot should we require one at this point on the layout. Luckily we can, if we want to, take the easy way out so far as station buildings and public access is concerned and assume a road crossing the tracks on a bridge, with the main station buildings on the level of the road at right angles to the platform. (See fig 38.) This is a common working arrangement, especially in towns and congested built-up areas—in fact, just the same sort of situation we find ourselves faced with in our model. As it happens, there would be a particularly desirable side effect if we used such an arrangement because, you will remember, the station we are developing is to be used in conjunction with the layout shown in fig 34, where part of the continuous oval passes behind the station in a tunnel hidden from view by a high-level scenic section. The road crossing the station on the bridge could therefore be made to join this high-level section, which scenically could be developed to represent a town landscape. This is probably the best solution for this particular dilemma. This practical demonstration shows how layout planning can be approached and how a fully developed plan is often the culmination of a lot of separate decisions which are made step by step as they occur.

The central point of any plan is invariably

the station and we have already seen how its length can be governed by the traffic requirements and how the station itself can dictate the ultimate shape and character of a layout. As in real life, the station should reflect the type of traffic you wish to operate. The grander and more express the train, the longer the platform and, unless space is unlimited, the bigger your problems. I think you will begin to see why the smaller type of branch line layout is so popular as, although many actual branch line stations had quite long platforms, in model form we can get away with relatively short platforms provided our trains are kept short. The platform must be long enough to hold the longest train, and in 00 gauge, 4 mm scale, 2 ft 6 in to 3 ft can be ample for a two- or three-coach branch line train.

As another exercise in layout planning, let us build up step by step a branch line terminal station. There are, or were, any number of actual stations we could use and the model press is full of examples, but rather than pick on one of these ready-made samples, let us build up one of our own to cover the particular type of traffic we wish to operate. Firstly, let us assume the branch line has been built to serve a small country market town some five or six miles from a junction with the main line and about 15 to 20 miles away from a larger commercial centre. The latter will justify the operation of a reasonably comprehensive passenger service since we can assume a residential population and a sprinkling of commuter traffic. For this we need to run a three-coach locomotive-hauled train at peak hours and perhaps a diesel railcar or steam-hauled railmotor during the off-peak times. The locomotive-hauled train will require a run-round loop to enable the engine to uncouple and run round the train. We may also need some siding accommodation to stable the early morning commuter train carriages overnight and the railmotor or rail car during the peak periods when it is out of use during the day. So already we need something similar to that given in fig 39.

Now the overall length of this little lot would work out at something like 7 ft in 00 4 mm scale. The next step is perhaps to consider the goods traffic. We have already established that it is a small country market town, so it is reasonable to assume the following types of traffic:

**Inward** Coal (mainly domestic); general merchandise; parcels; fertilisers; timber; possibly oil and petrol; agricultural machinery.
**Outward** Agricultural and dairy produce; milk; livestock (eg, cattle, sheep and pigs).

To cater for this traffic we would need the following facilities:
**1** Coal bins for coal merchants to unload and store coal.
**2** A goods shed to unload inward coming general merchandise and fertilisers and to load outward going agricultural products, fruit, vegetables, small livestock, etc.
**3** A crane to help offload containers, timber and agricultural machinery.
**4** An end loading bay to offload agricultural machinery.
**5** A cattle pen for loading and unloading cattle and sheep, and which must be reasonably near road access.
**6** A dairy to load milk tank wagons.
**7** Possibly an oil and petrol storage depot.

The plan in fig 41 covers all these points and is probably rather more elaborate than most branch line terminal stations were in practice. But I have attempted to cater for a large volume of traffic and a large number of traffic movements, since we want to provide our model with as much operating scope as possible. For instance, the goods arrival loop is something that may not always be found in a small terminal station, but I have installed it deliberately so that the arrival of a goods train need not interfere with the working of the passenger service. On arrival, the goods train would run into the loop and detach the goods brake van at the end which would be run into the storage siding at A. The engine would then uncouple, run round the train, and proceed to push the waggons into their respective sidings—B for general merchandise and fertilisers, D for coal, C for storage and off-loading when convenient, and E for

**Fig 39** *A track plan for a simple branch line terminal station.*

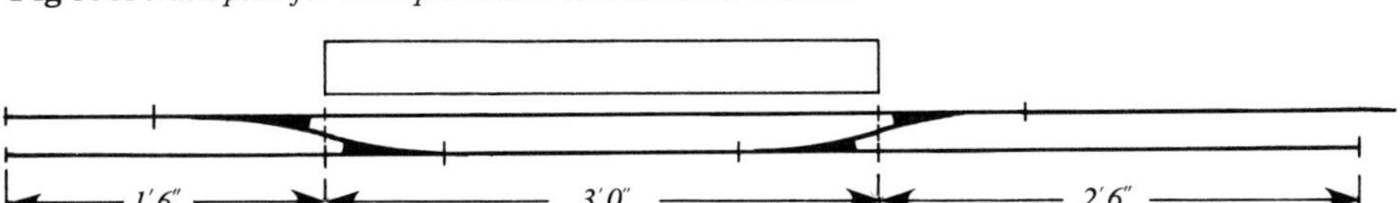


*Fig 39*

end unloading of agricultural machinery. It is assumed that the sidings would be cleared as far as possible beforehand of any empty wagons, which would already be made up into a train waiting in the departure road. You will see that, compared with fig 39, we have moved the carriage storage road to a bay platform at the side of the passenger station main platform. A bay platform such as this can be very useful for handling parcel traffic or for accepting extra trains during market or fair days. All the loading and unloading facilities listed earlier have been provided and sidings have been incorporated leading to the dairy and oil storage depot. In addition, provision for an engine shed has been made alongside the siding reserved for brake vans. Perhaps a loco coal wagon could be allowed to stand on the brake van siding, which would provide a reserve coal supply for the small locomotive depot.

As I said earlier, probably the track layout of fig 41 is over elaborate compared to many prototype branch line terminal stations. The very famous Ashburton station in Devon, so beloved by branch line enthusiasts and once the home for locomotives belonging to the Dart Valley Railway, is a case in point. The track layout of Ashburton is shown in fig 40.

Here a very long run round loop is provided, in fact the locomotive released from the front of the train after it arrived at the station had to travel right beyond the engine shed before it could come forward again to rejoin the train. The whole emphasis is on length rather than breadth and in fact in 00 gauge you would require a space of at least 10 ft in length to accommodate this quite simple design if you wanted to model it accurately, whereas it need only be about 1 ft 6 in wide. A long goods siding is provided, but access to it is in the middle. If any wagons have to be moved out of the left-hand end of the siding opposite the locomotive shed they have to enter the right-hand end where the goods shed is situated before they can be moved on to the main line. As the engine itself has to make a similar move, only a few wagons can be moved at a time and then only if there are a limited number of wagons on the goods shed road. Frankly, I am not over-enamoured with Ashburton as a track layout for a terminal station as it has such limited operating possibilities, although I join with everybody in regretting the reason for its closure as a branch line terminus. I am sure that it must have been mainly the buildings, particularly the overall station roof, that attracted so many people to it. If you want a much simpler branch line terminal station, but one that still provides some operating scope, fig 41 could be pruned quite extensively and still leave a number of interesting facilities.

In fig 42 we have cut out the goods arrival and departure loops. As a result it will be necessary to use the running line for a shunting spur, which is more in keeping with a small branch line terminal. Only one road has been provided for the milk depot and it will be necessary for the bay platform cum carriage siding to be nearly empty before any wagons can be worked into or out of the depot. The oil depot and engine shed can change places if you wish. Dispensing with the goods arrival and departure loops and moving the run round loop crossover further down the line away from the buffer stop has had the effect of extending the length of the run round loop, and at the same time has enabled the goods and coal sidings to be extended, which is probably a worth while advantage. I think you will agree that fig 42 is much less cluttered up than fig 41 and, bearing in mind the example set by Ashburton, is probably more authentic in appearance.

In drawing plans for these suggested

**Fig 40** *Ashburton station. This simple branch line terminal station occupies approximately ¼ mile in real life, which is about 15 ft in 00 gauge.*

**Fig 41** *and* **fig 42** *Each measure represents 6 in in N gauge, 1 ft in 00 gauge and 21 in in 0 gauge.*

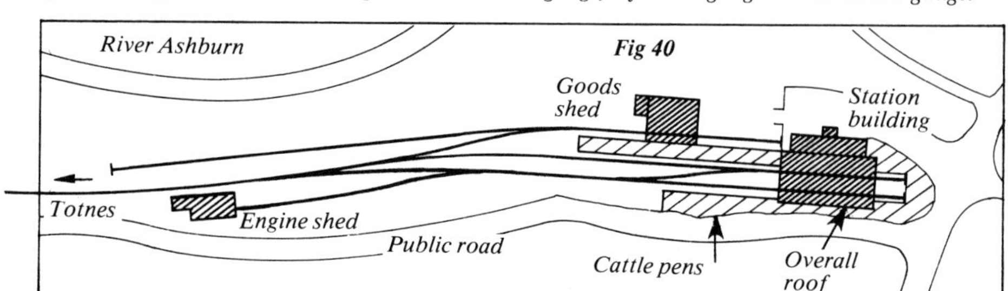

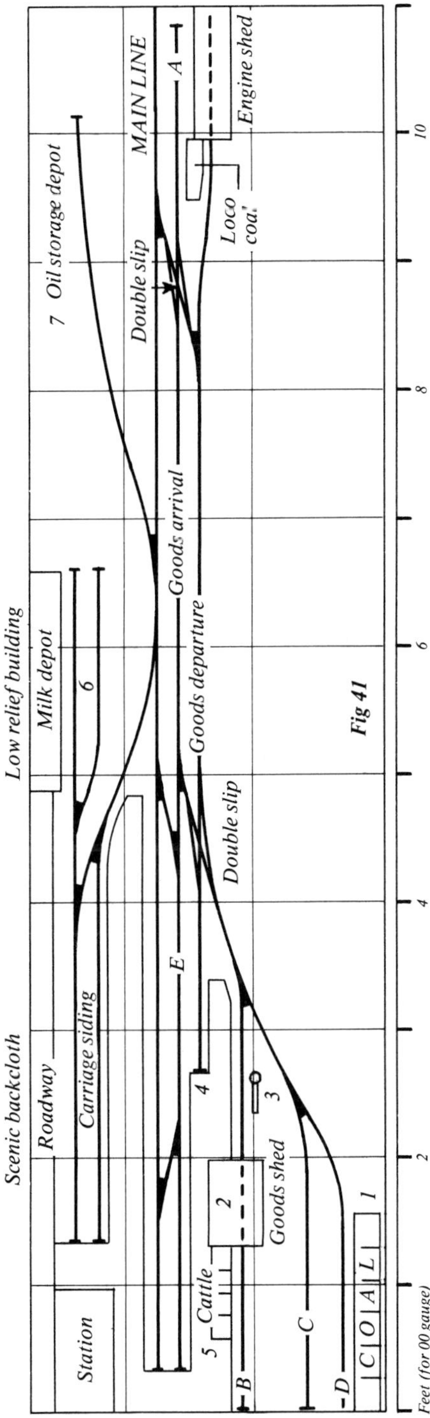
Scenic backcloth
Low relief building
Station
Roadway
Carriage siding
Milk depot
6
7 Oil storage depot
MAIN LINE
Double slip
Goods arrival
Goods departure
Double slip
Engine shed
Loco coal
A
B
C
D
E
5
Cattle
2
Goods shed
3
4
C O A L
1
Feet (for 00 gauge)
1
2
2
4
6
8
10

Fig 41

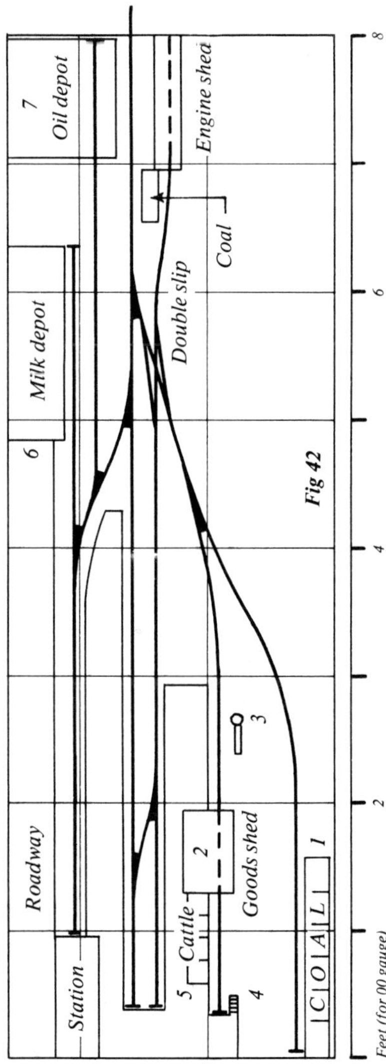
Station
Roadway
6
Milk depot
7
Oil depot
Engine shed
Coal
Double slip
5
Cattle
2
Goods shed
3
4
C O A L
1
Feet (for 00 gauge)
2
3
2
4
6
8

Fig 42

layouts it is always much easier to use a straight line for most of the running rails but, if possible, it adds considerably to the realism of a station layout if a slight curve can be introduced into the main track roads. Again, Ashburton is a good example as the layout is on a gentle curve, at least it looks gentle on a track plan but it is quite noticeably curved in real life when the eye is nearer to ground level. The inclusion of a gentle curve into the plan of a layout is not always possible if you are using proprietary ready-assembled track since, with few exceptions, the majority of commercially produced points and crossings are designed with a straight stock rail. There are, admittedly, such things as points on curves but the radius of these curves is much sharper than I have in mind for this particular application. If, however, you propose making your own trackwork the introduction of a gentle curve does not present too insurmountable a problem.

If you are intending to purchase ready-made track and points, the points themselves can be an expensive item since a fair number are usually required, even for the most basic layout plan. (Four are needed for the simple run round loop shown in fig 39.) Incidentally, we refer to points as left-hand or right-hand and in fig 39 we have two right-hand and two left-hand points; the right-hand points are in fact on the left-hand end of the loop and the two left-hand points are shown on the right-hand end of the loop, just to be awkward! Two points of the same hand make a crossover from one straight running rail to another, eg, figs 43 and 44. A crossover on a curve, however, uses points of opposite hands, as shown in fig 45. Another type much favoured by manufacturers is the 'Y' point, where the two diverging rails curve at an equal radius and angle, eg, fig 46. The crossing in fig 47 has a number of uses, depending on the angle of the crossing. A shallow angle such as 12 degrees is used for making what is known as a double

Fig 43

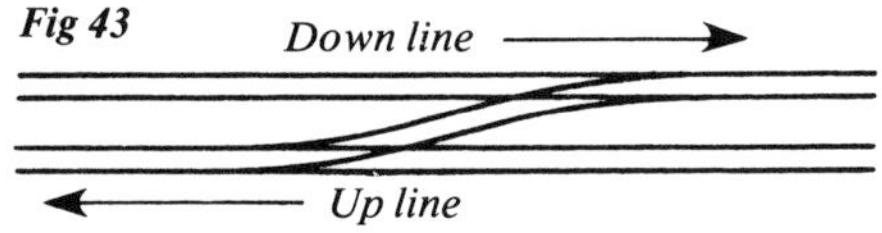


Fig 44

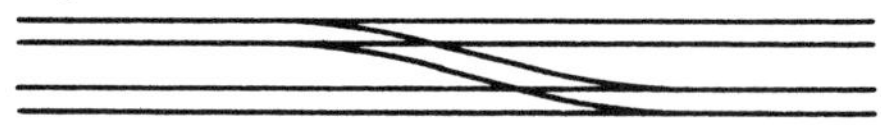

Fig 45

Fig 46

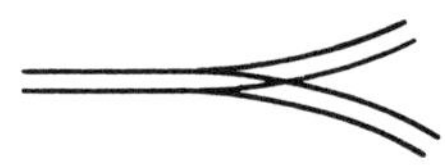

Fig 47

Fig 48

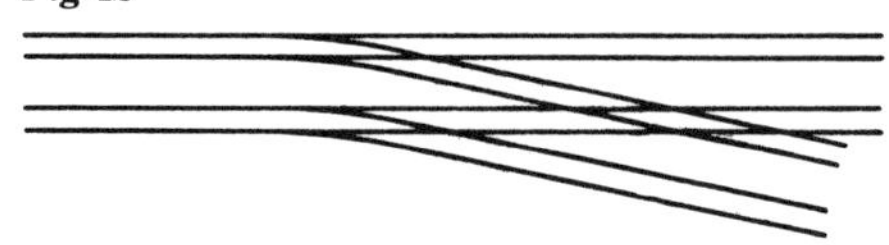

Fig 49 Fig 50

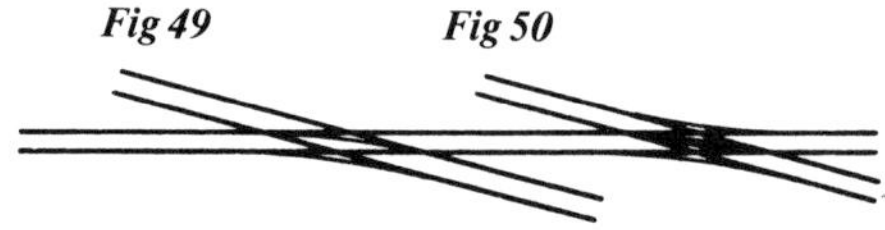

Fig 51

Fig 52

**Fig 43** *Two left-hand points make a trailing crossover.* **Fig 44** *Two right-hand points make a facing crossover.* **Fig 45** *One left-hand and one right-hand point make a crossover on a curve.* **Fig 46** *'Y' point.* **Fig 47** *Crossing. 'X' marks the angle—in this case 12 degrees.* **Fig 48** *Double junction, using two left-hand points and one 12 degree crossing.* **Fig 49** *(left) Single slip.* **Fig 50** *(right) Double slip.* **Fig 51** *Two points placed back to back have the same effect as a double slip, but take up twice as much room.* **Fig 52** *Three-way point—a useful space saver.*

junction, eg, fig 48, where two sets of running lines diverge from each other. Yet another type of pointwork is the slip, either a single slip or a double slip (see figs 49 and 50).

These slip points are very common in prototype practice, particularly in station goods yards. They were always regarded as a bit of a challenge to scratch builders and as ready-made commercial items they were very rare and almost unheard of at one time. But such is the development of mass-production technology in the model railway world that several manufacturers now offer double slips in 00 gauge and even in N gauge. A double slip virtually combines two points together. The same effect can be obtained by using two points, but as the expense of using more track space. (See fig 51.)

There is one other type of point which ought to be mentioned, and that is the three-way type (see fig 52), also quite common in prototype practice but rather rare in the commercial model world. On the full-size railway most pointwork is tailor-made to fit the location and more often than not the points are built on curves and do not assume the straight geometrical form that used to be adopted by model manufacturers. Points on curves are, however, becoming more common and several firms are beginning to include such items in their range. For really authentic track formations you cannot do better than build your own track, but if you feel you are unable to spare the time or you think it may be beyond your capability, the range of points and crossings available from commercial manufacturers in the two most popular gauges, 00 and N, is such that really comprehensive layouts can be built with very little trouble. But, as I said earlier, points are relatively costly items in comparison, say, to a yard of flexible track. When you find yourself being carried away and sketching in sidings and junctions all over your layout plan, remember that if you are going to purchase your track ready-made, it is probably going to cost more than £2 per point—even a little more after you have purchased the necessary point lever or operating mechanism. We will discuss these later in chapter 7. Fig 42 is not too bad in that it only uses seven points; four right-hand, two left-hand, one 'Y' point and one double slip. The probable cost of these items in 00 or N could be around £25, which is something that needs to be considered, although it must be emphasised that, once laid, track is a capital investment which need not be repeated and will last as long as the layout. Fig 41 uses 14 points—six right-hand, seven left-hand and one 'Y' point, and two double slips; the probable cost of this little lot could be as much as £50. This is for the pointwork alone, to which must be added the cost of the ordinary running rails you will also need.

In case you are worried about these kind of figures I would hasten to add that points and running rails need only be purchased as and when they are laid. It can take several weeks to lay a complete track formation for a station, such as shown in fig 42, since there is more to it than just connecting points up together, as I will show in succeeding chapters. Three or four points and half-a-dozen yards of track can be purchased to begin with, and this will enable you to make a start. The rest can follow later as and when funds permit.

Talking about the cost of trackwork, points and running rails reminds me to refer to point number 7 in the list of desirable features for layout planning—conform as far as possible to acceptable railway practice. I think the full-size railways are as mindful as anyone of the necessity to keep trackwork down to a minimum compatible with the job in hand. In many cases of railway construction, where single track only was laid, provision was made in the accompanying earthworks and civil engineering structures for laying double track on the assumption that if traffic expanded the second line could be added later. The capital cost of laying a double line and the continual drain on revenue of having to maintain a second line unnecessarily was avoided when it could be, but the relatively slight extra cost of building the earthworks and civil engineering structures to double track standard was accepted at the time as being cheaper than having to face the possible total conversion at a later date. Most prototype station track plans, although they sometimes seem to be festooned with points and sidings, are often very simple when you look at them closely and make a detailed study of each particular track and the likely operating movement. These days especially, tracks are not left in place any longer than they need to be. If you are modelling a modern image layout some provision ought to be made on the plan for a disused siding, or a branch line which perhaps can be made to disappear into a bricked-up tunnel mouth, or even a cutting with a row of hen houses standing where the track used to be.

One of the most basic rules to follow when trying to conform to prototype practice is to avoid the use of facing points on passenger carrying lines. The simplest illustration and practical application of this is the installation of a crossover between an up and down main line. The crossover should always be laid in a

*WD 2-8-0 No 90332 (a plastikard rebuild based on a Fleischmann 2-10-0) hauling a coal train out of Springwood station on Bob Denham's N gauge layout based on British Railways in the fifties. The siding ending at the buffer stop and the stone buttresses in the foreground which once supported an overbridge are all that remains of a truncated branch line. The layout is built on four baseboard sections occupying a total space of 20 ft × 3 ft 6 in—the classic N gauge long and narrow formula* (Brian Monaghan).

trailing fashion so that the train has to reverse if it wishes to travel over the points. (See fig 43.)

This is not to say that facing points never occur, because there are occasions, particularly at junctions where one main line diverges from another, where they are essential. However, in these situations special protective apparatus such as facing point locks and locking bars are needed, which in the old days of manual non-automatic control invariably required the nearby presence of a signal box. On single track lines, where trains travel in opposite directions on the same length of line, facing points cannot be avoided. In these cases added protection is provided by the single line train staff.

Another feature of prototype practice which can be copied so far as through station track plans are concerned is to avoid fouling the main line where possible. A shunting spur can often be laid parallel with the main line to take care of any movements of the locomotive, shunting in the goods yard, without the locomotive itself having to stray on to the main line. (See fig 53.)

Catch points are a necessity in a number of cases to protect the main line against runaway vehicles. Peco have thoughtfully provided such items in their range of N and 00/HO trackwork. A typical installation for a catch point would be where a siding joins a main line, as at A on fig 53, or on the main line itself at the foot of a gradient (see fig 54). In the absence of a special catch point, ordinary points can sometimes be used to provide a similar safety facility in the situation such as at A in fig 53, in which case the short length of track leaving the point would finish up in a sand drag and a pair of buffer stops (see fig 55). There are any number of Government-enforced regulations controlling safety arrangements for trackwork which manifest themselves in the layout of stations and goods yards. However, the subject is complex and in practice it need not concern the average modeller beyond the points I have just mentioned.

Lastly we come to point number 8 in the list of features to consider when making layout plans, which is the necessity to provide adequate provision for working and storing your proposed fleet of rolling stock. It is probably fair to say that however strong willed you may be you will soon amass a collection of rolling stock which is way beyond your needs, and the problem arises of where to put it all. I think it is impossible, and in fact unnecessary, to provide siding accommodation for *every* item of rolling stock you possess. It is nice instead to ring the changes from time to time and it is a sound practical idea to have a few alternative locomotives or sets of carriages to vary your workings, but which do not necessarily have to be kept in readiness on the layout itself. You only need enough sidings to take care of your immediate working stock and a few spare locomotives. The rest can be shunted into a fiddle yard or put on display somewhere away from the layout itself. If you have the room, of course, it is nice to fill up sidings with spare wagons and coaches and the locomotive depot with an impressive stud of locomotives, but I do not think you have to do this just because you are lucky enough to have the stock. And likewise do not feel that it is necessary to stop adding to your stock just because all the sidings are filled up. Imagine your surplus rolling stock has gone off to Thurso or Fishguard or somewhere or, better still, into 'works' and hand shunt them away out of sight for a while. One thing that will be required is adequate length storage roads to receive the trains you are intending to despatch around your layout. You will need sufficiently long goods roads to receive the goods trains and passenger station platforms to receive the passenger trains. Also, loops will have to be long enough for engines to run round the train, turntables and engine sheds long enough to take the largest engine, and bay platforms long enough to take the coaching stock *and* the engine. These are just common sense things which should be in your mind all the time you are preparing your layout plan.

Now we come to the actual job of planning itself. As I said earlier in this chapter, layout planning is a subject that most railway modellers love to get their teeth into. I find it

**Fig 53** *Shunting spur.* **Fig 54** *Catch point installed at the foot of a gradient on a double track main line for the purpose of derailing runaway rolling stock running back down the hill, a not uncommon occurrence in the days of loose coupled freight trains. Only the up line is so equipped, in this case with a right-hand point to ensure that rolling stock derails clear of the track and away from the down line.* **Fig 55** *An ordinary turnout employed as a catch point. The shunting spur finishes up buried in a deep layer of sand which, together with the buffer stop, should stop any runaway rolling stock and thus avoid fouling the main line.*

*Fig 53*

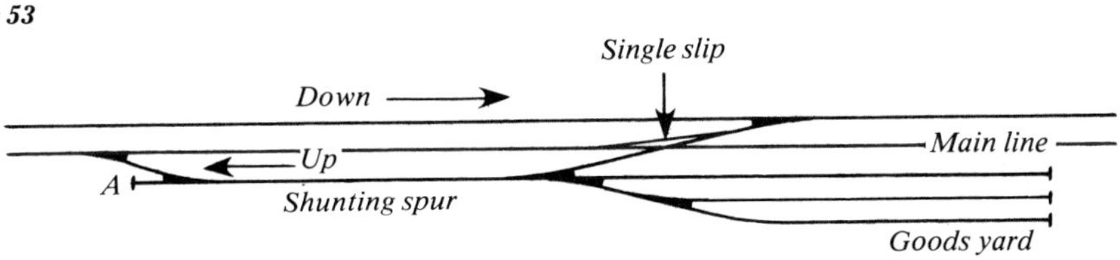


*Fig 54*

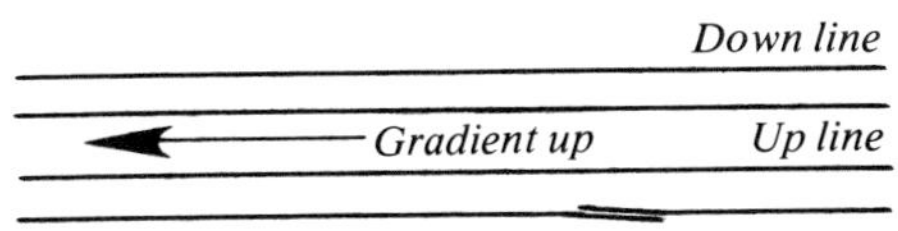


*Fig 55*

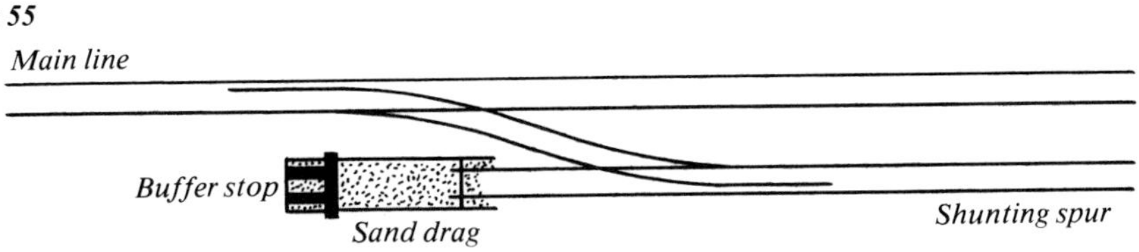

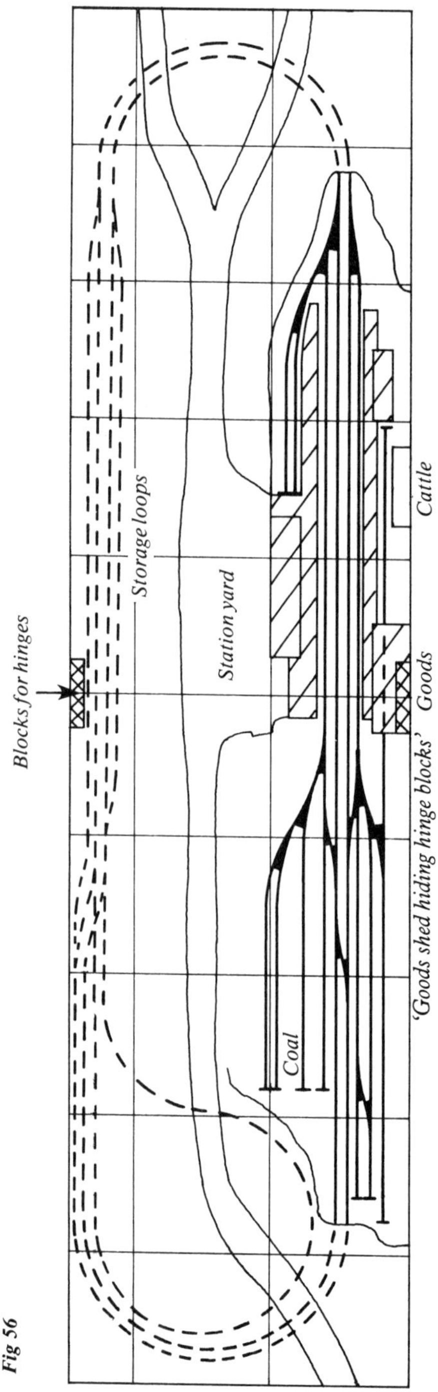


Fig 56

a very relaxing way of passing the time. Instead of a crossword puzzle or a pocket chess set I can find plenty to amuse myself with paper and pencil working out plans for the ideal model railway. At least it's one branch of the hobby that costs nothing! For 00 gauge layouts I always use a scale of 1 in to the ft when planning. Using a ruler with a 12th scale is an advantage since 1/12 in then equals 1 in. It is necessary to bear a few facts in mind when planning layouts and fig 57 gives some details of the clearances which should be allowed between parallel tracks and between the tracks and lineside structures such as bridges, station platforms, etc.

When working on layout plans you need to allow a 2 in wide strip for a single track in 00, so it follows therefore that double tracks need to be 2 in apart. I always work on the centre line of the track when drawing plans and only draw a single line rather than go to the extent of marking in both running rails. Tracks should not be brought nearer than 2 in from the outside edge of the baseboard. A fair average length is 9 in for a point in 00 gauge, so you can reckon on a crossover being about 18 in long. As mentioned earlier in this chapter, bogie passenger coaches in 00 gauge are approximately 9-10 in long so once again your platforms must be long enough to take your longest train. Four-wheeled wagons are a shade over 3 in long so you can accommodate approximately four to every foot of siding space. Locomotives can be anything from 3 to 10 in long, according to the type, but the average mixed traffic loco is approximately 9 in long. A 60 ft turntable which was quite a common size in prototype steam locomotive days and which is big enough to take all but the largest Pacific type is about $9\frac{1}{2}$ in long. However, if you are equipped with a 70 ft turntable, scale size approximately 11 in, you will take care of any British-type locomotive you are likely to come across.

Station platforms are invariably things that modellers are tempted to skimp on so far as the width is concerned on layout plans, but I do think you want to leave as much space as you possibly can. I think a reasonable *minimum* width might be $1\frac{1}{2}$ in for a single platform and 3 in for a double, that is with a running line either side of the platform, but I emphasise minimum width and something wider can always be made use of. In goods yards one should try and leave room for road vehicles to manoeuvre and to back up to wagons. Where a

**Fig 56** *An N gauge layout, 10 ft × 2 ft 6 in. Each square represents one square foot.*

lorry has to drive between sidings full of wagons I would suggest spacing the sidings at least 6 in apart, centre line to centre line, in 00 gauge.

All this basic information is just for drawing 1/12 scale layout plans which later become the subject for detailed planning using, where possible, full-size templates and plans. Seeing the plan laid out full-size on the baseboard may make you change your mind about a number of things and you should be fully prepared to expect this when the time comes. Be careful about sticking rigidly to a plan which you have drawn in 1/12 scale and do not make too many positive steps which will commit you to it, such as buying all the necessary equipment and so on, until you have started to see what it will look like full size.

The figures and dimensions quoted in the last three paragraphs refer to layout plans for 00 gauge systems. For N gauge you need to halve the dimensions, eg, single track needs a 1 in strip, points are approximately 4½ in long and so on. 00 gauge plans can, of course, be used for N gauge layouts and vice versa, but you must be careful not to fall into the trap when using 00 gauge plans scaled down for a N gauge layout of also scaling down the baseboard so that you only leave yourself half the space in which to gain access to some parts of the layout. A gap of approximately 2 ft to provide access to 00 gauge will still be needed if the layout is N gauge. You can, similarly, use 00 gauge layout plans for 0 gauge, in which case nearly double the space will be required, whilst TT gauge layouts will be approximately three-quarters the size of 00 gauge layouts.

Whilst it is perfectly possible to adapt some 00 gauge layout plans for N gauge, within the limitations referred to in the last paragraph, it is as well to bear in mind—and profit from—the special advantages of N gauge which sets it apart from the other larger scales and gauges. Curves of 1 ft radius are perfectly possible and this means that a continuous oval layout can be built on a baseboard not much more than 2 ft wide. Furthermore, N gauge locomotives and coaches are only half the length of 00. A four-track main line only needs a space of 5 in wide, and a station platform long enough for a six-coach train need only be a yard long. For the first time for many modellers it is possible to consider building and operating a main line layout with long fast straights and scale length trains.

The layout plan shown in fig 56 has been designed on this principle. It depicts an important country station with platforms served by loops off a double track main line, the fast roads of which pass through the

**Fig 57** *Minimum clearances, showing dimensions in feet. It is important to remember that additional clearance for platform edges, bridge piers, etc, should be allowed in the case of curved track.*

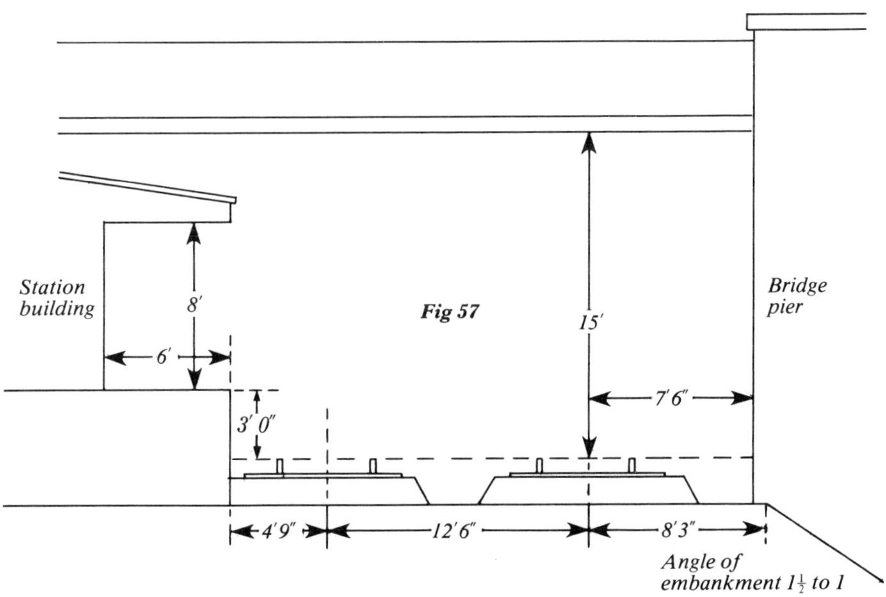

station unhindered. Just imagine the sight of a Peco Jubilee or a Minitrix Britannia romping through the fast roads heading a 10- or 12-coach train whilst a Graham Farish 'Black 5' and train waits on one or other of the platform roads. An extensive goods yard is provided with siding space for approximately 40 wagons, and there is also room for a locomotive depot. All this in an area only 8 ft × 1 ft! The additional space required to incorporate the station plan into a continuous oval layout with hidden storage loops and one or more reversing loops brings the total area to only 10 ft x 2 ft 6 in.

The plan has been devised to enable the baseboard to be constructed in two halves each 5 ft × 2 ft 6 in (less than the size of a door), which could be stored under the bed or hinged to the wall as described in Chapter 2. Such things are within the realms of possibility in N gauge but are less likely to be possible in 00 gauge, where no less than eight baseboard sections each 5 ft × 2 ft 6 in would be required for a comparable layout, which would measure 20 ft × 5 ft overall.

Narrow gauge layouts are also in a world of their own and deserve special attention when it comes to layout planning. This is mainly due to their special space-saving properties and the remarkable performance of the miniature locomotives and rolling stock. In 00-9, gradients of 1 in 20 and curves of $5\frac{1}{2}$ in are not impossible, so it is obvious that either a lot of narrow gauge layout can be built into a given space or else the space can be reduced to the minimum and still be adequate for a reasonable layout. I have given two plans which have been devised using proprietary 9 mm gauge 00-9 equipment. The larger of the two, fig 58, measures 4 ft × 3 ft and incorporates a harbour as the main feature. The smaller layout, fig 59, measures only 3 ft × 2 ft and is suggested as an example of what can be accomplished in the very minimum of space. Both plans can be enlarged with advantage, either by increasing the radius of the curve or extending the length of the sidings, etc.

Apart from the attractive scenic possibilities of fig 58, its one big feature is that the model railway has a purpose, namely the transport of stone from the quarry to the quayside. It is therefore primarily a freight line, although

**Fig 58** *A narrow gauge 00-9 layout 4 ft × 3 ft. Each square represents one square foot.*

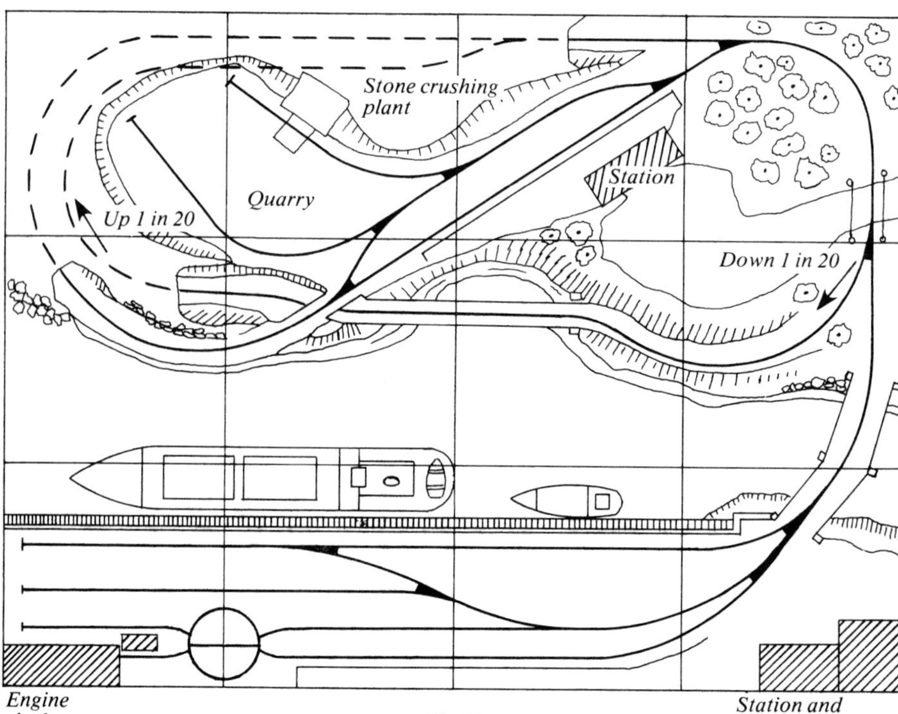


*Fig 58*

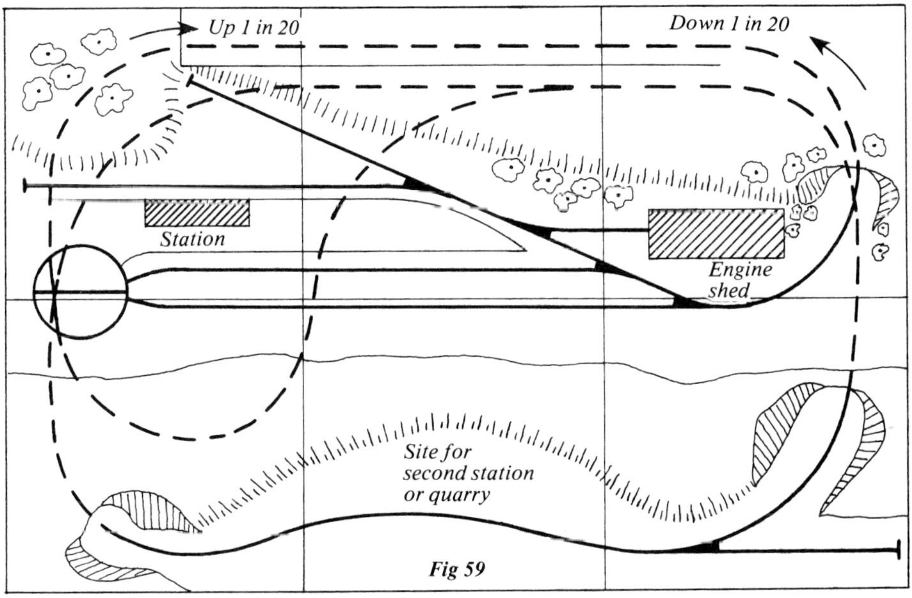


**Fig 59** *A narrow gauge 00-9 layout 3 ft × 2 ft. Each square represents one square foot.*

provision has also been made for operating a passenger service. Trains of tip wagons such as were once made by Jouef or the Minitrains ore wagons would, after loading up in the quarry, run round the continuous circuit for as many times as required to simulate a lengthy run, then leave the main circuit, cross the bridge spanning the river feeding the harbour estuary, and thread their way on to the quayside. As the wagons are unloaded they would be drawn clear and stored in the sidings until there were sufficient to make up a train to run back empty to the quarry.

It is suggested that all the track on the quayside would be level with the road surface. One of the points on the quay is intended to be a Peco 3 ft radius N gauge type which would have its standard gauge sleepers disguised by the road surface. The road surface could be made out of card strips or balsa wood packed up to the height of the tops of the rails. There is room, too, for a reasonably scale-sized ship along the quay. A full-size 300 ton coastal cargo boat measures about 145 ft in length and about 25 ft in breadth which works out at something under 2 ft × 4 in in 00 4 mm scale, making it a distinct possibility on this plan. The quayside would need to be at least 2 in above sea level but the space underneath the model quay could be utilised for hiding the electrical control equipment or for storing spare rolling stock.

Fig 59 incorporates many features which I consider add interest to a layout, but for which space cannot always be found. Thanks to the forementioned valuable climbing powers of narrow gauge locomotives and the fantastically sharp radius curves some of them will traverse, almost all things are possible in this branch of modelling. The features incorporated are a terminal station with adequate storage space, a hidden continuous run and a reverse loop. It is therefore possible to make up a train in the terminal station, despatch it to run on the continuous circle for as long as you like, reverse its direction on the reverse loop and bring it back to the station again. An alternative to the reverse loop might be to install a second station on the lower level with a loop line so that trains could be stopped and reversed and then sent back to the first terminal station.

## Chapter 6

# Electrical equipment

An electric motor powered by electricity conducted through the running rails is the most favoured method of propulsion for most model railways. In the smallest scales this is the only practical method although clockwork and even live-steam have been used in HO and 00 gauges. Appendix 5 includes a reference to a range of live-steam 00 gauge models. The foremost advantage of electric propulsion is that the speed and direction of travel of model locomotives can be altered by remote control, an accepted requirement of most railway modellers. In 0 and 1 gauges the larger scale permits other means of propulsion, even remote control of steam locomotives through the sophistication of radio control (see illustration on page 16) but such models are something of an exception. Because rail-conducted electric propulsion is the predominant source of motive power and potentially one of the biggest headaches for newcomers to railway modelling, no book on the hobby would be complete without a detailed reference to the subject.

In the majority of cases, electric model railways today use the two-rail system, where the current is passed to the locomotive through the two running rails which, of necessity, have to be kept insulated from each other. This in turn requires the wheels on one side of the locomotive to be insulated, either at the centre where they are fixed to the axle, fig 60, or in the wheel itself, usually at the rim or tyre which can be made separate from the wheel centre. (See fig 61.) The current is conducted to the motor through the chassis on the non-insulated wheel and by current collectors or pick-ups on the insulated wheel. Pick-ups can be a source of trouble if not properly cleaned and adjusted. They can be avoided on tender locomotives by insulating the tender wheels on the opposite side to the locomotive. The non-insulated wheels then become conductors on both locomotive and tender, requiring only a wire or conductive coupling between the two to complete the electrical circuit. This system is also applicable to bogie fitted diesel locomotives and DMUs. Another way of avoiding pick-ups is to split the axle across the centre and join the two halves with an insulated collar. (See fig 62.) The current is conducted through the axle bearings which in turn requires that the two sides of the chassis are insulated. Prior to World War 2 when two-rail electrification was little known, the accepted practice was not to insulate the wheels or track but to install a third insulated rail either inside (fig 63) or outside the running rails (fig 64) to complete the necessary electrical circuit.

With the post-war development of plastics, two-rail insulation of wheels and track became more of a practical commercial proposition. Eventually most of the main pre-war manufacturers converted their whole range to the two-rail system and all the major post-war developments have been in two-rail. One manufacturer, namely Marklin of Germany, still sticks to non-insulated running rails and wheels on the three-rail system, but the third rail is no longer a rail but in fact a row of studs which transmit the current to the locomotive via a skid underneath the engine. The skid is so designed that it is kept clear of the running rails but is allowed to come into contact with at least one stud at any one time. (See figs 65 and 66.) This is known as the stud contact system and is rather unusual in the smaller gauges. However, it is quite common in 0 and 1 gauge, where it is a practical alternative for anyone who does not want to go to the trouble of converting all his three-rail rolling stock, or perhaps wishes to operate live steam or clockwork locomotives in conjunction with his electrically powered fleet. Both the studs in the tracks and the skid underneath the locomotive can be made quite unobtrusive and the appearance of the trackwork is very little different from the ordinary two-rail type.

In order to move a locomotive (or railcar, multiple unit, etc) backwards or forwards at a realistic speed we require a variable source of electrical power to be taken to that part of the layout where the locomotive is standing and to where we want it to move. On a very simple layout where there is only 'one engine in steam' this presents few if any problems; just two wires connecting the outlet of the variable source of electrical power, ie the power unit, with the two running rails of the track. However, there are two factors to be considered as the layout is extended. Firstly there is the necessity to retain the purity of the electrical circuit as the track formation is expanded. You will recall it is the running rails that convey the electricity to the locomotive and the two running rails form part of an electrical circuit. As with any electrical circuit, the two running rails must not be allowed to touch each other anywhere on the layout. There is a danger of this happening with some track formations and these are referred to later in the chapter. The second factor to be considered arises when you have two or more locomotives and you only wish to run one, or you may wish to control more than one locomotive independently at the same time.

With a conventional electrically controlled layout where it is necessary to run one locomotive on a length of track whilst keeping another locomotive stationary it is necessary to electrically isolate that part of the track on which the locomotive is required to remain stationary. The situation arises, for example, when you use a second locomotive to detach coaches from a train which has run into a terminal station. Another example arises in the case of an engine shed or motive power depot where any number of locomotives can be expected to be in close proximity to each other on the same length of track. This is quite simply arranged and is shown in fig 67. One rail is broken and an on/off switch is wired across the break. The two ends of the broken rail are best joined by an insulating fishplate or rail joiner.

Whilst planning a layout, it is important to decide how many track sections will be required and their exact location since the insulated rail joiners must be put in at the same time as the track is laid. It is possible to make alterations afterwards by cutting through the rail with a fine saw and soldering the rail ends to pins driven into the baseboard, but there is less chance of damage to the track if all the insulated rail joiners which are likely to be needed are put in at the start. (You can

**Fig 60** *Two-rail wheel insulated at centre.* **Fig 61** *Two-rail wheel insulated at rim.* **Fig 62** *Two-rail wheel insulated by split axle.* **Fig 63** *Three-rail centre pick-up.* **Fig 64** *Three-rail outside pick-up.*

*Fig 60*

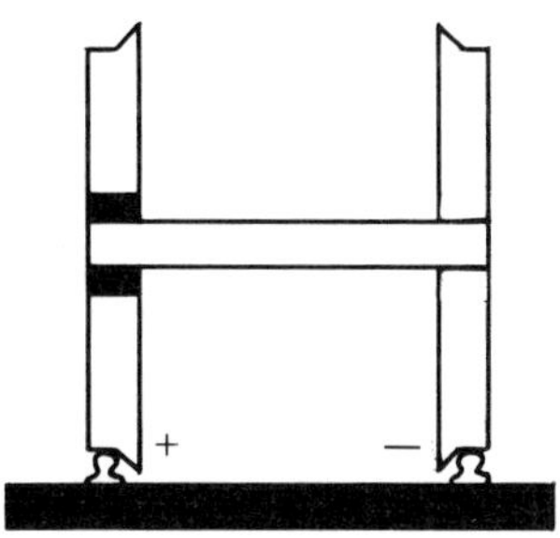


*Fig 61*

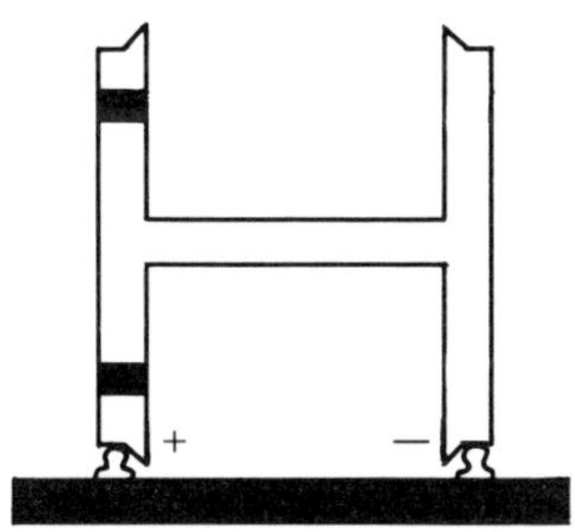


*Fig 62*

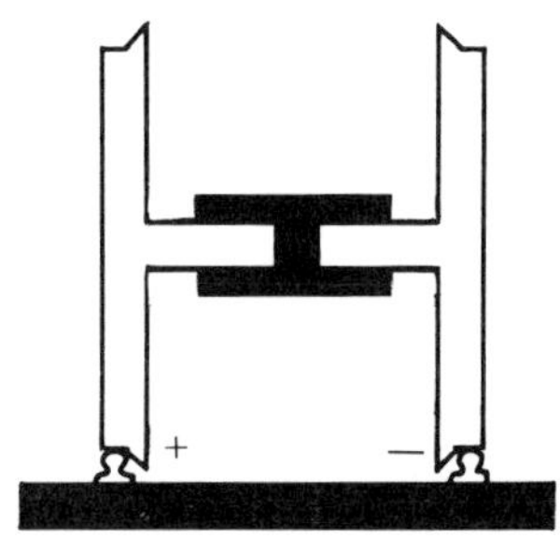


*Fig 63*

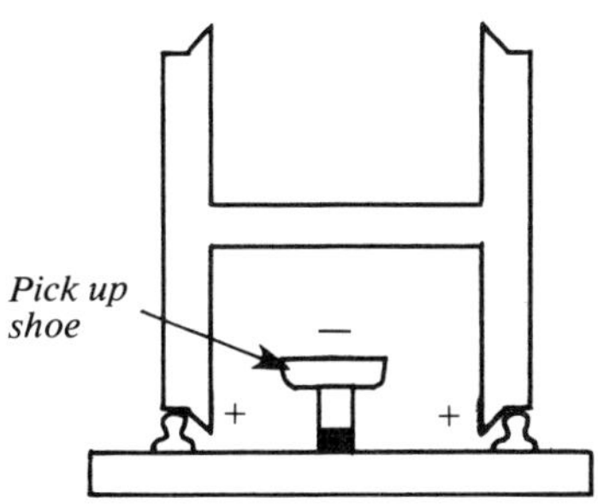


*Fig 64*

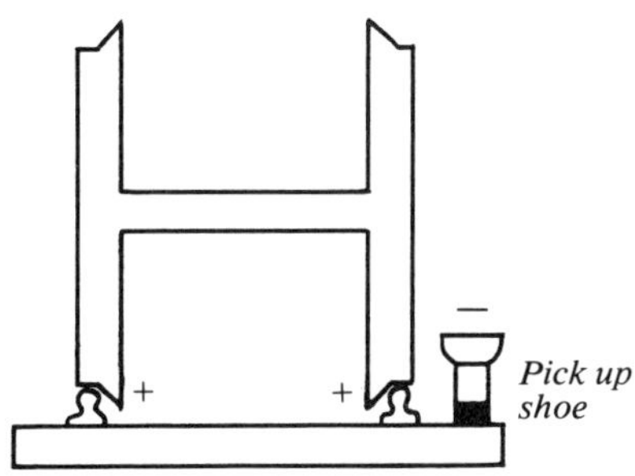

*Fig 65*

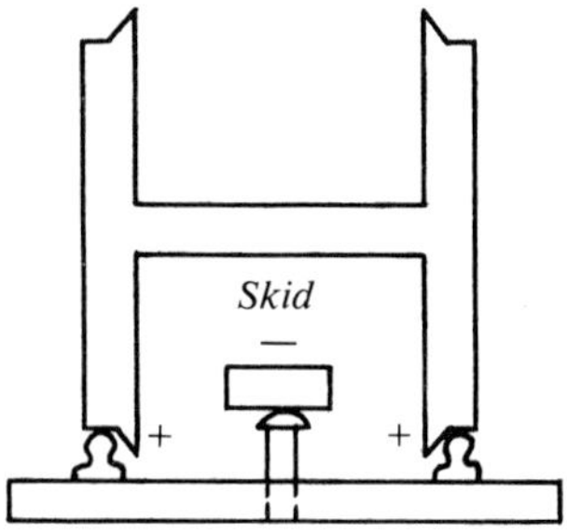


*Fig 66*

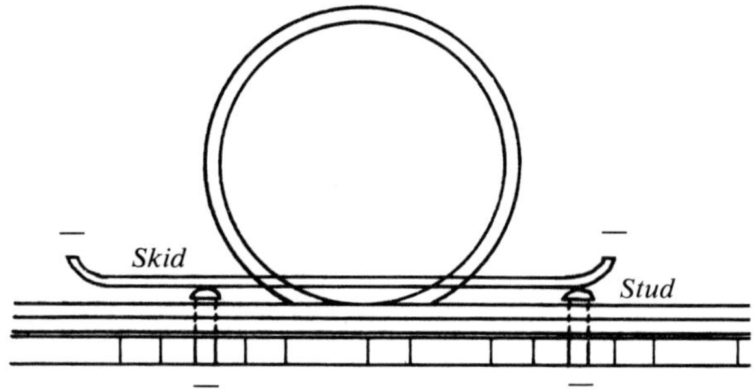


*Fig 67*

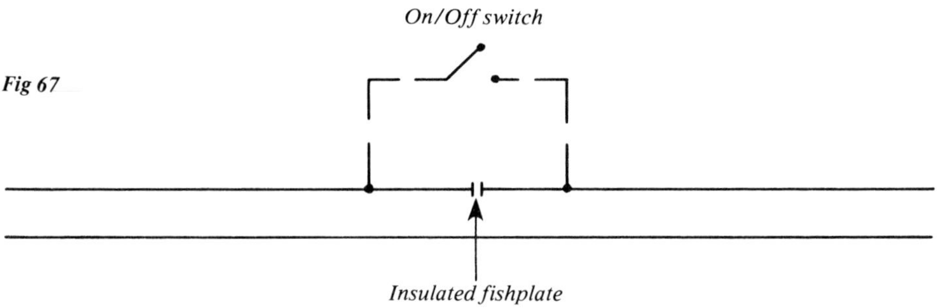


**Figs 65 and 66** *Stud contact—cross-section and side view.* **Fig 67** *Isolating rail and switch.*

always bond a wire across those which are not immediately needed.) How many isolating rails and switches you will require will be dependent on the size of the layout and the number of locomotives you are fortunate enough to possess but it will be readily appreciated that with some layouts the numbers can rise to an appreciable amount.

Realising the difficulties that the planning and installation of isolating rails can present, the trade has been quick to take note of the latest computer micro-technology and to respond with some revolutionary new control systems which entirely eliminate the need for isolating switches with all the attendant wiring problems associated with conventional electrical control systems. I am referring to the Hornby Railways Zero 1 control system, the Airfix MTC Multiple Train Control system and the ECM Selectrol 12 Channel Command Control. With only two wires to the layout these control systems have the ability to call up any one of a number of different locomotives; 12 in the case of ECM Selectrol and 16 in the case of the Airfix MTC and Hornby Railways Zero 1. Furthermore, parked locomotives can be held anywhere on the layout; a tremendous advantage in a locomotive depot where it is difficult to plan the optimum spacing of isolating rail sections with locomotives of different lengths. Rather like parking meter slots where a Mini looks lost in a space large enough for a Rolls Royce. The Airfix MTC and Hornby Railways Zero 1 have the added ability to call up and operate independently up to four locomotives at any one time. The calling up process is by means of a coded signal from the controller to an electronic 'chip' or module which is installed in the locomotive. Each module is programmed to react to a different coded signal and only after the appropriate signal is given will the module, and the locomotive in which it is installed, respond. In a conventional electrical system, locomotives are 'called up' by switching on the current to that part of the track where the locomotive is standing as previously discussed.

There is another method of calling up locomotives which can be applied to conventional electrical control systems and that is to install a switch on the locomotive itself. The basic principle has been used for a very long time in the case of model overhead electric locomotives fitted with working pantographs. Some of these models incorporate switches which enable the operator to choose between picking up current from the rails or from the overhead wiring. When switched to the overhead wiring one simply lowers the pantograph to isolate the locomotive completely from all sources of power. The one obvious disadvantage of locomotive on/off switches is that they have to be operated by hand but on the average size layout, where most parts of the track are likely to be reasonably accessible to the operator, this is unlikely to be a major problem. Full size locomotives do not operate by remote control. They require a driver to mount the footplate and start the machine going. It is not unreasonable to undertake that duty ourselves.

The ability to selectively call up individual locomotives is only one manifestation of the application of multiplex techniques to model railway control systems. By itself this is a sufficiently exciting prospect—the greatest thing since electrification in fact—but multichannel control systems offer far more than just the ability to simplify wiring and to accommodate up to 16 locomotives on a layout. Such features as independent control of more than one locomotive, remote uncoupling, constant train lighting when stationary or at whatever speed when moving, remote control of points and signals, improved electrical contact and synthesised sound effects are some of the possibilities and all with just two wires to the track. Readers are advised to consult the firms' brochures and catalogues to help themselves make up their mind on which system is most likely to suit their needs. Regular reading of the model railway magazines is also desirable to keep up to date with new developments which are coming thick and fast in this field. One thing that should be borne in mind is that conversion to either the Hornby Railways Zero 1 system or the Airfix MTC has to be total since these two systems, besides being non compatible one with the other, operate with alternating current (AC). The AC supply is converted to 12 volts DC by an electronic chip receiver module which must be fitted to every locomotive. Space permitting, any locomotive can be converted to either Airfix MTC or Zero 1 control whether it be Airfix, Hornby Railways, or any other make but locomotives not so fitted would be damaged if placed on the track and subjected to the AC supply. The ECM Selectrol system, however, obviates this difficulty since it operates on 12 volts DC. Receiver modules are still required to be fitted to locomotives to operate under ECM Selectrol control but the system also allows unmodified locomotives to run on the same track as modified locomotives.

The remainder of this chapter is devoted to convential electrical control systems starting first with the variable source of electrical power or power unit as it is usually referred to. This consists of a transformer to reduce the mains voltage to a level suitable for the motors in the locomotives, a rectifier to convert the alternating current (AC) from the transformer to direct current (DC) and a means of varying the level of the DC voltage output. It is in this means of varying the voltage level that the various types of conventional power unit differ.

The simplest and oldest method is to place a variable resistance in the circuit between the rectifier and the motor. This works on the principle that the greater the resistance in the circuit the less the current that can be delivered to the motor. Thus, by varying the resistance, the motor speed is altered. The second method is also simple and utilises a variable transformer which, as its name implies, supplies a variable AC voltage to the rectifier which converts it to the variable DC output.

The third method is less simple. After DC has been obtained from the rectifier, it is fed to a transistor regulator to obtain the variable voltage. I will not attempt to describe the workings of such a regulator, but power units are available in this category ranging from a simple speed control and reversing switch to very complex ones which can give predetermined rates of acceleration, coasting and braking, in addition to being used as a simple means of controlling the speed of a train in the normal manner.

Besides controlling the speed, we also need to control the direction in which the train travels, and two methods of doing this are available on power units. In the first, the control knob or lever has an 'off' position in the centre of its travel, one side of this travel being designated 'forward', the other side 'reverse'. The other method has a separate switch for reversing the direction of the train, thus leaving the whole of the movement of the knob or lever for speed control. The former method is common on variable resistance and variable transformer types, whilst most transistor units use a separate switch.

Many conventional controllers of both variable resistance and variable transformer varieties have a facility called 'pulse power' enabling better control to be achieved at low speeds. This works by applying what is known as half wave rectification to the AC voltage rather than the full wave recitification which is normally used, and gives a series of continuous instead of separate pulses of electricity to the locomotive.

All types of power unit in commercial production feature some kind of overload protection. The traditional type is the electromagnetic cut-out in which a button pops out of the power unit when an overload such as a short circuit occurs. You only have to depress the button in order to reset the unit and continue operation, having of course cured the cause. A second type, called the thermal cut-out, is very reliable but unfortunately gives no indication that it has operated. Thus it can cause a little confusion when fault finding, since the symptom of lack of power and a short circuit are the same. This type is, however, self-resetting after a time delay of a few seconds. Variable resistance and variable transformer units may be fitted with either of these types of cut-out, which do not act with sufficient speed to prevent damage to transistor circuits. Thus transistorised units contain electronic circuitry to limit the maximum current which may be delivered by the unit in case of a short circuit. However, they may have one of the above types of cut-out as well.

When choosing a power unit the modeller must base his choice on a balance of performance and cost. The variable resistance power unit is quite adequate for many purposes and is relatively cheap. The variable transformer power unit will generally give improved control of a locomotive in the low speed area but, as with all good things, you have to pay extra for it. The transistor power unit will give very good control but is, generally speaking, the most costly of all. When buying a power unit, don't forget that if you are going to operate your points and signals electrically you will need the extra uncontrolled outlets available on some units, typically 16 volts AC. An extra 12 volt DC outlet can be useful for a further control unit without its own transformer and rectifier (see below). If your friends own model railways, no doubt you could try out their power units and see how you like them and, if you are going to buy one, your dealer should be able to show you a selection.

As mentioned above, the various components forming a power unit can be obtained separately. Some complete power units have auxiliary 16 volt AC and 12 volt DC supplies, and extra control units of the variable resistance and transistor types can be obtained to 'add-on' and control an extra train. Remember, however, that if the auxiliary supply is AC, a rectifier will be required in the 'add-on' unit in order to give DC for the track.

At this stage, I would like to give a warning. Power units which include a transformer are almost invariably constructed so that it is difficult to get inside them. This is for a good reason since, besides being generally dangerous, mains electricity can be lethal. Under no circumstances should the modeller attempt to open a power unit unless he is a qualified electrician. He should take it to his dealer or send it to the manufacturer for repair.

Having obtained our source of power, we must now consider how to get it to the track by means of wires and connections. Suitable wire may be obtained from your model railway dealer or your local electrical shop. Multi-strand flexible wire is better for our purposes than single strand types, which tend to break if they are repeatedly flexed. The designations 7/.0076 and 14/.0076 (metric equivalents 7/0.2 mm and 16/0.2 mm) are used in the trade for wires which are admirable for our needs and which will easily carry all the current we are likely to require.

If the type of track you are using includes in its range a terminal connector, then by all means use it and attach the wire securely to the terminal fixings. If a terminal connector is not available, the alternative is to solder the bared end of the lead to the outside web of the rail. If you are using plastic-based track, apply the soldering iron for the minimum time possible, as it is easy to melt the plastic base if the iron is left in contact with the rail for long periods. You can avoid this by soldering the wire to a rail joiner which is the preferred method.

Normally, tight fitting fishplates or rail joiners should be adequate for conducting electricity across rail joints, but if the layout is likely to be subject to large temperature changes it is advisable to 'bond' the joints by soldering a loop of wire to the outside web of the rail about $\frac{1}{2}$ in each side of the joint. If one is lucky enough to have a large layout, trouble may be experienced with 'voltage drop' which is caused by the resistance of long lengths of rail and joints and manifests itself as diminished power when a train is a long distance from the control point. The cure is to bond the rail joints and, if necessary, to take extra leads from the power unit to the point on the track where the trouble occurs, taking due note of the polarity and using reasonably large-section wire, at least 14/.0076 as mentioned above, and preferably larger.

A subject which often causes confusion is the different types of turnout or point. There are two types, known as 'dead frog' and 'live frog', the difference being that the frog (the 'X' crossing part of the point) is electrically isolated from other pieces of rail in the former type, ie, it is electrically 'dead'. In live frog

*Fig 68a*

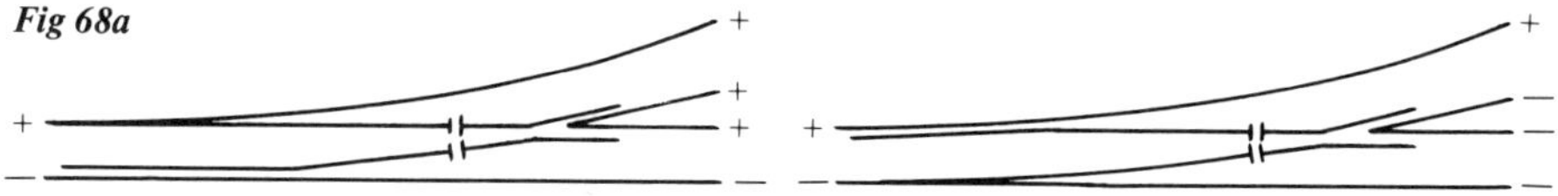

*Fig 68b*

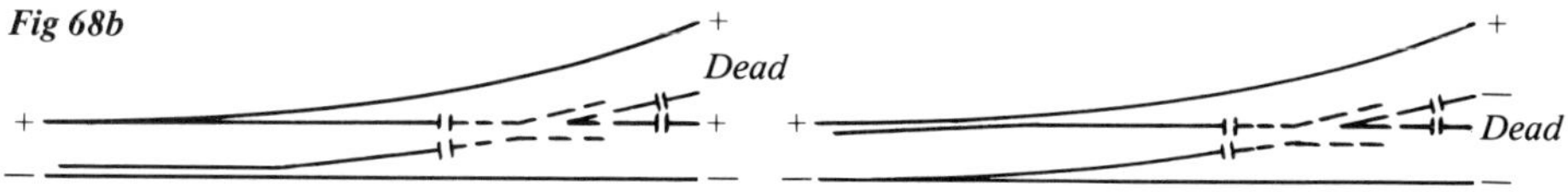


*Fig 68c*

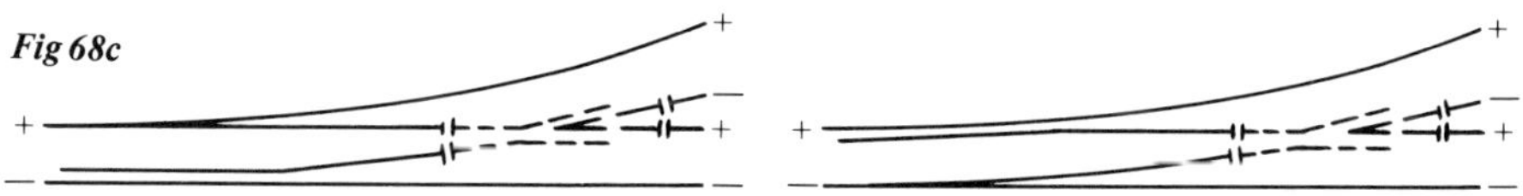

**Fig 68a** *Live frog isolating.* **Fig 68b** *Dead frog isolating.* **Fig 68c** *Dead frog non-isolating.*

parts, the frog carries electricity, although its polarity must change when the direction of the point changes. (See fig 68a.) Fig 68a also shows that the track which is not selected by the point will be 'dead', since it has the same polarity on both rails. Points with this switching feature are sometimes known as 'isolating' points and are not necessarily live frog types. Fig 68b shows a dead frog point which is an isolating type, and Fig 68c shows a type of dead frog point which is non-isolating, ie, both divergent tracks are electrified, irrespective of the track selected by the point blades.

The question arises as to which is the best type for the modeller to use and, as often occurs, there is no straightforward answer. The best approach is to discuss the relative advantages of each. Perhaps the greatest advantage of the live frog point is that there is an uninterrupted path for current as a locomotive traverses the point, whereas a dead frog cannot pass current through the wheel which is in contact with the frog. Despite the fact that on a locomotive there should be more than one wheel picking up current on each side, the rocking of a locomotive on any slight unevenness in the track can reduce the number of pick-up wheels on one side of the locomotive to one. This could easily be the one on the dead frog, with the result that the locomotive would 'stall'.

Isolating points are preferable to non-isolating ones in conventional electrical control systems since, if you need to leave a locomotive in a siding, it is necessary only to operate the point to the direction against the locomotive when power is automatically cut off. With isolating points it is impossible to run a train over them when they are set against the train—a feature which can prevent many a derailment! When using isolating points it is important that the power supply is connected to the toe, ie, blade end of the point, otherwise it will not be possible for electricity to be passed down the divergent track. If 'kick-back' sidings are included in the layout, such as in fig 69, then it is necessary to arrange an extra electrical feed into the headshunt in order to take power to the sidings and ensure that it is fed from the 'toe' of point A.

Reference to fig 70 will show that, when live frogs are used, their polarities on a diamond crossing will need to be switched according to which direction it is desired to run. Since we are not dealing with isolating points but with a crossing with frogs having rails of differing polarities next to them, insulated fishplates will be necessary where shown. All this will be unnecessary, of course, with dead frog diamond crossings and with dead frog slips. Live frog slips, however, are very difficult to electrify and this can only be done by using electrical relays which involve techniques beyong the scope of this book.

I previously referred to the necessity for isolating sections in conventionally wired

Fig 69

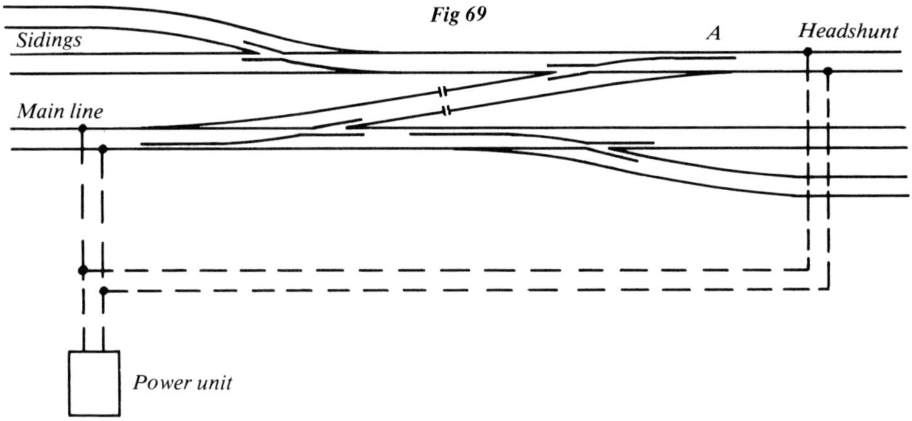


Fig 70

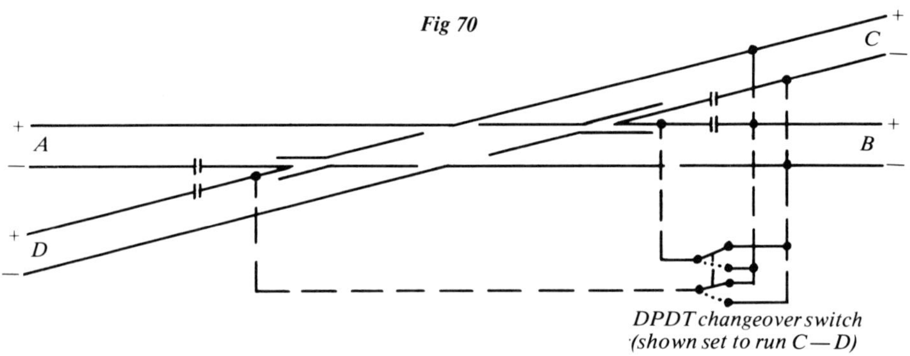


Fig 71

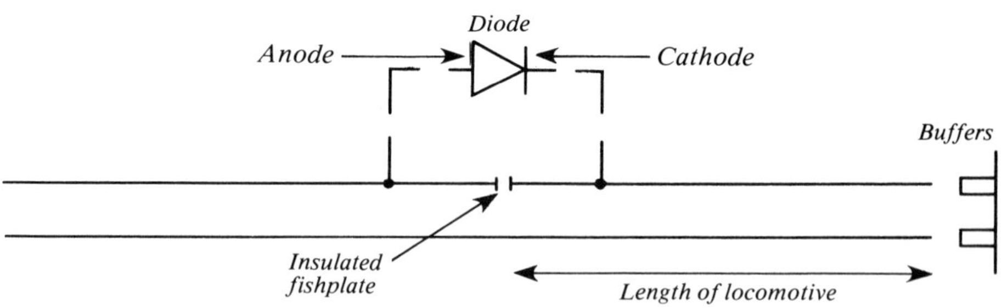


Fig 72

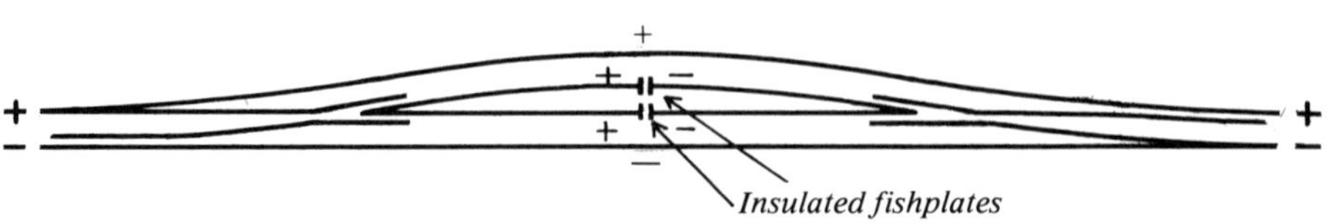

layouts and instanced the case of a train arriving at a terminal station where it is necessary to isolate the train engine. Where it is difficult to see the terminal station buffers from the control position, a useful precaution to prevent a train hitting the buffers is to instal a diode in the wiring connecting the isolating section (see fig 71). Diodes have the property of conducting electricity in one direction from positive to negative (anode to cathode) but not in the other. As shown in fig 71 the diode will cause the locomotive to stop as soon as it passes the rail break when driven towards the buffers but will enable the locomotive to be driven away from the buffers when the controller is reversed. The cathode is generally distinguished by a band or lip as an aid to correct installation but should the desired effect not be achieved at the first attempt, simply reverse the connections to the diode. The type of diode used must be capable of passing a continuous forward current of 1-1.5 amps.

Fig 72 shows the arrangement of insulated fishplates necessary to make a pasing loop work properly with live frog points. This is necessary since, as is shown in fig 72, if the two points were set for different tracks a short circuit would result if the insulated fishplates were not used. Such insulated fishplates are not required when points with dead frogs are used, since the polarity of the tracks beyond the point is not reversed, as is shown in figs 68b and 68c.

Reversing loops as shown in fig 73 require special attention. Tracing the polarity round the outer rail will show that, without the insulated fishplates, a short circuit will occur. The train must be driven into the loop, stopped, and the direction of the point and the DPDT (double pole, double throw) switch changed. The train can then continue its circuit by reversing the controller. The method shown in fig 73 can be simplified when, as happens in most cases, the point itself can be relied upon to change the polarity of the inner rail. In such circumstances insulated fishplates are not required in the inner rail and the DPDT switch can be replaced by a SPDT (single pole DT) switch.

A few modellers with sufficient space may wish to incorporate a triangle in their layouts and this can be done by following fig 74. The locomotive is driven from A round the curve and is stopped after passing over point B. Points A and B are changed and the DPDT switch is operated. With the controller in the same direction as previously, the locomotive may be driven towards point C and any further movement carried out at will. Connection X and the insulated fishplate between A and C are necessary to ensure continuity and avoid short circuits.

Some layouts are sufficiently simple to need only one train running at a time, and indeed on some it would be almost impossible to operate two trains at once for fear of conflicting movements and collisions, etc. Probably the simplest form of multiple train operation is where, as shown in fig 75, two terminal stations are connected by a single track, but separated electrically by insulated fishplates.

*Fig 73*

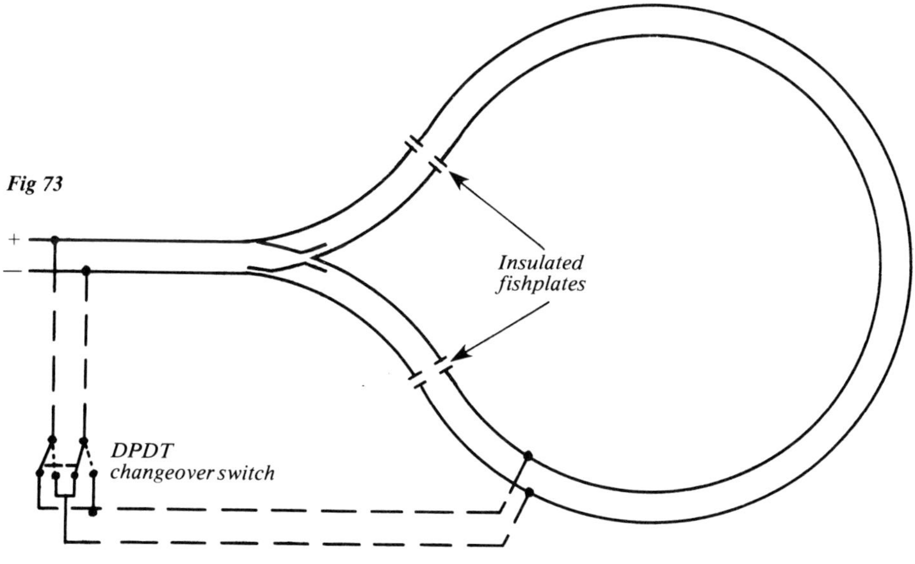

In this example, the operators at both stations could shunt and make up trains and, when the time came to exchange trains between stations, say from A to B, operator A would run his train towards the insulated joint, whilst operator B, having got his line clear in order to accept the train, would turn his controller knob so as to allow the train to carry on into his section at the same speed, so avoiding jerks. With practice, this can be done to a fair degree of accuracy, but if it is not, and particularly if operator B has the direction of his controller set wrongly, the train will either have a jerky passage across the joint or will oscillate back and forth, possibly to its mechanical detriment.

This disadvantage may be overcome by allowing operator A to drive the train to its destination in operator B's territory and vice versa. This system, which virtually involves each operator being able to run a train over any part of the layout, is known as 'cab control', the operator position being known as a 'cab'. The switching required to achieve this is shown in figs 76 and 77, but the exact form required depends upon the types of controllers in use. If you are using controllers which are not completely separate electrically (eg, an 'add-on' unit mentioned previously) then double pole switching is required as in fig 76. If, however, your controllers are electrically separate (ie, each has its own transformer, rectifier and controller) then 'common return' wiring, as shown in fig 77, can be employed with the advantage that it uses only single pole switching, ie, the switches themselves are simpler and the number of wires needed is reduced. Neglecting the detail, the principle is the same in either case, which is that the switches connect the track section to whichever controller is required.

The same ideas apply to a double-track line

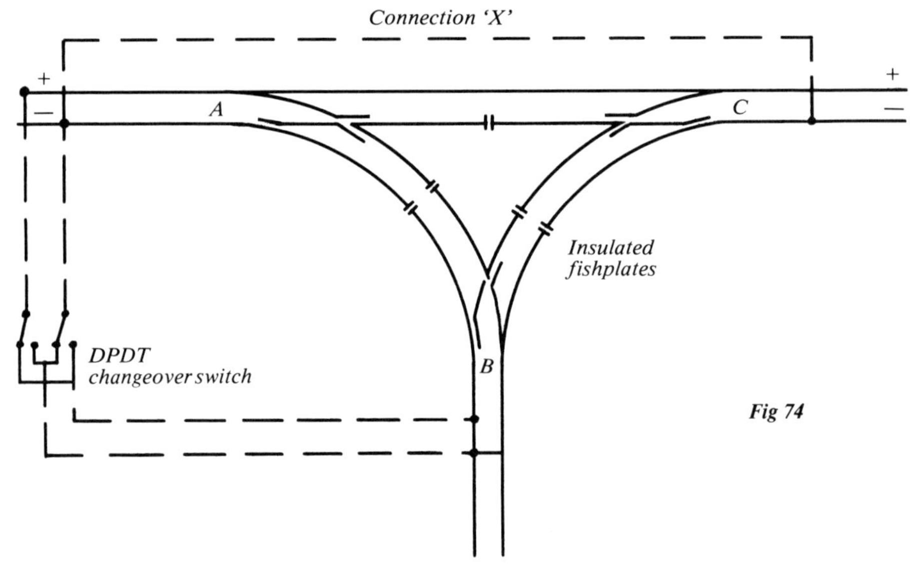


**Fig 74**

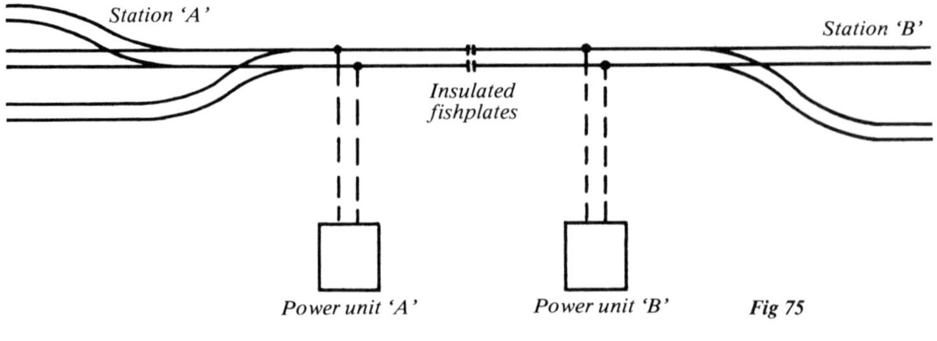


**Fig 75**

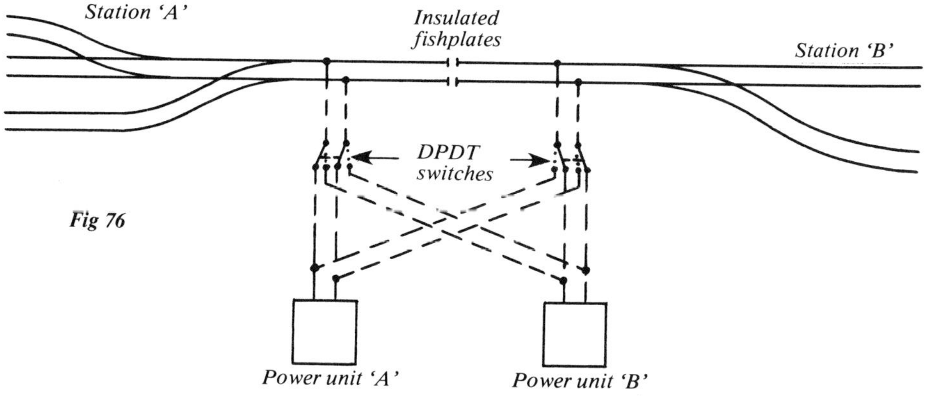


*Fig 76*

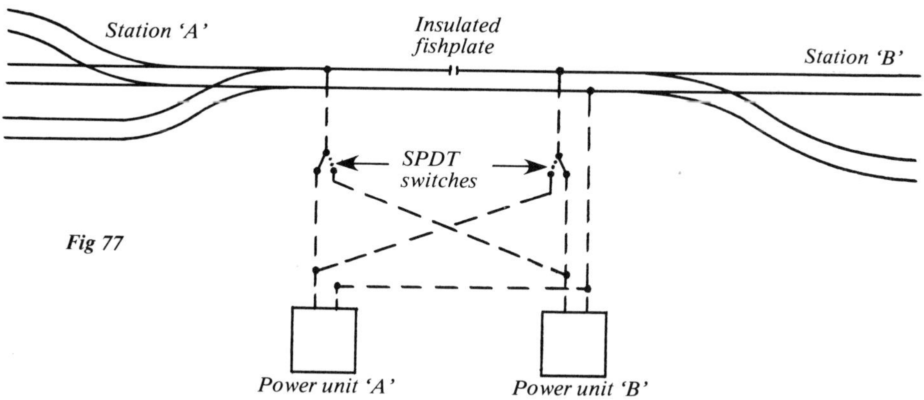


*Fig 77*

**Fig 76** *Double pole switching.* **Fig 77** *Single pole switching 'common return'.*

where each track is a separate section, as shown in fig 78, which includes a crossover. Common return wiring is shown but, for double pole switching, both fishplates between the points should be insulated and the wiring of the two sections to the controllers is similar to fig 76. Fig 78 shows one insulated fishplate and one described as 'X'. This fishplate may be metal when dead frog points are used since, depending on whether or not it is an isolating point, the piece of rail between the frog of the lower point and 'X' will be either dead or common (see figs 68b and 68c) with the point set straight and no short circuits will occur. With live frog points, however, 'X' must be an insulating fishplate, since the piece of rail in question would be the same polarity as the frog (ie, live and opposite to common) and a short circuit would result if an insulating fishplate were not included here.

Whilst planning a layout, it is important to decide how many track sections will be required and their exact location since the insulated fishplates must be put in at the same time as the track is laid. It is possible to make alterations afterwards by cutting through the rail with a fine saw and soldering the rail ends to pins driven into the baseboard, but there is less chance of damage to the track if all the insulated fishplates which are likely to be needed are put in at the start. (You can always bond a wire across those which are not immediately needed.)

The terminal stations arrangement in figs 75, 76 and 77 would entail only relatively limited use of the cab control idea, since it would be very likely that the two section switches would be mounted one at each control point. A more flexible use of cab control would be in, say, a station having both passenger and freight facilities, with separate sections for each and for the main line(s) as well. If there were two controllers, one could work the passenger service, whilst the other shunted the freight yard, but each operator would be able to run his train out on to the main line and towards its destination and the main line, station platforms, freight yard, etc,

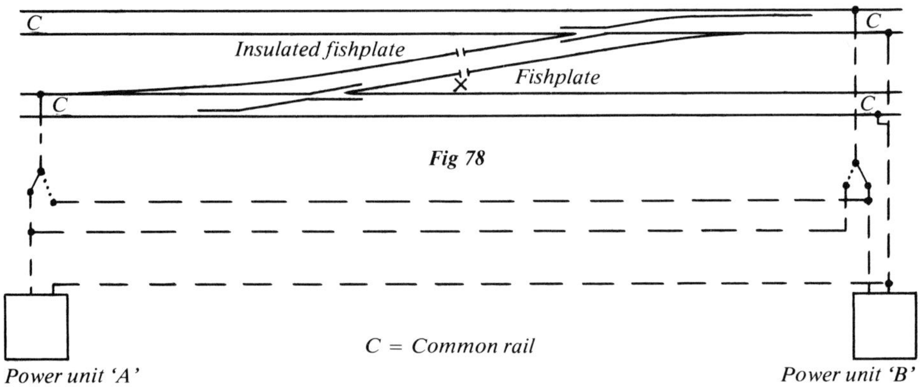


*Fig 78*

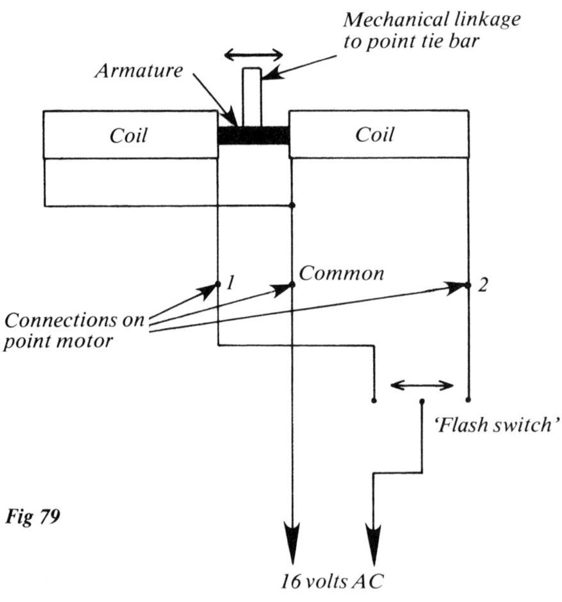


*Fig 79*

**Fig 79** *Diagrammatic view of the operation of a point motor and its associated wiring.*

**Fig 80** *Wiring diagram for an 'electric pencil'.*

would each form a section. The control panel shown in the photo on page 102 controls such a station, in this case a terminus.

There are switches on the market designed for use with cab control systems and these can be obtained from your local model railway dealer. They are not cheap, however, and radio and surplus shops may prove to be a source of suitable switches. It is very useful if switches can be obtained having a 'centre-off' position, since this means that a section need not be permanently connected to one or other controller, but could be switched off, thus reducing the need for some isolating switches on the layout.

It will be appreciated that, with larger layouts, more than two cab positions may be required, and in this case the best switches to use would be multi-way rotary types. The only source of these to the average modeller would probably be the radio shop.

Fig 79 shows diagrammatically the operation of a point motor and its associated wiring. In order to change the direction of the point an electrical pulse is applied to one coil. This attracts the magnetic armature, which is able to slide between the coils. The movement is then transmitted to the point tiebar. The usual means of applying the electrical pulse is with a 'flash' or passing contact switch which ensures that the coil is not permanently connected to the electrical supply, otherwise the coil would heat up and eventually burn out. Two designs of point motor on the market have their own internal switch which cuts off the power once the point has been operated, thus enabling the function of a passing contact switch to be achieved with a permanent contact type. If you are in doubt as to whether your point motors are of that type, the best advice is to play it safe and use 'flash' switches.

An alternative method of operation is by what is termed the 'electric pencil' and this is shown is fig 80. The common lead from the coils is taken to the 16 volt AC power supply, as before, but leads 1 and 2 are soldered to the undersides of round-head wood screws driven into the control panel (see later). The other lead from the power supply is taken to an electric pencil which can be made by threading the lead down the outer tube of an old ball point pen, soldering it to the metallic point of the pen, and finally pushing the metallic part back into the tube. Upon momentarily touching either of the screws with this 'electric pencil', the point motor will operate in either direction.

If possible it is best to use the 16 volt AC output of a power supply for point operation as this will give better results than 12 volts DC. Most power units are not capable of giving sufficient current to operate more than one point motor at the same time (eg, arranging for both points of a crossover to operate at once) but this can be overcome by using a capacitor discharge power unit. Such a unit has the effect of storing electrical energy

*Point motor connections* ***Fig 80***

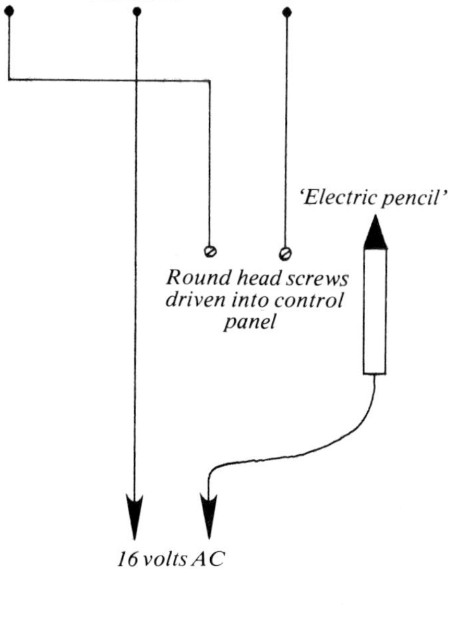


and releasing it when required in a sudden burst. This is exactly what is required to obtain maximum efficiency from a solenoid operated point motor and there is the added advantage that the capacitor will protect the point motor from burning out in the event of a passing switch jamming. Such units are comparatively inexpensive, simple to install and are readily obtainable from specialist suppliers such as ECM Control Systems Ltd. ECM also produce a range of plug in control units for the electronic automation of layouts. Only brief mention can be made here but the three basic units are an automatic station stop, a controlled signal stop and a train operated relay. The latter can be used for a number of different purposes such as providing a section and route indicator on a control panel, operating signals, controlling following trains, route setting and controlling the starting and stopping of trains in other parts of the layout.

Signals may be electrically operated using point motors and suitable mechanical linkages. A description of making your own solenoids to achieve this is rather beyond the scope of this chapter, but may be found in the *Railway Modeller* issues of October 1961 and June 1967.

Those wishing to illuminate buildings will probably find that the best way is to use 'grain-of-wheat' bulbs which can be obtained from model railway suppliers and which will work directly off the 12 volt DC supply of a power unit. As the name implies, these bulbs are very small and will fit into most buildings so as not to be directly visible through the windows, but will light the building itself in a realistic manner. The 3 volt screw-cap bulbs as fitted to cycle lamps can be used with suitable holders, but remember to connect enough of them in series to use up the whole 12 volt output of the power unit or you will blow the bulbs. Unfortunately, this type is not nearly as unobtrusive as the 'grain-of-wheat' sort. Furthermore, such cycle-type bulbs consume more power than the 'grain-of-wheat' variety and consequently give out more heat. Take care, therefore, that your buildings do not overheat when the lighting is left on for a while.

As to lighting the train itself, some manufacturers market locomotives with headlights and coaches with interior lighting, but with conventional electrical control systems these only function when power is applied to the train, ie, when it is moving.

The simplest layouts will have no need of a control panel as such, since a convenient grouping of the switches around the power

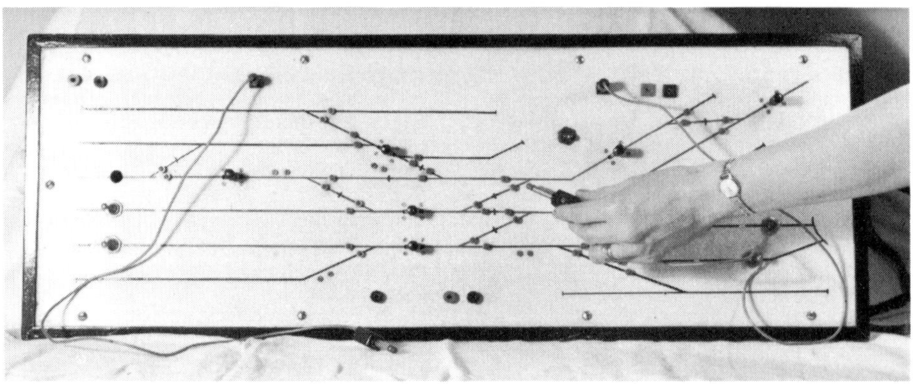

**Top** *An ECM capacitor discharge power unit for point motors.*

**Above** *A control panel for a terminal station as referred to in Chapter 6 (page 100 and below) showing the 'electric pencil' for point motor control. Note how the section switches are located in the position of the tracks they control.*

unit usually suffices. This arrangement is quite all right as far as the owner of the layout and regular visitors are concerned, but when we have to take occasional visitors into account the very least we need is a key to the functions of the switches. This is best done by indicating their purposes on a plan drawn on cardboard (it can also help the owner in case of small lapses of memory!).

An extension of this idea is to make the plan the central feature of the controls and to build the latter around it as shown in the photo above. The procedure here is to obtain a suitably sized piece of about $\frac{1}{4}$ in plywood (rather than hardboard, which will not easily take small screws) and, as neatly as possible, draw the track plan on it in black paint, having first painted the wood in a light colour. Optionally, the plywood may be covered in Formica or some similar material and the track plan either painted on as before, or gouged out using the tang (or non-business end) of a file. The groove is then filled with paint. Whichever method is used, about $\frac{1}{8}$ in is the right width for the groove. If you are going to use the electric pencil method of point control now is the time to insert the screws into drilled pilot holes. Round-headed wood screws $\frac{1}{2}$ in long serve well here and, having been driven right through the panel, soldered connections are made on their undersides. Wander plugs and sockets suitable for connecting the power unit to the control panel are obtainable from radio shops and clearance holes must be drilled for the sockets. The switches giving cab control are positioned along the various track grooves in the section which they control, and the boundaries of sections are marked by short lines across the track grooves. In the photo on page 102 panel-mounting switches have been used, which have the advantage that only the operating level is above the control panel with the 'works' and wiring below, which gives an unencumbered panel. These switches are mounted so that the operating levers swing from side to side, and thus point towards the direction of the controller which is switched to that track section, there normally being in this instance one controller placed at each end of the control panel.

It will be noted that there is no labelling of switches, etc, on the control panel. This is because it controls a portable layout which can be arranged to have the control panel at either side of the baseboards, thus the labels would be upside-down at times. Any switches which are not concerned with the supply of power to the track, such as point motor 'flash' switches and switches for lighting control, are conveniently mounted alongside each other in groups and should be suitably identified. Some power units are obtainable as 'panel mounting' types, and all that is necessary with these to install one neatly is to cut a hole of suitable size in the panel, drop the power unit in and screw it to the panel. A control panel should be framed with timber of a suitable size and a bottom provided to complete a 'box' which will ensure that wires cannot be accidentally pulled from their connections ununderneath the panel, as well as giving a good finished appearance.

The control panel should not be rigidly attached to the baseboard, but should at least be hinged to it to allow maintenance and such alterations as may be necessary. The modeller who owns a portable layout must, unless it is all contained on one baseboard, use multi-pole plugs and sockets for inter-connections between the control panel and baseboards and between the baseboards themselves. Unfortunately, such plugs and sockets are usually expensive, but Government Surplus shops may be a source of suitable types. Care should be taken when wiring these plugs and sockets to use only the minimum of solder needed to make a good joint and to ensure that the insulation of the wire is stripped back no more than is necessary, otherwise short circuits may well result from wires touching each other.

Leads between the control panel and the baseboard should be brought together and tied in a neat bundle with insulating tape, or lacing cord, which looks like connecting wire but has cotton instead of wire within the insulation. Connecting wire itself may be used.

Connections between baseboards on a semi-permanent layout which needs to be moved only infrequently can be made by using 'tag strips'—available from radio shops—which may be mounted alongside each other on the framing of adjacent baseboards. The inter-connections are taken to the baseboard side of the tag on each baseboard, the other sides of each tag being bonded together with bare wire.

Having provided power to the appropriate length of track, we must now ensure that it gets to the motor of the locomotive. This is mainly a question of cleanliness, since we rely on passing electricity between two pieces of metal which are in contact with each other and any dirt between them will not conduct electricity.

The track is probably the worst culprit so far as dirt is concerned and the surface of running rails must be kept clean at all times. It comes as a surprise to newcomers to the hobby just how much dirt and grease gets deposited on the rail surface. If you don't believe me, try running your finger on top of a yard of rail after a few hours' running session—the amount of dirt will probably surprise you. The time honoured method has always been to physically clean the rails with an abrasive cleaner (rather like a hard erasing rubber which is sold specially for the purpose) or to wipe the surface with a rag dipped in a solvent such as carbon tetrachloride (sold for removing stains from clothing). *But if you use this, it must be in a well-ventilated atmosphere since the fumes are toxic, and do not smoke until the fumes have cleared, as the smoke you inhale would be highly poisonous.* Another alternative is to use switch cleaner of which there are several proprietary brands.

Physically cleaning the track surface is a time consuming business and there never seems to be enough time to do the job thoroughly. Also there are invariably some parts of the layout where it is difficult to get at the rails properly such as underneath bridges and tunnels, or inside buildings such as goods sheds, engine sheds and stations with large canopies or overall roofs. The installation of a Relco High Frequency Generator between the power unit and the track will overcome the cleaning problem in the most efficient way. This is a very reasonably priced device which not only combats the effect of dirt, oil, carbon deposits and bad connections on the track, it also contributes to self-cleaning all the time it is in use. The generator works by producing a high frequency current which is superimposed on the normal DC supply to the track. When the locomotive wheels are making good contact with the rail surface the HF is automatically switched off but when the contact is poor the HF is instantly switched on, ionising the air gap. This will continue until the DC current is able to flow and re-establish contact with the locomotive. A lamp on the generator gives a visual indication of whether or not the track surface is clean. Relco HF Generators must never be used with multiple train control systems of the type referred to on pages 92 and 93.

Wheels also need to be kept clean and a wheel cleaning brush is available (in ap-appearance rather like a toothbrush) which, when connected to a power unit and pressed against the locomotive wheels, does the job well. Finally, watch for bits of fluff and dirt getting behind locomotive pick-ups; a regular inspection will ensure that you get no trouble on this score.

In spite of these precautions, it is still possible to get indifferent running and the following advice will help to improve reliability in this respect. Locomotives should have as many current collectors or pick-ups as possible, and in particular this should include all flanged wheels which make contact with the track. If you convert a locomotive to scale wheels, and the radius of the curves on your layout allows it, remember to put all flanged driving wheels on with a current collector for each. Often forgotten is the tender which, if it has metal wheels, can be the source of another couple of current collectors, although leads will need to be run between the tender and the locomotive. The more current collectors a locomotive possesses, the less likelihood there is of the current not being passed from the track to the motor. This provision of extra pick-ups is, if you can do it, a good method of eliminating 'stalling' on dead frog points. Current pick-ups are best made from thin phosphor-bronze wire or strip bearing lightly on to the backs of the wheels.

It will be found that plastic wheels on rolling stock have a far greater tendency to pick up dirt than metal wheels. The best wheels for rolling stock are the metal ones since, besides picking up less dirt, they are usually more accurate in manufacture. Unfortunately they are more expensive, too.

Lastly, although it would not appear to affect electrics, uneven track can be the cause of locomotive wheels failing to pick up electricity. The remedy is simple—lay your track as flat as possible. (A simple, effective way of checking this most important point is to mount a small spirit level across a two-wheeled truck, which will quickly show up any irregularities.)

If you still find the technicalities of electrical power a little baffling, a good model railway retailer will always be happy to advise you on the best equipment for your individual needs.

## Chapter 7

# Laying the track

By now I assume you have decided where the layout is to go, what sort of layout it is to be and what scale and gauge suits you best. You will also have some idea of the track you will require. Now, and really only now, is the time when you can safely make your first purchases and actually start work, assuming that you have already bought the timber and materials for the baseboard and have got most of this in position.

To a certain extent your initial purchases of model railway equipment will depend upon what scale and gauge you have decided to follow, and whether or not you intend doing most of your own construction work. If you have decided to follow EM gauge or Protofour, for example, there will not be many items that you will be able to buy ready-to-run and you will probably have to make your own track out of the basic materials and construct, or at least adapt from commercial models or kits, your own rolling stock. However, let us assume you have decided to start with 00 or N gauge, or some other popular scale and gauge which is well supported by the trade, and that, to begin with at least, you are buying all your rolling stock and trackwork ready made and ready to run.

First of all, select a retailer who takes the trouble to hold a good stock of model railway equipment. Appendix 4 gives a list of retailers who have at one time or another during recent years advertised in a British model railway magazine and therefore can be assumed to have a keen interest in the hobby. Apart from probably stocking the equipment you want to buy, he is also more likely to have an interest in, and a degree of sympathy for, model railways and therefore be in a better position to advise and assist you. If you tell the retailer you are just making a start and you are not too sure what is required, he will be glad to help you and, with the majority of responsible retailers, you need not fear you are going to be 'conned' into buying something you do not really want. A large number of shops in the model railway trade, certainly in England, have been in the business for many years, some of them since long before World War 2, and they are as keen on the hobby and as anxious to have your custom as you are to make a start. Make a friend of your retailer and I am sure he will look after you.

Now, the first items you will require will be a good power unit, as discussed in the previous chapter; at least one locomotive; at least one bogie vehicle of the maximum length you intend to use; a few yard lengths, say half-a-dozen, of flexible track; a pair of points and some rail joiners. You will need a minimum of two packets of rail joiners (or fishplates as they are sometimes called), one each of the insulated and non-insulated types. The necessity for a locomotive is obvious, since you will want to start things moving as soon as possible, even though you may have only a small nucleus of track parts to lay. In laying your track you will need to check as you go along that you are laying it properly and connecting up the electrical side of things correctly. There is no better method than to use a tried and trusted proprietary model locomotive which can be relied upon to work every time. I recommend buying a bogie vehicle, the longest type you intend using, to enable you to check clearances at vital points. You should have done this already on your track plan, but there is no substitute for a real practical test. You will observe that there can be a considerable amount of overhang with a large bogie vehicle when it passes round curves and over points and crossings. This is not always appreciated, neither is it always possible to make due allowance for it, until you can see and measure it for yourself. Clearances round curves are particularly important where lineside structures, eg, platforms, bridges, tunnel mouths and even the point motors on some proprietary points, are concerned and the sharper the curve and the longer the vehicle the greater the clearance required.

It has been my experience that, however well and detailed I may have drawn up a track plan, I have nearly always felt the need to amend it when it came to actually laying the track. The need for such change usually arises after the rails have been laid temporarily and a couple of items of rolling stock have been put into position, since it is only then that you can really judge your clearances and the overall effect of the plan. It is one thing planning the position of the trackwork, but quite another to judge the effect of the plan with the rolling stock in place. If you have purchased all your track in one go you will be able to lay out each item of trackwork to see how they look in relation to each other on the baseboard. However, if you are only buying a few items at a time and trying to keep within a limited budget, you may not be able to set up enough trackwork to gauge the overall effect. A useful aid at times such as these are the points and crossing plans available from Peco. A stamped and addressed foolscap envelope, together with a label from a length of Peco Streamline track, will entitle you to one set of plans. These are only available direct from the Peco Technical Advice Bureau, Pritchard Patent Product Co Ltd, Beer, Seaton, Devon, EX12 3NA, England.

In any case, whether or not you use Peco point and crossing plans, you will need to mark on the baseboard the position of each piece of point, crossing and trackwork, and to establish their relationship with each other. My own personal preference is to work out the point controls and electrical feeds at this stage before I actually start laying the track. I have done it the other way round in the past only to regret it later, since it is often easier to drill holes in the baseboard for the electrical wiring or to cut grooves for the point controls before the track is laid than it is after.

The electrical side of the business was explained in chapter 6, but perhaps now is the time to discuss point control. There are a number of alternative methods and the decision as to the best one to use is largely a matter of choice. With some installations, particularly in goods yards and locomotive depots convenient to the operator, it is not necessary for points to be remotely controlled. In these cases a simple point lever is all that is required and is more appropriate to prototype practice. However, where the main line points are concerned, which in prototype form would be controlled from a signal box, or in cases where hand-operated points would be difficult for the operator to reach, remote control is essential. Possibly the easiest and best remote-control method is the individual electrically operated point motor. The only disadvantage with these is the cost of the motors and switches, which add at least 50 per cent to the price of the points. Manual remote control is, generally speaking, cheaper and the best method is the tried and trusted wire in tube, rather similar in principle to a Bowden cable on a cycle or motorcycle brake. Either copper

**Fig 81** *Wire-in-tube point rodding.*

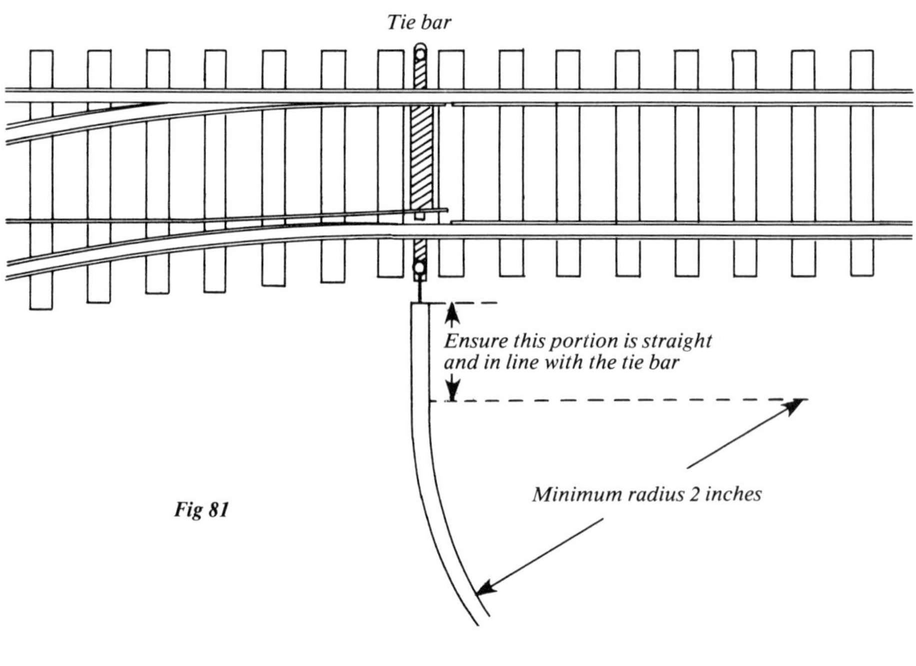


*Fig 81*

*Fig 82*

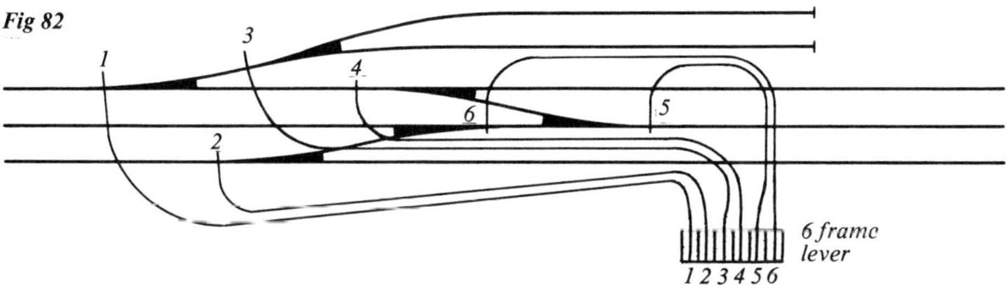


*Fig 83*

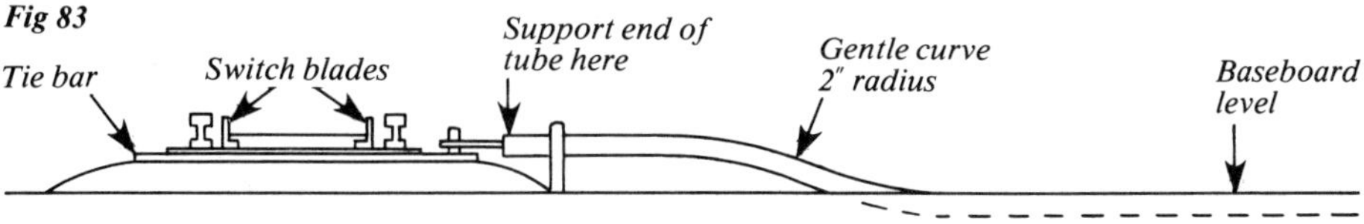


**Fig 82** *Typical layout of point control tubing.* **Fig 83** *Bending wire-in-tube, buried in the surface of the baseboard, to match the level of the point tie bar.*

or plastic tubing can be used for this purpose, and most model railway retailers maintain a stock of it and the lever frames by which the points can be operated. Ideally, the wire and tube joining the point to the lever frame should be in as direct a line as possible, avoiding sharp bends. Also, at the end of the tube, where the wire joins the point switch blades at one end and the lever frame at the other, the tube should be straight in line with the throw of the switch blade tie bar and the point lever. (See fig 81.) Where bends in the tubing are essential they should be of not less than 2 in radius, and when bending the tube you should always insert the wire first.

When it comes to installing these point control wires and tubes on the layout I place great emphasis on the necessity of doing as much preparatory work as you can before all the track is laid. Ideally you should lay track from the far edge of the baseboard working forward, connecting up each point as you go along. Grooves to take the point control tubing can then be cut in the top surface of the baseboard and the tubing fixed in place before the next rail is laid down. Fig 82 shows what may be considered as a typical installation. The first point to be laid would be no 3, together with the two sidings leading from it to the right. With these in place as a fixed datum point the position of the rest of the trackwork can then be planned and the grooves for the point control tubing cut into the top of the baseboard. Points nos 1 and 4 would then be fixed into position, followed by nos 5, 6 and 2. Finally, the running lines which in places overlay the point control tubing can be fixed in place.

Laying the point control tubing in grooves cut in the baseboard surface is far better than laying them on top. The main reason is that, provided the groove is cut with a reasonable degree of accuracy, it will prevent the tubing from moving, which is most essential. An additional advantage is that the tube will be hidden from sight and will not interfere with the running rails that pass over it. Remember, if you are using copper tubing and you lay it under the rails between the sleepers, you must avoid the tubing coming in contact with the two running rails, otherwise it will cause a short circuit. It is imperative that the tubing is held in place and, whereas copper tubing is relatively easy to fix, since you can simply solder it to pins driven into the baseboard, I have found that plastic tubing is rather more difficult. The 'U'-shaped tags supplied specially to hold the tubing in place can, if you are not careful, pinch the tubing and restrict the movement of the wire inside. Burying the tubing in the baseboard surface will of necessity require the tubing to be bent at each extremity to gain height to reach the level of the switch blade tie bar or point lever. However, this can be done very gradually and will not affect the performance (see fig 83).

It will be appreciated that, since the point control tube and wire is sold by the foot or yard, the further the point is from the point lever the more expensive manual control becomes. In some circumstances it is conceivable that electric point operation will be cheaper, but in any case there is a physical limit to the length of control that can be successfully carried out by manual means, and points more than 6 ft away from the lever should be electrically operated. If the point control wire needs to traverse sharp right-angled corners the best method is to use an angle crank such as that shown in fig 84. The arrows indicate the line of movement in one direction. It is possible, using these angle cranks, to connect up two sets of point blades to one lever. This is perfectly satisfactory in the case of manual control, but it is not usually possible with electric point motors since in my experience they have insufficient power to move more than one set of blades at a time. One thing to remember with the operation of points is that all things connected with them should be fixed immovably to the baseboard—the point itself, the point lever, point control tubing and the electric point motor. Looseness or slackness in any of these fittings will offer the line of least resistance and, instead of the switch blades of the point moving, it will be the point itself, the control tubing or the lever frame that moves. Peco have devised a particularly neat method of fixing for their own electric point motors which overcomes this problem. They snap to the underside of the base of the point itself, thereby providing immediate positive action without any movement between the point and the point motor. The advice given earlier to make provision for the point controls before the track is laid is even more necessary in the case of Peco points and point motors since to fit the point motor to the underside of the point base a rectangular shaped hole approximately $1\frac{1}{2}$ in × 1 in needs to be cut in the baseboard to accommodate the point motor—an impossible job once the point itself is laid. Should you forget to make provision for this or you are unlucky enough to find you have an obstruction under the baseboard just where the point motor is to go the Peco point motors can be adapted to fit above the baseboard surface. Whatever point motors you use make sure you have access to them after they are installed since it is possible for them to burn out and it may be necessary to replace one.

Before you actually start to lay your track, it is worth paying a visit to your nearest railway line to have a look at the real thing and see the effect you are trying to aim at. Most main line track that has been in use for some time appears a uniform rust red-brown in colour; with just the shiny top surface of the rails to break the dullness: A recently re-laid section of track will, however, have dark, almost black, creosoted sleepers laid in grey stone ballast, but after a time the creosote fades to a brown colour matching the rust of the rail, and the dirt and mud swept up by passing trains makes the ballast take on a similar colour. A look at the full-size track will emphasise just how important ballast is to help create a realistic appearance. In practice it forms a well-drained, slightly cushioned base for the sleepers, which also prevents their forward or lateral movement. Visually, the most important point to notice is that the ballast almost reaches the level of the top of the sleepers. For realism, therefore, it is not good enough to lay miniature track straight on to the baseboard, we also have to give it the effect and appearance of being ballasted.

One method of ballasting is to lay the track on a liberal quantity of glue and sprinkle on miniature ballast while the glue is still wet. When the glue is nearly dry the surplus ballast can be swept away and the remainder lightly pressed into place to ensure that it is stuck firmly and fills every nook and cranny. Small granulated cork is an ideal medium, since it is very near to the colour of well-used ballast and is readily stuck by most adhesives. To represent newly laid track, scale-size granite chippings can be used. Both these products are obtainable from most model railway stockists.

This method of track ballasting is very realistic, but slow and a bit messy, and the glue ensures a rather too long-lasting fixture of the permanent way which makes changes in the layout plan a major upheaval. For 00, HO and N gauges using proprietary track such as Peco Setrack, Peco Streamline, Airfix,

**Fig 84** *Action of an angle crank. The arrows indicate direction of movement.*

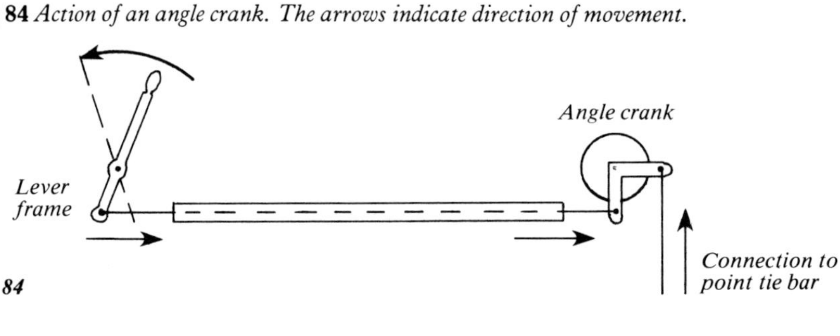


*Fig 84*

*The Peco point motor which clips to the underside of their range of Streamline points is shown here with an accessory switch which can be used to operate signals or for switching live frog points and other accessories* (Peco).

Mainline or Hornby Railways, an equally realistic, but far easier and cleaner, method is to use the pre-formed ballast inlays that are supplied. On first acquaintance these may be regarded as inessential luxuries which, if the budget is stretched, could be dispensed with but the opposite is true. Ballast inlays possess a number of practical features apart from the obvious one of adding realism to the track. Not least of their qualities is their sound-cushioning effect compared to track pinned or glued to a baseboard. The inlays also help with laying the track, especially lengths of flexible track, since the accurately moulded recesses for the sleepers and sleeper ties help to space the sleepers squarely and evenly. They also help to hold the track into place and the process of lining up flexible track into straight lines or round curves is far easier when the track is inserted into a ballast inlay. One of the reasons for this is that the back of the inlay has a rough surface which adheres quite readily to the surface of the baseboard, especially wood fibre insulation board, to prevent most lateral movement. On portable layouts or lifting sections of permanent layouts it is necessary to fix the inlay in place either with a spot of impact adhesive (be careful not to use too much) or by strips of double-sided adhesive tape. On a permanent layout I prefer not to stick the ballast inlay but to pin the track lightly at approximately 9 in to 12 in intervals.

Points need holding down with pins to enable the point-operating mechanism to function, as referred to earlier, and occasionally on the tightest and sharpest radius curves, say 2 ft or less in 00 and 1 ft or under in N, one or two pins in a few chosen sleepers can help the track retain its required curvature. The tighter the curve, the more pins may be required, but this is something you can judge for yourself as you go along. When drilling the holes for the pins (always drill them beforehand, as forcing the pins through may split the plastic sleepers) make sure the pins are a loose fit and see that they are not pushed home so far that they bend or strain the sleepers and squeeze the plastic foam ballast strip. Another thing to ensure with points is that the straight stock rail is in fact perfectly straight. Sometimes the tension produced by the curved stock rail can bend the point base slightly and curve the nominally straight stock rail out of line. This can be cured easily if a straight edge is held along the straight rail at the time the point is fixed to the baseboard. At least three pins should be used to hold the point in position, one at each end and one in the middle near the frog (the part of the point where the lines cross). Some brands of points have fixing holes ready marked or drilled.

Laying curved track calls for special attention since there are a number of additional points to watch. I have already mentioned the possible need for holding the track in place with pins to avoid any movement. In practice, you will find that track not held in place round curves will spread outwards in the direction of the trains, owing to the persistent force of the train's movement. Obviously this cannot be tolerated, otherwise a break in the running rails will occur at one of the spots where rail joiners are fitted. It is assumed that the position of the curve will be drawn in on the baseboard surface. Quite a practical compass can be devised for this purpose using a length of string with a pencil attached at one end. If the baseboard is wide enough the other end of the string can be held or pinned at the correct radius and the curve drawn in with the pencil. If, as is most likely, the centre point of the arc is off the baseboard, the string can be tied to a broom or carpet sweeper handle which, when held upright, can form the centre point for a makeshift compass. One recommended commercial aid to laying accurate radius curves is the Tracksetta Templates. These are available in five different radii for 00 gauge and six for N gauge. The firm also supplies straight sections for 00 and N gauges. They consist of accurately cut stout metal templates which fit in between the two running rails. Slots at intervals in the templates enable you to fit pins into the sleepers whilst the templates hold the track in place. I have found them particularly useful in lining up curves at joins in the baseboard as referred to in Chapter 2, fig 10.

It will be necessary to square up the ends of the flexible track when laid through a curve, since the inside rail will extend beyond the outer rail. The rail can be cut relatively easily with a pair of wire cutters. The cut will inevitably need cleaning up with a file so make due allowance for this when you make the incision and apply the wire cutters just a shade past the spot where you want the rail to end. It is a good tip to examine the ends of all rails, flexible track and points, since it will most likely be necessary to smooth the ends of the rails with a file to help them slide into the rail joiners. You will also need to cut the chairs from under the rails at the ends of the track where the rails are to be joined, as most rail joiners are longer than the regulation gap between two sleepers. A very useful little gadget to use when laying double or multiple tracks in 00 and N gauges in the Peco 6 ft Way Gauge. This not only ensures that double tracks are lined up exactly parallel to each other on straights and round curves it also makes the job that much easier.

For trackwork which is not supplied with plastic foam ballast strips or specially made point pieces there are a limited number of alternatives. I previously referred to the method of sprinkling ballast on glue spread between the sleepers. It is always much easier when using this method to fix the track and the ballast together rather than lay the track first and try and spread glue around and between the sleepers. The latter method is particularly tricky, since it is seldom possible to effect a complete covering with the glue. At the same time it is all too easy to get glue on to the rail or the top of the sleepers where it is most definitely not wanted. Then the problem is to scrape it off and, worse still, remove all trace of the glue which tends to leave a shiny tell-tale smear that is difficult to erase. I prefer to use a moderately slow-drying water-based glue for sticking ballast, since this enables you to tamp the ballast home really firmly while the glue is setting, but before it is thoroughly dry. Inevitably some parts of the track bed will have no ballast after the surplus has been dusted away, whilst others will probably have too much. Therefore, before the glue has thoroughly set, you have an opportunity to go over the whole installation, pushing ballast into place and tamping it home thoroughly. Any particularly bad spots can be given a drop or two of glue and another sprinkling of ballast. I like to use a small screwdriver as a tamping tool, employing the handle end to push the ballast well into the glue and the pointed end to pick out the odd bits that stray over the edges of the sleepers or between the check and wing rails. Whatever instrument you use, make sure that you keep it clean for if there is one little spot of glue on the screwdriver the ballast would rather stick to it than to the track bed!

One thing I would like to emphasise *very* strongly is to establish where the point switch blade tie bar and operating mechanism is going to be *before* you spread the glue on to the track base. Whatever else happens you must avoid fouling the switch blades with glue and/or ballast, since you will put an undue strain on the point-operating mechanism. In severe cases you can completely glue-up the point, making it quite useless. I speak from experience, as I have made the mistake more than once. I have spread the glue, pinned the point in place, sprinkled the ballast, and only when I have dusted the surplus away have I realised that I cannot move the switch blades. It is quite a miserable experience, for it is not at all easy digging out the offending mixture of glue and ballast from around the switch blades and the tie bar. You have to keep moving them until the glue dries thoroughly for fear that it will hold them permanently in one position and the vital full free movement of the switch blade will be lost.

Mention should also be made of the very good 'bonded ballast' system used in the USA. The ballast (granulated cork) is placed loosely in position round the track after the track is laid. This is then sprayed (using an old hair or scent spray) with an adhesive consisting of water with $\frac{1}{6}$ part size or artist's polymer varnish. This is transparent, sets the loose ballast solid with the track, and the edges of ballast can be shaped and adjusted while setting. Another method is to mix the ballast with glue powder, sprinkle the dry mixture evenly between and to the sides of the sleepers and spray the track with water.

Laying track may at first glance seem an easy, quick thing to do, especially when you are using ready-made proprietary items, but there is a bit more to it than meets the eye. The point control, electrical feeds and ballasting have all to be considered and it is far better in the long run to move slowly and surely than in great haste. After all, the track is likely to be left down for a long while, and it is best to ensure that it is laid properly in the first place. It is understandable that there could be a feeling of impatience to get something running, especially if this is your first model railway. Give yourself the occasional break from the slow, tedius process of laying points, crossings and sidings and get on with the far more satisfying job of laying the main line. You will find this easier and quicker, thereby raising your spirits again. In fact, it could be preferable to obtain some practical experience in track laying at the country end of your layout, where the track is most likely to be straightforward and devoid of complicated pointwork.

Certainly, if you have a lifting section across a doorway, it would be best to start here. When laying track across such sections it is essential to line up the tracks correctly from all angles and great care should be taken here. If you have to err at all, err on the side of cutting the rail overlength for the lifting section, assuming that this lifts upwards, since it will not matter if the ends of the rails slightly overlap the fixed baseboard section. On the other hand, if the rails on the fixed section were to overlap the lifting section they would either become damaged when the section was raised or they might prevent it from being raised at all.

Most of the foregoing has been written on the assumption that you are going to use proprietary ready-made track. There is no shortage of suitable material and if there is one area of model railways that is blessed by the trade it must surely be trackwork. One particularly noticeable development in recent years has been the improvement made to the fixed geometry track associated with toy railways and train sets. At one time most of this had to be discarded when a youngster grew up and made the transition from a toy railway to a model railway but, so far as 00 gauge is concerned, this is not the case today. Peco Setrack and the trackwork included in the Airfix Railway System and Mainline Railways is compatible with the more advanced pointwork and flexible track in the Peco Streamline range. A fixed geometry track such as Peco Setrack holds considerable advantages for the younger or less experienced railway modeller. Because the rails are fixed in length and curvature and each section of track has the rail joiners fixed in place at each end, a layout can be planned and laid in a very minimum of time. Furthermore, if the layout is found not to be interesting enough it can be dismantled and relaid in a different form, again and again. The standard radius curves will ensure that the layout is workable when finished provided the right number of track sections have been used. It is a very good way of cutting your teeth on a model railway and, as I said before, there is no need to give it all away when you are ready to move on to more advanced schemes. Admittedly, some of the curves down to $14\frac{1}{2}$ in radius would be unrealistic in a scale model railway setting but you might be able to hide some of them in tunnels or incorporate short pieces between two flexible track transition curves in the less noticeable parts of the layout. Despite the enormous variety of brands of track in most gauges from N to 1, there are many people who prefer to make their own for a number of good reasons. There is the obvious one of gauge. If you are intending to be a 4 mm scale modeller and you are not content with the underscale 00 gauge of 16.5 mm then you will have to make all your own points and crossings as there are none ready assembled in EM or 18.83 mm gauges. There is also the question of the type of track. Most proprietary 00 and HO flexible gauge tracks use flat bottom rail, most universal in Europe and America for decades, but which was used very little on British railways in pre-nationalisation days. Most main lines use flat bottom track today, but there is still some of the old bullhead rail laid in cast metal chairs about. This rail is of a noticeably thinner and shallower section than most of the proprietary makes of model track. If you do want to model the pre-nationalisation scene and you want authentic bullhead track this is now available in ready assembled flexible track form in 00 and EM gauges and in easily assembled kit form in 18.83 mm gauge but you must be prepared to make all the points and crossings yourself.

Most of the flexible HO/00 gauge tracks and nearly all proprietary 'snap together' tracks are in what is called Code 100 section. This figure actually refers to the depth of the cross-section of the rail, 100 referring to 100 thousandths of an inch. While, to the human eye, Code 100 track looks commendably close to scale (and certainly is close to scale compared with the very coarse section tracks of years gone by) it is worth pointing out I think that track to this Code 100 section really represents the very largest, deepest track you are likely to see on modern main lines, and then by no means everywhere. Almost everyone overlooks this as it does not worry the average modeller.

If you want a finer 'vintage' appearance you need a track with a smaller code number, such as Code 70 which gives a true scale depth. This is the favoured 'fine scale' in America, though in Britain Peco offer Code 65, and Code 80 which are very nearly the same in appearance. For the average modeller, however, this is an academic consideration because Code 100 track takes virtually all standards of proprietary rolling stock wheel, and track sections smaller than this will only take wheels to fine scale standards, ie, with small flanges. Deep flanges used on fine scale track will bump on the sleepers and not ride on the track at all. Thus Code 70, 65, or 80 track remains for the fine scale modeller prepared to do his own track laying. However, one range of Japanese-made Code 70 flexible track is available from a few shops in Britain specialising in American and Continental models. On the subject of codes, mention must be made of the Peco 'Code 100 Fine' range of points and crossings. These have been specially designed for the finer wheel standards now fitted to the latest ready-to-run products and they differ mainly in the wing rail and check rail clearances. It is also worth mentioning that the leaflet enclosed with Peco Universal points and crossings explains how these track parts can be adapted to fine scale standards and I can vouch for the improvement these simple modifications can make.

In the smaller gauges below 0 gauge, one of the most popular methods of track building which has been developed over recent years is the method of soldering rail to sleepers cut from copper-clad plastic, similar to that used in printed circuits. Strangely enough, this goes back to the old pre-war days when practically all so-called scale 00 gauge track was built by soldering the rails to brass sleepers. This, of course, was the three-rail track, since the brass well and truly conducted the current across to the two running rails. With the printed circuit material, however, it is a perfectly simple matter to scratch the top of the sleepers lightly with a saw blade after the rails have been soldered in place. This will make a gap in the copper cladding which will in turn effectively insulate the two running rails. Sleepers can be purchased ready cut or alternatively, you can cut your own from sheet material—not to be recommended unless you have a strong guillotine or access to other suitable machinery. Another method is to use thin wooden sleepers stuck to a sleeper base and to solder the rails to the heads of pins driven into the sleepers. The uniform size of the pin heads help to ensure that each blob of solder is roughly the same size and shape which assists in creating the illusion of a cast metal chair. A similar method to this is the one recommended by the Protofour people.

Whatever you are working with, an accurate track gauge is essential and there are a number of different types available. The use of jigs is also advised whenever scratch-built track using copper-clad printed circuit material sleepers is built, not only from the point of view of accuracy but also because of the speed with which it enables the work to be done. The simplest form of jig is shown in fig 85, and it consists of blocks of wood glued or pinned to a wooden base. Sleepers are laid in the gaps left between each block and one rail is laid along the edges of the blocks and soldered to as many sleepers as are slotted into position at any one time. The rail and the sleepers can then be removed from the jig, the rail slid along and soldered to another batch of sleepers inserted in the jig, until sleepers have been soldered throughout the whole length of one rail. Not until the track has been laid in position and ballasted will the second rail be soldered into place and this is when the track gauge will be required. This method will enable the track to be curved into any desired formation and multi-radius or transition curves will present no problem. A similar system can also be used for constructing points.

The larger gauges such as 0 and 1 normally use cast metal chairs and wooden sleepers

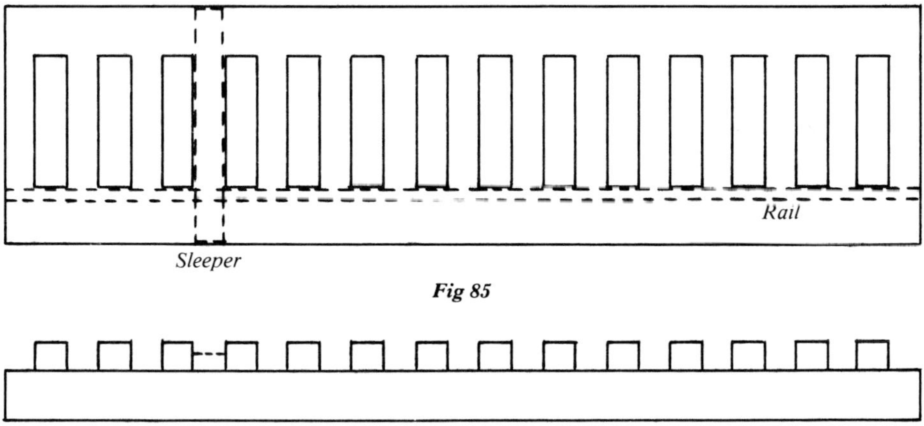


**Fig 85** *A jig for making track, using rail soldered to copper-clad printed circuit material sleepers.*

as do full-size railways, and this must surely be one of the attractions of these gauges. Track can, in fact, be made 100 per cent realistic, since we are using the same basic materials as the full-size railway. Rails still tend to have too heavy a section, but if you are worried by this there is the possibility of using a rail that is really intended for a smaller gauge. Proprietary ready-assembled track is available in 0 and 1 gauges, although not to the same extent as with the smaller gauges. Scratch-built track is generally accepted in 0 and 1 and is catered for by a number of firms who produce rail lengths, cast metal chairs, wooden sleepers and all the other parts required for home construction. Peco have extended their range of 'Streamline' flexible track to include 0 gauge, and very nice this is too, with proper bullhead chairs moulded in plastic and integral with the sleepers which have a very nice wood grain effect.

The importance of joining rails properly cannot be over-emphasised. Apart from the necessity to provide electrical continuity which we discussed in Chapter 6, it is essential that the rails be connected thoroughly to avoid the possibility of misalignment and derailment of the rolling stock. This is particularly true of pointwork and curved track, where there seem to be so many opposing forces intent on removing passing trains from the rails. When laying flexible track round curves, it is preferable to avoid having a rail joint too near the point where the curve starts and finishes. If by mischance you find it necessary to have such a joint, you will possibly find it necessary to bend the rail between your fingers into the curve required, rather than let it bow into its own curve. Fig 86 is an exaggeration of the bad effects of joining flexible track at the point of transition into a curve, whereas fig 87 shows the correct method. With joins between two curved rails on the curve itself the effects are not quite so bad, but it is important to watch the joints carefully and perhaps solder the rail joiners in position.

I mentioned earlier the point about curved track and the necessity to cut the inside rail shorter than the outside rail. It is quite amazing how a slight adjustment to the curvature can affect the relative lengths of the two rails and it is important to get the measurement as accurate as possible before you let the saw cut into the rail. It is preferable to ask someone to give you a hand, since the rails often slip unnoticed when you are marking them for cutting, especially if you are tackling a yard length of track and you have to take your eyes off one end to deal with the other. Another helpful aid when using proprietary flexible track is to try and arrange it so that two or three spare sleepers extend beyond the end of the rails at the end of a section of track, thus allowing the rail from the next section to be led into them. This is not essential but sometimes it helps. The situation can arise when one rail is shortened when it has been laid round a curve: the subsequent rail joint mid-way along a length of plastic sleepering can be just that little bit less strained than a joint between the ends of two separate lengths of sleepering.

Some proprietary track units, eg, Trix and Fleischmann with Code 100 rail, can be joined to Peco or Graham Farish flexible track. For trackwork in tunnels and other locations where it is hidden from view it is

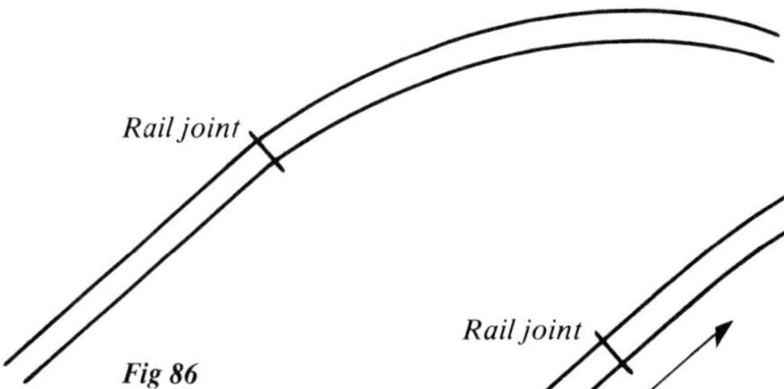


*Fig 86*

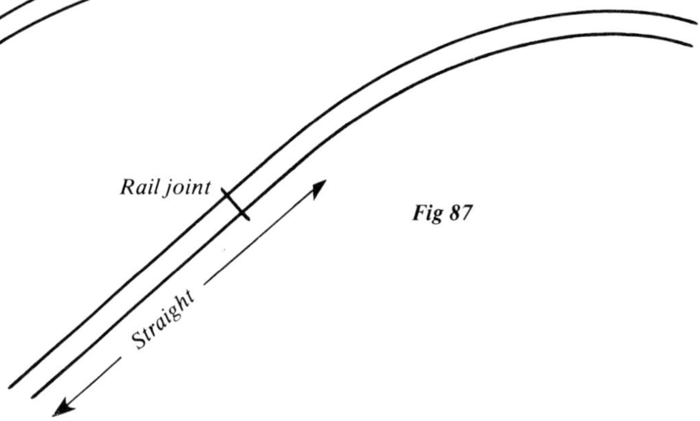


*Fig 87*

**Fig 86** *An exaggerated drawing of the bad effects of joining flexible track at the point of transition into a curve.* **Fig 87** *The correct method.*

sometimes an economic proposition to use secondhand or sale price items of proprietary track instead of using brand-new flexible track, especially since secondhand curved rails are invariably cheap items to buy. Another method of economising with scratch-built track in tunnels is to dispense with all the sleepers, leaving, say, one out of every four or five, just sufficient to hold the track in place but without making any attempt at realism. Sleepers can, in fact, be dispensed with altogether if you care to solder the rail to pins laid directly into the baseboard.

Thankfully wheel standards and track standards (the two go inseparably together) have improved tremendously in recent years and with the current range of products from the commercial manufacturers in the two most popular gauges, N and 00, we do not have the wide disparity between course and fine standards or between the standards of one manufacturer and another that once bedevilled the hobby.

## Chapter 8

# Scenic settings

In the early days of model railways, and I am thinking largely of 0 and 1 gauges in the pre-00/HO era, scenic effects were virtually unheard of. Practically no attempt was made to embellish the model railway beyond the bare bones of rolling stock, essential railway buildings such as stations and signal boxes, signals, and of course the track. Even the track itself was neglected from the appearance point of view and in the majority of cases it looked very crude with thick, heavy rails and widely spaced sleepers. Yet somehow or other these were accepted, and the obvious faults, at least they appear obvious now, were either ignored or glossed over. Very soon we began to see an improvement in track and additional sleepers were added to make it look a little more presentable. Even so, the whole effect was often marred by fixing the track to wooden battens which raised it high into the air and no attempt was made to hide the unsightly effect by sprinkling the whole lot with a good covering of ballast. The remedy always seemed so obvious, but in only a few instances did it appear to have been considered or applied. There probably was a good reason, but it has always escaped me.

The coming of 00 gauge seems to have done more to change things than anything else, especially when the two-rail system of electrification overcame the necessity to fit the unsightly and unrealistic third rail. At one time it appeared to be accepted that you had to make concessions and some departures from the real thing if you were going to make a practical success of a working model railway. But when people began to realise that there was less and less necessity to depart from the real thing and fewer concessions needed to be made, the quest for realism became greater, until we have reached the state of perfection we know today. This change in attitude was resisted at great length and even now there are many people who feel that scenic effects are to a certain extent overdone. 'Too much scenery and not enough railway,' some people say. As with many judgements about model railways this is largely a matter of opinion, but it is probably fair to say that the majority of people accept the need for a certain amount of scenery to embellish their model railway and that few are considered complete without it.

Another factor which has had a considerable influence on the changed attitude to scenery is, I think, the increasing number of illustrations of model railway layouts that appear in books and magazines. You can often be quite oblivious to the faults in the appearance of your own layout, since it is possible to be so absorbed in its operation that you never notice them. This is probably a slight case of familiarity breeding contempt. Yet the moment it is photographed and a copy of the photograph is examined critically or, worse still, published in a magazine, the areas at fault will stand out like sore thumbs, just as much to you as to other people. Critical examination of other people's layout photographs has probably made us more aware of the obvious visual pitfalls and has made it much easier for us to diagnose and apply the remedy to our own layouts.

When considering what can be done to add a scenic setting to the bare bones of our model railway, we can best start with the track itself. We have already discussed in the previous chapter the necessity for ballasting, strictly speaking a scenic addition since it is perfectly possible to run a *model* railway without ballast, but it looks so much better with it. Another aid to realism is to paint the rails a rusty-brown colour as it is most unnatural for the whole depth of the rail to be shining bright. Only the top running surface of the rail is in this condition and this can be achieved by wiping the top of the rail with a rag after it has been painted. It is probably easier to paint points before they are fixed in position, but it is not possible to do this with flexible track, since the chairs and sleepers will more than likely slide along the rail during the laying of the track and this will reveal patches of unpainted rail. Be careful not to get paint on to, or too near, the moving parts of the points, as one coat of paint is sufficient to stop the switch blades from functioning. Also, when using proprietary points with plastic sleeper bases, it is advisable to experiment first on a small section of track with the paint you intend to use because some types of paint can have a harmful effect on plastic. While we are dealing with colour it might be as well to mention that not all track is brown. There are many places on a railway system, especially in the old steam days, where coal, ash, water, oil and soot were deposited and covered the whole track, sleepers, ballast and rail, with a black gooey mess. Locomotive depots are the obvious places for such treatment, but other spots are the ends of platforms where engines frequently stand at the head of a train, or in coal yards and goods depots. Frequently, little-used sidings can be found that rust very quickly, and it is sometimes effective to model such a siding using brass rail instead of nickel silver. There is an added advantage in that brass rail is usually cheaper.

Moving outwards from the rails themselves, the first item we are likely to meet with, at least on an open country stretch of line, will be the boundary fence. On British railways anyway, it is an essential statutory requirement since by law all lines have to be fenced. There are a number of different types of fencing to be found on the full-size railway, as anyone keen enough will observe. In all gauges our requirements are fully met by the trade and a number of different types of fencing are available from several different manufacturers and suppliers. One recent innovation has been the use of etched-brass techniques to produce iron railings, chestnut paling, chicken wire and even barbed wire—in N gauge as well as 00! These are available from John Piper (Accessories) Ltd. In 00 gauge, Peco produce field gates, wicket gates and stiles. Of course, you can construct most types of fencing yourself out of basic raw materials and in some specialised applications this may be necessary. But out in the country section of the layout, where several yards of fencing are required on both sides of the line, the installation of ready-made proprietary fencing can save a lot of time. Just a word of warning though—some proprietary fences are made from white plastic material. Now, fences painted white may be found around stations or specially protected areas, but it is most unusual to find ordinary lineside fencing painted white. Some concrete fences or fence posts appear an off-white colour, but usually wooden fences are creosoted, if they are protected at all, and over the years they become almost black in colour. This effect can be achieved by dabbing on washes of black and brown paint in haphazard fashion. A useful paint to have by for a large number of model railway applications is Humbrol Track Colour, which is a dull rust-brown. It is worth while buying a $\frac{1}{2}$ pint tin since there are so many potential uses for it.

There are very few railways that run through the countryside as flat as a model baseboard, and some means are called for of adding realism and variety to an otherwise monotonous landscape. Although the track base itself may need to be level, inevitably the country on either side of it will rise and fall. The rising bit is simply done on a model railway, since we can build up from the baseboard level without difficulty, but the falling part is a different matter, and we will deal with that later. The rising parts, ie, the land either side of the track that rises above the level of the track in the form of hills, cuttings and tunnels, can be represented by an almost endless variety of methods and materials. To a certain extent what you use is dictated by the size of area and type of hill, cutting or tunnel you wish to represent, but let us assume a normal rolling or undulating countryside. For scenery such as this, the generally accepted method is to build some sort of framework over which can be stretched a suitable covering material. Fig 88 shows a cross-section of a typical stretch of lineside scenery modelled in this fashion. When planning the framework for a scenic setting such as this, it is a good idea to take the fencing line as a datum point for working out the height and shape of your high ground. Inevitably the fencing will follow the contour of the land either side of the railway line, since it would have been the railway in all probability that was responsible for cutting into that land and changing its shape in the first place. Anything within the cutting will be railway property, so the fence that runs along the cutting edge will mark the end of that property.

Now we need to establish a reasonably reliable foundation on which to build the boundary fence, so the framework we use for hills and cuttings can also provide the foundation for the fence. My own personal preference for making such a framework is to use offcuts of insulation board which are left over from the baseboard itself. These can be cut roughly to the shape of the hill and glued on edge to the baseboard. The open spaces between the framework should be filled in with something to stop the covering material sagging, and crumpled newspaper is very suitable for this. It can be simply rolled and screwed up in the hand, then glued and pinned into position. The material I have found most effective for covering hills such as

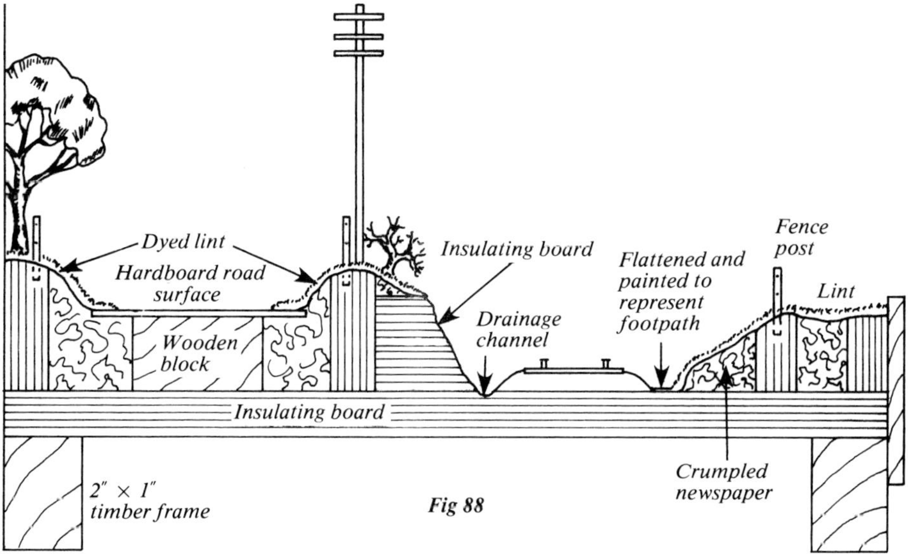


**Fig 88** *Cross-section of a typical stretch of lineside scenery. Dyed lint, representing grass, is laid across a foundation made from pieces of insulating board. Note how the tree, telegraph pole and fence posts fit into the insulating board. Crumpled newspaper helps to support the lint.*

these is medical lint, dyed green. An 8 oz roll of lint measures over 4 yd long and 9 in wide and a packet of dye costing a few pence is more than enough to colour the lot. Ideas vary as to what constitutes a natural grass green, depending on the time of the year, the dryness of the weather, and other variable climatic conditions, but I try to avoid too bright a colour and prefer olive green. The lint should be glued along the edge alongside the track and over the framework of the hills. Joins in the material can be covered up by carefully brushing with a stiff nylon nail brush, which is also an effective method of bringing up the 'pile' in the material to give a realistic grass effect. Alternatively, the lint can be coated with a size solution and painted, using matt oil paints or poster colours.

There are any number of alternative covering materials and one variation which has had the accolade of being demonstrated on television is the Jack Kine method which consists of building up a framework of card strips over which are pasted 2 in squares of tarlaton (a type of thin open muslin) or buckram. The paste used is a modelling compound specially formulated by Artex which when mixed with water can be worked into the landscape to form varying textures and finishes. Full details of the method are given in an instruction booklet which is supplied with the Jack Kine modelling powder and having seen this remarkable material and method of scenic modelling demonstrated several times I can vouch for its excellence. Another popular method is to use a proprietary material known as Mod-Roc, which is a form of plaster-impregnated bandage. Alternate layers can be soaked and placed across each other to build a cover over the scenic framework, and when the plaster dries, which it does quite quickly, it forms a thin but reasonably robust 'crust'. The surface can then be painted to represent a basic earth colour and sprinkled while the paint is wet with the various scenic dressings which are available from model shops. I advise that you experiment with scenic dressing and I would hesitate to recommend any specific brand or colour. I do, however, suggest that a mixture of two or more colours gives the best result, say yellow and green, or two shades of green, when it comes to representing grass. There is endless scope for imagination and originality in the application of these materials.

Another very useful material to use when building up a scenic landscape is expanded polystyrene. You can buy this in the form of ceiling tiles, or you can do as I do and beg, borrow or scrounge odd pieces used for packaging which in normal circumstances would only be thrown away. I keep a cardboard box to store the odd bits in and add to it any time a piece comes my way. 'Never throw anything away' is the model makers' maxim—'you never know when it might come in useful.' Expanded polystyrene is so light that it is absolutely perfect for portable layouts. It is even possible to carve out the track bed for a layout from a solid block of expanded polystyrene, using a soldering iron or some other heat source to burn your way through the material to make cuttings and gorges in a realistic rocky mountain setting. Where weight is no problem almost any material can be used as a foundation for the scenery—blocks of wood, chipboad, softboard, cardboard, or anything that comes to hand and is not otherwise wanted. Similarly, there are countless alternatives for covering surfaces. Old worn-out sheets, shirts or blankets can be used and these can be pre-soaked in size to hold them stiff when set. Alternatively, you can consider pasting paper over a chicken wire frame or spreading a coat of plaster over some stiff hessian or rug canvas. Again, I can only recommend that you try the different methods and find which one suits you best. It might be as well, before you place your covering material, to establish where any firm and flat surfaces such as roads or foundations for buildings are to be positioned, since it is preferable to fix these first. They can be made of pieces of hardboard or cardboard supported on wooden blocks.

A rocky landscape is easy to build with the materials available. We have already mentioned the possibility of expanded polystyrene, but one of the best and most widely used materials for simulating rocks is cork bark. This is available in packets from most model shops and is easy to apply and most effective in use. It is, of course, very light in weight which makes it suitable for portable layouts. The cork bark should be pinned and glued to the baseboard, with perhaps a light supporting wooden framework behind, and any gaps between different pieces can be filled in either with offcuts of cork bark or with plaster. The softer limestone rocks, or such features as sand and chalk pits, can be represented by gluing layers of soft insulation board on top of each other so that the rough edges face outwards. The edges can be roughened up still further with a stiff wire or nylon brush to represent a lush growth of foliage, ferns, etc, which often congregate in places such as these, especially if there is any water around. Alternatively, the edges of the insulation board can be smoothed over with plaster which, if left in its natural colour, will look like a chalk pit. Plaster can also be used on its own to represent rock faces, where paint will need to be added to complete the effect. A favourite dodge is to imprint the impression of a piece of coal on the face of the plaster before it finally sets. Even a lump of coal itself can be used to represent a rock face and so can actual pieces of stone or rock, but this will give you a weight problem which will rule out the use of these materials in a portable layout. Smaller, lighter pieces of rock or stone can, however, be used in places such as river beds, rocky streams and at the foot of a cliff or cutting, where loose boulders can be expected to be lying around. Small pieces of real coal can also be left lying around on the coal yard siding and employed as loads in wagons and locomotive tenders and bunkers.

Water always adds interest to any scenic setting, in real life as well as in miniature, and I suggest finding an excuse for simulating a water effect somewhere on your layout, whether it be a harbour at one extreme or a duck pond at the other. How you can best do this will depend on the particular location. For a large, deep water area like a harbour or river, I find a sheet of ripple glass such as Stippolyte gives a realistic result, especially if it is held about 1 in clear of the river bed. The higher the glass is held above the bed the more obscure the river bed becomes and the more realistic the whole affair looks. There are many simple ways of achieving extra realism, such as streaks of green paint applied to the underside of the glass to represent weeds floating in the water, or actual rocks placed on the bed of the river so that they just show below the surface of the glass. The river bed or harbour bottom can be a piece of hardboard painted according to the type it is to represent. If the scene is set in a heavy industrial area it could easily be painted black! On the other hand, a tidal creek could be painted sea green, with perhaps the natural hardboard colour at the edges to represent the sand banks just appearing below the surface. The natural hardboard colour will also be perfectly satisfactory for the average muddy brown river.

On a portable layout you will hardly want to use glass for obvious reasons, in which case you can use other lighter and potentially less vulnerable materials such as clear plastic. Another method which is very popular, especially for smaller streams, is to apply successive coats of varnish. Allow each coat to dry before applying the next and, over a period of time, you will build up a thick semi-clear layer which looks very much like a smooth flowing stream or brook. This method is particularly suitable for waterfalls and streams, where the varnish can be allowed to tumble and find its own level just as the water would do. One of the most realistic artificial rivers I have ever seen was on the Johnshaven Branch constructed by Les and Richard Parker, which has been exhibited on several occasions. Here the material used is a sheet of silicon rubber known as Midland Silicon, and the effect is quite tremendous.

Foliage, bushes, trees and plants present quite a challenge to modellers, if only because in real life there are so many of them. Most modellers do not have the time to devote to tree making and fall back on the various proprietary models that are available, either ready assembled or in kit form. Some of the latest products attain a very high level of realism and two particularly noteworthy brands are the Model Accessories Landscape Series from John Piper (Accessories) Ltd (available ready assembled and in kit form) and the Woodland Scenics range of tree kits from Hammant and Morgan. Also, Britains Ltd produce a range of plastic model trees which are very simple to assemble, reasonably realistic in appearance and are passable on either 00/HO or 0 gauge model railways. For the smaller trees and bushes, green lichen—which can be bought in packets from most model shops—is ideal, either glued direct to the ground to represent bushes and hedgerows, or placed on suitable twigs which can be made to look like tree trunks. Home-made trees can be fashioned out of multi-strand wire, bound with tape at the base and progressively unwound towards the top of the tree to represent the diverging branches and twigs. The branches can be dipped in glue and sprinkled with green-dyed sawdust, scenic dressing or dyed tea leaves for summer foliage, or they can be left to represent the bare winter branches. Various other ways have been demonstrated or described in the model railway press from time to time and, as with most other aspects of scenic modelling, there is considerable scope for ingenuity in adapting different materials and devising new methods.

I mentioned earlier the rise and fall of the

*'Woodland Scenics' trees have been skillfully planted in this attractive scenic setting* (McLeish Associates Ltd).

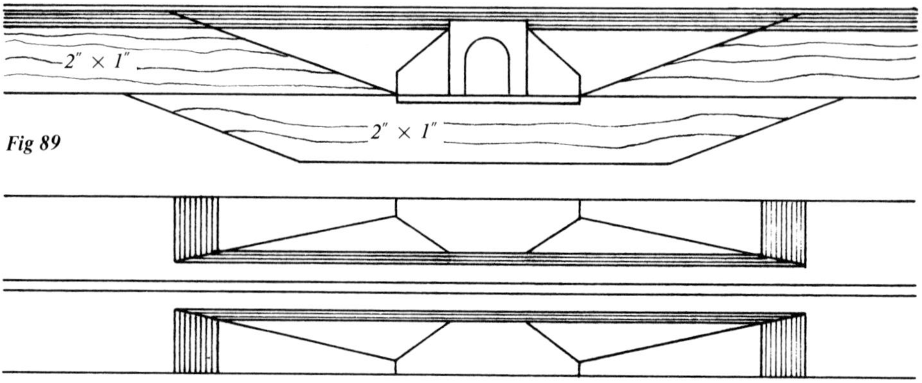


Fig 89

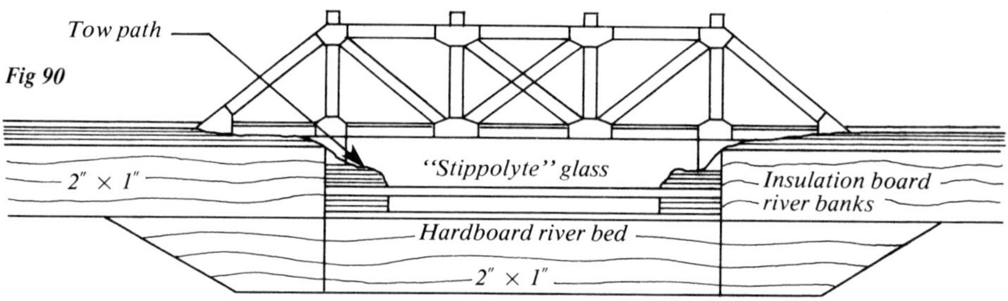


Fig 90

**Fig 89** *Dropping the datum line of the baseboard surface to provide scope for embarkments and bridges.* **Fig 90** *A bridge across a river.*

countryside and said that the rising part was easy enough but that the falling part is another matter. The difference lies in the fact that we usually build our model railways on flat baseboard, below which we cannot normally go. With the open framework type of baseboard we can sometimes cut and lower a section of the framework to build some scenery below the level of the railway line. Figs 89 and 90 illustrate two alternative schemes. The first illustration shows the railway line crossing a shallow valley on an embankment; the small bridge or culvert is optional. The second illustration shows the line carried across a river by a bridge, such as the Airfix Girder Bridge.

In an undulating landscape a railway is just as likely to burrow through hills and cuttings as it is to be carried above the surrounding countryside on embankments, bridges and viaducts. It follows, therefore, that wherever you can it is desirable to build scenery *down* from the track and baseboard level as well as up. In a scheme such as that in fig 89, the insulation board forming the baseboard surface and track bed would be cut to approximately 2 in wide (assuming a single track in 00 gauge) for the embankment section, and the embankment sides and valley floor can be built up by using dyed lint or whatever surfacing material you have decided on. The bridge or culvert can be a simple cardboard structure faced with brick or stone paper or can be adapted from ready-made proprietary parts. Fig 90 is perhaps self-explanatory and you can see that I have used a sheet of Stippolyte glass to represent the surface of the river, as described earlier. The river banks can be formed from strips of insulation board and shaped to represent sloping banks with a level tow path either side of the river. The insulation board can then be covered with dyed medical lint to represent grass and the ragged edges painted with dabs of brown, grey and green paint. The banks themselves can form unlimited scope for artistic enterprise in the application of paint, lint and lichen to represent weeds, rushes and overhanging trees. There is also scope for modelling landing stages, boat houses, boats and marine equipment of all kinds. If the railway is planned in detail before constructing the baseboard, it is an advantage to consider features such as these when the baseboard framework is being constructed. If, however, you already have your baseboard in place, it is a relatively simple matter to adapt it, especially if you are using insulation board since this can be cut so easily, even when *in situ*.

To augment the natural scenery and scenic effects there are any number of man-made items which either form part of the actual railway scene or are frequently to be seen adjoining the line. The obvious ones are, of course, buildings and bridges, but there are others like telegraph poles, overhead electric pylons, roads, level crossings, road vehicles, and street furniture such as lamps, road signs and advertising hoardings, etc. Model railway buildings fall into two categories, depending upon which side of the railway fence they are to be found. On one side are the railway-owned properties such as stations, engine sheds, goods sheds, signal boxes, etc, and on the other side the privately owned properties such as houses, shops, industrial premises, farms, etc. There are a limited number of ready assembled models of railway-owned properties (currently there are two very nice ranges available in N and 00 by Graham Farish and Hornby Railways respectively) but there is also a very wide range of construction kits that afford a relatively quick and easy way of adding buildings to your layout. Most British-style kits take the form of printed card parts and perhaps the best known are Bilteezi (some available in TT as well as 00), Prototype Models (available in N, 00 and a limited range in 0) and Superquick (available in 00 only). One highly recommended kit in 4 mm scale which uses a combination of moulded plastic and coloured paper brick outer walls and interior details is the semi-detached house by Scalerama. Some of the smaller buildings are available in cast white metal kits and another method of establishing relief detail in model buildings is to use moulded plaster. This was the method adopted by Ossett Mouldings in their range of building kits. Another development in this field is the Linka model building system which is a range of kits not for specific buildings but for making interlocking parts in different architectural styles which can be assembled into an endless variety of buildings suitable for HO and 00. There are a few British-style moulded plastic building kits such as Airfix, Cooper Craft, Hornby Railways, Peco and Wills Finecast, but the most prolific source of plastic building kits emanate from the Continent where, of course,

*Superquick buildings have been cleverly adapted to make this impressive motive power depot on John Woodman's 00 gauge model railway. In the foreground is the diesel locomotive refuelling point* (Tom Boulter).

they are built to Continental styles of architecture and to the Continental scales, 1:87 for HO, 1:100 for TT-3 and 1:160 for N. The exception to this is the Danish firm of Heljan who have produced a limited range of British-style building kits in 00 including a very attractive and authentic looking signal box. Admittedly some of the Continental kits are unsuited to British layouts. I have in mind the typically Bavarian and Alpine buildings with low pitched overhanging roofs. But many more can easily be adapted, in some cases simply by leaving off the Continental embellishments such as window shutters, a feature not often found in Britain. The question of scale need not be all that important especially if the buildings are placed nearer the back of the layout where in all probability most scenic buildings will be placed. The quality and attention to detail in these Continental kits has to be seen to be believed and they have the added attraction of being moulded in different realistically coloured plastics, sometimes multi-coloured, which gives a natural and realistic random effect. Therefore, there is absolutely no painting required and this more than offsets the slightly higher cost of these kits.

As nice as all these building kits are, and let there be no mistake, some of them are superb little gems, there is no substitute for the scratch-built tailor-made model. There are many different styles of architecture and even in these days of 'shoe box' office blocks there is still a lot of individuality to be found in buildings, particularly railway stations. Many railway companies had an individual 'house style' (no pun intended) and numerous small characteristics, such as chimney pots, barge boards and awnings, bore the stamp of the owning company. The types of material used in the construction of the building, whether wood, brick or stone, varied according to the company or location of the line, and there were even variations in the type of brick and stone used. There is little doubt that a model

*A grimy SR L1 4-4-0, partly obscured by a cloud of smoke, is seen after being coaled on John Woodman's 00 gauge layout. The coaling stage is made from Superquick water tower kits. Note the ash pits in the foreground liberally covered with ash* (Tom Boulter).

built to represent an authentic railway in an authentic location ought to have authentic-looking buildings in the style of the owning company and with representative local materials. Back numbers of the model railway magazines will provide a number of photographs and drawings of buildings and these should be scanned as a first source of inspiration and information. There is, however, no real substitute for field observation and a visit to a railway station, taking with you a camera, notebook, pencil and tape measure, will pay dividends. There is little doubt that a model of an authentic railway station will be admired much more and will add more atmosphere to your layout than a kit-built structure which has possibly already been seen on countless other model railway layouts. I would suggest using building kits as an expediency, to get something assembled quickly, and then after the rest of the layout is finished you can again turn your attention to the buildings and replace them one by one with scratch-built models. But remember, if you do intend doing some field observation in a particular area there is no time like the present. To delay the job for a week or two may be too late, since many of the most interesting railway structures are being pulled down or rebuilt beyond all recognition, and if your interest is primarily in the past it is important to get out and about now.

The materials which can be used for making scratch-built buildings are generally simple to work with, easy to come by and inexpensive, which is not something we can always say. They need not be difficult to construct or call for a great deal of manipulative skill or architectural knowledge. What model building construction does need, however, is an artistic eye, an appreciation of colour, a keen sense of observation and in some cases the ability to concentrate the subject matter in such a way that the overall effect is retained without overburdening the model with a lot of unnecessary detail and without spreading it over too large an area. Some railway buildings would take up more space on the baseboard than we have room for and it is sometimes permitted to reduce the ground area by perhaps restricting the length or width of a building, so long as it does not unduly affect the overall appearance.

Balsa wood is a good basic material to use for the main structure of buildings. It cuts easily, is light in weight, does not twist or warp and can be stuck easily with balsa cement. It can be obtained in a wide range of thickness, thereby allowing the correct depth to be given to window and door openings. As an alternative to balsa wood, card (either the normal paper-fibre type or the modern plastic or styrene sheet variety) is often acceptable, but it can bow or warp if subjected to heat or damp, especially when building papers are glued to the outside. If you prefer to use card rather than sheet balsa, I would suggest gluing a framework of bracing struts made out of balsa or hardwood strip behind the walls. The printed paper building sheets representing brick or stone can be obtained in a variety of styles and can be thoroughly recommended. An advance on these printed sheets is, however, to be found in the embossed card or moulded plastic sheets which show the individual brick or stone course in relief. These moulded plastic sheets generally require some painting since they are invariably moulded in a basic brick colour, which does not differentiate the pointing. Thus, whether you prefer these to printed paper sheets may depend upon your skill as a painter. My view is that where brickwork is concerned the relief effect is less important than accurate colouring, and I think it is no easy task to match the accurate random brick shades that some producers of the best brick papers manage to achieve.

With stone work, however, I consider the relief effect of moulded plastic, provided it can be painted reasonably well, is worth the extra expense and effort. Roofs should be given particular attention, since they are invariably the parts of the model which we see the most. For slate or tile roofs a favourite dodge is to cut out the roofing tile papers into strips and overlap each succeeding strip. This is a long and tedious process, but it is worth while if you can do it neatly and evenly and you have the time to spare. If you are in any doubt on any of these points it is probably better to leave well alone. The process can also be used to represent weather boarding on timber buildings, but the same reservation applies, and you may find it easier just to score the planks rather than build them up one by one. However, weather boarding can also be bought ready-made in moulded plastic which is probably a lot more satisfactory. Finally, when it comes to mentioning ways of representing surfaces of buildings, there are a number of methods in which a relief finish can be built by hand. Scraper board is a favourite material, since brick or stone courses can be scratched out readily from the surface. Also plaster itself can be used, or modelling clay, Plasticine, or any other fine grain material which will set firm in relatively shallow areas and which will allow you to gouge out courses between the stonework. Peco Scene texture

*Llareggub, the seaport terminus of David Rowe's 009 'Under Milk Wood', heavily inspired by Dylan Thomas and the Welsh narrow gauge railways. Llareggub town is built in a cabinet 4 ft 6 in long and 1 ft 6 in wide and is one of three such cabinets, each one portraying different aspects of the welsh narrow gauge scene. Note the beautifully executed relief stonework of the walls and buildings using a modelling compound such as Peco Scene* (Brian Monaghan).

modelling compound is particularly suitable. This is the material used by David Rowe when constructing his well-known 'Under Milkwood' layout.

Plastic card or styrene sheet is a tremendous asset to miniature building construction because it simplifies making many smaller detailed architectural features, such as foundation and corner stones, window frames, bay windows, doors and door frames, dormer windows, sills, lintels, barge boards, cornices, facias, buttresses, plinths, canopies, balconies, chimneys, steps and staircases, to name several. The advantage of plastic card is that it can be cut and cemented together so easily. It is not necessary to cut right through the material, you just score it with the tip of a craft knife blade, bend the two halves of the material either side of the score mark and the pieces will snap in two. After the light application of a brush full of liquid cement the two pieces can be joined together again in any position. The liquid cement evaporates very quickly and leaves little or no mark, unlike glue for example, which can leave a blob mark unless it is put on sparingly, when it may not have sufficient strength. To cement two pieces of plastic card together you should use tweezers to avoid undue handling of the material, because there is a danger that the liquid cement will get on to the fingers and dissolve the card, leaving an impression of the finger tip on the plastic. One particular asset of plastic card is that it is possible to cement two pieces together along their edge and, because the liquid cement dries so quickly, they can be held together long enough for them to set firm. If, after you have cemented the two pieces together, you find they are in the wrong position, a quick stroke with another brush full of liquid cement is enough to free the two parts so that they can be re-positioned and cemented together again.

Umbrella ribs have been suggested more than once for guttering, which is all right if you have a ready source of such material. However, an alternative which is probably better, at least in the smaller scales, is to use plastic rodding which can be obtained in a number of different sizes, and to flatten or scrape along one side to produce a 'U'-shaped cross-section. The fact that it is a solid 'U' will not be visible in the finished model, especially if the top part is painted black. Plastic rodding can also be used for the down pipes, which can be bent in almost any fashion by warming them between the fingers, in hot water, or over a candle flame.

In Britain, Slater's Plastikard Ltd produce a number of different materials specially made for model building construction in all gauges up to '0', and a copy of their catalogue would be an advantage to any would-be modeller. One of the firm's most ingenious products is the Grid System for constructing windows, ventilators, etc. This consists of strips of Plastikard precision cut with halved joints at regular distances which form glazing bars. These glazing bars are supplied in an amazing number of sizes which can be built up into a grid pattern to form window frames. Assembly is quick and easy with liquid cement and an almost unlimited variety of window patterns and sizes can be constructed speedily and accurately. You should try to make the window aperture fit the window frame rather than the frame the window aperture since this will reduce the number of different-size window frames and window glazing bars you will need to carry in stock. The Slater Grid System is undoubtedly better than cutting window frames from sheet material or making them from overlapping strips—or, worse still, painting or drawing the window-frames on to celluloid or acetate sheet with paint or white Indian Ink! Window frames are more effective when glazed, since the the glazing reflects the light.

If you want to hide the lack of detail inside the building you can always draw curtains across behind the window, which will also add a splash of colour and realism to the finished model. Whilst it is by no means essential to furnish the interiors of buildings, since in miniature they are so dark that nothing can be seen in normal lighting, it might be necessary to fit interior partition walls in some locations. It would spoil the effect if you were able to see right through the building from one side to the other or down from the third floor to the basement. Apart from the extra realism it will also add strength to the building if an intermediate floor and interior partition are included. The fitting of lights inside miniature buildings can add a large measure of interest to a layout, but at the same time it is necessary to provide ready access to the building interiors. This can be achieved in a number of different ways, but the most effective is to fit the roof so that it can be lifted off the sides rather than make the whole building lift off the baseboard surface. We generally look down on to a model railway and any gap that it may be necessary to leave around the edge of the roof and the walls of the building can be largely obscured by the overhanging eaves. If the whole building is removable from the baseboard it may not be possible to hide the gap around the bottom edge of the building so easily and if there is one give-away feature that detracts from the appearance of a model building more then any other it is the sight of the building standing suspended above the baseboard, albeit by only the barest fraction of a millimetre. The base lines of all buildings should be well and truly wedded to the ground on which they stand, and it is a useful aid to sprinkle some scenic dressing around the foundations to help simulate this effect as much as possible.

Apart from the painted woodwork and curtains, a welcome splash of colour can also be given to painted walls of buildings which need not always be white, cream or grey. A few stucco or plastered wall buildings can liven up and add variety to a row of houses built of brick or stone. The roughcast effect can easily be achieved by using sandpaper or glasspaper of the appropriate grade and suitably coloured. Such material is also useful for gravel or stone paths and terraces or station platforms. Station platforms are almost a subject in themselves. There appears to be an unlimited variety of styles and materials used in their construction, from the simple timber wayside halt built out of old railway sleepers to the modern pre-cast concrete structures of today. In Britain, the most common form is a brick or stone retaining wall surmounted by paving stones forming the platform edge, behind which there is a mound of earth and rubble finished with tarmac, paving stones or some other suitable surface. In many cases there is only a paved surface near the station buildings and gravel or ashes suffice elsewhere. The retaining wall can be

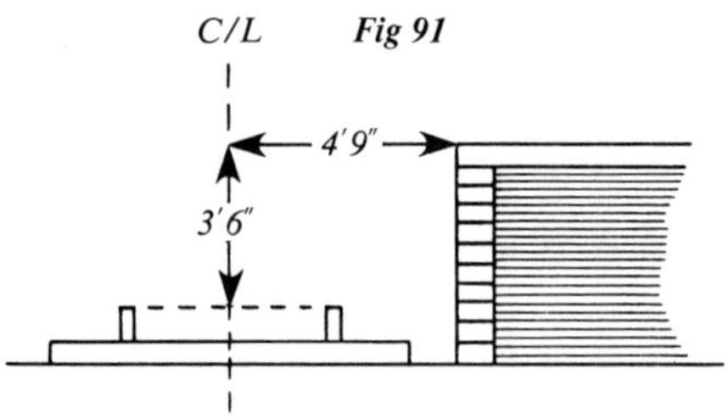


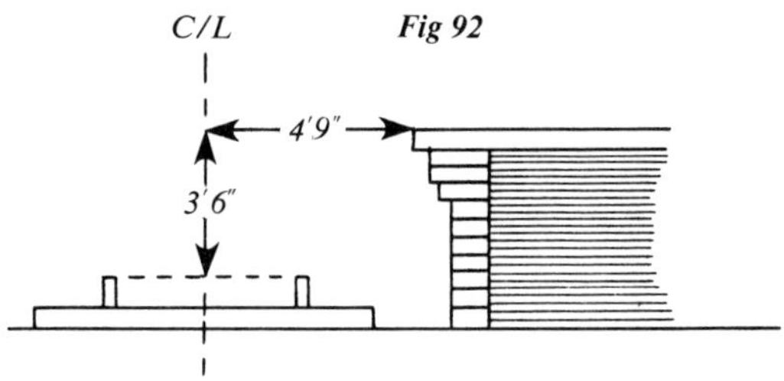


**Fig 91** *A simple brick platform wall.* **Fig 92** *A platform wall with a protruding edge.*

a simple brick one ending abruptly at the top, or else it can have one or more courses of bricks brought forward at the top to support a protuding edge, eg, as shown in figs 91 and 92.

One aspect of real railways that never ceases to amaze me is the number of huts and small buildings that you can usually see scattered around stations, station yards and goods depots, to say nothing of the main line itself. Alongside the main line they provide shelter and toolstorage for the permanent way staff and a number of them fulfil a similar function around the station and goods yards. The huts come in a variety of structures from brick-built to corrugated iron and even the familiar railway van or coach body. The railway coach body minus bogies that you find dumped along the lineside, or possibly resting on wooden or brick-built blocks, is now almost a hackneyed subject amongst scenic railway modellers. There has been at least one commercially produced model of this most scenic feature that I know of, but far less commonly seen in models is a wagon body used in the same way, whereas in real life they appear in large numbers on both sides of the railway fence. They are popular amongst farmers and many can be seen miles away from the actual railway, but still bearing signs of their former lettering and painting details.

Reverting back to railway uses, old wagons are often converted to mess wagons, either on or off their chassis, and the conversion usually takes the form of the insertion of a couple of windows and the inevitable addition of a stovepipe through the roof. For small details, such as huts and old wagon and coach bodies, etc, it is worth giving a little thought to the subject and paying attention to those you see in real life, since often a lot of small items pass unnoticed individually but collectively add up to a sense of realism. I mean such things as the use of an old enamel advertising sign to patch up a rotting body panel; an extra piece of roofing felt nailed to the roof (which can be represented by sticking on a square of tissue paper painted black); a broken window pane; a lean-to fitted at one end or side of the body to provide additional storage, perhaps for a bicycle or wheelbarrow, etc; a water tank on the roof and guttering draining into a water butt; old wooden boxes stacked at one end; and perhaps storage for firewood and boiler fuel. You can spend hours detailing mundane structures such as these and there is no end to the variety of work you can find when adding realism to scenic models.

Scenery is not only decorative, it can also perform a useful function on a model railway as an aid to illusion. We have already discussed in the chapter on layout planning the desirability of breaking up the circle effect of a continuous run layout. Tunnels built at each end of a continuous oval will not only help to conceal this they will also hide the curves, thus permitting the use of a sharper radius without offending the eye unduly. There is something fascinating about the sight of a train entering or leaving a tunnel. The tunnel mouth itself can provide scope for an interesting architectural feature, since there is so much variety in their style and method of construction. (See fig 93.) Tunnel mouths can be purchased ready made in N, HO, 00 and 0 gauges in a variety of styles, or they can be built by hand using balsa wood covered with brick or stone paper. If the tunnel is to be installed on a curve or near the entrance to a curve, do not forget to allow extra clearance for the overhang either side of the longest vehicle in your rolling stock fleet, or for the outward swing of the front buffer beam of your longest locomotive. The general construction features already described for scenery can be applied when building the rising ground between the two tunnel mouths, ie, a framework over which can be stretched a covering of some suitable material. Rarely will it be necessary to build a lining actually inside the tunnel, although you may feel it is a good idea to have one for the first few inches inside the mouth of the tunnel, especially if at that point the tunnel is in line with the viewer and clearly visible. The tunnel mouth itself can be supported with a framework of wood blocks or strips, or alternatively expanded polystyrene is a useful material to use. Blocks of expanded polystyrene can be built up to make an arch entrance to the tunnel and the tunnel mouth can be simply glued in place. Don't forget to paint some tell-tale black soot marks on the tunnel arch if you are modelling a steam railway. You can use a lighted candle to do this job, but I do not recommend it if the tunnel is made of inflammable material which it is most likely to be!

Another way in which scenery can be applied for practical purposes is to disguise the entrance to a fiddle yard or a bank of hidden storage sidings. A gap in a scenic backcloth can sometimes be used this way, as shown in fig 94. The backcloth in this instance is a row of buildings facing on to a high level road, the road being supported by a retaining wall made to represent a row of brick arches (there are ready-made proprietary models of such things). The buildings facing on to the street can, if they are normally viewed from one side, be built in low relief, that is they only have a false front to them and have no back or depth, thus reducing by at least half the space taken up. Kits for such low relief models are made and sold specially, but

**Fig 93** *Three different styles of tunnel mouth.*

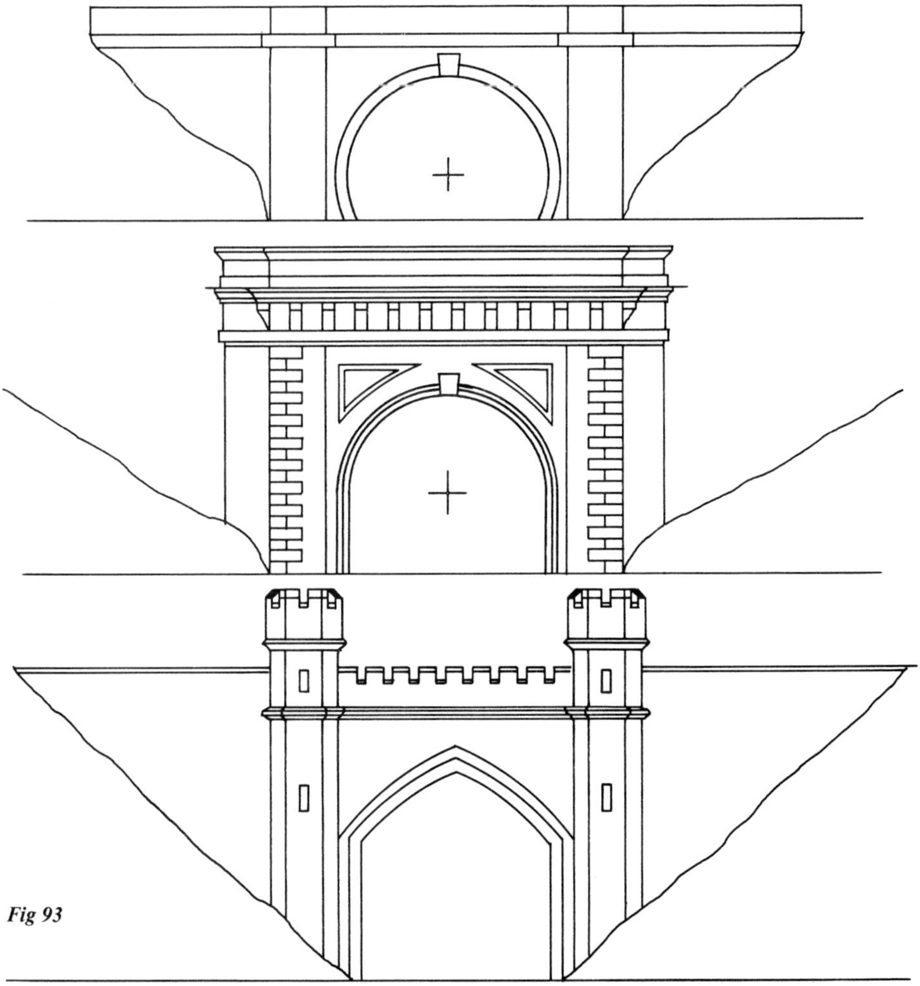

*Fig 93*

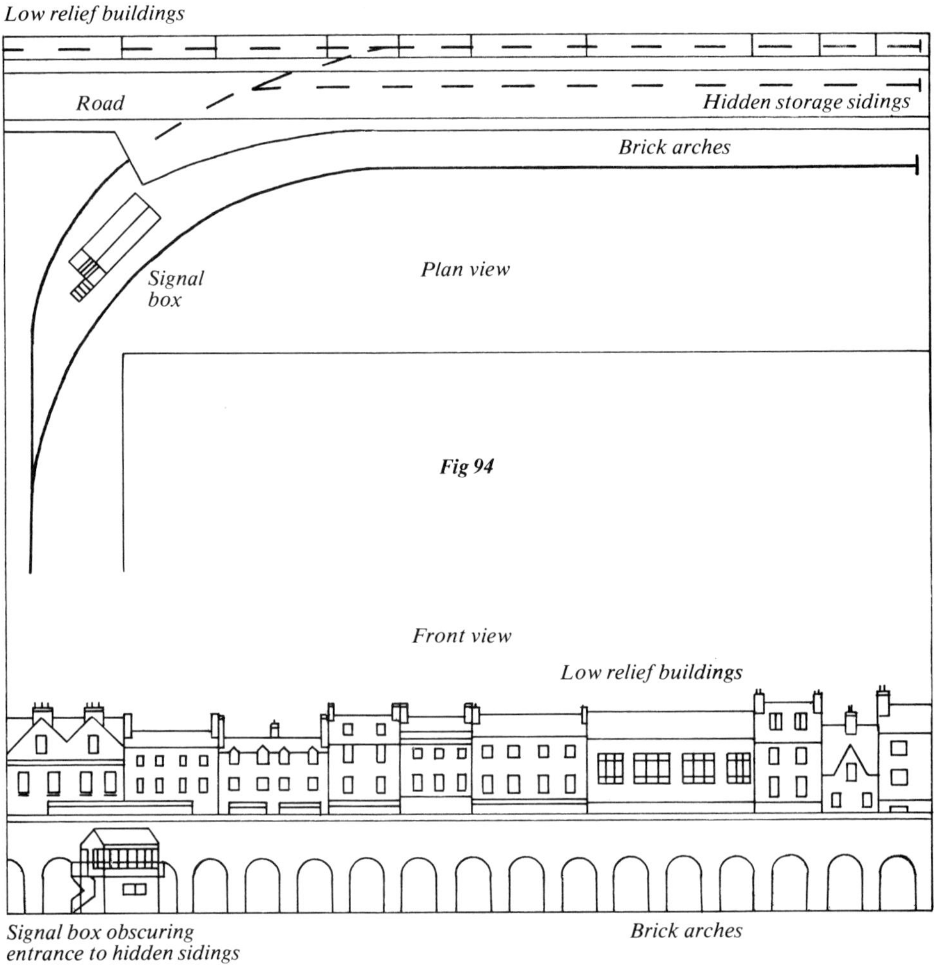


**Fig 94** *High level road and low relief buildings obscuring hidden storage sidings. The entrance is obscured by the signal box.*

alternatively you can adopt a number of ordinary kits, simply by cutting them in half, or you can make up your own. The scenic backcloth effectively becomes a tunnel and the entrance to the 'tunnel' can either be disguised as an ordinary road bridge, or else there need be no proper entrance at all, and the railway line simply disappears behind a building or a row of trees.

Scenic features can also provide operating scope for a model railway. The obvious example is, of course, the station itself which provides a focal point for the operation of the railway, from where the traffic originates. In discussing the plan for a country terminus in the chapter on layout planning, I mentioned a dairy and a petrol and oil storage depot as a source of traffic for the railway. Lineside industries such as these can make interesting scenic features in their own right. There are any number in this category that not only provide traffic for the railways, but form interesting subjects for modelling or adding scenic interest. Timber yard, iron and steel merchant, scrap merchant, stonemason, brickworks, power station, gasworks, stone crushing plant, quarry, coalmine, cement works, oil refinery, tar distillery, whisky distillery, china clay works, army depot (scope for army vehicles and tanks travelling on bogie flat and well wagons, to say nothing of squads of soldiers lined up on the nearby station platform), canal wharf, harbour (either deep sea, river estuary for coastal shipping or inland waterway), or simply a straightforward factory are just some examples of what I mean. Any one of these industries can provide traffic for the railway, and some will require special wagons, possibly privately owned and painted in attractive and colourful liveries. Also, at the same time, the industrial premises themselves can provide unlimited scope for creative modelling and for artistic expression.

There are bound to be a number of places on the model where the railway comes in close proximity to the road and road traffic, for example in station forecourts, goods yards, level crossings, road over and under bridges, and in the straightforward case of a road running alongside the railway line. In all these cases there will be an opportunity to display a collection of road vehicles, and here special care is needed to select the right vehicles in order to create an authentic atmosphere. It is regrettable that of all the hundreds, if not thousands, of miniature die-cast model cars and commercial vehicles that are mass produced as toys, but which are made to such incredible precision as to raise their status to the level of scale models, so few are built to a scale which makes them suitable for incorporation into the scenic effects of most of the popular model railway gauges. 0 and 1 gauges are perhaps the best served, but generally speaking the space required for these larger gauges leaves precious little room for scenic effects, at any rate in any large quantity, and therefore road vehicles are not so much in demand in these scales. For HO gauge Continental modellers there are a number of firms that produce a wide range of road vehicles, both mechanical and horse drawn, and these are available in Britain where in a few cases their use can pass muster on the larger British 4 mm scale 00 gauge layouts. But true scale 4 mm models have always been comparatively scarce and not all those produced in the past are still currently available. For instance, Dinky Toys produced a few cars before World War 2 that were suitable for 00 gauge and at one time hardly a layout was complete without one or more of them, together with at least one example of their fine double deck bus. Despite the fact that the bus was modelled on a London Transport STL type, which was practically unheard of outside London, the model looked good repainted in other liveries and served its purpose in providing suitable passenger road transport on many a model layout based on country and provincial practice. Alas, this model is not available today, unless you can track down a secondhand example, and the cars that were also supplied are very difficult to obtain even secondhand.

It can be quite entertaining trying to find past or present die-cast models that may be suitable for use in a model railway scenic setting. A few of the Lesney Matchbox models are produced to something near recognisable model railway scales, but this prolific supplier produces the vast majority of its models in a size which will fit its own Matchbox covers rather than to a scale which will suit railway modellers. Most of the best models near to 00 gauge have now, in fact, been withdrawn and some of these are being offered at very high prices on the secondhand market.

Therefore, so far as 4 mm scale road vehicles are concerned, there is not a very large or representative collection of ready-made models from which to choose. Luckily, commercial vehicles such as buses and lorries are perfectly practical models to make. They can be scratch-built from simple materials like card (the paper type or plastic card and styrene sheet) and wood, and only the wheels need to be obtained commercially. Special wheels for lorries and buses can either be bought ready made or they can sometimes be modified from other kits. Generally speaking, older vehicles, such as those built during the 1930s, 1940s and early 1950s, are easier to make than the more modern ones, since the later vehicles contain a large amount of body pressings with multiple curves and, even worse, they invariably include multiple-curve windscreens and windows. Even these features do not rule out home construction entirely, but they do make the job that little more difficult, since the glazing material has to be specially moulded to help create the shape of the original, whereas bodywork with flat plain glass windows is so much easier to model.

Windows are one of the biggest difficulties with model cars because in 4 mm scale they are rather small and difficult to glaze individually using flat strips of clear styrene sheet. It is possibly best to mould the entire top half of the bodywork out of perspex and simply paint on the roof and window pillars, or even carve the bodywork out of wood and just paint the windows on. On the other hand, buses and lorries with predominantly flat sides are relatively simple to make using two sheets of card for each side with the windows cut out and a strip of glazing material sandwiched in between. Each of the three layers of material forming one side should be cut progressively shorter at the corner ends so that they form steps which will fit into each other when two side panels are placed

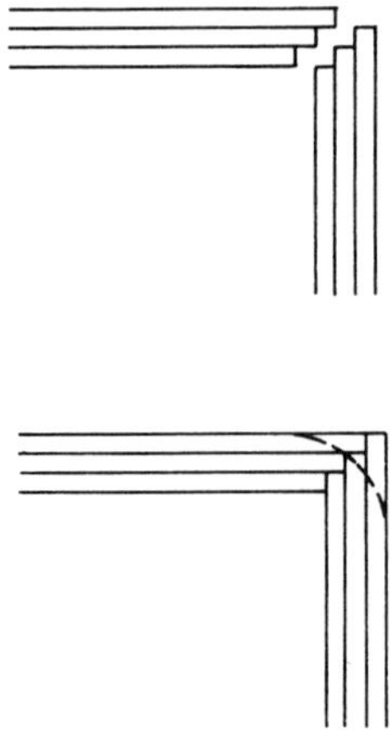

*Fig 95*

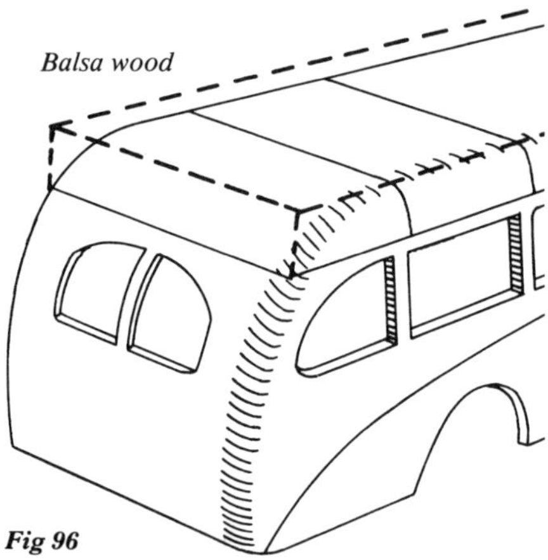


*Fig 96*

**Fig 95** *Stepped balsa wood corners are strong and easily rounded.* **Fig 96** *A square piece of balsa is ideal material for a bus roof.*

**Above right** *Dennis E type with Dixon body built for West Bromwich Corporation in 1929 as modelled from a Cotswold 4 mm scale cast metal kit* (Sutherland Model Casters Ltd).

**Right** *Three types of Leyland buses from the Anbrico range of 4 mm scale bus kits* (Anbrico Scale Models).

**Below right** *Steam road locomotives such as this model constructed from a 4 mm scale W&T cast white metal kit were to be seen hauling heavy loads on the roads of Britain in the 1920s and 30s. It was not unknown for them to be seen shunting railway wagons* (W&T).

together at the corners (see fig 95). Not only will this give added strength to the corners, it will also provide a sufficient depth of material at the corner to enable it to be rounded in prototype fashion, using at first a craft knife, followed by a file and sandpaper to smooth the surface. On a bus, the rear dome is usually the part of the bodywork with the most curves and a smooth gentle curvature at this point can often be obtained by using a block of balsa wood for the roof which can be made to smooth into the sides and rear panel. (See fig 96.)

The importance of road vehicles has now been fully appreciated by the trade and there are a growing number of kits available in N and 00 gauges covering horse drawn vehicles, traction engines and steam lorries as well as cars, lorries and buses. A few of them are in plastic but the majority are cast white metal. Bus models predominate due in part to the hobby of bus modelling which is a recognised branch of model making in its own right but it has a very welcome spin off for railway modellers. In catering for the needs of bus modellers Mabex Products who produce a commendably wide range of water slide transfers of bus fleet names, destination blinds, bus stop signs and advertisements, also assist the railway modeller. The bus modelling fraternity appear to go in more for the post-war or modern day prototypes which form the majority of bus model kits.

This is, of course, no disadvantage to the railway modeller modelling the contemporary railway scene but one of the most popular periods for railway modelling is the late 1930s when the big-four railway companies were at the height of their existence. There does appear to be a tendancy with some model railway layouts based on this period to include vintage and veteran cars and an over-abundance of steam vehicles more reminiscent of pre-World War 1 rather than pre-World War 2. It is important to get the right model when selecting road vehicles and to ensure that you have a type appropriate to the period you are modelling. To come back to the 1930s and knowing that not everyone can remember them; horse drawn vehicles especially railway owned ones, were abundant at that time and there is no shortage of kits for these.

Despite the predominance of modern day bus kits there are sufficient bus model kits covering the 1930s to suit most people's needs. Cars are more of a problem. Although there are some very nice kits available they can become an expensive item when you take into consideration the numbers you need.

WEST BROMWICH CORPORATION

HF 4109

ROWLAND MINIATURES

*The BR Scarab mechanical horse and trailer constructed from a 4 mm scale Eckon plastic kit* (CCH Models).

Whereas buses come in ones and twos, cars even in the 1930s, came in dozens and a representative street scene in 4 mm scale could cost in kits nearly as much as half the price of a brand new car in 1939. The toy market which is the only hope for a cheap source of lineside road vehicle pays little attention to the popular saloon cars of the 1930s which were the main inhabitants of the streets and station forecourts at the time, and in fact went on doing so well into the 1940s and 1950s.

Some of the manufacturers of die-cast miniature road vehicles produce lorries suitable for model railway use and other sources of supply are the softskin military vehicle kits by Airfix and Matchbox, either built as intended or converted for civilian use. Mention must be made of the never to be forgotten Scammell mechanical horse and trailer. Most model railways portraying the 1930s onwards can justify one or more of these. The post-war BR Scarab version is illustrated above. There is, however, a die-cast metal kit available from Langley Miniature Models which represents the earlier type of mechanical horse so widely used by the big four railway companies as well as British Railways and which is therefore of greater potential use, since it can be incorporated in pre-war as well as post-nationalisation layouts.

Trams also have a great following and they can form an excellent scenic feature on a model railway, with the added advantage of being working models. Several cast metal kits are available in 4 mm scale, together with a number of accessories. There is also the Continental firm of Eheim which makes working model trams and trolley buses down to as small a scale as N. A number of working roadway systems can also be incorporated in a model railway layout although I have never been particularly impressed with the realism or practicality of any I have seen. There are some working scenic models that can form arresting scenic features. The Continentals are great ones for scenic attractions such as working cable railways, working windmills, waterfalls that are operated by a concealed electric pump, chiming church bells, flashing neon signs and various other ideas which add rather more novelty than realism to a scenic setting. Nevertheless, they are still desirable provided they are not overdone or obviously installed just for effect's sake.

One branch of the commercial modelling world which provides poor service to railway modellers is that concerned with shipping, since there are so very few ship models, either ready made or in a kit form, which are to a scale suitable for incorporation as a scenic addition to the most popular scale model railways. Yet a harbour can provide a most attractive and practical scenic feature on a model layout. The majority of ship kits seem to be galleons, liners or battleships, which are either of the wrong scale or the wrong vintage for a model railway. What would be most desirable for an 00 gauge layout would be a nice 4 mm scale model of a typical 300-ton coastal cargo vessel, the sort that sails up river estuaries to take on loads at small docks all over the country and also many other parts of the world. Apart from being a scenic addition, such a ship would also be an excellent model to make in its own right and the techniques of plastic kit manufacture would appear to be ideally suited to producing the usual deck trappings, winches, derricks, lifeboats, dinghies and other nautical paraphernalia which usually accompany such vessels.

In the absence of almost any suitable kits,

you have to be prepared to scratch build if you want to add a boat or boats to a harbour setting, but thankfully this is not such a difficult task and is one that can give a lot of pleasure. Balsa wood or ordinary hardwood is perhaps the best material to use for the hull, the plastic card can be used to build up the superstructure and deck fittings. The model itself can be a long-term project that can be fitted in as and when time permits and can be regarded as a kind of relaxation when something other than model railways is required. There are many more types of suitable ships and boats other than 300-ton coastal cargo vessels that would look equally at home in a harbour setting alongside a model railway. However, it is a good idea to select a vessel which will provide an excuse for operating traffic to and from the harbour, thereby justifying the construction of the harbour branch and the running of trains to and from the quay. For example, you could operate a passenger ferry service and run trains on to the quay, such as is done at Weymouth for the Channel Islands service or at Ryde Pier Head on the Isle of Wight. However, most of these models demand more space than can usually be spared in the majority of scales, but they might make ideal subjects for N gauge. Coming down to a much smaller size, canals form a very interesting scenic subject for a model railway and almost any space can be utilised for adding at least one canal feature. Locks and lock gates are perhaps the most noteworthy features of such systems, which can be easily fitted into either the corner of a layout or else across the width of a baseboard, where the railway line can perhaps cross the canal on a bridge similar to the one shown in fig 90. Langley Miniature Models supply kits in N and 00 gauges for modelling canal scenes.

Lastly, on the subject of scenery, we come to the animal kingdom—farmyard animals and, most important of all, human beings. Luckily there is no shortage of material here in almost any scale. The Continental manufacturers look after their own scales of N and HO very well. For British N gauge Peco have their 'Petite People'. 00 gauge is well catered for by the wide range of Airfix figures which are unpainted and are therefore commendably cheap. John Piper, Merit and Slater's

*Good use has been made of Slater's Huminiatures in this attractive 4 mm scale station scene. Note also the horse drawn parcels van in the station yard. The buildings have been assembled from Prototype Model kits and the LMS brake van and NE hopper wagon from Slater's wagon kits* (Slater's Plastikard Ltd).

Huminiatures also offer a good selection; the latter can also be bought for 0 gauge. 1 gauge modellers can make use of the wide range of Britains' models, which include a number of farmyard items ideal for a model railway. Some modellers are particularly adept at miniature figure conversion. This is easily enough done with plastic figures, since it is possible to cut them in half and fit the top half of one figure to the lower half of another, thereby changing its shape in as many ways as you like. Similarly, running figures can be converted to standing figures and standing to sitting figures, or any other combination you want. Simple conversions, either by the use of the craft knife or the paint brush, can also be done to alter dress and uniforms to make, for example, soldiers into ticket collectors. To add variety to your layout don't just take your figures at face value, but see what you can do to alter their pose, shape or dress, to represent a variety of figures not covered by the normal range of commercially produced models.

Farmyard animals used as scenic features in lineside fields can often be adapted in the same way. Horses can always be hitched up to horse-drawn vehicles, and there are a number of kits that are sold principally for their military interest but which can be adapted or converted to a civil function appropriate to a model railway setting. The Airfix American Civil War Artillery or Royal Horse Artillery sets, for example, contain horses, guns and limbers which provide excellent material for making a horse-drawn delivery van or farm wagon. With human figures, which normally stand on a heavy base, it is desirable to remove as much of the base material, all of it if you can, to improve the appearance of the figure. Then you can either glue the figure in position to keep it upright or you can cut a groove along the inside of one of the legs into which can be cemented a small length of pin, leaving the pointed end to project out of the sole of the foot. The pin can then be pushed into the baseboard and will be sufficient to hold the figure up, but at the same time will allow it to be moved whenever you want to. Another alternative which can be used is to cut out depressions in the baseboard, platform or pavement where the figure is to stand so that the top of the base is level with the floor. One particular point to watch is to ensure that there are no flash or moulding marks on the figure. In other words, it should be given a good clean up with a craft knife blade so that all traces of its moulded-plastic origin are removed.

The smaller scenic features, such as human figures, milk churns, platform barrows, luggage on platforms, street furniture (eg, lamp-posts, pillar boxes, telephone kiosks, sand bins, fire buckets, posters, hoardings, notice boards, etc) are the sort of things that can always be added to a model railway layout at any time, as and when funds and time permit. In actual fact they cost very little individually, but collectively they could amount to a considerable sum, if only because there are so many of these features that you can add to a layout. This is perhaps one of the attractions of a model railway—it is never really finished. However complete the layout may become there is always somewhere where a little added detail can be attended to. The commercial model railway trade is bringing out new accessories all the time and new ideas are always being discussed in the model railway magazines which give you inspiration to alter or make additions to your layout. One small enterprising firm brought out a range of 4 mm scale model birds in different shapes and sizes, some with wings outstretched and others perched as on fences or roof tops. It is quite amazing the amount of extra realism these models give to a scenic setting, yet how often do you see features such as these modelled? After the main expense of equipping the layout has been completed, small details like this can always be added to make a valuable contribution to the overall effect of the layout.

*Cement mixing and road mending plant and figures in N gauge* (Fleetline Model Co).

## Chapter 9

# Locomotives

Of all the many different and separate items that go to make up a complete model railway the one that probably has the greatest universal appeal is the motive power—the locomotives, whether they be steam, diesel or electric, that haul the trains. There are exceptions, of course, and for example there are some people who specialise in railway signalling, electronic control, architecture or a scenic landscape setting who may pay scant regard to the locomotives and the rest of the rolling stock. However, the majority of us build our model railways so that we have somewhere on which to run our locomotives and their carriages and wagons.

It is important not to lose sight of the fact that most locomotives were built for a purpose. Some cynics may argue that certain classes of locomotives were built just to satisfy the vain glory of a particular locomotive engineer. There are certainly cases where there seems little justification for the introduction of an entirely new class of locomotive, and an existing and, on the face of it, perfectly adequate design appears not to have been persevered with because of a personality change in the locomotive design office. But this is not by any means true in all cases and there are probably more examples of locomotive engineers perpetuating the designs of their predecessors than there are the other way round. Consider, for example, the continued construction of the Great Western Railway 'Castle' Class from 1923 when the first was built until the last one which was constructed as late as 1950. The building period of 28 years not only covered the reign of two Great Western Railway Company locomotive engineers but also the transition into the Western Region of British Railways. On British Railways the classic example of longevity of a locomotive design is the J72 Class of 0-6-0T designed originally by Wilson Worsdell for the North Eastern Railway in 1898. Seventy-five were built by the NER before the grouping, another ten were built by the LNER after grouping and a further 28 were made by British Railways after nationalisation. The final eight locomotives were built in 1951, 53 years after the construction of the first J72 in 1898.

The design of a locomotive is influenced in a great number of different ways. The weight and speed of the train, the length of run, the ruling gradient, the curvature of the track, the condition of the permanent way and the civil engineering structures are probably the most important factors. This is, of course, ignoring the all-important aspect of power source; steam (coal, oil fired or wood burning), diesel (electric, hydraulic or mechanical transmission) or electric (overhead, third rail or battery) to name some of the most important types. A steam locomotive carries its own source of power, namely the boiler, and a heavy long-distance train will of course demand a big locomotive with a large boiler to provide a plentiful supply of steam. A heavy but relatively slow-moving freight train will need maximum power for starting and for plodding up the gradients which, with a steam locomotive, can best be met by a larger number of relatively small diameter coupled wheels. On the other hand, the requirements for a high-speed passenger train steam locomotive are best met by large diameter driving wheels.

Since it is necessary to keep the weight of high-speed reciprocating and moving parts down to easily manageable proportions, and because it is necessary for the rigid part of the locomotive chassis to pass round curves with ease, the number of coupled wheels on express passenger locomotives has to be kept within limits—more often six but, rather exceptionally, eight in number. With the most powerful locomotives, poorer quality coal will demand a larger and wider firebox which, because it cannot be contained within the space between the frames and the coupled wheels, will invariably require the added support of a trailing pony truck or bogie. Leading bogies or pony trucks are required at the front end to spread the weight of the locomotive over as many axles as possible, to keep the individual axle weight down and also to guide the locomotive into curves at speed. This is why the majority of latter day large

**Top** *The long established Wills Finecast range of cast metal kits now includes this fine model of the GWR 'Castle' Class. The kit is supplied with either the small 3,500 gallon tender (as shown here) or the later 4,000 gallon tender. Interior cab details are included together with alternative front ends, chimneys etc, covering most of the modifications made to the prototype over the long years of its existence. The etched nickel-silver chassis has brake gear even for the bogies which were fitted for a short time when the class was first introduced* (Wills Finecast).

**Above** *Mainline Railways' 00 gauge model of the LNER J72 0-6-0T shown here in the early BR livery.*

high-speed passenger steam locomotives tended to have the 4-6-2 wheel arrangement. In contrast, heavy goods engines were invariably of the 2-8-0 or 2-10-0 type and their smaller diameter coupled wheels allowed them to carry boilers with large fireboxes without the necessity for trailing pony or bogie carrying wheels. A short-range medium- or lightweight goods engine can be built on an 0-6-0 chassis. If the range of operation is limited to short transfer goods, branch line or shunting duties, sufficient water for the boiler and coal for the firebox need not be carried in a separate tender but can be accommodated on the locomotive chassis in tanks alongside the boiler and a bunker behind the cab. A locomotive intended for very sharp radius curves will, however, need to have the rigid wheelbase as short as possible. This is why many dockyard, colliery or factory shunting locomotives have only four coupled wheels or, if they have six, why they are close coupled.

With most locomotives the reason for their particular shape, style or design becomes obvious once the subject is given some thought. It is certainly no accident or personal whim on the part of the designer that some classes of locomotives had more or less wheels than others, larger or smaller boilers, tenders or side tanks, or the many other distinguishing features which make one type of locomotive different from another. They were designed for a particular purpose and the design that was ultimately evolved was considered to be the most suitable for that purpose. It follows, therefore, that if we want to make our model railway as authentic as possible we have to consider the same factors when we choose a model locomotive for our layout. If we have the space to run heavy main line express passenger trains or long haul mineral or goods trains we can justify having a fleet of large 4-6-0, 4-6-2, 2-8-0 or 2-10-0 tender engines. If, on the other hand, our layout is restricted by the space available and we have to run lighter, smaller trains, we may have to limit our stud of locomotives to smaller 4-6-0, 4-4-0 and 0-6-0 tender engines, or the even more compact tank locomotives of possibly 2-6-4T, 2-6-2T or 0-6-0T designs.

There are, of course, exceptions to these guide lines as there are with most rules. For instance, immediately after World War 2 the Southern Railway started a big engine policy and built a fleet of 4-6-2 locomotives that were designed to operate both heavy main line passenger trains as well as relatively lightly loaded feeder services in the remoter outposts of the Southern Railway system in the West Country. For someone who likes Pacific type locomotives but does not have the space for a large layout this is a golden opportunity to have the best of both worlds since you can build a small country branch line and still operate large locomotives. This is also an illustration of applying knowledge of actual railway operation and drawing from authentic locations and authentic railway practice. If you search hard enough you will most likely find an example of almost anything for which you are looking.

If, as I strongly recommend, you are modelling your railway to represent a particular company or a certain period in time then, if you are to retain an air of authenticity, your choice of locomotives should be further restricted to the types of classes that are representative of that company or could reasonably be expected to be seen in service during the period or in the geographical location you have selected to model. I have already mentioned in Chapter 3 some of the many varieties or types of model railway you can build. The fact that there are so many accounts for the commendably wide range of ready-to-run model railway locomotives that are currently available. Yet, despite this, there is still a persistent clamour for more and it is not difficult to understand this when you consider the tremendour number of different locomotive designs and classes there have been in the past and still exist in one way or another today. Many attempts at standardisation and rationalisation have been made by locomotive designers to limit or reduce the number of classes. The trouble with standardisation is that every locomotive designer has his own idea of what should be a standard

*This diminutive Avonside 0-4-0ST made from a Centre Models 4 mm scale cast metal kit demonstrates the extremely short wheelbase of some industrial locomotives.*

**Top** *410 of the LNER B1 Class 4-6-0's were built between 1942 and 1952. This well finished 4 mm scale model was constructed from a Nu-Cast cast metal kit* (Nu-Cast Model Engineering).

**Above** *The Graham Farish N gauge Black 5 in BR lined black livery* (Model loaned by Barlow's).

class. When a change of leadership, ownership or organisation takes place a new set of standard designs emerges. We thus had the picture in England in the 1930s and early '40s of the four main groups, the GWR, LMS, LNER and SR, each attempting to rationalise their stock of locomotives obtained at the grouping and trying to establish a range of standard designs which, when the companies were nationalised to become British Railways, were added to by yet another set of standard designs. Even more variety of motive power came when the diesel locomotives began to emerge in the late 1950s.

It is absolutely impossible for one manufacturer to keep abreast of all developments such as these. Model locomotives are expensive things to produce and the cost of tooling, making moulds and dies, etc, can run into several thousand pounds. All the manufacturers can hope to do is to produce a range of models which, as far as can be judged, will be popular amongst the majority of people and which possibly has been requested by customers. Even so, there have been some surprising choices of prototypes and one wonders what thought processes have been responsible for some of them. Some locomotives have more visual appeal than others. Some for reasons unconnected with the hobby attract widescale publicity. The 'Flying Scotsman' is a case in point. Who amongst the general public had not heard of this locomotive? Other locomotives that perhaps are potentially more useful for the railway modeller because they are, or were, to be found all over the railway system and thus can be used on a variety of different duties, are slow to attract the manufacturers' eye. Perhaps the most ubiquitous locomotive ever to run on Britain's railways was the LMS 'Black 5' 4-6-0. No less than 842 engines of this handsome class were built over a period of 16 years from 1934 and they could be seen anywhere on the LMS system, stretching from Wick in Scotland to Bournemouth on the South Coast, on all kinds of duties, passenger as well as freight. As a further incentive for its choice as a model the class had a lifespan covering both pre- and post-nationalisation periods, right up to the very last days of steam on BR in 1967, and no less than 15 locomotives from the class are currently preserved. It was 1973 before a ready-to-run model of one of these locomotives became available in 00 gauge and 1978 before an N gauge version was introduced.

Another oddity, or so it appears to me, is the ex-South Eastern Railway R1 Class, which was selected by Hornby-Dublo as the basis for their model 0-6-0T. Only 13 of these R1 locomotives were ever built and in actual fact there were detailed modifications to the class affecting their appearance which reduced to six the number of actual engines identical with the Hornby-Dublo model. Consequently this class of locomotive was not a very common sight on the Southern Railway, likewise the ex-London Brighton and South Coast Railway E2 0-6-0T, which has been faithfully modelled by Hornby Railways, but was nonetheless a comparatively rare Southern Railway class. Only ten of these locomotives were ever built and there are detailed modifications on this class which reduce the number of engines comparable with the model to five. Furthermore, they were not successful when tried on passenger trains and they spent their time mostly on shunting or short trip freight workings. Not an engine likely to be in great demand by Southern Railways modellers as grateful as they may be for any consideration by manufacturers in this most neglected of railway companies.

I always feel that a railway modeller should have a balanced stud of locomotives which is representative of the company or region which he is modelling. By balanced stud I mean a collection of models of different classes which could commonly be found at the majority of locomotive sheds of the company you have chosen to follow. Normally speaking a balanced stud is likely to include representatives of the large classes, ie, those which were built in the largest numbers. Some railway companies are easier to cater for in this respect than others. The GWR for example, through its policy of standardisation, had comparatively few basic classes of locomotives but each class was built in large numbers and could be found in most parts of

**Below and bottom** *It needs a close-up picture to show the detail in Mainline Railways' GWR Collett Goods, here shown in BR lined black livery.*

**Top** *Mainline Railways 00 gauge model of one of the original parallel boilered 'Royal Scot' Class – 4-6-0's No 6127 'Old Contemptible'* (Mainline Railways).

**Above** *There are relatively few ready-to-run Southern Railway locomotives but the Hornby Railways 'Schools' Class No 928 'Stowe' is a welcome addition to the ranks* (Hornby Railways).

the system. By combining the products of Hornby Railways: 'King', 'Hall', 'County' 4-4-0, 2721 and 8750 Pannier Tanks; Airfix: 'Castle', 61XX Prairie Tank, Dean Goods 0-6-0 and 14XX 0-4-2T; Lima: 'King', 4575 Prairie Tank, 94XX Pannier Tank, Diesel Railcar and Parcels Car; Mainline Railways: 'Manor', 43XX Mogul, Collett Goods 0-6-0 and 57XX Pannier Tank; and Wrenn: 'Castle', the 00 gauge GWR modeller can build up a balanced stud of GWR locomotives to suit almost any region of the GWR system he wishes to model. The GWR, always popular amongst railway enthusiasts, is amply catered for.

On the other hand the Southern Railway enthusiast is not so well served. There are the R1 and E2 0-6-0Ts I spoke of earlier and the Hornby Railways 'Schools' and 'Battle of Britain' but the Southern Railway enthusiast still has a fair way to go to build up a balanced stud with just these four locomotives. To a certain extent one can understand the dilemma of manufacturers when faced with the multitudinous classes that made up the Southern Railway. Many of the classes were small in numbers and had a limited regional distribution over the system. There is however one class I can think of which ranged wide from Kent to Cornwall and numbered 80 locomotives in the class and that is the N Class Maunsell Mogul but it probably lacks the visual appeal I spoke of earlier.

The LNER is another difficult railway for manufacturers to cater for. In many ways it is similar to the Southern Railway since it also has strong regional tendencies. Large numbers of locomotives from the constituent railway companies continued to be built after the grouping and it was very late in the life of the company before it embarked on a measure of standardisation like the GWR and LMS. In 00 gauge there is no shortage of express passenger locomotives with no less than three manufacturers producing an A4 Pacific: Wrenn, Hornby Railways and Liliput and two producing a 'Flying Scotsman': Hornby Railways and Liliput. For the middle range of mixed traffic and passenger locomotives Lima have announced a V2 'Green Arrow' and from Hornby Railways there is the B17/4 4-6-0 and D49/1 'Shire' 4-4-0. At the bottom end of the scale is the Airfix N2 0-6-2T, and three 0-6-0Ts: J52, J50 and J72 by Hornby Railways, Lima and Mainline Railways respectively. Noticeable absentees are heavy goods and 0-6-0s which were very much in evidence on the LNER as they were with most

**Top** *Lima's 00 gauge model of No 50043 'Eagle', shown here in the latest BR livery, is bound to be popular with the many Class 50 fans* (Lima).

**Above** *Despite the fact that BR have withdrawn all their 'Westerns' the class has a tremendous following amongst diesel enthusiasts and seven of the class are preserved. This Hornby Railways 00 gauge model of 'Western Courier' is bound to be a popular model* (Hornby Railways).

pre-grouping railway companies. Not quite a balanced stud for the LNER.

To complete this summary of pre-grouping railway companies in 00 gauge and to turn attention to the LMS, this company is much better served. At the top end we have two 'Duchesses': Wrenn and Hornby Railways; two Rebuilt Scots: Airfix and Mainline Railways; two unrebuilt Scots: Mainline Railways and Wrenn; a 'Jubilee' from Mainline Railways; an unrebuilt 'Patriot', 'Black 5', Compound 4-4-0 and Fowler 2-6-4T from Hornby Railways; an 8F 2-8-0 from Wrenn; a 'Crab' 2-6-0 from Lima; a 4F 0-6-0 from Airfix; the well loved 'Jinty' 0-6-0T from Hornby Railways; and a Caledonian Railway 0-4-0 Saddle Tank from Hornby Railways. A very well balanced stud from which the majority of LMS enthusiasts can find enough ready to run motive power to operate a representative 00 gauge layout covering most regions of the system and all types of traffic.

The post-dieselisation era is very well covered and most modern diesel locomotives and even those diesel classes now extinct are well represented in 00 gauge by combining the products of all the manufacturers. Airfix: Class 31; Hornby Railways: Classes 25, 29, 35, 37, 47, 52 and Classes 253 and 370, the High Speed and Advanced Passenger Trains; Jouef: Class 40; Lima: Classes 09, 33, 42/43, 50, 52, 55 and the Pressed Steel Class 117/2 DMU; Mainline Railways: Classes 42/43 and 45; and Wrenn: Classes 08 and 20. Electric locomotives of the type built for the West Coast main line electrification from Euston to Glasgow are represented by the Class 83 from Liliput, Class 86/2 from Hornby Railways and Class 87 from Lima.

I hope I have shown that, whereas one manufacturer on his own may not be able to build up an entirely representative collection of models the 00 gauge modeller in Britain today can build up a varied stud of locomotives covering most of the popular periods and companies (SR and possibly LNER excepted) in a way that he has never been able to achieve or even dream about before. The added marvel is that all the models are compatible in respect of couplings and wheel and track standards, so that they can all run on one and the same layout together. Furthermore, the universal standards set by manufacturers in their attention to detail, accuracy of outline, paint finish and faithful reproduction of

*Hornby Railways excellent model of Class 86 No 86219* Phoenix *is representative of the electric locomotives used on BR's West Coast main line from Euston to Glasgow* (Hornby Railways).

liveries, which have reached such heights of perfection, ensures that no one manufacturer's product looks out of place alongside another. There has been such an improvement in the quality and authenticity of ready-to-run models in recent years that it is to be hoped that any vestiges of compromise that were once considered to be necessary in the early days of model railways are gone forever, now it has been shown that these departures from scale which always were of doubtful necessity, can no longer be tolerated by the discerning modeller.

The main European manufacturers catering for the needs of Continental model railway enthusiasts generally show an awareness for a balanced stud of locomotives in the wide variety of models they produce. To a certain extent the problem has been simplified by the fact that most of the Continental railways were nationalised many years before their British counterparts, thereby achieving a greater degree of standardisation of locomotive classes. Fewer classes of prototype locomotives make it easier for the model manufacturers to cater for majority tastes. Also the fewer the classes the larger they become, thereby giving each type of locomotive a wider distribution. In Germany, for example, the standard DB class 38 (ex-Prussian P8) 4-6-0 dates back to 1906, whereas in Britain the BR standard 4-6-0s did not appear until 1951. Close to 3,800 locomotives of the DB class 38 4-6-0s were built. Other large German classes include the ex-Prussian G8 0-8-0 which numbered approximately 5,000 and the World War 2 austerity class 52 2-10-0s of which more than 8,000 were built. These massive production totals cannot be matched by any British locomotive class, where quantities of 800 are considered to be high. It follows that the larger the number of locomotives produced in any one class the more common it becomes and the fewer different classes that result makes it much easier for model railway manufacturers to cover the needs of enthusiasts for a balanced stud of locomotives.

By combining the products of Piko, Roco, Fleischmann, Liliput, Marklin, Rivarossi and Trix it is possible in HO gauge to build up a comprehensive stud of German ready-to-run locomotive models. Even in N gauge, German locomotives are well represented, with several different Pacific designs, 2-10-0, 4-6-0, 2-6-2, 2-6-0 and a host of different tank engine classes to choose from, to say nothing of diesel and electric locomotives and railcars. Arnold Rapido, Minitrix and Atlas are responsible for most of these. The principal manufacturer of French locomotives in HO scale is Jouef but other suppliers include France Trains, Fulgurex, Lima, Metropolitan sa, Roco and Rivarossi. K's also produce cast-metal kits of French locomotives. Also in HO, the Italian firms Lima and Rivarossi produce a comprehensive range of Italian locomotives and the Austrian firms Kleinbahn, Liliput and Roco include a representative selection of Austrian locomotives in their international ranges. Swiss locomotive models (some steam outline as well as electric) feature in the catalogues of most European manufacturers including Hag which originates from Switzerland. To complete the Continental picture, several manufacturers include Belgian, Dutch and Swedish locomotives in their ranges and there are just a few Norwegian, Portuguese and Spanish locomotives available. One factor which assists manufacturers catering for Continental modellers is that large numbers of German locomotives were used as reparations after World Wars 1 and 2 and were absorbed into the stock of other railways, such as the French, Belgian and Austrian. In fact, at some time or another, German locomotives could be seen over practically all the standard gauge lines in Europe.

In America the situation is potentially not so easy as far as steam locomotives are concerned since there were many railway companies which built their own individual designs. Even so, it was the practice of a number of other railroads to buy their locomotives from builders who offered a range of 'standard' designs. This practice has become even more noticeable with the advent of diesel locomotives, and in many cases it is only the livery that distinguishes one railroad company's locomotive from another. Many European and Japanese manufacturers produce ready-to-run models of American prototype locomotives—both steam and diesel—and consequently it is possible, by combining the products of several different manufacturers from within the USA itself, as well as from Japan and Europe, to assemble a comprehensive and representative stud of locomotives for practically any major American railroad. Expense is probably the only limiting factor, since although some of these models (eg, Tyco, Rivarossi and Pocher in HO gauge and Arnold, Minitrix and Atlas in N gauge) are no dearer than accepted British and European products, some of the limited-run Japanese built brass models available from specialist stockists in Britain cost, even in HO scale, anything up to £500 each, depending on the length of the production run and the size and complexity of the model! Prices of between £100 and £300 are perhaps nearer the average. The quality of these models, however, matches the price and they have become collector's items to many people who purchase them for display on the mantle shelf rather than for their intended use as working models.

So far as British protoype railways are concerned, although it is possible to build up a balanced stud of locomotives from ready-to-run products, there are some railway companies not so well blessed or there are some regional locations within the best served companies where it is necessary to resort to constructing your own model to fill in one or more gaps in the stock list. Resort is probably the wrong word to use, however, since we do not make our own model locomotives simply because we need to. The majority of railway modellers also *enjoy* making them.

For many years the traditional method of

*The Marklin Gauge 1 range includes this well proportioned 4-6-0 ex-Prussian P8 Class (DB Class 38). It is available with smoke generator and simulated sound and when seen in action belies the fact that it is electrically operated* (Marklin).

building model locomotives was to use tinplate, brass or nickel-silver sheet cut, bent and soldered together. For many people this is still the preferred method, but the higher standards of the art demand a fairly fine degree of skill and patience which not all of us possess in sufficient quantities. Fortunately, many of the specialist model railway firms have come to our aid with a range of locomotive kits which today is truly outstanding. Their numbers are continually being expanded and new firms are entering the field to widen the choice of models even further. Appendix 5 gives a list of representative classes of locomotive from the pre-nationalised railway companies and British Railways, showing what ready-to-run models and/or kits are available in the popular N, TT, 00 and 0 gauges. It will be seen that, in the most popular 00 gauge at least, the kit manufacturers have filled in most of the gaps in available ready-to-run models left by the larger manufacturers.

There are three basic types of locomotive kits: sheet metal, cast metal and plastic. Sheet metal kits can be subdivided into two types; pre-cut nickel silver sheet metal kits such as Jamieson in 00 gauge and CCW in 0 gauge, and etched brass kits such as Mallard models in both 00 and 0 gauges. There are also one or two kits by Craftsman Models and MPD that combine etched brass and cast metal parts. All these kits are an excellent introduction to the classic method of model locomotive construction as practised by serious railway modellers for many years. In the Jamieson and CCW kits the various parts are cut out from a nickel-silver sheet or strip and bent to the correct contour so that virtually only assembly is required. This overcomes the necessity for two tricky operations since metal cutting and bending can be difficult to someone inexperienced and/or ill equipped for the operation. It still leaves the assembly problem to be solved, however, and this can be equally as off-putting to some since, with brass or nickel-silver, the only practical assembly method is by soldering.

It is easy enough to give reassuring advice about soldering and to say that there is really nothing to fear or worry about, but the person who has met with little success in his early pioneering days will take a lot of convincing. Soldering is a knack which can only be mastered after a degree of practice and the best advice I can give is to suggest practising on some scrap pieces of brass, nickel-silver or tinplate before you risk making a mess of a relatively expensive pre-cut metal kit. The main requirements for successful soldering are to transfer sufficient heat from the iron on to the metal parts you are joning, and to scrupulously clean the metal surfaces so that the solder will flow and adhere evenly to the parts to be joined and not simply run off in a blob. To one who is more used to assembly by glue or cement, soldering can be rather frustrating since it is rarely possible to hold directly the metal pieces you wish to join. The only sure way out of this dilemma is to jig everything up so that you have, as far as possible, both hands free and you can keep your fingers out of the way.

Another difficulty that occurs with soldering, unlike glueing or cementing is that once you have assembled two pieces together you have to be very careful not to allow the soldering iron to linger too near and too long so that the pieces come apart again. It is, of course, possible to use different types of solder which melt at different temperatures and to make the first prime assembly using the highest melting point solder. However, this usually means using silver solder which is again an art in itself, requiring different techniques from ordinary soft soldering. Possibly the easiest way to solve the problem of having lots of separate parts together in close proximity to each other is to make a series of separate sub-assemblies which can eventually be bolted together. Sub-assemblies such as these can also be an asset when it comes to painting since it is often difficult to get at some parts of a locomotive model after it is completed. The worst part is the underside of the boiler and it is frequently a practical idea to make the boiler, firebox and perhaps smokebox as a separate assembly which can be removed from the running plate and cab. To return to the subject of soft-soldering again, there is no value in leaving large blobs of solder at a join between assembled parts unless you are deliberately trying to fill up space or build up sufficient thickness of material for subsequent shaping, eg the front corners of a belpaire firebox. Large blobs of solder do not necessarily add strength to the join. It is far more desirable to give the parts to be assembled an overall thin coating of solder (referred to as tinning), which will fuse together when the two parts are brought into contact and the hot iron applied. Only a little additional solder is then needed to complete the joint.

One of the advantages of solder is that it is much quicker than glueing. The solder 'sets' in seconds as soon as it cools, whereas most glues take quite a long while to set thoroughly and there is a danger all the time that the parts may be disturbed and become misplaced. After a soldered joint has set it is a pleasure to

*GWR Class 1101 0-4-0T assembled from a Cavendish N gauge cast metal body kit fitted to the Arnold-N 2242 chassis.*

clean up with a file and emery cloth and to feel the solid construction of the finished assembly. Finally the model should be washed and scrubbed in mild detergent to remove all traces of the solder flux and metal dust which is liable to lurk in unsuspecting places and will only reappear when a paint brush is brought to bear! There is little doubt that there is a great deal of satisfaction in handling a model constructed from sheet nickel-silver or brass and, if not to begin with, I recommend you to try your hand some time at locomotive building this way.

When you do decide to build your first sheet nickel-silver locomotive, whether from a kit or from your own home-cut parts, it is a good idea to choose a simple locomotive design, preferably one with a straight running plate without drop ends and with a parallel boiler. Taper boilers can be a bit troublesome to a beginner, whereas parallel boilers need be nothing more than a length of brass tubing—and it is sometimes possible to find tubing of exactly the right diameter. Tank locomotives often provide suitable prototypes for beginners since the large flat area of the tank and the bunker sides forms a solidly constructed unit which can be jigged up between blocks of wood during assembly to facilitate soldering. A perfectly flat surface, such as a sheet of plate glass, is a great aid to accurate assembly.

The choice of a simple straightforward locomotive design is also recommended for your first attempt at assembling one of the cast metal locomotive kits. The type that has been designed to fit on a proprietary chassis is perhaps the best since you will not have the added worry of getting the chassis to work properly. Some kits take a proprietary chassis without modification, whereas others require the chassis to be adapted in some way, possibly involving the removal of certain areas of the die-cast metal chassis block. In many cases this is easily enough done with a hacksaw blade, but it is sometimes preferable to strip the chassis first to avoid damaging the wheels and motion and to ensure that no metal dust from the hacksaw gets into the commutator of the electric motor. If you do dismantle a proprietary chassis in this way remember to make some notes as you unscrew each nut and bolt and remove each part so that you know where they go back again when the time comes to reassemble them. It is also a wise precaution to have a small box or container at hand so that the parts can be put in straight away without fear of losing any.

The parts in most cast metal kits require a great deal of cleaning up and preparation before they can be assembled. Very often 'flash' from the casting process needs to be removed and marks where the two halves of the casting mould were brought together need to be cleaned up. In some cases parts have also to be bent flat or straight and this can be done

*Langley Miniature Models produce a number of body kits for adding variety to an otherwise limited range of available N gauge locomotives. The LNER A3 Pacific shown here is designed to fit on the Minitrix Britannia chassis* (Langley Miniature Models).

easily since the metal is relatively soft and responds well to careful manipulation. The parts should be held firmly and only a slight deflection made at any one time, gradually applying even pressure so that the parts are eventually brought back to shape. It is very important that parts which should be assembled vertically are, in fact, vertical. Cabs on locomotives are a notoriously bad spot for this since any lean forward or backward at this point, however small, is immediately noticeable and stands out like a sore thumb.

Sometimes you will find that certain parts do not fit together very well. This may be due to bad design or it may be that they have shrunk or become distorted after removal from the mould. It will depend on each individual case, but you should be prepared to do some filing or trimming with a knife to get some parts to fit properly. Always be careful when faced with problems such as this, for you may be trying to fit the wrong two parts together! Parts often look very much alike and the illustration in the instruction sheet may not be all that helpful. I cannot emphasise too strongly the necessity to study the instruction sheet carefully and check the fit of *all* parts before you actually start to fix any two of them permanently. It has been known for instruction sheets to make mistakes and this is another reason why I consider it necessary to go through a dummy run with *all* parts. If you come across any snags and it is late in the day it is sometimes a good thing to go to bed at this point. The solution to assembly problems can become crystal clear in the morning!

Assembly of cast metal kits can be accomplished in a number of different ways. The most common method is to use a clear cellulose adhesive. I have some models assembled in this way which have been in use for 20 years or more and they are still perfectly sound today, largely I suspect because a number of parts on such kits are designed to interlock with each other, thereby adding strength to the joins. But in cases where moving parts or those under stress are involved (for example fixing points where the body is connected to the locomotive chassis) I recommend the use of something stronger, such as an epoxy resin adhesive or the special type of low melting point solder which is available for use with cast metal kits. One of the objections to epoxy resin adhesive has been that it takes time to cure or set, particularly because the parts cannot be heated in the oven as the adhesive instructions recommend since the heat would simply melt the cast metal. However, there are now on the market some new epoxy adhesives which are claimed to set within five minutes, and these appear to be absolutely ideal. There are also the latest cyanoacrylate adhesives such as Loctite Super Glue-3 and Mr Slater's Cyanobond 'Kung-Fu Glue' which can also be used for sheet metal as well as cast white metal kits. I am still a bit wary about these glues having heard some awful tales about what they can do but with a little practice you soon get used to them and avoid the all important thing of not getting the stuff on your hands. I prefer to use cyanoacrylate adhesives on fitting smaller parts such as footplate steps but definitely not chimneys, domes and safety valves where I like to take my time and stand back to view the model to make sure they are upright from all angles. For those who prefer soldering, and most people do once they have broken the ice, special low melting point solder and a 12 volt iron which can be controlled by a normal model railway power unit take the worst headaches out of the job. Be careful though, since a cast metal kit can turn into a pool of virtually valueless molten metal quicker than the time it took you to hand over the cash to pay for it, so if you are in doubt about your soldering ability, stick to glue! On the other hand, once the technique has been mastered, a soldered cast metal kit is quicker to assemble and is unlikely ever to come apart, provided it has been carefully made.

There is a great deal more to building locomotives from cast metal kits than simply sticking them together. The finished assembly also needs a lot of attention to fill in cracks and gaps between parts and the minute blow holes or pit marks that sometimes appear on the surface. I have used a proprietary brand of wood stopping paste known as 'Brummer' stopping for all such jobs, and since the tin I bought over ten years ago is still going strong I see no point in changing to any other method! The paste is soluble in water and, since only very little is required each time, I find it satisfactory to wet the end of the finger and transfer the paste on the finger-tip to the locomotive body where it can be rubbed in. Sometimes a craft knife blade or the end of a screwdriver can be used to get at areas which cannot be reached by your fingers. The paste dries reasonably quickly, after which it can be smoothed down to provide an almost indiscernible cover to a badly fitting joint, hole or gap in the cast metal parts. There are also several proprietary putties or body filling pastes such as Isopon which are useful for

**Below** *The handsome lines of the North British Railway Reid Atlantic, shown here in LNER livery, are well captured by this superbly constructed GEM 00 gauge cast metal kit. GEM include a comprehensive collection of NBR locomotives in their wide range of kits* (GEM).

**Bottom** *LNER V1 2-6-2T made from an 00 gauge McGowan Models cast metal kit.*

filling in the larger gaps and even for building up extra detail.

It is advisable to inspect the assembled body again after the first undercoat to ensure that there are no imperfections in the surface or at any of the joins and that the stopping paste or putty filling has been thoroughly smoothed into the surrounding surfaces. Boiler mountings also need special attention when assembling cast metal kits. Apart from the obvious necessity to fix them upright, the flare at the base of the chimney or dome often needs special attention to ensure that it blends in perfectly with the top of the boiler and that the flare itself is kept as thin and as unobtrusive as it is on the prototype. For detail points such as these it is essential to have as many good photographs of the full size locomotive you are modelling as you can lay your hands on and also at least one detailed drawing. Gathering facts around you of the locomotives and rolling stock you think you may one day want to build is one of the fascinations of the model railway hobby. Squabbles do arise from time to time about the accuracy of published drawings, but on the whole the hobby is well served with prototype information and new drawings appear regularly in the model railway press.

It is, of course, perfectly possible to assemble a model railway locomotive kit without the use of prototype drawings and photographs but if you want to make a really authentic job then drawings and photographs are essential. The range of drawings produced by John E. Skinley are perhaps the best known. It is always being extended and the choice of prototypes is now quite formidable. The Ian Allan books of locomotive, carriage and wagon drawings in 4 mm scale are also good value for money and, although at first glance you may think that you will never need all the drawings in these books, you will be surprised at the inspiration they will give and the pleasant hours you can spend studying them. For accurate and authentic models you simply cannot have too much prototype information.

One of the big advantages with cast metal kits over any other form of locomotive body building is their weight. This can be demonstrated easily if you care to make one of these locomotive kits that fit to a proprietary chassis and compare the performance of the chassis fitted with the original plastic body with its capabilities when fitted to the new cast metal one. The extra weight provides greater adhesion and hauling capacity and often has a beneficial effect on the noise of the motor and gear train, which in turn creates the illusion of smoother, silent power. It is not an exaggeration to say that cast metal locomotive kits have revolutionised model railways. They have vastly extended the scope and variety of locomotives beyond the ready-to-run models and they have made scratch-building possible to anyone with average manual dexterity.

Some people despise cast metal kits because of the thickness of the parts. With one or two exceptions I fail to see the justification for this since it is an easy matter to taper to a scale thickness the visible ends of such parts as cab roofs, smoke deflectors and tender sides. Note that I say the visible ends, since it is only the edges of these parts that can be seen and it is only at these points that any thinning is really necessary. The parts can be tapered to a scale thickness at the edge without detracting from the appearance or weakening the structure in any way. It surely does not matter that a cab roof is not the scale thickness throughout the whole of its length since it will, after all, only be the edge that is seen. One advantage with cast metal as opposed to plain sheet metal parts is the relief detail that can be incorporated. Etched brass kits are, of course, the exception. This is perhaps a little overdone in some cases, and on certain models rivets look more like saucepan lids. However, where they do offend they can always be removed and the state of the art is improving all the time so we may be spared these oversize details in time. It is a funny thing how points like this always look worse in photographs. In actual fact, overscale relief detail is much more bearable than photographs would have us believe.

When it comes to building model locomotives, plastic has not had the same revolutionary effect on railway modelling as it has for example in the field of solid scale model aeroplanes, where there is a vast range of constant scale plastic kits available at commendably low prices. The accuracy and attention to detail in these plastic aeroplane kits show a degree of sympathy for the prototype on the part of the designer, tool maker and manufacturer which is not so apparent in all cases in comparable locomotive kits. Plastic is, however, very successfully used for complete ready-to-run model locomotive bodies and I see no basic reason why it should not be more widely used for kits and home construction work. However, the cost of tooling-up being what it is, manufacturers—if they are to be commercial—are only interested in models which will have very wide sales. Unfortunately, many locomotives that would form ideal subjects for models are not million-sellers. Such plastic locomotive kits that do appear on the market sometimes have a limited production run so I recommend you

*The ubiquitous GWR Pannier Tank came in many shapes and sizes. Here we have the small wheeled 2021 Class, No 2082, as built from the Cotswold 00 gauge cast metal kit. A most useful locomotive for almost any GWR model railway as the prototype lasted from the turn of the century until the early 1950s.* (Sutherland Model Casters Ltd).

to buy as many as you think you are likely to need when you see them. As straightforward static models they can be made to look attractive on the mantlepiece or railway bookshelf, or they can be displayed in or around the locomotive depot on the model railway itself. In many cases they can also be motorised using special adaptor kits for the locomotive chassis, by modifying an existing proprietary model locomotive chassis or, in the case of a tender locomotive, by fitting a motorised chassis into the tender. The latter method is most effective and is not at all noticeable in practice. Many of the recognised proprietary model locomotive builders such as Airfix and Hornby Railways successfully use powered tenders for propelling their locomotives. Most locomotive tenders are capacious enough to take a fair amount of ballast weight as well as the motorised chassis itself. Ballast weight for adhesion is a factor which has to be given serious consideration with plastic-bodied locomotives, and as much weight as possible should be inserted in the body above the traction wheels.

As well as making attractive models in their own right, many plastic locomotive kits are capable of modification or conversion into other prototypes. In any case, practically all plastic model locomotive kits are capable of improvement by the constructor and it is seldom good enough to make the model straight as it comes in the kit. Some of the details I mentioned with regard to cast metal kits also apply to plastic kits, eg attending to the flash which sometimes adheres as a result of the moulding process, and the marks where the two halves of the mould have come together. These blemishes, and any others, should be thoroughly cleaned up before you commence assembly. Also the thick visible edges of cab roofs and sides, smoke deflectors and the tender body (as I mentioned with cast metal kits) can all be reduced in thickness to near scale proportions without weakening the structure in any way. Most Airfix kits make a point of moulding the lining detail on the body parts. I always think it is rather like moulding RAF roundels on the wings of an aircraft model and I am sure aeromodellers would soon be up in arms about that. The lining detail is fairly easily removed, although in one or two cases care has to be taken not to erase other detail which *is* wanted. I have found a $\frac{1}{4}$ in wood chisel to be my best tool for removing moulded plastic lining. For example, on that most useful kit for conversion purposes, the Airfix 'City of Truro', the lining on the tender can be peeled off like the skin off an orange.

A desirable modification which can be made to some plastic ready-to-run and kit model locomotives is to fit wire handrails instead of the solid plastic one moulded on to the model. With ready-to-run models the problem is not so persistent as it used to be since the manufacturers that erred in this respect have come to appreciate the improvement that separate wire handrails make. Most new models are being introduced with this feature and there has been at least one case where a model was originally produced with solid plastic handrails and has now been modified. However, where you do wish to replace old solid plastic handrails it is necessary first to remove them (once again the $\frac{1}{4}$ in chisel is useful for this), and drill holes either to take the specially made handrail knobs that some manufacturers, namely Bonds and K's, produce or else the handrail split pins which are also available from most model railway suppliers. I prefer the split pins myself since the length of the pin is adjustable and also it is much easier to anchor the ends of the pins simply by spreading the split ends inside the body. A spot of epoxy adhesive or a Polyfilla mix poured into the boiler will ensure that the handrail split pins never move again. Handrail wire is available from model railway retailers and can be bent easily with fingers and pliers. On a locomotive boiler handrail, remember to thread on whatever handrail knobs or pins you require for the front of the smokebox before you fit the handrail wire into the knobs or pins alongside the boiler. I suggest that you cut the wire overlength and drill a couple of holes, one each side of the cab spectacle plate, to take the loose ends of the wire. The wire can then be bent inside the cab to hold it securely in place. Not all handrails are secured by knobs and many are simply 'U'-shaped pieces of wire. When fitting handrails such as these it is advisable to bend over the ends of the wire behind the assembly, thereby fixing the wire firmly in place. If the spread-over ends of the wire are also sealed by a piece of plastic card or dabbed with a spot of epoxy adhesive they should withstand handling.

One of the finest finishing touches for any locomotive whether it be metal or plastic is the fitting, where appropriate, of the correct type of engraved brass name and/or number plate. These sometimes appear expensive items—and in the case of a plastic kit they can cost more than the kit itself—but the improvement they bring about cannot be measured in monetary terms. There is such a wide range of these that it is asking a lot of retailers to expect them to maintain a complete stock, but most good shops keep a fair selection. For special locomotives not listed in the current catalogues name plates can be made to order, although I have heard these orders sometimes take a long time to fulfill. The engraved brass name and number plates usually have to be trimmed to size, which I find easy to do with a pair of scissors and a needle file. With plastic locomotives I recommend sticking the name plates with epoxy adhesive to a piece of plastic which can in turn be fixed with polystyrene cement to the locomotive body. With metal locomotives the name and number plates can, of course, be soldered in place. Just recently a new type of self-adhesive name plate which simulates an engraved brass plate has been introduced and has found favour amongst many modellers.

In talking about plastic locomotives we have so far only mentioned ready-to-run models and plastic kits. Another medium which can also be used with great success in locomotive body building is plastic card, or styrene sheet as it is sometimes referred to. This is an excellent raw material for making cab side sheets, tender bodies, belpaire fireboxes, coupled wheel splashers, tanks and bunkers for tank locomotives or any number of different features. Admittedly, working parts in plastic are not suitable for serious or prolonged use in model locomotives but, as we have shown earlier, it is perfectly possible to combine a plastic locomotive body with a metal chassis. It is also possible to combine plastic and metal together in the case of body parts. Such fittings as chimneys, domes, safety valves, buffers, name and number plates, handrails, smokebox doors, handbrake columns, etc, which are produced in metal by various model railway accessory firms and which are usually readily available from most retailers, are quite capable of being fitted to an otherwise all-plastic model. Even a piece of brass or copper tubing can be used to represent the boiler. In fact, it is probably worth while having an item such as the boiler made out of metal to give added strength and rigidity to the finished model, though plastic card is well capable of standing up on its own right. It is possible, using laminations of two or more sheets of plastic card, to make a very robust structure and you are nearly always able to hide bracing struts and reinforcements behind the assembly and out of view. Before the days of plastic card I once made a GWR 57XX Pannier Tank from ordinary card of the sort used for filing cards and postcards and reinforced the model with 1 mm plywood and $\frac{1}{8}$ in obeche. A liberal coat of shellac afterwards ensured a pretty strong model which, because of the solid square-shaped construction of the Pannier Tanks, lasted for quite a long while. The body outlasted the mechanism, in fact! Although the 4 mm scale model was only wood and card I was able to ballast it with lead shot and it turned the scales at 12½ oz. I would suggest not being the least bit shy about using unorthodox materials for locomotive building. Use those materials you find best, since it is more likely you will meet with success that way. A good plastic or plastic card model can often fool the expert—if not at close quarters, at least at the usual distance from which you view a model on someone else's layout.

So far I have said nothing about locomotive chassis other than refer to the stripping down of proprietary models. Building locomotive chassis from scratch really has to be done thoroughly and there is simply no room for bodged work or half measures. The job is by no means impossible, however, and should you at any time find the necessity to make one it is not something you should feel you need avoid. The main reason it sometimes has to be done is usually because you want to build a particular locomotive whose wheelbase or coupled wheel diameter does not match any existing proprietary models or because existing commercially made chassis will not fit inside the locomotive you have selected. This question of wheelbase and wheel diameters is a vexed one. At one time, manufacturers catering principally for the toy market were prone to depart from prototype dimensions in the design of their locomotive chassis and it was common practice to utilise a standard mechanism with a wheelbase or wheel diameter unsuited to the prototype being modelled. Furthermore, on some six-coupled locomotives, there appeared to be an inexplicable desire to give an even spacing to the wheels.

However, not all locomotives have the coupled wheels evenly spaced. The standard dimensions for GWR 4-6-0s, for example, were 7 ft between the first two wheels and 7 ft 9 in between the last two. This applied to all GWR 4-6-0s except the 'Kings', and if you look at photographs of GWR locomotives for any length of time you will soon become conscious of this fact. I have always assumed the extra length between the rear two coupled wheels was designed to give greater clearance for the firebox ashpan. But suffice it to say that both the former Hornby-Dublo model of the 'Castle' locomotive and the Tri-ang 'Hall' model had wheelbases a scale 7 ft 3 in between each of the coupled wheels whereas, of course, they should be 7 ft and 7 ft 9 in. Furthermore, the Hornby-Dublo 'Castle' model has wheels the correct scale diameter for a 'Hall'. Now I always think that the chassis is just as much an important part of the locomotive as the boiler, cab or anything else. In fact, I would go further and suggest that the driving and coupled wheels are the parts that hold the greatest fascination for observers of steam locomotives. It is the magnificence of the large-diameter coupled wheels of express passenger locomotives which gives the steam locomotive such distinction and helps to distinguish an express passenger locomotive from a mixed traffic one. It seems such a pity to spoil an otherwise good model by using the wrong size wheels, wrongly spaced. Thankfully this is another area where standards have improved. The old ideas which insisted that departures from scale had to be made have been successfully challenged and are no longer acceptable. Most manufacturers nowadays aim to produce models with correct diameter wheels, correctly spaced *and* with all six coupled wheels flanged.

It is usual to make locomotive chassis from strip brass material. In 00 gauge, ½ in by 1/16 in is the size commonly used. The first essentials in a locomotive chassis are the accurate spacing and pairing of the axle holes, from one side of the chassis to the other, so that from whatever angle the chassis is looked at—top, bottom, side, front or rear—the axles are dead in line and all wheels are in contact with the rails. This is not always so simple as it sounds, for it is very easy for a drill to slip slightly, which causes the hole to go out of line. Assuming you are to use sheet brass for the chassis frame, the usual dodge when drilling out the axle holes is to solder the two frame pieces together so that cutting out and drilling the axle holes for both frames can be done in one go. This will help considerably, but even so you must still be careful to ensure that the drill is kept absolutely upright. Needless to say, a drill stand is a welcome asset in a situation like this. It is a good idea to drill the coupling rods at the same time as the axle holes, which will help to ensure that both sets of holes match up correctly and is essential to avoid the coupling rods binding when they revolve. A small pilot drill, sufficient for the coupling rod crank pin holes, will make a useful start to the axle holes themselves. Once the crank pin holes are drilled in the coupling rods with the pilot drill the coupling rods can be lined up on the frames and the axle holes drilled. Once again, pilot holes are advisable, and these can then be opened out with a larger drill to take the axles.

The normal method of assembling the chassis is to bolt the two side frames to a pair of frame spacers, one at each end of the chassis and perhaps a third one amidships on which to locate the electric motor. In 4 mm scale these frame spacers are available from model railway stockists and, since they are relatively cheap, they can be recommended as a worth

L M S
4454

6103
L M S

80033

while timesaver. The fore and aft frame spacers can also form fixing points for the body and this should be borne in mind when determining the position of the spacers. The gear wheel should be mounted on the driving axle before the frames are assembled. The placing of the third spacer will be determined by the position of the motor, which in turn will be partly dictated by the position of the driving axle and gear wheel. It is assumed that before they have reached the stage of building their own locomotive chassis most modellers will have had some experience of proprietary ready-to-run models. You can learn most of what you need to know from examining these chassis; for example, the positioning of the motor, the gears, the electrical pick-up, body fixing points, cylinders and valve gear, etc. Basically all you are trying to do when making your own chassis is to fabricate the frame out of sheet or strip brass instead of a die-cast metal block as produced by the commercial manufacturers.

It is often possible to adapt a commercial chassis frame to a particular prototype, either by drilling alternative axle holes in the die-cast metal frame itself or by lengthening the frame by bolting on brass strip extension pieces. Marking off the centre points for the new axle holes should, of course, be done either side of the driving axle hole which, together with the motor mounting bracket, should be left undisturbed. It is the meshing of the worm and worm wheel gears and the positioning of the motor which usually give the most trouble to model makers and, since most manufacturers invariably make a thorough job of this, it is as well to profit from their precision tooling and use their parts whenever you can.

Among the most popular proprietary chassis for adaptation in 16.5 mm gauge are those in the Hornby Railways range. They are all well designed and made and their performance is greatly respected by most modellers. The availability of spare parts, motors, gears and brushes, etc, is another reason why they are so popular. One of the most common modifications that modellers have to make to these chassis is the fitting of alternative size driving and coupled wheels. Usually this means installing either Romford or Hamblings wheels, whose standard axle is smaller in diameter than the Hornby Railways equivalent. Special brass bushes are available to enable such a conversion to be carried out, and most model railway retailers stock them. The Hornby Railways wheels can be removed by knocking out the axle from the wheel. I have an old nail with the pointed end cut off which I use together with a light hammer to tap out the axle. This can be done fairly easily, provided you give support to the chassis frame as close as you can either side of the axle. Extra resistance will be felt with the driving axle since this also needs to be knocked out of the worm wheel. It is even more important to ensure that the chassis frame is well supported for this operation, otherwise it is all too easy to bend and ultimately break it. I have found in practice that it is rare to find all axles revolving freely in their bushes immediately they are inserted, and it is often necessary to bore out one or more of the holes very slightly to overcome a tight spot. The boring out can be done quite easily with the tapered handle end of a file, but take care to ensure that the hole is bored out evenly and is not enlarged too much. Finally, a small piece of very fine emery cloth wrapped round a length of rodding, dowel or stout wire, inserted into the bush and twisted a few times will ensure a smooth bearing surface to present the very minimum resistance to the axle. In case you think this is too crude which I admit it is, the preferred method is to use a $\frac{1}{8}$ in diameter parallel reamer and a tap wrench but these two little items will cost about £6. It rather depends on how many locomotive chassis you wish to make but money spent on tools is always a good investment.

As anyone will find out when they strip down a Hornby Railways six-coupled chassis, the coupling rods are fitted rather ingeniously in that the coupling rod is only held in place by means of a 10BA bolt to the centre driving wheel. In the case of the leading and trailing wheels, the crank pins are fixed to the coupling rod and simply fit loosely into the wheel faces. This system works very well with Hornby Railways wheels and I have never found any necessity to change the practice when fitting Romford wheels. There is normally adequate material in the Romford wheels to drill out the relatively large crank pin holes to take the Hornby Railways types. A No 51 drill is required for the front and rear wheels and a No 54 drill for the centre driving wheel. No 54 is the correct size for tapping out a 10BA thread to replace the Hornby Railways crank pin screws. Hamblings'

**Top and centre left** *The Airfix tender locomotives such as the Fowler 4F 0-6-0 and the rebuilt Scot 4-6-0 shown here are powered by motors in the tender.*

**Left** *The Wrenn BR Class 4 2-6-4T is a most useful mixed traffic tank engine. The heavy cast metal body ensures an excellent performance.*

wheels have the crank pins already fitted and a special tool for fixing the wheels to the axles also ensures that each pair is properly quartered during assembly.

K's 4 mm scale locomotive driving wheels have a number of practical features which put them at an advantage over some others. To begin with they have 'D' shaped ends to the axles which ensures that when the screws holding the wheels in place are tightened up, the wheels on both ends of the axle are properly quartered, ie the crank pins either side of the chassis are in the right position relative to each other. The second advantage is with the crank pins themselves since they are threaded at the ends to take 14BA nuts which are supplied with the wheels. It is a relatively simple job to assemble the wheels and motion and, even more to the point, should you find there are any tight spots in any of the moving parts, it is just as simple to remove the 14BA nuts and strip the motion down to check where the fault lies. The latest K's chassis as supplied in their kits are also well designed with $\frac{1}{16}$ in brass frames which are screw assembled to the chassis cross members—the result of over 20 years practical experience in the business. The chassis which cover a wide variety of wheel spacings are available separately.

Wills do chassis kits specially to suit some of their range of Finecast locomotive kits. The earlier Finecast chassis have jig drilled main frames, brass bushed and designed to take Hornby motors and Romford wheels and gears of 40:1 or 30:1 ratio. The latest Wills chassis are based on etched brass, or more precisely, etched nickel silver techniques. Another exponent of these techniques is Kemilway who produce chassis for motorising Airfix plastic kits such as the 'Battle of Britain', BR Class 4 Mogul and the 'Schools'. GEM produce a 4-4-0 locomotive chassis kit which replaced the Tri-ang L1 chassis when it went out of production. It has basically the same dimensions and fixing points and was designed for use with those GEM kits that formerly took the Tri-ang L1 chassis but it can, of course, be used for any model requiring a 10 ft four-coupled wheelbase. GEM also produce chassis for the remainder of their wide range of kits. In fact most of the 00 gauge locomotive kit manufacturers are now supplying chassis with their kits and less reliance is being placed on using chassis from ready-to-run models supplied by the larger manufacturers. Mention must also be made of the fantastic range of chassis supplied by Studiolith Ltd for Protofour. These are the ultimate in 4 mm scale modelling since the frames, supplied already cut to shape, are based exactly on the full-size locomotive and the coupled wheels are designed to be sprung also in prototypical fashion. There are, in fact, a large number of commercial possibilities and sources of locomotive chassis, particularly in 00 gauge, and space does not permit me to mention them all. There are also a number of commercially available sets of valve gear parts and also cast metal cylinders which can help to take some of the drudgery out of this operation, which is generally considered difficult. However, should you decide to scorn all or most of these readily available commercial aids, and because I have only the space to touch lightly on the subject in this chapter, I would recommend as a further source of reference reading the late John H. Ahern's book 'Miniature Locomotive Construction' published by Model & Allied Publications Ltd, which, though written more than 20 years ago, still contains a lot of solid, practical and sound advice on the whole aspect of miniature locomotive building, with a particular emphasis on chassis construction.

*An assembled Kemilway chassis kit for motorising the Airfix plastic kit of the Battle of Britain Class Pacific* (Kemilway).

One piece of advice I would like to mention, born out of painful experience, is to make thoroughly sure whenever you are building a model locomotive, either from scratch or from a kit, that you keep a constant running check throughout every stage of construction that the body fits comfortably on the chassis. Wherever possible, make the chassis first and tailor the body to fit. I would certainly not attempt to make the body first without having the chassis parts available to check it against. One of the easiest mistakes to make is to forget that the boiler is round. You line up a mechanism alongside a scale drawing to check that the motor will fit inside the boiler, forgetting that the square corners of the motor will not fit inside the curvature of the topmost part of the boiler. Allowance must also be made for the brush gear, electrical wiring, TV suppressor, etc, on the motor and for any projections inside the body, such as handrail knobs or split pins. Some locomotive bodies are a very tight fit on the chassis, with limited clearance around the motor, and a cast metal body or metal projections inside a plastic body can easily cause a short circuit by coming into contact with the motor. To avoid this danger it is often a wise move to stick some insulating or self-adhesive tape inside the body at any point where there is the likelihood of contact being made, for it is difficult if not impossible to check thoroughly what is happening when the body is in place on the chassis. One way of finding out is to stick some Plasticine inside the body, fit the body to the chassis, then remove it and note the impression the motor has made on the Plasticine. One of the last features to fit to the body might well be the smokebox front, since it is sometimes possible to see through the front of the boiler whether or not all is well.

I would also suggest that you concentrate on the main assembly first of all and leave the smaller details such as steps and boiler mountings until last. For one thing they can be knocked off when working on other parts of the model, but with the footplate steps the particular trouble is that they can so easily foul the wheels. The leading bogie or pony wheels are the most troublesome, and on some locomotives where the clearance is particularly tight at these points it may be necessary to reposition the steps or leave them off entirely. The trouble only shows itself as a rule when the locomotive is travelling round a curve, and of course the sharper the curve the worse the trouble is likely to be. Some manufacturers overcome this by fixing the steps to the bogie, but you want to try and avoid these artificial dodges as far as you can. With boiler mountings, chimney, dome and safety valve, it is so essential to have these fittings dead upright that I always prefer to leave their assembly as long as possible so that the finished model can be set up and viewed from all angles.

So far I have made no mention of diesel or electric locomotives, and any reference to locomotive building until now has been concerned with steam versions. I realise that many people find great attraction in the latest forms of motive power and either combine diesels with their steam locomotives or else concentrate entirely on diesel or electric locomotives. The writer has had no practical experience of scratch-building a diesel outline model locomotive and there seems little point in referring to the subject since the railway modeller is so well served by the trade. This is particularly the case for British modellers in 00 gauge. There are no significant locomotive classes in British Rail's diesel locomotive fleet, past or present, that are not available either ready-to-run or in kit form, or in most cases both. With the Class 42/43 'Warship' and Class 52 'Western' there is even a choice

*Mainline Railways' 00 gauge model of the popular BR WR Warship Class No 827 'Kelly'* (Mainline Railways).

of more than one ready-to-run model and more than one kit. N gauge modellers are not quite so well off but even so, out of the current BR diesel fleet, Classes 03, 25, 37, 45/46, 47 and 50 are represented in kit form and Classes 08, 27, 31 and 55 are available ready-to-run. Details will be found in Appendix 5. In 0 gauge there is the former Tri-ang 'Big Big Train' Class 35 Hymek which is now back into production by Novo Toys Ltd and the Lima Class 33. The latter has incorrect bogie sideframes but there are cast white metal parts available for converting them into something resembling the prototype.

Continental and American modellers in N and HO gauges are also very well served with ready-to-run diesel outline locomotive models covering a wide variety of types from most European and American railways. Electric railways working on the overhead catenary system are far more extensive on the Continent than they are in Britain and this is reflected in the catalogues of Continental manufacturers of model railway equipment. I am able to account for no less than 165 different ready-to-run HO gauge models representing over a hundred different classes of electric locomotives. Truly a staggering figure. In contrast to this there are only three ready-to-run 00 gauge models of British prototype electric locomotives available to British modellers but such are the limitations of overhead catenary main line electrification in Britain that these three models together with the APT pretty well cover the UK scene. To the layman, the Classes 81-87 Bo-Bo electric locomotives used on the LMR West Coast main line out of Euston look very much alike since they all have a similar looking basic shape and they are all finished in the monotonous BR livery, unlike some of the French locomotives, for instance, that sport cheat lines and very rakish colour schemes. There are subtle outward differences in the LMR locomotives as well as technical specification variations which justify their separation into different classes and some of the locomotives are distinguished by being named. Details of all BR electric locomotive classes currently modelled in kit or ready-to-run form can be found in Appendix 5. Sadly the one-time Tri-ang ready-to-run 00 gauge model of the Class 76, which class was introduced in 1950 for the Manchester to Sheffield route, has been out of production for some time. Models of overhead electric locomotives will, of course, run without an overhead wiring or catenary system but for realism, if for no other reason, a model electric railway would not look authentic without one. I appreciate that not everyone relishes the thought but as with most things connected with the hobby, the trade is there to give support. There are a number of Continental manufacturers of working overhead catenary equipment in N and HO gauges. Probably the best known since they specialise in the subject is the German firm of Sommerfeldt who produce HO gauge systems representative of the German, Swiss and Italian railways. Yes, even overhead wiring, or more particularly the supporting structures, have recognisably different shapes and styles. Lima also produce a neat and well designed catenary system which can be used either as a scenic accessory or, with the aid of the special Lima pantograph adaptor kit, can be used to carry the electric current to their locomotives.

Though an important source of railway motive power, diesel or electric multiple units and diesel railcars are, from the modeller's point of view, little more than ordinary carriages fitted with a power bogie at one or both ends. The problems involved in their construction are more appropriate to the chapter dealing with carriages and wagons, but some reference should be made here to the subject. Ready-to-run models of diesel and electric multiple units, or DMUs and EMUs as they are often referred to, have never been very prolific. The EMUs once made by Hornby-Dublo and Tri-ang have long since been out of production and they have now been elevated to the status of collectors items. The Hornby Railways Metro-Cammell DMU set ceased to appear in the firm's catalogue after the 1977 edition. The only 00 gauge ready-to-run BR multiple units currently listed are the HST and APT from Hornby Railways, the Swindon built Trans-Pennine unit originally produced by Trix and now available from Liliput and the Lima version of the Pressed Steel Company's Motor Brake 2nd and Lavatory Composite Car. MTK Ltd, however, produce an extensive range of kits and also a 4-wheel motor bogie kit useful for making your own multiple units or railcars. The ever popular GWR diesel railcar is well provided for. In 00 gauge Lima produce two ready-to-run models and 4 mm scale kits are available from

**Opposite** *Continental electric locomotives come in a variety of styles. These three HO gauge models are; DB Class 132 2-6-2 by Fleischmann, DB Class 191 0-6-6-0 by Roco, and OBB Class 1020 Co-Co by Liliput.*

2
132 101-7
1

OBB

**Above** *'Express Parcels' Railcar No 34 is one of two GWR Railcar models produced in 00 gauge by Lima. The other model is the passenger carrying version* (Lima).

**Right** *A relatively cheap form of motive power for a 16 mm scale gauge 0 narrow gauge railway is this Faller Playtrain cleverly modified by John Edwards for his garden railway.*

**Below right** *GWR steam railmotor constructed by Norman Bradley from a Mallard Models etched brass kit crossing the overbridge outside Butley Town station on Ken Ball's 4 mm fine scale layout* (Brian Monaghan).

Anbrico, K's and MTK Ltd. Langley Miniature Models produce kits for different versions in N gauge. Mention must also be made of the 4 mm scale kit for the 3 ft gauge Isle of Man Railway railcar as shown on page 62. K's also produce a delightful model Ro-Rail bus of a type which once saw service on the LMS. The prototype was fitted with both rail and road wheels and could leave the track at, say, the end of a branch line and carry on the journey over public roads. In appearance it resembled an ordinary single deck half-cab bus.

Buses were also used by a number of Irish railways at one time. They were converted to permanent rail use by the substitution of flanged wheels for the normal road wheels. There are a number of actual prototypes of single unit railcars that once existed in the past to provide inspiration for an attractive and unusual model for a branch line or light railway layout. Mention must also be made of the steam railcars that once existed on Britain's railways since these make very attractive models, combining in some cases a normal type coach body with a very short stubby locomotive at one end, complete with boiler mountings, outside cylinders and valve gear and all the other paraphernalia of a steam engine. There were also the Sentinel steam railcars of the LNER which were operated in some numbers. In their case the method of propulsion was rather more disguised than the earlier form of steam railcar and outwardly they could only be distinguished by the chimney on the roof. Their colourful green and cream livery makes them attractive subjects. Nu-Cast Model Engineering and Langley Miniature Models produce kits in 00 and N gauges respectively.

The final operation with most model building is painting and it is at this point that many otherwise fine models are spoilt. By finding out what not to do you perhaps stand a better chance of avoiding the usual mistakes and thereby achieving some measure of success. There is no doubt the best finished models invariably turn out to have been spray painted—brush painting rarely reaches the same standard. If you intend to take up modelling locomotives and rolling stock seriously, money spent on an airbrush would be a wise investment. The cheapest one on the market, the Modeller's Air Brush by Humbrol Ltd, is not at all expensive, costing around £8 at 1981 prices excluding the aerosol power pack but you can spend over £100 if you go in for the more expensive equipment and use a compressor as a propellant source. A comprehensive review of airbrush equipment was conducted in the January and February 1978 issues of *Model Railways* by John Talbot-Jones—recommended reading for anyone contemplating branching out into this aspect of the hobby. Paints are no problem and there are any number to choose from

TARMAC
ROBERTS JENKS
CARDIFF
G W
JOHN NICOL LTD
COAL & COKE MERCHANTS
VAT 69

including matching railway colours covering most railway liveries. Possibly the best known is Humbrol who supply 15 ml tinlets of authentic railway colours covering GWR, LMS, LNER, SR and BR, as well as their standard range of colours for which you can find many uses. The most extensive railway colour range for British railway modellers comes from the Precision Paints Co who cover pre- and post-grouping railway companies as well as BR and even authentic bus company colours. Their smallest tin size is 50 cc which is quite a lot when, for example, you just want signal red. One thing you must not try and skimp on, assuming an airbrush is beyond your means, is paint brushes. Always buy the best, and this generally means the dearest, which are sable. I recommend having at the very least two sizes to work with, one small, say 0 or 1, and one medium, say 3 or 4. For locomotives I prefer smaller brushes since the areas to be painted are not usually very large, but for bigger areas such as the sides and roofs of railway carriages I favour the larger sizes.

The main mistake with painting is to do the job in a hurry. One is invariably told that it is better to put on two thin coats rather than a single thick one. Before the second thin coat can be applied the first thin one needs to dry thoroughly, and this will take time. The more coats of paint the more times the surface is made wet and tacky and liable to attract dust and fluff. These really are enemies to watch and every effort should be made to avoid them, eg by not wearing woollen or fluffy clothes or working in a dusty room and by covering up the model in between painting sessions. One trouble I have often found when applying the second of two coats is that the first coat tends to lift and become mixed with the second. This is annoying since you feel you might just as well have painted one thick coat in the first place. The only cure so far as I can see is to give the paint longer time to dry or not to work in the second coat too much but to lightly sweep the brush across the surface with a smooth even movement. This sounds all very well but any features in relief on the model, such as a row of rivets or a boiler band, have the effect of dragging extra paint off the brush at one edge and leaving bare metal at the other. You simply have to go back over relief detail such as this and work the brush in both directions.

There is no doubt that some colours are much easier to use and work with than others. For instance, I find black and most greens, particularly GWR green, easy to apply since they cover well and need the minimum number of coats. On the other hand, red, yellow and cream, to say nothing of white, I have found to be very difficult, especially in glossy form. The covering power is increased in matt paint but there is a disadvantage in that it seems to dry up in the tin much quicker and therefore will not keep so long as glossy paint. A possible compromise is to keep stocks of different colour paints in glossy form and mix a flattening agent with them when they are used. Only enough paint to do the job you have in hand needs to be treated on each occasion. I have found storing paints in tins upside down helps them keep longer, and they then also appear to be easier to mix when they are turned the right way up ready for use. For one thing the sediment in the paint will be found on the lid where it can be easily scraped off and thoroughly mixed in with the rest of the paint. Inverting the tin also forms a seal round the inside of the lid, which helps to keep the air out should the lid not be fitting properly. If the lid is such a bad fit then, of course, the paint will run out, which will be a tell-tale sign that all is not well! It is far better to find out in the early stages than wait until you want to use the tin when you might find that all the paint has dried up. Upside-down storing also helps to avoid the formation of a skin on the surface of the paint. I always try and keep the lid and edge of the tin free of paint before sealing it after use. With paints in bottles this is particularly important, for it is easy to seal up the bottle so that it becomes impossible to unscrew the cap without breaking the glass. I find that paint stored in corked bottles becomes useless after a relatively short while, but happily, few paints appear to be sold that way today.

I assume most modellers will acquire a quantity of thinner and are aware of the necessity of having appropriate thinners for the paints they are using. Whilst most paints are ready for use without thinning, it is necessary eventually as the paint becomes thicker due to evaporation every time the container is opened. On this account it is essential to keep the paint container closed as much as possible, and also to avoid dust and fluff getting into the paint. Thinners are also required for cleaning brushes. I usually keep a separate bottle of dirty thinner which is good enough to use in the early stages of brush cleaning, and clean thinner can be reserved for the final stage. It is an idea to keep a few old empty paint tins or lids in which to pour out small quantities of thinner for brush cleaning. They can also be used when mixing colours or for making up small quantities of matt paint using a matting agent.

It is essential that the model should be clean and free of grease before and during painting. Most models collect a fair amount of dirt during their construction, as well as swarf, dust from filing and sandpapering and grease from your fingers. What action you take to clean a model will to a certain extent depend on the materials used in its construction. An all-metal model can most likely be safely immersed in warm water containing detergent and scrubbed with a brush. A final rinse in running water will also do it little harm. Greater care needs to be taken with a plastic card structure, however, especially if you have used a water-soluble wood filler. A wipe over with a clean rag or a light brush is probably all you can do in a case such as this.

The first undercoat is important to 'key' the paint to the surface. It will also serve to show up any blemishes in the material or finish of the model, so a rub down with fine sandpaper or flour paper will not only improve the model but it will also help the finish of succeeding coats of paint. Each coat of paint should in fact, be allowed to dry thoroughly and be rubbed down with flour paper before the next coat is applied. I do not think there is any merit in putting on too many coats of paint since they begin to obscure the detail, however thinly and carefully they may be applied. Such details as the undersides of beading round cab entrances, boiler wash out plugs and boiler bands seem to collect more than their fair share of paint. I do, however, like to give a coat of varnish. Apart from anything else it preserves any decals or rub-on transfers you may have applied and in some cases helps the life of bright metal surfaces. I do not like matt varnish since this gives an artificial matt surface which I consider is rarely seen on railway rolling stock. I know they get dirty but the dirt is often accompanied by an oily sheen which is far from a flat matt finish. Certainly high-gloss paint looks out of place and artificial on a model, but a dead flat matt finish looks just as bad. Somewhere in between, such as a semi-matt or eggshell varnish, is in my opinion to be preferred. For many years I have used Bonds Eggshell Varnish and there is still plenty left after applying it to more than 40 or 50 separate items of rolling stock. Take care when applying this varnish since it will begin to dissolve the paint if it is worked in too thoroughly. It does, however, dry reasonably quickly, which is a great asset.

Lining and lettering locomotives can be a difficult art. Thankfully, there is an impressive range of aids in the form of decals or transfers which cover a wide field of prototype styles. Until recently most transfers produced in the model railway trade have been of the rub-on variety or require varnish or a solution of methylated spirits and water for their application but water slide transfers are now becoming available. I must admit I like the ease of water slide transfers, although I know there are objections to the ring or halo effect that sometimes goes with them. Rub-on transfers are fine except that you have to be careful to position them accurately when making the application as there is little or no room for manoeuvre afterwards like there is with a water slide transfer. Most model railway transfers are very thin, which is commendable from the appearance point of view but it does make the job of applying them rather critical. Lining and lettering can be applied direct to a model with a bow pen or a brush using ordinary paints if there are no suitable transfers, or alternatively the lining can be painted on to thin cigarette paper which can afterwards be fixed to the model with varnish. Another method is to paint self-adhesive tape which can afterwards be cut into strips and applied to the model. This is particularly suitable for locomotive boiler bands since the thickness of the tape will be just about right for the boiler band itself. I often wonder why we make boiler bands on our models and paint them afterwards, only to put transfers on top of the lot. Why not leave the boiler bands off the model until after painting at the end when a strip of painted self-adhesive tape will do the job just as well and make painting much easier?

The difficulty with painting lining is that if you make a mistake and have to remove the lining there is a chance that the base colour will also come away or, at the very least, be damaged. One way of avoiding this difficulty in the case of a metal locomotive is to paint the base colour with a cellulose paint and do the lining with an oil paint. Unfortunately all the special model railway paints I know of are oil based. It is possible that amongst the very wide range of car touch-up kits and aerosols there may be some colours that approximate to recognised railway liveries, in which case you could use these. Aerosol spray cans are not, however, terribly easy to control over such small and intricate areas as a model locomotive and you cannot hope to achieve as good a result as you would say, with an expensive airbrush. When applying oil paint lining with a bow pen always give the paint a start by drawing on a surface before you apply it to the model. Try and get the job done on one fill of the pen, but if you have to reload clean the pen first. It is important not to allow any paint to clog on the surface of the pen. To me, lining with a bow pen is far easier than with a brush, but not everyone finds it the same. Lining freehand is not an easy job, however, and you should not get discouraged if you find you cannot achieve the same results as the professionals. Two essential aids are good lighting immediately over the work to avoid shadows plus adequate support for the model and for your arms and hands. It is preferable to build up the working surface where your hands are resting to the same height as the model you are painting.

Most model locomotives begin to take on a more natural look after they have been running for a year or more and have been subjected to some handling. Whilst you should always be careful not to over-oil the working parts of electric propelled locos there is no harm in rubbing a light smear of oil over the bodywork from time to time. This is very often how the full size locomotives, particularly the steam locomotives, retained their sheen. One enemy of miniature locomotives and rolling stock, and in fact anything connected with model railways, is dust and you will need to give your models a clean up from time to time. An old shaving brush is ideal for this purpose.

Some modellers consider that it adds realism to their layout to 'dirty up' their locomotives a bit. The degree to which you apply such realism depends partly on your taste and possibly also on the type of locomotives and layout you are operating. For instance, most main line express passenger locomotives could be seen at one time in reasonably resplendent condition compared to freight locomotives which are generally allowed to become dirty. Locomotive depots in areas of high unemployment usually found it easier to recruit adequate cleaning staff compared to some other depots which were forced to employ all their available labour on maintaining and running the engines. Locomotives operating in predominantly industrial areas will also stand a better chance of getting dirty quicker than other engines which operate in the quieter and more remote country districts. It cannot be assumed that before World War 2 and nationalisation of British railways all locomotives looked bright, shiny and brand spanking new. Equally it is a mistake to think that after 1939 all locomotives were dirty, rusty and neglected. Even during the war years some locomotives were cleaned and they had to be repainted on occasions so it was by no means impossible to see a shiny, sparkling locomotive. Even those that only received an intermediate overhaul often left the works with a glossy coat of black paint on the smoke box and a bright red buffer beam, which made the whole locomotive look good and new.

One thing that is pretty certain is that all steam locomotives first entered service with a shiny coat of paint—or more likely several costs of paint and coats of varnish to top it off. The larger and more important the locomotive the greater the attention given to the paint finish. As anyone who runs a car will know, the glossy finish becomes dulled after a while by dust and dirt from the air or by mud thrown up from the road and the movement of other passing vehicles. Even the rain is not blameless, as it is either dirty if it falls through a smoke haze for example, or else it makes a solution of the dust and dirt already present and spreads it all over the surface in streaks. Something similar happens with a steam locomotive, but in addition there are the hazards of coal dust, which can be a menace at any time but is particularly troublesome when the bunker or tender is refuelled; soot which blows about from the chimney or when the interior of the smokebox is cleaned; ash from the firebox; over-generous lubrication; scruff marks from the feet and hands of the maintenance staff clambering over the engine; and the effects of water, hot or cold, and escaping steam from leaky glands, safety valves and cylinders, etc.

Whilst, as I have said earlier, I prefer not to paint a model initially with a dead matt finish I am the first to admit that with the effects of weathering, and all the other hazards mentioned, a locomotive that is never cleaned will lose its glossy varnish finish. At the same time, however, it will also lose most of its basic colour. Black will become grey and the pigment in other colours will be considerably toned down. In my opinion, therefore, it is not enough to paint a locomotive with authentic railway colours and simply finish with a dead matt varnish. If you want to show the authentic colours then there should at least be a trace of gloss or semi-gloss finish, otherwise the colours would not be so prominent. A matt finish only comes with dirt, in which case the colour of the dirt itself will show, or the matt finish will come with age, in which case the colour pigments will lose their intensity.

The colour of dirt varies according to what sort it is. Wheels and motion get coated with a rust brown colour, which is a mixture of mud and rust thrown up from the rails and augmented by the 'filings' from the cast metal brake blocks. A similar colour can be detected on passenger coaching stock where it often rises above the waistline and on to the windows. The deposits of coal dust, soot and ash will result in various shades of grey and grey/black and escaping water or steam will often leave whitish/grey streaks as well as rust. Priming via the chimney can also cause whitish streaks down the sides of the smokebox as well as on the outside of the chimney itself. Over-lubrication can produce black marks which spread far from the source of the lubrication itself. If it mixes with dirt or dust it will form a heavy shiny sludge, which will collect in pockets wherever there is somewhere for it to lie. There are, of course, plenty of places on a steam locomotive where rust will appear, unless it is kept down by regular cleaning or greasing. There are parts like buffer heads, coupling hooks, brake blocks, valve gear and connecting rods that lack a protective covering of paint and therefore become subject to rust and cause it to spread to other nearby areas. Other parts that are painted initially lose their protective covering either by wear and tear, such as on footplates, steps and handrails, or by overheating such as sometimes occurs round the base of badly fitting smokebox doors. Or it could simply be because it is a long time since the locomotive was last painted and the paint is beginning to wear thin!

Steam locomotives used to get pretty dirty at times, but diesel locomotives seem to have reached an all-time low. Even some main line diesels at the head of important passenger trains appear in an unkempt and neglected state. Paint becomes chipped and whole areas are allowed to flake off. The usual muddy rusty brown colour creeps upwards from the wheels, bogies and lower body side panels and, worst of all, apparent over-filling around the fuel tank fillers either causes a creeping black mixture of oil and dirt to spread or else it helps to remove yet more paint from the locomotive. Another oddity is the bluish 'rainbow' effect that can be observed sometimes on the windscreen glazing.

All these features may be an aid to realism, but whether you want to go to this extent is up to you. My own personal view is that unless you are modelling a particular area, period or setting that demands this treatment you might prefer to imagine that the local motive power depot has a full complement of cleaners who are able to do their job properly! I am sure locomotives, whether they be steam, diesel or electric, look better for a spot of cleaning. A natural weathered look will come soon enough after regular handling of the model.

Finally, when it comes to finishing your model locomotives, don't forget to put some coal in the tender or coal bunker. When in service it also helps if there is a crew on the footplate and other little details like lamps or destination boards can all help to give the finishing touch to a model.

## Chapter 10

# Carriages and wagons

If locomotives are one modelling field where plastic is not recognised as a universal construction medium this is not so of carriages and wagons. The vast majority of proprietary ready-to-run wagons and coaches are based on plastic mouldings and it is difficult to imagine what the hobby would be like today without this material. The old tinplate and lithograph models of yesteryear leave a lot to be desired in comparison with today's efforts which, thanks to modern plastic technology, can show in relief every small detail such as strapping, rivets, door handles, hinges, ventilators and planking, and even simulate the wood grain. The light weight of plastic is a virtue when it is applied to wagons since we do not want to increase the weight of the trailing load behind our engines any more than we need to. A certain amount of weight is necessary to give the wagons and coaches stability and such weight should be installed as low down as possible to keep the centre of gravity in the right place. Many manufacturers install a piece of heavy metal between the chassis and the body on their wagon and coach models and this is the ideal place. Metal wheels, insulated of course for 2-rail layouts can add a little extra weight in an area where it is most wanted although the rolling quality and profile of most of the latest 00 gauge plastic wagon and coach wheels is so good there is not the overriding necessity to replace them with metal wheels that there once was.

It is probably true to say that there are very few model railways that could accommodate every one of the different examples of ready-to-run wagons that are now commercially available in N and 00 gauges and most manufacturers appear to be adding to their ranges all the time. One factor which contributes to the variety is the large number of private owner wagons that once existed on Britain's railways prior to the outbreak of World War 2. The bulk of these were coal wagons owned (or sometimes hired) by coal mining companies and coal merchants, factors and traders. The reason for this was peculiar to Great Britain where at their inception railway companies were not required by statute to supply wagons for coal traffic as they were for other kinds of merchandise. The railways did in fact supply some wagons in certain districts, the Southern Railway in the Kent coalfield, for instance, but in general coal was transported in privately owned wagons of which at one time there were over 600,000 belonging to no less than 5,000 separate owners.

There were other privately owned wagons besides coal wagons as there still are in limited numbers today, but instinctively one thinks of coal wagons when thinking of privately owned wagons. The wagons themselves were made by different wagon builders based on a standard 'Railway Clearing House' specification which laid down standard dimensions for the chassis but allowed the body to be built to suit the owner's requirements in such features as the height of the body sides (largely identified by the number of planks used in their construction; 5, 6, 7, or 8 usually) and the number and types of doors, eg end, side or bottom, or a combination of two or more of each. With perhaps the exception of the bottom doors, all these features were readily discernible close to although at a distance the wagons all looked very much alike in overall appearance apart from their varying heights and, of course, their distinctive liveries. Here there was such a tremendous variety, both in the basic body colour and the colour and style of the lettering. Model railway manufacturers have unlimited but legitimate scope for imparting variety to an otherwise undistinguished basic shape of wagon and they have not been slow to appreciate this potential. I do not want to be accused of being a kill-joy but as nice and colourful as all these wagons are, they did have their regional limitations. For instance,

**Top to bottom** *A selection of 00 gauge 5- and 7-plank Private Owner coal and mineral wagons from Airfix; LNER brake van, BISC hopper wagon, TCD high sided coke wagon and three colourful 7-plank Private Owner coal wagons from Mainline Railways.*

The Harts Hill Iron Company Limited
Nº2
Brierley Hill
BROADOAK
460
SPENCER
St Paul's
Halifax

Gloucester Gas Light Company
Gloucester
JOHN ARNOLD & SONS
CHIPPING SODBURY
HIGHLEY MINING COMPANY
LIMITED
HIGHLEY
Nr KIDDERMINSTER
425

N E
IRON
B.I.S.C.
ORE
T. C. D. Ld
171

FOR
EVERYTHING
WASHABLE
C. W. S. Ltd
Coal Dept
London
Railway Wagon Builders & Repairers
London
COAL
FOR
COLMAN'S
MUSTARD WORKS

**Top** *No model railway based on the north east of England would be complete without a train of hopper wagons such as this pair made from Slater's plastic kits. Notice how well the strapping and rivet detail has been brought out in the plastic moulding* (Slater's Plastikard).

**Above** *The Peco range of wagon kits is now enhanced by the 'Wonderful Weathered Wagons' which feature unpainted replacement planks (a common feature when these wagons were in service), chalked destinations and a generally run-down weathered look* (Peco).

wagons owned by coal merchants could find their way almost anywhere since they could be sent to any colliery for loading, but unloading would normally only take place alongside the coal merchant's yard. Colliery wagons, on the other hand, could be sent to and unloaded almost anywhere although each colliery district had its traditional outlets that were frequently dictated either by the proximity of the customer to the colliery of the existence of a direct railway route and the influence of the adjoining railway company. Long haul coal trains en route from collieries to consumers, or going back empty in the opposite direction, would include a varied selection of wagons, possibly even every one different, but in a country station coal yard the variety is likely to be restricted to those wagons owned by the local coal merchants (or merchant depending on the monopoly situation in the district) or those colliery owned wagons most likely to serve that particular district. In all probability, there would have been more than one wagon from each of an unrestricted range of owners.

Whether or not you stick to such rules is up to you but it is worth considering if your layout is based on any particular region, railway company or, especially in the case of a branch line terminus, one particular town. Some coal mining companies ranged wider than others. The amalgamation of private collieries that took place before the war resulted in the formation of some very big companies having collieries in more than one coalfield in different parts of the country. One such, and possibly the largest, was Stephenson Clarke & Associated Collieries Ltd who had a very large fleet of wooden bodied wagons attractively finished in grey with 'SC' in large white letters shaded red. They bore the inscription 'Empty to Toton LMSR, Doncaster LNER or Aberdare GWR' which is an indication of their widespread distribution. Personally I am always finding SC wagons popping up in the background of pre-war railway photographs. Somehow the potential usefulness of these particular wagons appears to have escaped the notice of all but one N gauge manufacturer yet other far more obscure and locally restricted private owners receive attention. As I say, whether you bother about such things or not is up to you but it is worth a thought.

As well as the commercially produced ready-to-run wagons in plastic there is a growing range of plastic kits for scale model wagons both in 00 and 0 gauges and their various parts can also be adapted for conversions into other types of wagon. There are also a fair number of cast metal kits and separate parts such as axle guards, bogie side frames, brake gear and buffers which can be used for scratch-building wagons. Mention must also be made at this point of the Peco Wonderful Wagons which have been available in 00 gauge for a number of years. These come in kit form and are probably unique in the world of small scale model railway wagons since they contain so many desirable features. Foremost are the sprung axle boxes and buffers which operate just like they do on the full size wagons. The springs transmit the load of the wagon on to the axle boxes which can move up or down in the axle guard, the spring being deflected in the process. The main structure of the lower part of the body is a metal casting which gives the body rigidity as well as the necessary amount of weight in the place where it is most wanted. The visible body sides take the form of embossed and colour-printed card, requiring no additional painting or artwork to complete a thoroughly authentic and in many cases colourful wagon. A large range of prototypes is available and they can be highly recommended. The chassis is available separately as a set of parts to enable modellers to construct their own bodies should they so desire. Peco also produce their N gauge Quality Line Wagons in unpainted and easily assembled kit form as well as the fully painted and lettered ready-to-run models.

Scratch-building wagon bodies to be fitted on chassis, using sets of proprietary parts such as the Peco Wonderful Wagons, material taken from other plastic kits or even chassis from commercial ready-to-run models, is

*Scribing planking for plastic card wagon bodies using the point of a pair of dividers.*

simple with plastic card or styrene sheet. Basically a wagon body is nothing more than a box with or without a roof, and the body structure is easily enough assembled. It is only in the detailing that any particular skill is required. For 00 gauge I recommend using 40 thou plastic card to make up the four sides and the base of the 'box' and if you use black plastic card it will save you having to paint the interior. The planking and such features as doors can be represented by scoring the face of the card with a pointed instrument (not too sharp, otherwise it will only cut or scratch the surface). I use the pointed arm of a pair of adjustable dividers, sliding the other arm alongside the edge of the card to act as a guide. With this tool it is easy to score accurate parallel lines over as long a length of material as you like. I prefer to cut enough material for the two sides and two ends of the body in one strip so that all the planking can be completed in one go. This way the planking will be completely parallel and even around all four sides and there will be no difficulty in matching up the planking where it meets at the corners. For the average 00 gauge wagon a strip of plastic card 8 in long will be enough for all four sides.

When scoring, take care not to dig too deeply with the pointer otherwise you may find the card will bow or, at worst, crack in two. The sides and ends can be assembled round a plastic card floor, also similarly scored for planking, and the body cemented to whatever chassis you have chosen. Strapping can be cut from 10 thou plastic card and cemented in place using liquid cement such as Mek-pak supplied by George Slater. (The chemical name of the solvent used for cementing plastic card is methylethylketone.) Bolt head detail on the strapping looks very nice and completes the effect, but only if it is done neatly. The bolts can be represented by pressing a blunt pointed instrument such as a knitting needle or a centre punch on the

**Below** *The conversion possibilities of plastic kits are shown by these two 9 ft wheelbase 1-plank wagons built from two 12 ft wheelbase Maj Models kits* (Maj Models (Poulton) Ltd).

**Bottom** *No GWR locomotive depot would be complete without this GWR 10 ton iron Loco coal wagon. This 00 gauge model has been constructed from a Cooper Craft plastic kit which in common with the rest of the range comes complete with wheels, couplings and transfers* (Douglas Allen).

**Top** *Swiss railway carriages have a distinctive low slung appearance which is well portrayed by this Liliput HO 2nd class centre entrance coach* (Liliput).

**Above** *6-wheel carriages are a thing of the past so far as British railways are concerned but the type is popular on the Deutsche Bundesbahn. This 2nd class coach is an HO gauge model by Roco* (Richard Kohnstam Ltd).

reverse side but this is rather tedious. Unless you make each impression with equal force and dead in line the result will look worse than no rivets or bolt heads at all.

A gear wheel rolled along the back of the strapping so that the teeth leave an impression would be ideal provided you can find an old clock gear wheel with the right spacing of teeth. Another snag with rivet embossing is that is comes out well on large areas but with narrow strips it is difficult to get the plastic card to withstand such treatment. It is probably much better to mark the rivets before you cut out the strapping. Better still, use thin metal foil for the strapping detail which can withstand greater distortion from the embossing tool. Some bracing and strapping on the outside of wagon bodies takes the form in cross-section of 'L' or 'T' shaped sections which can be built up from strips of plastic card very easily. First the base of the 'L' or the top of the 'T' is cemented in place and then the stem of the 'L' or 'T' can be held on edge with the aid of a pair of tweezers and fixed with a wash of liquid cement.

One point that calls for particular attention when assembling wagons (and indeed all vehicles such as locomotives and tender chassis, coach bogies, etc) is to ensure that all the wheels sit fairly and squarely on the rails, which will not be the case if you assemble a wagon with a twist in the chassis! Once completed that way it is difficult to correct. It is a wise precaution to have a dead flat surface such as a piece of plate glass handy when you are assembling wagons and other items of rolling stock to ensure that all the axles are in the same plane and that all the wheels are in contact with the ground. It is just possible that the running surface or tyres of the wheels are true but that one or more of the flanges may be uneven. So, to be thoroughly sure, stand the wagon on a length of track which is itself on the glass. When assembling plastic models in particular it is necessary to check constantly since it is possible for the model to be assembled correctly but to find that the action of the cement drying shrinks, twists or pulls the body and chassis slightly out of shape. You cannot be too careful with this point since a

*BR 16 ton mineral wagons in real life and as modelled in 00 gauge by Mainline Railways* (Mainline Railways).

wagon with uneven wheels will be a sure source of derailment. In extreme cases it looks pretty horrible too.

For those who model prototypes other than British the rolling stock situation differs to some degree. Anyone who has already studied the windows of shops selling imported model railway items will already be aware that a vast range of ready-assembled, ready-to-run stock is available. Most enthusiasts could completely stock a Continental or American-style layout 'off the shelf' with no need for kit-building at all. The ranges of Jouef, Rivarossi, Liliput, Fleischmann and so on between them offer almost anything needed for running passenger or freight trains of almost any period from about 1900 onwards. Such is the availability of stock that kits seem virtually non-existent for Continental models and anyone who *did* want to build up something in this line would have to resort to scratch-building, perhaps using underframes 'cannibalised' from a ready-to-run wagon. However, with such a wealth of stock to hand even the effort of doing this seems hardly worth while. What can be done, however, is a good deal in the way of super-detailing, for instance replacing moulded handrails with wire and adding brake pipes, parts often missing even from the highest quality Continental models. Ideas for wagon and coach conversions using readily-available items as a basis appear frequently in the Continental model railway magazines such as *Loco Revue* and *Rail Miniature Flash*. Anyone modelling Continental lines would be well advised to invest in these magazines, and others, in any case.

The situation with American stock differs again. Not only is there a huge range of ready-to-run items, but there are also scores of kits varying from the 'craftsmen' kit in wood and metal up to 'CKD' (completely knocked down) types which can be assembled with screws and cement in as little as 30 minutes. The quality of the latter type of kit is very high indeed, Trains-Miniature and Athearn products being notably good, offering models which are virtually exhibition class. The choice is large, 'steam age' rolling stock predominating. Both freight and passenger cars are available (as indeed are locomotives) in this type of quality kit. The 'craftsmen' type kits are obviously more basic and require rather more skill, not far removed from scratch-building, but even here body parts often come ready painted and lettered. Victors of Islington and Millholme Models are two principal British stockists of American and Continental models but there are others. Tyco are the principal producers of ready-to-run American rolling stock and the quality is excellent. Airfix, Rivarossi and Fleischmann also offer a limited amount of ready-to-run American stock.

While most of the foregoing applies to HO gauge, the same remarks apply to N and O gauges, though there are fewer or no N gauge kits and a relatively limited range either in kits or ready-to-run as far as 0 gauge is concerned. However, Rivarossi and Pola each have ranges of ready-to-run 0 gauge items in both American and Continental ranges.

For scratch-builders following American prototypes there is quite a big range of components including wheels, trucks, doors, grab-irons, rainstrips, roofs, car ends, and so on.

Painting wagons needs care, not only for the elaborate colour and lettering schemes that were to be found on some of them (principally the privately owned coal and mineral wagons), but also because of the amount of dirt and rust that—in recent years especially—more and more of the modern all-steel wagons tend to attract. It is not difficult to see why they soon lose their ex-works newness when you consider the treatment they get. To begin with, they are probably loaded under a hopper which discharges into the body of the wagon 16 tons of coal in about as many seconds. Unloading can involve the wagon in being rotated full circle in a rotary discharger or tilted at one end to discharge through the end door. Alternatively, a mechanical grab may be employed which, however careful the operator, is bound on occasions to knock against the sides of the wagon. Inevitably paint becomes chipped and worn and rust forms to take its place—in some cases there appears to be more rust than paint. Though this may look rather drab, if you are striving after realism you will want to consider how to create this dirty neglected effect in miniature. This calls for a little creative artwork which can be applied to all forms of railway modelling—locomotives, coaches, wagons, road vehicles or any painted structure which sees the ravages of wear and tear and wind and rain over a period of time. (See photo on page 170.)

Assuming that your model is already painted, the first thing to bear in mind when applying paint to represent rust or weathering is to avoid using a heavy coat which will obliterate the prime colour. Use your paints well thinned and never apply straight from the tin. Keep a pallet or small tin lid handy in which you can play about with your paints and thinners, and perhaps have a spare piece of scrap plastic to experiment with before applying paint to the model. In your tin lid put a dab of black paint, a dab of brick red and a brush full of thinner. Keep adding one or more of these items until you have a weak, watery solution that can be slapped liberally all over the model. If it settles into corners and crevices so much the better, for these are the very places where dirt and rust are likely to congregate. Rust on wagon body sides usually appears in patches, mainly in the centre of large panels where the sides have been dented and the paint has flaked off.

I use an old paint brush that has seen better days, and cut off whatever hairs remain until there is just a stump about 1/16 in long. This brush, used end-on, produces a good stipple effect with diluted brick red paint. Dirt can be washed on using dirty thinner—the remains from a bottle which has been used for cleaning paint brushes is ideal. Add a spot of brick red and black if it is not dirty enough. Wash the dirt solution with vertical strokes to represent streaks caused by rain carrying coal dust and grime down the body sides. White lettering can also be toned down using a wash of dirty thinner since it is unusual to see an old rusty wagon with bright white lettering. Another obvious way of adding realism to wagons is to put a few chalk destination markings on the body sides, using a mapping pen and white Indian ink. Parcels vans are particularly prone to this type of decoration and a widely spaced range of destinations, such as Edinburgh, Bournemouth, Cardiff or Liverpool, can often be seen scribbled in chalk on these wagons. It is a wonder the operating staff know which one to take note of.

Wagon loads is a subject in itself since there is so much variety of merchandise and so many different methods of loading. Also, of course, they provide a lot of operating scope since open wagons can be loaded and unloaded just like the real thing. In the majority of cases it is preferable to 'package' the load so that it can be put into the wagon and taken out with the least difficulty. For example, a load of coal for a coal wagon can be represented by a lightweight block of balsa wood with the top shaped and sprinkled with a layer of coal dust or small chippings glued to the wood. Alternatively, the excellent Airfix mineral wagon dummy load can be used. Timber loads can be represented by one single block of wood with the planks scored along the top, ends and sides. Many loads such as milk churns, cable drums, containers, barrels and packing cases are available as ready-made accessories from a number of manufacturers and there are many more than can be scratch-built at home from scrap materials. Another source of wagon loads can sometimes be found from within the range of die-cast miniature vehicles such as Lesney's Matchbox series. All too frequently these are not built to recognised model railway scales but sometimes you can find one that is not too far removed, and there are also some items such as boats and caravans that can be made use of. Military vehicles also make good subjects for wagon loads, especially as the army seems to be a good customer of British Railways.

Mention must also be made of tarpaulins since these were at one time regularly used for sheeting open wagons to protect their contents, the classic example being the Hybar wagon which had a bar that could be swung into place especially to take a tarpaulin. They were also commonly used to drape over a

*LMS 6-wheel bogie dining car built in 7 mm scale by D.C. Lawrence. The close-up picture opposite taken from the reverse side gives a glimpse of the furnished interior* (Larry Goddard).

quantity of timber stacked in the wagon in such a way that it overlapped the edge at one end. Invariably the tip of the timber could be seen poking out from below the tarpaulin. I have found crumpled tissue paper painted with black Indian ink produces an effective miniature tarpaulin. They are also available commercially in N and 00 gauges. There is practically no limit to the ingenuity you can put into the subject of wagon loads, both by thinking up new subjects for loads and in the various ways of modelling the loads themselves.

I mentioned in the previous chapter the difficulties that large scale manufacturers must have in trying to produce a range of model locomotives which will satisfy the largest proportion of their customers. It is difficult enough with locomotives and it must be well nigh impossible with railway carriages. The trouble with model railway carriages is that, to a layman, most of them look alike. There are obvious differences such as four-wheel, six-wheel and bogie coaches, non-corridor and corridor coaches, first class and second class coaches, and restaurant, buffet and sleeping cars. In reality, however, these are just broad categories and in actual fact, as with locomotives, there are many different styles and designs. At the same time as there were attempts by the various railway companies to produce standard designs of locomotives, every company had a succession of carriages and wagon engineers who had their own ideas on how railway carriages should be built and what they should look like. They all left their mark in various ways and degrees to produce a variety of coaches which, though basically built to a similar pattern, were quite distinguishable in detail. These details are important when it comes to building an authentic model railway, and to create the right atmosphere when modelling a particular railway company you should be as particular about your railway carriages as you are with the locomotives and other items that go to distinguish one company, period or location from another.

To begin at the bottom and work up, all the pre-nationalisation British railway companies had different designs of bogies. The dimensions of the wheelbase differed for a start: the GWR had mostly 9 ft wheelbase bogies, but there were also quite a number of 7 ft bogies, a dimension which was peculiar to the GWR. The LMS standardised on 9 ft and the SR 8 ft. The LNER used 8 ft 6 in bogies but they had a very distinctive appearance since the springing gear was hidden behind the bogie frames which were attractively curved in shape—unlike some outside frame bogies used at one time by the SR which were straight and somewhat ugly in appearance. The shape of the frames also distinguished the GWR 9 ft bogies from the standard LMS bogies which had the same wheelbase. The

*The Airfix 00 gauge model of the GWR Centenary stock 1st/3rd Composite. Strictly speaking this model should be limited to main line running on GWR layouts only, as the prototype had a severely limited route availability due to its exceptional width of 9 ft 6 in and was not allowed to run over other Company's lines* (Airfix).

type of springing also affects the appearance. In the past most bogies have had leaf springs but in recent years BR have used coil springs which markedly change the appearance of a bogie. There is little excuse for running rolling stock with the wrong sort of bogies in 00 gauge, and even in 0 gauge, where there is a fair selection of bogies or bogie parts.

Bogies are the most noticeable feature of the underframe but there are others that have to be considered, such as the size, shape and position of battery boxes, vacuum brake cylinders, truss rods, buffers, buffer heads (whether round or oval), footboards, etc, and they are all items that sometimes differ from one design to another and which need to be considered when building a particular coach model.

The coach body also has infinite scope for detail variations. To begin with, let's consider the curvature of the body sides, as seen end-on. The majority of designs have sides that curve inwards starting from a point below the waistline so that the overall width of the lower part of the body is less than the middle and top. This is known as 'tumble home' and is a most noticeable feature which must be reproduced correctly if an authentic appearance is to be given to a model. The post-war Bulleid coaches of the SR were unusual in that they had a continuous curvature to the sides, some of them even having curved glass in the windows, whereas the post-war Hawksworth coaches of the GWR had nearly straight sides. This is just one example of different thinking by different designers working for separate railway companies at the same period in time. Another distinctive and unique feature of the SR Bulleid coaches was the pronounced rounded corners of the window frames. The size and shape of windows and ventilators are themselves distinguishing features which help to make one design different from another.

The roof is a further area where design differences show up. The curved drop ends to the roofs of the Gresley coaches on the LNER were very striking and no model LNER train would really look right without them. At about the time when the LNER broke away from this unique tradition, and started to build their coaches with normal straight tops to the roofs, the GWR inexplicably began building theirs the other way. The positioning of rain strips on the roofs and the type, location and number of ventilators also help to distinguish one coach design from another. At each end of a coach the identifying features can be the number and position of handrails, steps, jumper cables and corridor connections, plus the shape of the end itself and whether it is flat or curved.

With all these individual variations in design it was thought at one time it would be very near impossible for the large 'toy' model railway manufacturers to produce a range of ready-to-run models which would cover the needs of all modellers. However, such has been the expansion in the manufacturing side of the hobby that this undreamt of possibility has now become a reality so far as 00 gauge is concerned. We have now in 00 gauge a range of authentic ready-to-run coaches covering the basic needs of most modellers of the GWR, LMS, LNER, SR and British Railways. The latest products from Airfix, Jouef and Mainline Railways make little or no concessions to mass production and they all faithfully follow their chosen prototypes in matters of detail such as the bogies and interiors, and adherence to the prototype dimensions. For example, the two Airfix

*Graham Farish produce an attractive range of passenger coaches in N and 00 gauges. Shown here is the 00 gauge Southern Railway Brake Third Corridor.*

LMS corridor coaches are of different lengths and in their GWR 'B Set' coach the seating in the one solitary first class compartment is distinguished by armrests. Of the pre-nationalisation companies the GWR and LMS are presently the best served but devotees of the earlier days of BR can obtain these coaches in BR livery which, of course, can be combined with BR Mk 1 stock which is available from Lima and Mainline Railways. Later day BR coaches in the form of Mk IIs and Mk IIIs are also well covered by Airfix, Hornby Railways and Jouef. Such is the state of the market that complaints are being made that some types of coaches are only represented by Brake Thirds and First/Third Composites whereas of course all-Thirds were one time more common than the composites and there were such things as all-Firsts. I think there has got to be a limit to what we can expect from manufacturers and personally I am grateful for what we have got already, which is far more than I ever expected only a few years ago.

Some of the Hornby Railways coaches lack the absolute authenticity achieved by other manufacturers, particularly in such matters as the bogies where there is no variation according to prototype, and the BR Mk I bogies are used in GWR, LMS and SR coaches alike. However, they have made amends with the LNER coaches since these are now fitted with the proper Gresley bogies. The earlier models were spoilt by this lack of attention to detail which was a pity because otherwise the distinctive but difficult to produce LNER teak finish is very well portrayed and overall the models are very convincing. If you run Hornby Railways' coaches with other makes you will soon appreciate the need to lower the bodies on to the bogies since they are pitched a scale 6 in too high to suit the standard Hornby Railways buffer height. If you decide to retain the bogies they are easily removed to enable the bolster to be filed down by the necessary amount. Overall, the railway modeller in 00 gauge is exceptionally well supplied with ready-to-run coaches and never in the history of the hobby have we ever had it so good.

Graham Farish upholds N gauge very well with two Pullman cars, a range of corridor and non-corridor pre-nationalisation style bogie and four-wheel coaches and two very realistic flush sided BR Mk 1 coaches in four types of BR livery. For BR stock there are also ready-to-run models from Hornby Minitrix and Lima and the coach kits of MTK Ltd. Cavendish also do a range of coach kits for authentic pre-nationalisation coaches including GWR and LNER. In 0 gauge Lima have at last produced the Brake Third to accompany their well established First/Third composite and these are both very good models of BR Mk I stock spoilt only by the bogies. Maybe they will get round to that one of these days as they have done with their 00 gauge range but meanwhile you should be able to convert them fairly easily or they can, of course, be replaced by bogie kits such as CCW. Coach kits in 0 gauge are available mostly in pre-cut aluminium body shells or etched-brass. I personally find the cost of some of these kits a little off-putting since at £20-£30 plus per kit a rake of four coaches can cost upwards of £100. There is no comparison with the smaller gauges such as 00 where a rake of ready-to-run coaches costs less than a fifth of this price. There is a great incentive in 0 gauge to stick to the BR period and use Lima coach bodies that compare very favourably with 00 gauge prices or else run a simple branch line with the minimum amount of coaching stock. The other alternative is to make your own bodies from basic raw materials.

There is an absolute abundance of coach

**Top** *The Graham Farish range of N gauge coaches includes this accurate portrayal of a BR Mk 1 Brake End Composite. A notable feature is the flush windows* (Graham Farish).

**Above** *Maj Models 00 gauge coach kits are moulded in clear plastic to which are stuck pre-coloured and lined self-adhesive sides. The range includes this impressive GWR 70 ft Brake Third* (Maj Models (Poulton) Ltd).

kits in 4 mm scale covering the pre-grouping, pre-nationalisation and BR periods and using a variety of materials; plastic, cast white metal, punched aluminium and etched zinc or brass. Harry Drummond did a most exhaustive survey of all these kits in the issues of *Model Railways* for November and December 1978. You are well advised to look these issues up not only as a well documented source of reference on the availability of models in kit form but also for the valuable hints and tips the author gives that were acquired as a result of constructing each of the kits.

To make a really good job of a model railway carriage can take as long as making a model locomotive. The kits that are available provide a great service to the modeller who wants to speed up his construction work. Even so, kit-built models take time in assembly and the whole job cannot be rushed. One of the big advantages with most coach kits is that the window openings are already produced for you. Windows are one of the big character-shaping features of railway carriage designs and it is essential to get them right. Almost without exception you should paint the windows before they are glazed, otherwise it is difficult to paint the edges of the window frames without some paint straying on to the glazing material. I have seen a method of scratch-built coach construction in 00 gauge using thin glass for glazing and I am convinced this is the best material and the best method of construction. Basically it is the well-known 'sandwich' type of construction in that three layers of plastic card are used to construct each coach body side. An outer and inner layer with the window openings cut out and a centre layer containing the glazing material form the sandwich. When cemented or glued together the three layers form a strong side which resists warping and pressure from the fingers when handling the finished model. If the inner layer is made of plastic card, just slightly thicker than the glazing, the panels forming the window panes can be lifted out after assembly of the side to facilitate painting. Any cement which may stray on to the glazing during assembly of the sides can also be removed from the glass. The three layers of plastic card in the lower part of the body make a strong three-ply structure which can be scraped, filed or sandpapered to produce the correct tumble home to the sides, while the separate layers act as contour lines and provide a useful visual aid to the accurate and even curvature of the sides.

Plastic card is also ideal material for constructing the floor, ends and interior partitions, and for making a false roof which is often necessary to stop the sides from bending inwards at any point where there are no interior partitions to add strength to the model—very necessary in the case of open saloon coaches. The roof is best made from wood, but I consider it preferable to use a lightweight wood such as balsa rather than some of the hardwood roofs especially produced for coach model building since these can be rather heavy, and put the weight in the wrong place. It is possible to fill in the grain of whatever wood you are using to produce a perfectly smooth finish, but it is worth remembering that some coach roofs were at one time covered with canvas and in these cases a super smooth gloss finish would be inappropriate. Here I suggest covering the roof with a sheet of tissue paper, which when painted gives the desired fabric effect.

As with wagons and diesel locomotives, railway coach bodies are basically nothing more than boxes in construction but the number of extra features they incorporate—the correct curvature of the sides and the roof, window openings, door handles, handrails, ventilators, rain strips, etc—call for much more detailed work which can add a lot to the construction time and can make or mar a model. The outside panelling, which was such a feature of the older coaches, can be represented by building thin strips of 10 thou plastic card which can easily be added to the main body structure by a wash of liquid cement applied by a brush. The only snag with this method is that the corners do not have the correct curvature which was invariably present in most panelling. The only alternative is the rather painstaking one of cutting out the panelling from a single sheet of plastic card. The thin spidery web of panelling calls for some delicate handling and some pretty accurate measuring since, if it is made all in one piece, it will have to fit around the window openings. Whichever method you use will depend on your skill and patience.

The rounded corners in window openings are also a problem when cutting out coach body sides from plastic card. One method is to drill holes in the four corners of the opening using a drill which approximates to the radius of the inner curvature. The window is finally cut out with a craft knife from corner to corner. I have never met with much success using this method since I have found it all too easy to misalign the drill holes and finish up with windows at varying heights and sizes. I prefer to cut diagonally across the corners with the craft knife and file out the correct curvature afterwards, using a small round Swiss file. I must confess, however, that I am not terribly happy either way and it is very much easier to cut out windows that have square corners. Luckily plastic card is such wonderful material to work with; should you find that you have gone too far with a craft knife and have cut across a pillar between two separate window openings you can usually repair the damage with a wash of liquid cement.

With all forms of model making using plastic card or wood I cannot emphasise too strongly the necessity to have really sharp tools. Craft knife blades are relatively cheap things to buy and there is no point in struggling on with a blunt blade when it is really time it was changed. The trouble with craft knives is that they are sometimes too useful and you find yourself using them as scrapers and for other purposes for which they are not really intended. I always have at least two knives in use at any one time; one with a new sharp blade which I reserve for the really delicate and precise cutting jobs and another with an older worn blade which is past its prime but is still adequate for the rougher jobs.

Another absolute necessity when it comes to model making, especially accurate cutting, assembly and painting work, is to have really adequate lighting. I speak from experience as I struggled for a long while trying to dodge shadows from a straight edge and wondering why cuts with a craft knife drawn along the straight edge did not always line up properly. I also wondered why model making made me feel so tired after an evening session. I invested in an adjustable studio lamp and it made the world of difference. To have the light immediately over your work and to be able to adjust it so that you can avoid all unwanted shadows is, in my opinion, absolutely essential, not only from the point of view of making worth while models but also for the sake of your eyes and your health.

The subject of model locomotives, carriages and wagons would be incomplete without some mention of couplings. Probably more ingenuity has been spent on this subject than almost anything else connected with model railways, and the multiplicity of different designs has perhaps been the cause of more dissatisfaction than anything else. At one time it appeared that no manufacturer would dream of fitting a type of coupling which would enable his rolling stock to couple up to anyone else's, and it seemed to be a point of honour amongst the different firms that they had to establish themselves by inventing their own coupling. By making them so wildly different one assumes that each manufacturer hoped to retain his customer's patronage by making it impossible for him to use any other manufacturer's product. There was probably also a question of copyright and patent rights.

Whatever the reason it was a great inconvenience to modellers who wanted to combine the products of different manufacturers on their layout. Thankfully the situation is nowhere near so bad today as manufacturers have developed a greater awareness of the needs for compatible couplings and the all round advantage to be gained by adopting common standards. The first realisation dawned with the introduction of TT-3 when British railway modellers accepted the Triang type coupler as standard for the gauge. With the coming of N gauge the process went a stage further whereby an international universal coupling was adopted by all British and Continental manufacturers. The latest of them all, Z gauge, is uncomplicated by the fact that there is at present only one manufacturer producing equipment in this gauge.

It is with the older established scales and gauges namely HO and 00 where the coupling problem still persists although to a lesser extent than it has done in the past. The majority of HO gauge manufacturers on the Continent use the NEM (European Model Railways Standard) Class A coupling which consists of a hook and a movable bow or loop. The bow pivots upwards to rise over and engages with the hook of the coupling to which it is to be joined. An important exception to the manufacturers using this coupling is Fleischmann whose coupling works on the opposite principle, ie the hook itself is pivoted and the somewhat narrower bow or loop remains in a fixed vertical position. The two types of coupling are incompatible.

The most common coupler used on American HO models is what is usually called the 'horn hook' type, sometimes erroneously termed the NMRA type though it has never been sponsored or approved by that body. The Airfix plastic railway kits use the same type. This coupler is very effective for coupling—it has a sideways pressure action—but is less effective when it comes to uncoupling. A simple uncoupler ramp is available but all uncouplers need to be well adjusted, all exactly the same height, and all equally well sprung for the uncoupler ramp to be foolproof. A stiff coupling can result in the vehicle concerned being pushed off the track sideways as the train is pushed over the uncoupler ramp. In practice (and with practice!) it is usually possible to uncouple the 'horn hook' coupler manually using a cocktail stick to force apart the vertical rods of two adjacent couplers. The most desirable American style coupler, though it can be expensive to install, is the Kadee magnetic type. This is a near scale metal knuckle coupler which uncouples

**Below far left and left** *1 European MR Standard Class A coupling. 2 Fleischmann coupling.*

**Above** *American NMRA coupling.*

**Above right and right** *Lima and Graham Farish versions of the tension-lock hook and bar coupling.*

automatically from magnetic ramps which are set inconspicuously into the track. A range of different types is available to suit virtually every make or type of rolling stock and locomotive (American prototype, of course), and it can be had in 0 and N gauge sizes as well as HO; Victors of Islington are the main British Kadee stockists. In America, of course, these couplers are widely sold in hobby shops.

For British outline 00 gauge the Hornby Railways, formerly Tri-ang, tension-lock hook and bar coupling has now gained ascendancy and close variants of it are now used by all manufacturers of ready-to-run locomotives and rolling stock and by a number of kit manufacturers. The coupling works on similar principles to Fleischmann in that the hook pivots upwards to rise over and engage with the loop or bar of the adjoining vehicle. There is no denying that the coupling works very well but in its most exaggerated form it is somewhat ugly and obtrusive. Aesthetically more satisfying is the Peco Simplex claw type coupler formerly used by Hornby Dublo and British Trix and currently included in the Peco Wonderful Wagon kits in the form of the uprated Magni-Simplex Auto Coupler. Whilst it is sometimes possible to engage a hook from the old Tri-ang type coupling on to the claw of a Peco Simplex coupling, for all practical purposes the two types are incompatible. Both types of couplings can be uncoupled remotely; the old Tri-ang type by a ramp between the running rails which lifts the hook and the Peco Simplex by a check rail which guides the coupler to one side. The

*Peco Magni-Simplex Auto Coupling and permanent magnet installed in the track* (Peco).

latest Peco Magni-Simplex Auto Coupler can also be operated by a permanent magnet.

Without an uncoupling ramp, disengaging the old Tri-ang and similar type couplings can be a troublesome business. Both hooks have to be disengaged simultaneously and I have wrestled many times with an item of rolling stock trying to separate one vehicle from another. The solution is simple. All that is needed is a thin piece of metal, wood or plastic that can be slid under the downward projections of the coupling hooks so that the hooks can be raised and disengaged. A thin metal ruler will sometimes do excepting that obstructions such as platforms, boundary fences or a line of wagons on an adjacent siding may prevent access with the ruler. The solution I have hit on is to make a spoon or shovel shaped object as shown in fig 97. The handle is a piece of plastic sprue left over from a kit. By lucky chance the piece I selected had a small cross piece at one end which I have found useful to hold the handle steady between the thumb and the first and second fingers. The flat plate is an offcut of 20 thou plastic card, 1 in × 1½ in. None of the dimensions are critical except the plastic card which must be thin enough to slide between the tops of the running rails and the downward extension of the pivoting hooks and be wide enough to operate both hooks at the same time. The angle of the plastic sprue is also not very critical but I have found that the one chosen, 110°, permits the uncoupling device to be manoeuvred between most obstacles including a line of high sided vehicles on an adjacent siding. It is a wonder such a device has not been offered commercially, but with offcuts of plastic card and plastic sprue being readily available to most modellers, it costs virtually nothing and is so easy to make.

So far, all the couplings I have mentioned have been the various proprietary type automatic couplings. Their obvious advantage is that they engage with each other automatically when two vehicles are brought together and most of them have the added capability of remote uncoupling. Another feature which they all possess which may not be readily apparent to newcomers to the hobby is that they prevent vehicles coming too close together when being pushed. This is done deliberately to avoid buffer locking. I have already referred to this in Chapter 5 and it must be appreciated that buffer locking is a very serious problem in model railways. It arises mainly due to the sharp radius curves that most modellers are forced by space limitations to use. The sharper the radius of the curve the worse the problem becomes. The length of the vehicle is also a factor to consider. The proprietary type automatic couplings are designed to cater for the extreme conditions found in toy model railways where curves of 1 ft 3 in radius in HO and 00 gauges and 9 in in N gauge are common. In coping with these extreme conditions manufacturers of ready-to-run rolling stock are required to ensure that the buffers of opposing vehicles never meet. The couplings in fact act as buffers. For practical purposes this is fine but from the point of view of realism it leaves a lot to be desired. If you are forced to use really sharp radius curves then you have little choice in the matter and you will have to stick to one or other of the proprietary couplings, but for larger radius curves, say 3 ft radius or more in 00 gauge you can consider the alternative of the hook and chain, or three-link and screw couplings (as the two types are referred to), as used by all main line standard gauge railways in Europe. Screw couplings are used on all passenger and continuous brake fitted freight stock and on locomotives used for passenger train working. Three-link couplings are only used on wagons without continuous brakes and on locomotives not required for passenger or fitted freight train working. Both types are available in model form down to 4 mm scale but the screw couplings are only representational and do not work like their prototypes. Three-link couplings and miniature screw couplings have been accepted in 00 for many years. Occasionally critics have referred to their over-scale appearance, in particular the over-size coupling links, and have pointed out that from the realism point of view the average commercial product is not a lot better than some much maligned automatic couplings. To a large extent such criticism is true and a hard look at the great dangling loops of chain on the end of the average British models fitted with three-link couplings, my own included, will confirm this. Like many things in model railways, the problem looks worse in a photograph than it does in the flesh, but with standards improving all the time it was inevitable that someone would point an accusing finger and at the same time come up with a solution. In 00 gauge, Protofour have produced a fine scale three-link coupling which really looks the part. The links are not only the right size but they are also the right shape and they are the right price as well. A further feature of note is that the links can be lifted by magnetism using a special illuminated shunter's pole which is supplied for the purpose. This overcomes what at first glance might be considered a difficult problem since the links are measurably smaller than the normal commercial 00 gauge 'anchor chains' and might be thought of as being fiddly things to handle. If anything, because of their unique magnetic properties, Protofour three-link couplings are easier to use than the other larger types. On all counts, therefore, they are to be recommended, whether or not you are using Protofour standards on the rest of your layout.

Generally speaking loose coupled rolling stock, that is wagons and coaches fitted with three-link couplings or the miniature representation of screw couplings, can only be operated successfully on layouts with curves of 3 ft radius or more. The short wheelbase four-wheeled wagons can sometimes be propelled over curves of shorter radius but, at the same time, longer wheelbase bogie stock requires curves of even larger radius. Therefore 3 ft is only something of a compromise and even larger radius curves are desirable where possible, to be sure of avoiding buffer locking if three-link or screw couplings are used on all rolling stock. The ideal is perhaps a combination of two different types of coupling; three-link for the smaller four-wheel and shorter wheelbase bogie freight stock and automatic for the longer passenger coaches. In a way this matches prototype British practice to a certain extent, since it is normally only the four-wheel and shorter wheelbase freight vehicles that are not fitted with the continuous vacuum

*Fig 97*

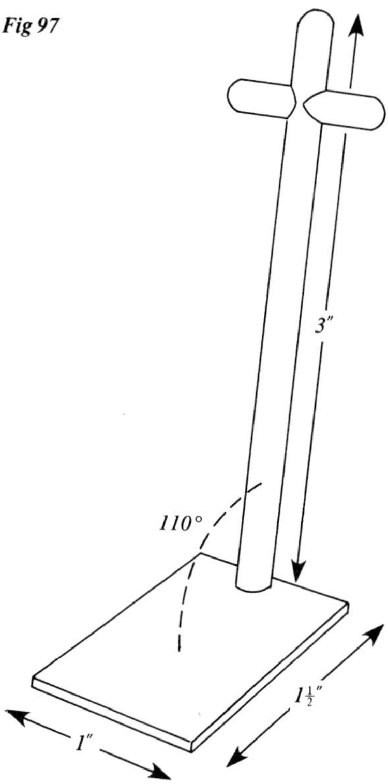


**Fig 97** *Uncoupling device for Tri-ang/Hornby Railways' type couplings.*

**Above** *Screw couplings can be clearly seen on this 4 mm scale LMS horsebox built by D.C. Lawrence which contains a wealth of fine detail* (Larry Goddard).

**Left** *Two couplings on one vehicle; 3-link and Hornby tension-lock.*

brake and are therefore loose coupled. The difficulty with mixing different types of coupling is that some vehicles and all locomotives, unless they are clearly made for one specific duty, will need to be dual fitted. The vehicles that will need special attention are those that can be seen in both freight and passenger trains, such as passenger luggage and parcel vans, perishable wagons, milk tank wagons and some freight vehicles fitted with vacuum brakes. Dual fitting can be accomplished, however, by having a normal coupling hook on the buffer beam of all vehicles and only fixing the three-link chains to the vehicles without automatic couplings.

Three-link and screw couplings are, of course, non-automatic but for 4 mm scale railway modellers who require an unobtrusive automatic coupling without the disadvantages inherent in most proprietary types I recommend the Alex Jackson coupling. The coupling itself is made out of .011 in diameter (32 gauge) spring steel wire and is therefore very cheap to make. Uncoupling is by electromagnet. The Alex Jackson coupling was fully described in the January 1960 issue of *The Model Railway News* and a revised description giving full constructional and dimensional details was given in the July and August 1977 issues of *Model Railways*. The minimum radius recommended in 4 mm scale is 2 ft 6 in and, bearing in mind my earlier comments about buffer locking, it must be remembered that the Alex Johnson coupling does not fulfil the function of a buffer. When pushing, the vehicle buffers themselves fulfil this role and curves must be laid out to ensure that your longest vehicles will not lock buffers. Something larger than 2 ft 6 in radius may be required depending on the length of your rolling stock. The Alex Jackson coupling is capable of adaption to all gauges from N to 0.

Many modellers prefer to assemble their coaching stock into permanently coupled rakes or trains of coaches and there is a lot to be said in favour of this. For one thing it accords with prototype practice since many companies operated their coaching stock in this fashion. The Southern Railway, in particular, even went to the extent of allocating set numbers to each rake of coaches, a set consisting of any number of coaches—two, three, four, six or whatever was required to operate a particular service. The advantage in model form is that corridor connections can be made to link up between the coaches and a rigid form of coupling bar can be used which will overcome the problem of buffer locking. The coupling itself can be little more than a metal bar with a hole drilled at each end, through which it is screwed to the floor of each coach. Normal couplings would, of course, be provided at each end of the rake of coaches for coupling to the locomotive or adding any other items of rolling stock such as extra coaches, parcels vans or express fitted perishable wagons. The one snag with a permanently coupled set of coaches is that units of more than about three coaches can sometimes be awkward things to handle should it be necessary to remove the rake from the layout at any time. Ideally, if you have enough siding space, this need not be necessary and the occasion would only arise infrequently when maintenance is required. If your siding space is limited and you frequently have to resort to hand shunting I recommend that you limit the number of coaches in each set to three.

One obvious candidate for assembly into a permanent rake of coaches is the diesel or electric multiple unit train. Here the more or less permanent connection of the carriages is necessitated by the push-pull method of propulsion since with a power bogie at only one end of a unit (it is hardly conceivable that with a model diesel or electric multiple unit you would need more than one power bogie) the train will be operating in 'reverse' for 50 per cent of its time. Coupling the coaches together provides an opportunity to spread the electrical pick-ups throughout the whole length of the train, thereby overcoming any possibility of the relatively short wheelbase power bogie stalling on the dead frogs of pointwork.

Rolling stock, whether it be coaches or wagons, has endless variety and one is constantly being tempted to add new items to a layout. Whether the inspiration is the introduction of a new proprietary ready-to-run model, or a new kit, or whether one has just seen a plan in a current issue of one of the monthly magazines, whatever the reason, one is constantly being tempted to buy or construct new items. There comes a time, and it happens all too quickly, when you reach saturation point and the available siding space or station terminal roads will not hold any more wagons or coaches without cluttering up the running lines. This will never do and you have to think about storage facilities off the layout, but at the same time in such a position that they are readily available when required. I do not think it is very satisfactory just to keep spare rolling stock in cardboard boxes. It is too fiddly opening and closing the boxes after each operating session and in any case the average cardboard box will not withstand unlimited handling.

A better way is to construct a series of shallow drawers or trays, just deep enough to cover the height of the rolling stock (in 00 gauge say about 2½ in) and devise some means of partitioning the interior of the tray so that each item of rolling stock can be kept apart from its neighbour, rather on the lines of a cutlery drawer. There are any number of extensions of the theme beyond the basic idea. You could, for example, cut grooves in the base of the drawer to take the wheel flanges. A further modification might be to make separate lift-out containers for each item of rolling stock, the containers being designed to fit over the rails and with one open end so that the vehicle it contains can be rolled out directly on to the track, along the lines of a re-railing device. Such an elaboration would be particularly useful for bogie rolling stock. Each drawer or magazine could be constructed internally to take the rolling stock for a particular service or train, such as 'newspaper/parcels train', 'milk train' or 'pick-up goods' to mention three examples. Any means you can devise to hold your spare rolling stock and at the same time make easy its transfer to and from the layout will increase enormously the pleasure of operating sessions. Storing rolling stock off the layout under cover will also help to diminish the cleaning problem!

# Chapter 11

# Operating

With the baseboard built, the track laid, the scenery installed and the locomotives, carriages and wagons either bought or built, what do we do now? Well, the whole point of all the foregoing activity, in case you had forgotten, is to provide a layout on which to operate working model trains. Some people tend to lose sight of this object, rather like some motoring enthusiasts who seem to spend all their time peering into the bonnet or clambering underneath the car but who never have any time (or inclination?) to take themselves or their family out in it. Sometimes it is a bit of an anticlimax, after all the feverish activity in building a layout, to find that it is virtually completed. But very rarely is it completely completed (if that is not too much of a contradition in terms!) as there is always something that can be done, in rather the same way as local authorities are always carrying out road improvements and developers are always pulling down houses and putting up new ones. You may well want to do something similar with your model railway: re-plan a particular track layout, extend a siding, replace a proprietary model goods shed with an exact scale scratch-built model or simply paint a zebra crossing on the road outside the station entrance.

Assuming all the really hard work is over, there is still plenty to keep you occupied when it comes to operating the layout. Exactly what pleasure and fulfilment you obtain will, to a certain extent, depend on your approach to the hobby in the first place. If you merely like to see a locomotive and train on the move then you will find enough pleasure in just that. Watching the motion of the locomotive, the movement of the valve gear, pistons, connecting and coupling rods and the gentle rock of the train as it passes over the points are just some of the things that fascinate the average person who likes to watch the trains go by. On the other hand, if you find the idea of train watching too mild and passive you can add purpose to the operating by running the trains to a timetable, which should embrace a complete service of trains—express passenger, local stopping passenger, goods, empty coaching stock, light engine workings, etc. A specially geared, speeded-up clock can be a useful mechanical aid. It scales down time and enables you to run a full day's service in something like one hour instead of 24, which will also cut out the waiting time between services.

One of the most fascinating operations on a model railway is shunting and the receiving and despatching of goods trains. You can naturally please yourself entirely how to make up your goods trains, and if you want you can do so purely to satisfy aesthetic considerations. For example, one grey wagon, one brown wagon, two white covered vans, one silver oil tanker, one green horse box and a dark grey brake van may make a satisfactory goods train in your estimation. However, it is as well to remember the considerations that dictate the formation of a goods train in real life and to profit from these when you can. The train will consist either of wagons carrying goods from one place to another or it will comprise empty wagons proceeding to a station or loading point to pick up goods. Some wagons (for example, covered parcel vans) will pick up and put down goods all over the system. Others, such as coal wagons, will only carry a load in one direction from coal mine to consumer and for 50 per cent of their time they will run empty.

If you have a goods yard you can add interest to its operation if you try and imagine a typical day's transit of goods, both inwards and outwards, and arrange the formation of the train accordingly. For instance, you may want to take delivery of two wagon loads of coal, some barrels of mineral oil, a combine harvester and the usual daily supply of sundries and parcels. You may have for forwarding some boxes of fruit and tomatoes, some livestock (say cattle or sheep) and a couple of empty coal wagons that have just been unloaded from a previous day's delivery. To cater for this traffic you will need to send to the yard the two loaded coal wagons, an open wagon containing the mineral oil barrels, a flat truck or Lowmac to carry the combine harvester, a couple of ordinary covered vans for

*A named Black 5 5157 'The Glasgow Highlander' meets 5234 under the signal gantry on the 0 gauge garden layout of Ken Longbottom* (Brian Monaghan).

the sundries and parcels and some empty cattle wagons to pick up the livestock. The fruit and tomatoes can probably be despatched in the covered vans after they have deposited the sundries and parcels, but it may be necessary to send in some empty fruit vans specially to pick up this traffic. You must ensure that you have siding space for all these wagons when they arrive, bearing in mind that you have empty wagons already in the yard waiting to be picked up. Also, there must be room to shunt the loaded wagons into the appropriate unloading bays and likewise for the empty wagons to be positioned to pick up their loads.

All this takes a bit of sorting out and if you add further complications, such as limiting the maximum number of wagons that can be hauled by different locomotives, applying weight restrictions which limit the types of locomotive that can enter each siding, plus trying to complete the operation against the clock to meet a timetable, you are likely to find yourself doing a bit of head scratching! To add a little more interest and variety to the method of determining inwards and outward loads, and to simulate the unpredictable daily fluctuations in traffic that often occur, you can write the description of typical loads on to cards which you can shuffle and deal to yourself. Alternatively, you can use ordinary playing cards and have a list of codes showing what each card represents, eg, Ace of Hearts for one combine harvester, Jack of Clubs for 16 tons of household coal, Nine of Spades for one loaded milk tank wagon, etc. The element of chance and surprise can add a little spice to the operation!

Further interest is added if the layout is fully signalled and interlocked, as in the case of the full size railway, yet very few models ever seem to reach this stage of perfection. Signals are all too often installed more for decoration than for actual control purposes. It is a pity really, as there is no doubt that proper signalling can add considerable interest to the operation. Unfortunately, it is a complex subject in itself and there are a number of mechanical and electrical problems to solve that the average modeller fears are either beyond his comprehension or his means. Fully operating signalling is certainly an added expense and complication that will delay the completion of a model layout and will not be absolutely essential for its operation. It can, then, if circumstances dictate, be dispensed with and a modeller working to a budget, with limited spare time available, may find the money he would need to spend on signalling more profitably employed on buying a new locomotive or laying a few extra yards of track. Model railways, unlike the full size ones, can operate without working signals and when modellers find this out, as they do very early on, they tend to neglect the subject. However, I do not want to be accused of encouraging this attitude.

One problem with miniature signals, particularly the mechanical semaphore type, is that they can easily be damaged. When it comes to siting signals you must consider the model railway operator as well as the imaginary driver of the train. Signals at the end of a station platform are a case in point since this is often the place where engines are coupled to or uncoupled from a train. If you are using non-automatic couplings you may find the presence of a signal post at this particular spot will make it difficult to reach the coupling, or you could even find that the signal becomes damaged because of frequent contact with your hand or arm, or the sleeve of your jacket. Where problems such as this are likely to occur it may be necessary to effect a compromise solution so far as siting is concerned or alternatively you may find a different type of signal, such as a bracket signal, may enable you to position the signal post on the far side of the track out of harm's way. Plastic signals such as Ratio's in 00 gauge are very good, but they are light and will not withstand clumsy or thoughless handling. Young children find signals particularly fascinating and they love to move the arms up and down. Unfortunately they are not deterred by the fact that the arms may be linked to a solenoid or a mechanical lever frame by a relatively fragile piece of wire, and either the wire gets bent or the arm comes off the pivot when they try to move it.

Certainly some practical aspects have to be considered when it comes to the installation of signalling and you may often find that you have to compromise with what is required by railway regulations and what you have room for on your layout. One book which I recommend on the subject, both from the point of view of content and value for money, is 'British Railway Signalling', first published by Ian Allen in 1963 and now revised. The book is a mine of information about different types of signals, their layout at stations and junctions, and the different rules and regulations governing their use and the operating of trains. In fact, it gives all the prototype information the modeller needs to

**Below and right** *The standard range of Eckon 4 mm scale colour light signals showing the wide variety of types available. Also shown is a working signal indicating 2 aspect junction signal* (CCH Models).

know to enable him to make an authentic installation on his layout.

There is no shortage of proprietary signals, ready-made or in kit form, both for the mechanical semaphore and the colour light variety in all the popular scales and gauges. The extent to which miniaturisation has been extended in the field of working colour light signals is very commendable even down to N gauge. For British prototypes Eckon produce an extensive range of 4 mm scale colour light signal kits in two, three and four aspects in a variety of different combinations and styles such as platform, lineside or wall mounted and ground signals. Built around grain of wheat lamp bulbs the housings are technically oversize but by no means excessively so. Small resistors reduce the normal 12-16 volt AC power supply to prolong the lamp life and avoid the risk of overheating which might otherwise distort the plastic housings. The range of Ratio 4 mm scale plastic kits covering GWR square and tubular posts, LMS upper quadrant, LNWR lower quadrant, LNER latticed posts and a gantry set are now well known. They have also introduced a range of working semaphore signals based on GWR square post prototypes which are a real break through for 4 mm scale modellers requiring a remote control mechanical system. The post and arms, including the operating wire and the special spring-return mechanism, are supplied ready assembled and painted where necessary and it only remains to fit the ladder, platforms and balance weights to complete the model. A particularly noteworthy feature is that the semaphore arms are fitted with correct colour see-through spectacle lenses. The operating mechanism in the base of the signal is encased in a tube which enables the signal to be installed in a $\frac{1}{2}$ in diameter hole drilled in the baseboard. The signal is operated by a remote control lever which can be similarly installed in a $\frac{1}{2}$ in diameter hole at any point in the baseboard convenient to the operator. The signal and lever are connected below the baseboard by a length of cord passing through small brass eyes at intervals of about 12 in. An adjuster tied into the cord ensures the correct tension. Other manufacturers supply a range of etched brass semaphore arms and signal ladder parts and cast metal brackets to aid home construction using basic raw materials such as metal bars or tubing or even lengths of rail section for the posts. Disc and miniature semaphore ground signals are also available in 4 mm scale.

Throughout I have emphasised the need for cleaning and maintenance. In the chapter on electrical equipment I stressed that rails and wheels should be clean to ensure electrical conductivity between the power source and the motor (page 103). A most useful aid to this is Electrolube MP-64X which is available from Peco stockists. Applied to a clean cloth and rubbed well on to rail surfaces and wheel tyres it removes contamination. A further thin coating improves electrical conductivity and reduces the need for frequent cleaning. It is also a mechanical lubricant ideal for all bearings, gear assemblies, etc, and is particularly suitable for cleaning the brushes and commutators of electric motors. With ordinary lubricating oils, any excess on the gears and wheels can get thrown around on to rail surfaces and electrical pick ups, interfering with the electrical conductivity.

Regular cleaning and maintenance of rolling stock wheels and bearings will reduce their drag resistance, this enabling locomotives to haul longer and heavier loads and improve their performance on starting and on climbing gradients. It will also increase their speed capabilities—but this can be a mixed blessing. Most model railway locomotives are capable of going far faster than their full-size counterparts. It is all too easy to turn the controller to the maximum notch and let the locomotive run away with its train, but the sight of a train lurching into a corner at a scale 150 mph looks utterly ridiculous.

By a simple scaling down you can work out the correct speed for your trains. If you time the train over a measured distance and use the figures in the table below you can calculate its approximate scale speed. For distances less than those quoted in the table the timings would be reduced in proportion, eg, over a distance of 35 feet a 4 mm scale train would take 30 seconds to approximate to a scale speed of 60 mph, or 12 seconds over 14 feet. It is interesting to note that in HO the figures for feet per minute are the same as for miles per hour.

After you have tried a number of runs you will soon get to know where to set the controller to obtain a realistic speed. Periodical timing checks are one way of keeping an eye on the performance of your locomotives and rolling stock. Longer and slower runs may well indicate that the rolling stock is in need of attention either because the rolling resistance is increased or because insufficient power is getting through the circuit to the motor.

Also there are the visual aspects to consider, which brings us to dusting the layout. Many model railway items, especially the smaller lighter scenic accessories, are comparatively fragile, and I find an old shaving brush is an ideal tool for most cleaning purposes. It is small enough to get into most nooks and crannies and to be manageable. Smooth, flat surfaces are the obvious places where dust shows most, and a regular cleaning will make all the difference.

Cleaning also presents the opportunity for inspecting the trackwork and lineside accessories. You should be particularly careful to ensure that there are no loose metal objects such as track pins, nuts or screws lying on or near the tracks. They can very easily cause short circuits across the rails or insulated wheels of locomotives, especially the Tri-ang/Hornby types fitted with Magnadhesion where pins sometimes get attracted to the magnets in the locomotive chassis. These loose objects are a potential source of trouble since they can cause derailment by jamming point switch blades or check rails. Any nuts, bolts or screws should be carefully examined since the odds are they have worked loose and fallen from a passing locomotive or train.

It can be annoying when you start what you hope and expect to be an enjoyable operating session to find things going wrong. Maybe a locomotive refuses to move or stalls on the pointwork, or a wagon or coach keeps derailing or uncoupling itself, or a thousand and one other mishaps. It is the nature of all working things that they do not go on forever, and inevitably something will move out of alignment or bend, break or simply wear out. It is very often the most trivial thing that is the root cause of the problem and it takes far more time finding the source than it does applying the cure. The only course is to approach the problem methodically and eliminate all possible causes one by one.

It is impossible to give a fault finding chart listing all trouble spots and their cure but the two most likely problems are derailments or an interruption or break in the electrical circuit. In the case of electrical troubles, first of all try another locomotive to see if the fault is with the locomotive or the track. If it is the track, check right through the circuit from mains plug to the electric motor. If it appears to be the locomotive attach the 12-volt power supply direct to the motor to check whether it is the motor at fault or the electrical pick-up. In the case of derailments this will be due to displacement of either wheels or track. If every item of rolling stock is affected it will most likely be due to the track but if only one item is troublesome it will most likely be the wheels of the offending vehicle. In both cases

| **Feet per minute** | | | | **Miles per hour** |
|---|---|---|---|---|
| N Gauge | HO | 00/EM/ Protofour | 0 Gauge | Scale equivalent |
| 6 | 10 | 12 | 20 | 10 |
| 12 | 20 | 23 | 40 | 20 |
| 18 | 30 | 35 | 60 | 30 |
| 24 | 40 | 46 | 80 | 40 |
| 30 | 50 | 58 | 100 | 50 |
| 36 | 60 | 70 | 120 | 60 |
| 42 | 70 | 81 | 140 | 70 |
| 48 | 80 | 93 | 160 | 80 |

check for gauge and for any vertical displacement. Wheels sometimes work loose on their axles and some of the lighter plastic items of rolling stock can warp and twist lifting one of the four wheels off the track. Trackwork is very much at the mercy of the baseboard which, if it shrinks, twists or warps, will take the track along with it. Check this with a straight edge laid along the top of the rails. Premature uncoupling, which is sometimes another source of trouble, is also likely to be caused by uneven track, especially if you find it happens on one particular spot on the layout.

To conclude, I have tried to show in this book that there is a lot more to model railways than may at first meet the eye. It has not been possible to touch exhaustively on every single aspect of the hobby, but the book should give you plenty of ideas on how you can go railway modelling at the present time. To a large extent the hobby is a personal thing. You can get out of it exactly what you want, and although there are certain conventions, rules and guide lines which should normally be followed you can, if you want, flout the lot and you will only have yourself to answer to. How *you* go railway modelling is in the end up to you.

# Appendices

## 1 Model railway and allied clubs

It is not practical in a book of this kind to give accurate details of the several hundred model railway and allied clubs that exist in Great Britain today. The majority of the organising committees of such clubs consist of spare-time volunteers who are elected to their posts and it is inevitable therefore that, with changes brought about by Annual General Meetings and with club officers having to resign for private or business reasons, alterations in the names and addresses of club secretaries will arise. Changes also occur in the clubs themselves, particularly in the case of local district clubs as new ones are created and some of the established clubs find for various reasons that they have to close down. A list of such clubs can easily lose its value by becoming out of date.

Readers in Britain who are interested to know whether there is a model railway club in their vicinity are advised to refer to back numbers of the main model railway magazines where club activities are reported regularly each month. The chances are that during the year most clubs will be referred to at one time or another. In addition *Railway Modeller* periodically gives an up-to-date club register. The number of such clubs is such that it takes more than one issue of the magazine to list and give details of them all.

Less liable to change are the clubs and societies serving a particular branch or aspect of the hobby which are organised on a national basis. A list showing the scope of such clubs follows. The club titles adequately describe the interests they aim to serve. Such clubs perform a valuable function bringing together modellers with a common interest throughout the country by means of club journals, publications and meetings. Very often these national clubs have their own local branches, autonomous organisations in themselves holding meetings in various centres and circulating their own news sheets to members. If you can identify your interests with any one of these national clubs or societies it can very often be to your advantage to apply for membership, since many such organisations offer facilities unobtainable elsewhere. For example, some of the societies who cater for particular scales or gauges produce for their members a range of essential items such as track parts, wheels, or even complete kits for making locomotives and rolling stock not normally available from ordinary trade sources. Demonstrating your interests by joining such a club also helps to establish the potential demand for certain items, and a healthy club acting on behalf of several hundreds or thousands of members can often bring influence to bear on manufacturers to produce the kind of equipment most wanted by members.

The following lists some of the national clubs and societies catering for specialised aspects of the hobby:

### Scales and gauges etc

Two Millimetre Scale Association
N Gauge Society
The 009 Society
Three Millimetre Society
EM Gauge Society
Protofour Society
Scalefour Society
S Gauge Model Railway Society
Gauge 0 Guild
Association of 16 mm NG Modellers
Gauge 1 Model Railway Association
Hornby Railway Collectors' Association (Gauge 0 and Dublo)

### Prototype interests

Great Western Society Limited
The LMS Society
LNER Study Group
Southern Railways Group
Industrial Railway Society
Tramway & Light Railway Society
Historical Model Railway Society
Locomotive Club of Great Britain
Railway Correspondence & Travel Society
Stephenson Locomotive Society

# 2 Railway books and magazines

There is a vast library of railway books, all of which are potentially interesting to railway modellers depending on the particular project they have chosen. The following is a limited choice, but the titles have been selected either because they have been written and produced with railway modellers in mind or because they contain a wealth of prototype information of general interest to modellers. No guarantee can be given for the up-to-date accuracy of all details. Many of the railway histories, such as those published by David & Charles, Ian Allan, Oakwood Press and others, contain prototype information, particularly drawings or photographs, on locomotives and rolling stock which can be invaluable to modellers.

## Magazines

**Continental Modeller:** Published bi-monthly. Peco Publications and Publicity Ltd.

**Model Railway Constructor:** Published monthly. Ian Allan Ltd.

**Model Railways:** Published monthly on the first Friday of every month. Model and Allied Publications Ltd.

**Model Trains:** Published for the proprietors Airfix Products Ltd on the second Friday of each month by Kristall Productions Ltd, 4 Surbiton Hall Close, Kingston, Surrey.

**Railway Modeller:** Published monthly on the 24th of preceding month. Peco Publications and Publicity Ltd.

**Rail Miniature Flash** and **Loco Revue:** French language magazines available from Peco Technical Advice Bureau.

**Model Railroader:** Published monthly. Kalmbach Publishing Co, 1027 N 7th Street, Milwaukee, Wisconsin 53233, USA.

**Railroad Model Craftsman:** Published monthly. Carstens Publications Inc, PO Box 700, Newton, New Jersey 07860, USA.

## Practical modelling books

**Miniature Building Construction, Miniature Locomotive Construction, Miniature Landscape Modelling,** by John H. Ahern, **Miniature Scenic Modelling,** by Jack Kine, **Painting and Lining Scale Models,** by R.C. Rogers, **Narrow Gauge Railway Modelling,** by D. Boreham, Argus Books Ltd.

**Model Locomotive Construction in 4 mm scale,** by Guy Williams, Ian Allan Ltd.

**Gauge 0 Guild Handbooks; No 1 Trade Directory, No 2 Standards & Trackwork, No 3 Coach & Wagon Construction, No 4 Locomotive Construction, No 5 Signal Construction.** Gauge 0 Guild.

**Wheel Specifications for the Modeller,** by M. Sharman, Oxford Publishing Co.

**60 Plans for Small Railways, Plans for Larger Layouts, Track Plans, A Home for Your Railway, Starting in Scale 00, Canals** (How to add a canal to your layout), **Railways in the Garden,** by Don Neale, **Period Railway Modelling—Buildings,** by Vivien Thompson, **Buckingham Great Central,** by Peter Denny, **Narrow Gauge Adventure,** by P.D. Hancock. Peco Publications & Publicity Ltd.

**PSL Model Railway Guides: 1 Baseboards, Track and Electrification; 2 Layout Planning; 3 Structure Modelling; 4 Scenery; 5 Operating Your Layout: 6 Branch Line Railways; 7 Modern Railways; 8 Narrow gauge Railways,** all by Michael Andress. Patrick Stephens Ltd.

## Locomotives

**Historic Locomotive Drawings in 4 mm Scale,** drawn by F.J. Roche, **BR Main Line Diesels.** Ian Allan Ltd.

**GWR Engines, Names, Numbers, Types and Classes** (1940 to Preservation), by B. Whitehurst, **The Engines of the LMS (Built 1923–51),** by J.W.P. Rowledge, **The History of Highland Railway Locomotives,** by P. Tatlow. **A Pictorial Record of Great Western Engines, A Pictorial Record of Great Western Absorbed Engines,** by J.H. Russell, Oxford Publishing Co.

**Locomotives in Outline,** by C.J. Freezer. Peco Publications & Publicity Ltd.

**The Locomotives of the GWR,** Parts 1-12. Railway Correspondence & Travel Society. **Locomotives of the LNER,** Parts 1-10, **Locomotives of the LB&SCR;** Parts 1-3, **Locomotives of the LSWR,** Parts 1-2, **Locomotives of the LC&DR, Locomotives of the SER, Locomotives of the SE&CR, Locomotives of the Southern Railway,** Parts 1-2, Railway Correspondence & Travel Society.

**Locomotives Illustrated.** Published quarterly by Ian Allan Ltd.

**Fowler Locomotives, Stanier Locomotives, Maunsell Locomotives, Bulleid Locomotives, Ivatt & Riddles Locomotives, Gresley Locomotives,** by Brian Haresnape, **Churchward Locomotives,** by Brian Haresnape & Alec Swain. Ian Allan Ltd.

## Coaches

**Preserved Railway Coaches.** Ian Allan Ltd.

**Great Western Railway Coaches 1890–1954, Gresley's Coaches,** by Michael Harris. David & Charles.

**Southern Railway Rolling Stock, Carriage Stock of Minor Standard Gauge Railways,** by R.W. Kidner, **Carriage Stock of the SE&CR,** by David Gould, **Carriage Stock of the LB&SCR,** by P.J. Newbury. Oakwood Press.

**The Coaching Stock of British Railways 1980,** by P. Mallaband & L.J. Bowles. Railway Correspondence & Travel Society.

**LMS Coaches (An Illustrated History),** by R.J. Essery & D. Jenkinson, **A Pictorial Record of LNWR Coaches,** by D. Jenkinson, **A Pictorial Record of Great Western Coaches,** Vol 1 1838-1913 and Vol 2 1903-1948, by J.H. Russell. Oxford Publishing Co.

## Wagons

**Historic Wagon Drawings in 4 mm Scale,** drawn by F.J. Roche. Ian Allan Ltd.

**History of GWR Goods Wagons Vols 1 & 2,** by A.G. Atkins, W. Beard, D.J. Hyde & R. Tourret, **The LMS Wagon,** by R.J. Essery & K. Morgan. David & Charles.

**Great Western Wagons Appendix, Great Western Wagons Plan Book,** by J.H. Russell, **A Pictorial Record of LNER Wagons,** by Peter Tatlow, **Midland Wagons,** Vols 1 & 2 by R.J. Essery, **Private Owner Wagons,** Vols 1 & 2, by W. Hudson. Oxford Publishing Co.

**The Modeller's Sketchbook of Private Owner Wagons,** Books 1, 2 & 3. Eames (Reading) Ltd.

**Petroleum Rail Tank Wagons of Britain,** Tourret Publishing, 5, Bryan Close, Abingdon, Oxon.

**BR Standard Freight Wagons, Private Owner Freight Wagons, Pre-nationalisation Freight Wagons, BR General Parcels Rolling Stock, BR Departmental Rolling Stock,** by D. Larkin. D. Bradford Barton Ltd.

## General

**Historical Model Railway Society Livery Registers: No 1 Caledonian Railway, No 3 LSWR & Southern Railway. Midland Style,** by George Dow, **Great Western Way,** by J.N. Slinn.

**British Railway Signalling,** by G.M. Kichenside & Alan Williams. Ian Allan Ltd.

**Railway Stations—Southern Region,** by Nigel Wikeley & John Middleton. Peco Publications & Publicity Ltd.

**An Historical Survey of Great Western Engine Sheds 1947,** by E. Lyons, **An Historical Survey of Great Western Engine Sheds—1837-1947** (including amalgamated companies) by E. Lyons & E. Mountford, **An Historical Survey of Southern Sheds 1923-1947** by C. Hawkins & G. Reeve. Oxford Publishing Co.

**A Pictorial Record of Great Western Signalling,** by A. Vaughan, **A Pictorial Record of LMS Signals,** by G. Warburton, **A Pictorial Record of Southern Signals,** by G. Pryer. Oxford Publishing Co.

**Road Vehicles of the GWR,** by Philip Kelley. Oxford Publishing Co.

**A Pictorial Record of Great Western Architecture,** by A. Vaughan, **An Historical Survey of Selected Great Western Stations, Vols 1 & 2,** by R. Clark, **Great Western Branch Line Termini, Vols 1 & 2,** by Paul Karau, **A Pictorial Record of LMS Architecture,** by V.R. Anderson & G.K. Fox, **An Historical Survey of Selected Southern Stations,** by G.A. Pryer & G.J. Bowring, **An Historical Survey of the Somerset & Dorset Railway** (Track Layout and Illustrations) by C.W. Judge & C. Potts. Oxford Publishing Co.

**The Watlington Branch,** by John Holden, **The Woodstock Branch,** by Richard Lingard, **The Calne Branch,** by G. Tanner, **The Ashburton Branch,** by A.R. Kingdom, **The Kingsbridge Branch,** by K. Williams & D. Reynolds, **Banbury-Verney Junction Branch,** by Bill Simpson, **The Bridport Branch,** by B.L. Jackson & M.J. Tattershall, **The Faringdon Branch,** by A. Vaughan (and other titles in preparation). Oxford Publishing Co.

**Eric Plans-GWR & LMS Buildings, Downesplans-Country Buildings,** by Allan Downes. Peco Publications & Publicity Ltd.

**An Index to Railway Model Drawings,** by S.A. Leleux. The Oakwood Press.

**Track Layout Diagrams of the GWR and BR(WR).** A series of publications in several parts, giving detailed diagrams of every station and siding layout, c 1880-1920, with details and dates of alterations up to 1973. Published by R.A. Cooke, 'Evergreen', School Lane, Harwell, Oxon, OX11 0ES.

**Copies of original drawings from railway archives.** Oxford Publishing Co/British Rail (Western Region) Joint Venture, Dell cottage, Bank, Nr Lyndhurst, Hants.

**An Album of Pre-grouping Signal Boxes,** by M.A. King. Turntable Publications.

**Beatties Comprehensive Guide to 00/HO British Outline.** Beatties.

**Along Hornby Lines,** by B. Huntingdon. Oxford Publishing Co.

# 3 Manufacturers and suppliers

This directory of names and addresses (or countries of origin) of manufacturers and suppliers of model railway equipment available in Great Britain has been compiled from advertisements appearing in the UK model railway periodicals and from firms' catalogues. The brief description of each firm's products is included as an aid to identification and is not intended to be fully comprehensive. The unit size of manufacturers and suppliers in the model railway industry varies considerably from private individuals working in their spare time producing one or two small accessories, to large public companies who manufacture and market a fully comprehensive range of items covering every conceivable aspect of the hobby. Within these two extremes there are, of course, any number of variations, and changes are forever occurring in the industry. Readers are therefore advised to scan the advertisement and editorial pages of the monthly magazines to keep abreast of new manufacturers, new products, new developments and changes in the marketing arrangements of existing firms.

The high quality of goods manufactured in France, Germany, Italy, Austria, Switzerland, Spain, United States of America and Japan attracts a large number of customers in the UK and there are a number of agencies specialising in the importation of these products. These arrangements alter from time to time as agencies change hands and it is not possible to give a complete picture of this important aspect of the hobby. No responsibility can be accepted for the goods or services provided by the companies listed, nor can we guarantee up-to-date accuracy of all addresses.

**ABS Models,** 39 Napier Road, Hamworthy, Poole, Dorset, BH15 4LX.
N, 00 and 0 kits, parts and accessories.

**A.C. Model Engineering,** 25, Oakhart Road, Whissendine, Oakham, Rutland.
Rolling bars and riveting tools.

**ADE** (West Germany).
HO track system and scale length HO DB coaches.

**AGW Electronics Ltd,** Hayford Way, Staveley, Derbys, S43 3JR.
Electronic controllers, sound unit.

**AHM—Assoc Hobby Manufacturers Inc (USA).**
American HO and HO9 rolling stock and building kits, etc.

**Airfix Products Ltd,** Haldane Pl, Garratt La, London SW18 4NB.
Airfix GMR (Great Model Railways) railway system—comprehensive range of 00, British outline ready-to-run locomotives, rolling stock and MTC (Multiple Train Controller) electronic control system.

Comprehensive range of plastic construction kits, including some railway items.
**Alco Models** (USA).
American HO etched brass locos and rolling stock manufactured in Japan.
**Ian Allan Ltd,** Terminal House, Shepperton, Middx TW17 8AS.
Model Railway and transport periodicals and books.
**Anbrico Scale Models,** 5 Perseverance St, Pudsey, West Yorks, LS28 7PZ.
4 mm scale cast metal railcar and road vehicle kits, coach bogie kits and parts. N diesel loco kits.
**Archangel Models,** 43 Cock La, High Wycombe, Bucks, HP13 7DY.
0 gauge live steam model locos and fittings.
**Argo Transacord,** The Decca Record Co Ltd, Decca House, Albert Embankment, London, SE17 SW.
Railway sound effect gramophone records.
**Arnold-N** (West Germany).
Comprehensive range of N gauge locos, rolling stock and equipment.
**Athearn** (USA).
Extensive range of HO diesel locos and rolling stock.
**Atlas** (USA).
0, HO & N American diesel locomotives manufactured in Europe.

**Bachmann** (USA).
American N and HO gauge locos and rolling stock.
**Badger.**
Airbrushes marketed by Humbrol.
**Bailey's Dailies Models,** 48 Sandy Park Road, Bristol.
00 & N number plates, accessories, etc.
**A. Barton (Electronics),** High Banks, Newport Road, Sandown, I of W.
Control units and components.
**R. Baxter,** 5 Manor View, Selsey, Stroud, Glos GL5 5LR.
4 mm scale cast metal accessories, bus kits, etc.
**Beaver Products Co,** 39 Napier Rd., Hanworthy, Poole, Dorset, BH15 4LX.
N loco kits, wheels and gears etc.
**BEC Kits,** PO Box 5, Aldershot, Hants, GU12 6JP.
4 mm scale cast metal tram kits.
**BEMO** (West Germany).
HO9 & HO12 German narrow gauge rolling stock.
**Berliner TT Bahnen** (East Germany).
Range of TT (1:120 Scale) locos, rolling stock, track and accessories.
**Bonds O'Euston Road Ltd,** Rumbolds Hill, Midhurst, Sussex.
0 gauge rail, chairs, sleepers, wheels, castings, motors, etc.
**Bowser** (USA).
American HO loco kits.
**D. Bradford Barton Ltd,** Trethellan House, St Aubyns Road, Truro, Cornwall.
Extensive range of prototype railway books.
**Brawa** (Austria).
N and HO trolley bus, motorway and cable cars, signals, lamposts, traverser, etc.
**S & R Brewster Ltd,** 86-88 Union St, Plymouth.
S & B Soldering irons & accessories suitable for modellers.
**J.W. Bricket,** 22, Shelley Road, Horsham, Sussex.
7 mm white metal figures.
**Bristol Models,** 76 Station Rd, Filton, Bristol, BS12 7JJ.
Range of 4 mm scale cast metal loco kits and chassis.
**Bristone Model Products,** 12A Farm Rd, Hove, Sussex.
The Western Rivet Press tool, rolling mill, wormgear puller, track cutting jig.
**Britains Ltd,** Blackhorse La, Walthamstow, London, E17.
1:32 scale models of farm machinery, figures, animals, trees etc.
**BSL Hobbytime,** 5 & 7 Ravenswood Cr, West Wickham, Kent.
Coach body kits and accessories in 4 and 7 mm scales.
**Builder Plus, B & G (Wetherby) Ltd,** York Road Industrial Estate, Wetherby, Yorks.
Cardboard & wood building construction kits.
**Busch** (Germany).
N and HO gauge building kits, light fittings and scenic materials.

**Cambrian Model Products,** Bethania, Llanon, Dyfed, SY23 5NS.
Plastic wagon kits, 3-link couplings, 4 mm & 7 mm scale.
**Cav'N'dish** (see W & H (Models) Ltd).
N loco and coach kits.
**CCW Model Manufacturing Co,** Unit 8, Green Lane Industrial Estate, Small Heath, Birmingham, B9 5QP.
Comprehensive range of 0 gauge kits and parts.
**Central Valley** (USA).
American freight car kits.
**Centre Models,** 51 Sparkenhoe Street, Leicester.
4 mm scale industrial locomotive kits, 009 Leek & Manifold loco, coach & transporter wagon.
**T.R. Charlton,** 206 Dower Rd, Four Oaks, Sutton Coldfield, Warwicks, B75 6SZ.
4 mm, 7 mm and 1 gauge panelled coach parts.
**Chivers Finelines,** 49, St Christines Ave, Leyland, Preston, Lancs, PR5 2YS.
White metal 0-16.5 mm narrow gauge loco kits.
**Classic Scale Models Ltd,** 79 Vyse St, Birmingham, B18 6HA.
4 mm & 7 mm coach kits.
**Coastway Models,** Stanage Works, South Coast Road, Telescombe Cliffs, Sussex.
Electronic controller kits.
**Cockrobin Controls,** 106 Drove Rd, Weston-super-Mare, BS23 3NW.
Quality components for electrical control.
**Codar Ltd,** PO Box 3, Rottingdean, Brighton, BN2 8AZ.
Electronic controllers, steamsound electronic synthesizer.
**Como Drills,** The Mill, Mill Lane, Worth, Deal, Kent.
Variable ratio gearboxes, complete with motor.
**Con-cor** (USA).
American HO, American passenger car kits, accessories and N gauge model railway system.
**Conrad** (West Germany).
HO track system.
**C.J. Controls,** Crofty Industrial Estate, Swansea.
Minitrol controllers.
**Cooper Craft,** 25 Swain Street, Watchet, Somerset. TA23 0AD.
Series of plastic wagon and building kits, 4 mm scale.
**Cornard Model Co,** Holt House, Caswell Bay, Swansea, West Glamorgan.
Wire and polythene tubing for point control system. Signal and point lever frames.
**Charles Covey Models,** 572 Kingston Road, Raynes Park, London, SW20.
0 gauge loco kits, parts and accessories.
**Cox Hobbies Inc** (USA).
Limited range of HO diesel locos & rolling stock.
**Craftsman Models,** 35 Willoughby Road, Langley, Slough, Berks, SL3 8JH.
4 mm scale locomotive kits.
**Custom Brass-NJ International** (USA).
American HO brass locos & rolling stock manufacturered in Japan.
**C & W Electronics,** 5 Rivoli Buildings, Chapel Road, Worthing, Sussex, BN11 1BS.
Gaugemaster electronic controller.

**Dart Castings,** 4 Bridgetown, Totnes, Devon.
4 mm cast metal figures, accessories, etc.
**David & Charles,** Railway Station, Newton Abbot, Devon.

Railway and transport books containing prototype material of interest to modellers.

**Davric Kits,** Distributed by: Marton Models Ltd, 33, Parliament Road, Middlesborough, Cleveland.
4 mm plastic road vehicle kits.

**D.G. Models,** 2 Linden Ave, Halesowen, W Midlands.
7 mm, 4 mm, 2 mm road vehicle kits.

**Digitol,** Southern Electronic Consultants (Gosport) Ltd, 26 Findon Road, Gosport, Hants.
Digital electronic controllers.

**Diorama Buildings,** 55, High St, Grantham, Lincolnshire.
4 mm card building kits.

**DJH Kits Ltd,** Leadgate Industrial Estate, Lore Hill Road, Consett, Co Durham, DH8 7RS.
4 mm scale cast metal loco kits.

**D & M Castings, Huddersfield.**
N gauge cast metal kits and accessories.

**D & S Models,** 46, The Street, Wallington, Nr Baldock, Herts, SG7 6SW.
4 mm white metal & etched brass wagon kits.

**Dundas Models,** 9 Dundas St, Bo'ness, EH51 0DF Scotland.
009 model railway specialists.

**Eames (Reading) Ltd,** 24 Tudor Rd, Reading, RH1 1NH.
Various kits and parts, low melt solder, etc, of great interest to modellers, Jamieson loco kits.

**East Coast Joint Models,** 10 Cowdray Avenue, Colchester, CO1 1UT.
4 mm scale locomotive kits.

**Eckon,** CCH Models, 5 Kings Ave, Holland-on-Sea, Essex, CO15 5EU.
4 mm Colourlight Signals, accessories.

**ECM Control Systems Ltd,** Blatchford Road, Horsham, Sussex, RH13 5QR.
Electronic controllers, components & accessories.

**Eheim** (Germany).
N and HO trolley bus and tram equipment.

**Ejay Models,** (RM8), 83, Prestbury Road, Cheltenham, Glos.
4 mm scale small parts.

**Electroten** (Spain).
Range of HO gauge items including loco and rolling stock.

**Ellmar Products Ltd,** 14 Cherston Road, Loughton, Essex.
British outline bodies for Marklin Mini-Club Z gauge. Distributor: A.M. Richards.

**Endura Ltd,** 161, Dugdale Hill Lane, Potters Bar, Herts, EN6 2DF.
ABS plastic structural steel sections.

**Faller (UK) Ltd,** 27 Richmond Place, Grand Parade, Brighton.
Extensive range of building kits, N and HO.

**Festiniog Railway Co,** Porthmadog, Gwynedd.
009 narrow gauge loco and rolling stock kits.

**Finecast** (See Wills).

**Fleetline Model Company,** 101, Jellicoe Ave, Alverstoke, Gosport, Hants.
N gauge cast metal accessories.

**Fleischmann** (Germany).
Comprehensive range of Continental N and HO locos, coaches and wagons, track and equipment. Sole UK Distributor: M & R (Model Railways) Ltd.

**Floquil** (USA).
Super quality paints.

**Fourmill Model Rly Kits,** 91, Edge Junction, Thornhill Edge, Dewsbury, W Yorks, WF12 6PY.
4 mm etched brass GWR carriage kits.

**France Trains** (France).
French railway coaching stock in HO and 0.

**Fulgurex** (Switzerland).
Craftsman-built brass locos and rolling stock in HO and 0.

**Garrick Leisure Consultants Ltd,** 32 High Street, Kingston-on-Thames, Surrey.
00 and N trees, 4 mm scale bus kits.

**Gaugemaster** (see C & W Electronics).

**GEM**—see under George E. Mellor.

**GEM Models** (USA).
Handmade brass models imported from Japan.

**Graham Farish,** Romany Works, Holton Heath, Poole, Dorset, BH16 6JL.
Extensive range ofN locos, coaches, wagons, Liveway track and points, 00 coaches, wagons and track.

**GS Models,** 19 Dolorme Street, London W6.
4 mm scale London Transport bus kits and Met Rly 'F' class loco kit.

**Gunther** (West Germany).
HO loco kits and accessories.

**Hag** (Switzerland).
HO Swiss prototype locos and coaches.

**Hallmark** (USA).
HO brass locos and rolling stock manufactured in Japan.

**Hambling's (Models) Ltd,** 29 Cecil Ct, Charing Cross Rd, London WC2.
Wide range of 4 mm scale parts and accessories, Merco lithos, Mercontrol point control, Bilteezi building and scenic model kits, etc.

**Hammant & Morgan Ltd,** Handem Works, Apem Estate, St Albans Rd, Watford, Herts, WD2 4AW.
Manufacturer of power units, point motors, etc. Distributor of "Woodland Scenics" tree kits and landscaping materials.

**Hamo** (Germany).
Marklin HO locomotives for 2-rail.

**Harbutt's Plasticine Ltd,** Bathampton, Bath, Somerset.
Manufacturers of 'Plasticine' the world-famous modelling clay.

**Hawko** (available from: Charles Covey (Models)).
Range of 0 gauge 2-rail pointwork.

**HB Models,** 12 Grove Park, Tring, Herts.
0 gauge live steam locomotives, kits and ready-to-run.

**Heljan** (Denmark).
N, HO and 00 gauge building kits.

**Herkat** (Germany).
N and HO gauge accessories, electrical equipment, etc.

**Highfield Models,** Highfield Hse, Bishop Thornton, Harrogate, Yorks, HG3 3JY.
0 gauge locomotive and rolling stock body kits.

**Highway Models,** 20 Cwmdonkin Terrace, Swansea, SA2 0RQ.
4 mm scale lorry kits.

**Hornby Minitrix.**
Range of British outline N gauge locos, rolling stock and equipment manufactured by Trix Germany.

**Hornby Railways,** Hornby Hobbies Ltd, Westwood, Margate, Kent, CT9 4JX.
Comprehensive range of 00 British outline ready-to-run locos, rolling stock, track and accessories. Zero 1 multiple train control system. 3½" gauge live-steam 'Rocket', coach and track.

**Humbrol,** Humber Oil Co Ltd, Marfleet, Hull, Humberside.
Manufacturer of enamels, modelling adhesives, craft knives, dopes, thinners, brush cleaners, authentic colours, metallics, poster colours and airbrushes.

**Ibertren** (Spain).
N gauge continental rolling stock.

**Industrial Display Co Ltd,** Lower Rd, Forest Row, Sx.
Manufacturer of Wills 'Finecast' kits.

**Intermodel** (W Germany).
N, HO and 0 continental brass locomotives, steam and electric outline.

**Jackson Evans,** 4, Dartmouth Rd, Coventry.
4 mm smoke deflectors, pre-cut GWR name and numberplates.

**Jackson Model Products.**
Range of 4 mm scale wheels now manufactured by Romford Models Ltd.

**Jamieson** (distributed by Eames).
4 mm scale nickel-silver locomotive kits.

**Jaycraft,** 45 Symonds Road, Preston, Lancs, PR2 3DH.
00 one piece moulded polyester resin loco and tender bodies.

**JC Models** (USA).
American HO passenger car kits.

**Jidenco,** 32, Coombe Court, Thatcham, Berks.
Etched brass loco, coach & wagon kits.

**Jouef** (France).
Comprehensive range of French HO model railway equipment, 00 British outline locos and coaches.

**Joy,** Turnbridges Ltd, London SW17.
Manufacturers of paints, dopes, thinners and model adhesives, etc.

**Kadee** (USA).
Range of American N freight car, N or HO magnetic couplers, etc.

**Kar-Line** (USA).
American HO freight car kits.

**Kean Components,** Tall Trees, Eastbourne Rd, Cross-in-Hand, Heathfield, East Sussex, TN21 0LT.
Car motors and gearboxes for 4 mm locos.

**Kemco,** 15 Calvin Close, St. Paul's Cray, Orpington, Kent, BR5 3LB.
4 mm scale transfers for locos & rolling stock.

**Kemilway,** PO Box 179, 12 York Way, London, N1 9DB.
4 mm scale etched brass rolling stock chassis & accessory kits.

**Kemtron** (USA).
HO & HO9 brass loco, passenger & freight car kits.

**Kenline Model Products,** 148 Lavender Av, Coventry.
4 mm scale wagon parts, castings and kits.

**Charles Kennion,** 2 Railway Pl, Hertford, Herts.
Hand tools materials and sundries for model engineers.

**Key** (USA).
HO brass models made in Japan & Korea.

**N. & K.C. Keyser Ltd,** Grimsbury South Industrial Estate, Banbury, Oxon, OX16 8SS.
Wide range of 4 mm and 7 mm kits, scale parts and accessories including K's cast metal kits, motors, wheels, chassis parts, etc.

**Keystone** (USA).
HO, HO9 & 0 Shay locomotive and American branch line rolling stock kits.

**Kibri** (UK): No 4 Factory Unit, Station Yard, Bala, N Wales.
Z, N, HO & 00 bulding kits & accessories.

**Jack Kine Models,** 10d, St Mark's Hill, Surbiton.
Modelling powder for landscapes.

**Kings Cross Plates & Kingsprint** (made by the Model Railway (Mfg) Company Ltd, 14 York Way, London N1 9AA).
Engraved brass or nickel silver name and number plates and dry print loco lettering and lining.

**Ian Kirk (Model Engineering),** 14 East St, St Monans, Fife, KY10 2AT.
4 mm, 009 and N gauge plastic rolling stock kits, cast metal loco kits, basic wagon kits.

**Kleinbahn** (Austria).
HO equipment, locos and rolling stock.

**Richard Kohnstam Ltd,** 13-15a High St, Hemel Hempstead, Herts.
Importers of several lines of model railway interest. Producers of RIKO scenic accessories.

**La Belle (USA).**
Range of HO freight and passenger cars. Imported by Victors.

**Lambert** (USA).
HO American locos & rolling stock made in Japan.

**Lam Models,** 88 Plumstead High Street, London, SE18 1SL.
4 mm scale pre-punched plastic Bulleid coach sides.

**Langley Miniature Models,** 166 Three Bridges Road, Crawley, Sussex, RH10 1LE.
00 and N kits and accessories.

**D.C. Lawrence (Scale Models),** 84 West Rd, Congleton, Cheshire.
Hand-built coaches, 4 & 7 mm scale.

**Lehmann** (West Germany).
'LGB' 1:22 1 gauge narrow gauge equipment, locos and rolling stock, etc.

**Chris Leigh,** 46 Meadow Way, Old Windsor, Berks.
4 mm scale cast metal accessories.

**Leinster Models,** 18 Monck Place, Phibsboro, Dublin 7, Eire.
0 gauge sheet metal loco kits.

**Leo Products,** 409, Tyburn Rd, Erdington, Birmingham, B24 8HJ.
4 mm small etched brass parts.

**Lesney Products & Co Ltd,** Eastway, London E9.
Die-cast miniature road vehicles of varying scales, some of which can be used as lineside accessories.

**LFC Models,** Lion Fireworks Co Ltd, 'Grandsire Well', off New Road, Netherthong, Holmfirth, Huddersfield, HD7 2XX.
2, 4 & 7 mm scale name and numberplates.

**Life-Like** (USA). N & HO American locos & rolling stock.

**Light Soldering Developments Ltd,** 97-99, Gloucester Rd, Croydon, Surrey, CR0 2DN.
'Litesold Super Iron', soldering iron made for modellers.

**Liliput** (Austria).
Extensive range of HO continental locos and rolling stock and HO9 Austrian narrow gauge models.

**Liliput Model Railways (UK) Ltd.**
Ex-Trix British outline locos & rolling stock.

**Lima** (Italy).
Extensive range of N, HO, 00 and 0 locos and rolling stock.

**Linka,** J. & L. Randall Ltd, Potters Bar, Herts.
Moulded building kits.

**Lionel** (USA).
HO and 0 American locos, rolling stock track and accessories.

**Locontrol,** Forgestone Colour Developments Ltd, Ketheringham, Wymondham, Norfolk, NR18 9RY.
Electronic controllers for all gauges N to 0.

**Mabex Products,** 31 Pevensey Rd, Eastbourne, Sussex.
Model bus transfers, eg fleetnames, destination screens, adverts, numbers, etc.

**Maidenhead Microsystems Ltd,** PO Box 22, Northwood, Middx, HA6 2PU.
Automatic colour signal controller.

**Mainline Railways,** Palitoy, Owen Street, Coalville, Leicester, LE6 2DE.
Comprehensive range of 00 British outline locomotives and rolling stock.

**MAJ Products,** 16, Market Precinct, Tiverton, Devon, EX16 6BL.
4 mm scale coach and wagon kits.

**Mallard Models,** PO Box 85, Camberley, Surrey, GU15 1JT.
4 mm and 7 mm scale etched brass loco and coach kits.
**Mantua Metal Products Co** (USA).
American HO kits and ready to run models sold under the name 'Tyco'.
**Marklin** (Germany).
Extensive range of model railway equipment in HO, 0 & 1 gauges, also Mini-Club System in Z gauge.
**P & D Marsh (Model Railway Accessories),** BBP House, 117 John Bright Street, Birmingham, B1 1BE.
N gauge loco and accessory kits. 0 gauge bogies and figures.
**Maygib Components,** F. Mayer, Mill Works, Mill Road, Salhouse, Norwich, Norfolk, NR13 6QA.
Loco kits, wheels, plunger pick-ups in 4 mm.
**MB Model Projects,** 109 Upper Holland Road, Sutton Coldfield, W Midlands, B72 1RD.
N and 2 mm scale coupling, loco and tender wheels, gear etc.
**McGowan Models,** 7 Ringley Park Rd, Reigate, Surrey.
Range of 4 mm scale cast metal loco kits.
**Mehanotehnika** (Jugoslavia).
N & HO American, French & German outline locomotives and rolling stock.
**George E. Mellor,** 31A Rhos Rd, Rhos-on-Sea, Clwyd, LL28 4RR.
Manufacturer of GEM cast metal loco and rolling stock kits, 'Flexi-Trak' and accessories in TT, HO and 00.
**Merco** (see Hambling's).
Litho coach and wagon sides and building papers.
**Mercontrol** (see Hambling's).
Wire-in-tube method of point control.
**Merit,** J. & L. Randall Ltd, Merit House, Potters Bar, Herts, EN6 3JY.
Wide range of N and 00 accessories.
**Merker & Fischer** (Germany).
N & HO craftsman-built locos and parts.
**Merten** (Germany).
Wide range of Z, N, TT, HO and 0 figures and lineside accessories.
**Metalmodels,** 59 Holman Road, Aylsham, Norfolk.
4 & 7 mm scale etched brass coach kits.
**Metropolitan SA** (Switzerland).
HO continental brass locomotives and plastic bodied rolling stock.
**MGW Precision Products,** Wade Road, Gorse Lane Industrial Estate, Clacton-on-Sea, Essex.
00 & EM wagon, coach, loco bogie & tender wheels.
**Micro-Rail,** 9 Mendip Drive, Nuneaton, Warwicks, CV10 8PT.
Etched brass 4 mm rolling stock.
**Midget Models,** 20 Ashmead Rise, Rednal, Birmingham.
4 mm scale cast metal vehicle kits.
**Midland Model Railway Suppliers,** The Woodlands, Green Lane, Clapham, Bedford.
Pre-formed scenic backgrounds and buildings, N, TT & 00.
**Mike's Models,** Holt House, Caswell Bay, Swansea, West Glamorgan.
Range of 4 mm, 7 mm and 009 cast metal kits and accessories.
**Millholme Models Ltd,** The Old School, Woodborough, Notts, NG14 7DX.
4 mm scale cast metal locomotive kits.
**Minitrix** (see Hornby Minitrix).
**Model & Allied Publications Ltd,** PO Box 35, Hemel Hempstead, Herts, HP1 1EE.
'Model Railways' and wide range of model and model engineer books.
**Model Design Company Ltd,** 4 Hayling Rise, High Salvington, Worthing, Sussex.
00 & N model railway accessories.
**Model Loco,** 42 Forest Hill, Carlisle, CA1 3HF.
Locos & loco kits.
**Model Power** (USA).
N & HO American locos, rolling stock & track.
**Model Railway Services,** 9 Burleigh Road, Shipway, Torquay, Devon, TQ2 6JX.
4 mm GWR whitemetal/brass broad gauge loco, carriage & wagon kits.
**Models & Leisure (Castings) Ltd,** 101, Sewall Highway, Coventry.
4 mm scale white metal loco kits & etched brass parts.
**Model Wagon Company,** 90 Ardrossan Rd, Seamill, West Kilbride, Ayrshire, KA23 9LX.
4 mm wagon kits.
**Modern Traction Kits Ltd,** 60, Queens St, Maidenhead, Berks.
Diesel, multiple unit, coach and wagon kits, N, TT & 00.
**Mod-Roc,** Smith & Nephew Ltd, Welwyn Garden City, Herts.
Plaster impregnated bandage used for scenic work in all scales and gauges.
**Mopok—Modern Prototype Kits,** 22 Longmoor Rd, Simondley, Glossop, Derbyshire.
Cast metal parts, kits, transfers, nuts and screws, etc.
**Motorway Model Kits,** 38 The Stirrup, Cashes Green, Stroud, Glos, GL5 4SG.
4 mm lorry kits.
**MSC Models,** 26 Surbiton Hill Park, Surbiton, Surrey.
0 loco brass body and chassis kits. 'Crailcrest' motor.
**MTK Ltd** (see Modern Traction Kits Ltd).
**MW Develolpment,** 165 Reading Rd, Henley, Oxon.
Manufacturer of five-pole motors.

**Nickel Plate Products** (USA).
HO American rolling stock.
**Noch** (Germany).
Complete formed scenic baseboard for compact layouts, HO, N and Z gauges.
**North Notts Scale Models & Engineering,** 11 High Street, Edwinstowe, Nr Mansfield, Notts.
7 mm scale coach kits.
**Northwest Short Line** (USA).
Craftsmen-built American brass locos.
**Nu-cast Model Engineering,** 189 Park Road, Hartlepool, Cleveland, TS26 9LP.
Range of 4 mm scale cast metal loco kits.

**The Oakwood Press,** Tandridge Lane, Lingfield, Surrey.
Railway and transport books containing prototype material of interest to modellers.
**Omega Model Co,** 67A, the Tricorn, Portsmouth, Hants.
4 mm wagon kits.
**Oryx.**
Miniature electric soldering irons.
**Ossett Mouldings,** J.R. & S. Clayton, 11 Hilda St, Ossett, West Yorks, WF5 0JJ.
Moulded plaster building and lineside accessory kits.
**Overland Models Inc.** (USA).
HO brass American locos and rolling stock made in Korea.
**Oxford Publishing Co,** 8 The Roundway, Headington, Oxford.
Publisher of railway books of interest to modellers.

**Pacific Fast Mail** (USA).
HO brass American locos made in Japan.
**Pads Electrical,** 45 Southward Rd, New Eltham, London, SE9 (post only).
Colour light signals and electrical/electronic parts for model railways.
**PC Models,** 2 Marsh Lane, Birmingham, B23 6NX.
4 mm scale coach kits and pre-painted sides, transfers.

**Peco** (see Pritchard Patent Products Co Ltd).
**Pendon Products,** Pendon Museum Sales Ltd, Long Wittenham, Abingdon, Oxon.
Dart castings, Springside Models and own accessories, 4 mm scale PO wagon kits.
**Phobec Ltd,** 31 Poole Road, Wimborne, Dorset.
'Linesman' tracktester.
**Piccolo** (Germany).
Comprehensive range of N gauge equipment manufactured by Fleischmann.
**Piko** (East Germany).
Range of N and HO locomotives and rolling stock.
**John Piper (Accessories) Ltd,** 2 Acre Road, Kingston-upon-Thames, Surrey, KT2 6EF.
Tree kits, fencing, 4 mm figures.
**Pirate Models,** 430 Hoe Street, London E.17.
4 mm and 7 mm scale cast metal bus kits.
**Pittman** (USA).
Electric motors.
**Pocher** (Italy).
HO scale models mainly of 'old time' American locos and stock. Made by Rivarossi.
**Pola** (Germany).
Building kits. 'Pola Maxi' 0 gauge locos and rolling stock. 'Pola-N' N gauge and 'Pola-Quick' 00/HO structure kits.
**Precision Paints Co,** PO Box 43, Cheltenham, Glos, GL51 5HR.
Authentic railway colour paints.
**Precision Petite Ltd,** 119A High Street, Teddington, Middx.
Miniature tools suitable for modellers.
**Precision Scale Models,** Gunby Road, Bubwith, Selby, Yorks, YO8 7DQ.
Copper clad sleepers, granite ballast, styrene sheet, n/s rail etc.
**Preiser** (Germany).
Range of figures in Z, N, TT and HO.
**Pritchard Patent Product Co Ltd,** Beer, Seaton, Devon.
Extensive range of kits and parts in all gauges N to 0. 'Streamline' track and points, 'Wonderful Wagons', etc. Publisher of 'Railway Modeller' and model railway books.

**Q Kits,** 8 Kirkwood View, Leeds, Yorks.
Fibreglass moulded diesel loco kits, 4 mm scale. Q-driver electronic controller.

**Ratio Plastic Models Ltd,** Butts Pond, Sturminster Newton, Dorset, DT10 1AZ.
Plastic loco, wagon, coach and signal kits in 4 mm scale, 'Emtrack' 4 mm scale permanent way.
**Ravenscale Model Co,** 587 High Rd, Leyton, London E10.
0 gauge ready-to-run locos and points.
**Alan Rawson,** 8 Hoo Close, Buckden, Huntingdon, Cambs, PE18 9TX.
Photo-etched GER number plates.
**Relco,** Rosefair Electronics, Shakespeare Street, Watford, Herts.
HF Generator track cleaner.
**A.M. Richards,** 6 Richmond Way, Fetcham, Leatherhead, Surrey, KT22 9NZ.
Distributor for Ellmar Products Ltd. British outline Z gauge locos.
**Ridley Photo-Electronics,** Box 62, Uckfield, Sussex.
Electronic controller, capacity discharge unit.
**Riko.**
Scenic accessories by Richard Kohnstam Ltd.
**Rivarossi** (Italy).
Extensive range of locos, rolling stock and equipment in N, HO and 0 gauges.
**RJH Model Railways Ltd,** 339 Poole Road, Poole, Dorset, BH12 1AE.
7 mm rolling stock.
**Roco International** (Austria).
Extensive range of N, HO9 & HO locos, rolling stock, track and accessories.
**Romford Models Ltd,** 14 New Cavendish St, London W1.
Locomotive wheels for TT and 00, and electric motors for TT, 00 and 0 gauges.
**Roskopf Miniaturmodelle** (Germany).
Horse drawn vehicles in N and HO.
**Roundhouse Products** (USA).
Range of American HO loco kits produced by Model Die Casting.
**Roxey Mouldings,** 83 Bridge Road, East Molesey, Surrey, KT8 9HH.
4 mm scale coach and building kits.
**Ruco** (Switzerland).
Limited range of HO Swiss wagons.
**Terry Russell,** Chaceside, St Leonard's Park, Horsham, Sussex.
7 mm scale tramway parts and plans.

**Scale Link Company,** 42 Appleby Close, Twickenham, Middlesex TW2 5NA.
Etched brass and cast metal accessories.
**Scalespeed Ltd,** 106 High Street, Lee-on-Solent, Hants.
Manufacturer of electrical control gear. Supplier of transistors, transformers, switches, relays, timers, etc.
**Schicht** (East Germany).
Range of HO locos and rolling stock.
**Seuthe** (Germany).
Smoke units for locos.
**Brian Sherriff Ltd,** 35, Cowgate, Dundee, DD1 2LW.
Backscenes, 'townscene'.
**Shinohara** (Japan).
Trackwork made to NMRA standards, HO, HO9 and dual gauge.
**John E. Skinley,** 23 Branscombe Gdns, Southend-on-Sea, Essex, SS1 3PH.
Extensive range of scale drawings for railways, tramways and ships.
**Slaters (Plastikard) Ltd,** Royal Bank Buildings, Temple Rd, Matlock Bath, Derbyshire, DE4 3PG.
4 mm & 7 mm scale wagon kits, 2, 4 & 7 mm scale prototype buildings, model making materials including Plastikard, Mek-pak fluid cement, Huminiture figures and many other accessories. Prototype Models building kits.
**S & M (Anglia) Ltd,** Queen Square, Haverhill, Suffolk, CM7 6JS.
Controllers, transformers, electrical and electronic components.
**Smiths Fittings,** 121 Wellsford Avenue, Solihull, W Midlands, B92 8HB.
4 mm scale wagon tarpaulin sheets and train nameboards.
**SMP,** Scale Model Productions, 46 Cromwell Rd, Cleethorpes, South Humberside, DN35 0AW.
'Scaleway' 00 and EM Bullhead flexible chaired track and point kits.
**SMS,** Scale Model Railways (Scotland) Ltd, 87 Wellington Street, Glasgow, G2 6DE.
Waterslide transfers, white metal & etched brass tramcar kits.
**SN Mouldings,** 'Annadale', Lopscombe Corner, Salisbury, Wilts, SP5 1BZ.
N gauge accessories, plastic building kits.
**Somerfeldt** (W Germany).
Range of authentic overhead catenary equipment based on German, Swiss and Italian prototypes, N, HO & 0.
**Southern Electronic Consultants,** (see under Digitol).
**Specialised Products Ltd,** 63, Gell St, Sheffield, S3 7QP.
00 gauge points, parts (copperclad).

**Sprat & Winkle Line,** Derek Mundy, 19 Forest Road, Chandlers Ford, Hants, SO5 1NA.
4 mm scale etched brass autocouplings, signal parts.
**Springside Models,** Units 1 & 2, Silverhills Rd, Decoy Industrial Estate, Newton Abbot, Devon, TQ12 5SJ.
4 mm & 7 mm small parts for locos.
**Studiolith Ltd,** Box 469 Rofford, Little Milton, Oxford, OX9 7QQ.
Manufacturer of Protofour equipment designed by the Model Railway Study Group.
**Sundeala,** Sundeala Board Co Ltd, 3 Aldwych, London, WC2B 4BZ.
Baseboard surface material.
**Sunset Models** (USA).
HO, HO9 limited production locos made in Japan.
**Superquick,** E. Keil & Co Ltd, Wickford, Essex.
Wide range of printed card 4 mm scale building kits.
**Swann Morton,** Penn Works, Owlerton Green, Sheffield, S6 2BJ.
Craft tools

**Taylectric,** 6 Daddlebrook Road, Alveley, Salop.
Point and signal control systems.
**D.R. Taylor,** 33, Trafalgar Rd, Southport, Lancs.
00 gauge live steam locos.
**Tenshodo** (Japan).
Brass HO scale locos.
**Three Aitch Mouldings,** High St, North Kelsey, Lincoln, LN7 6EQ.
Plastic wagon kits in 00 and 0 gauges.
**The Three Millimetre Society.**
Range of cast metal and plastic wagon and carriage kits for TT (available to members only).
**Tiny Signs,** PO Box 4, Henley-on-Thames, Oxon, RG9 1QQ.
Replica advertisement posters, N and 00.
**Tracksetta Templates,** Melcam Models, 36 St Margarets Road, Swindon, Wilts, SN3 1RX.
Templates for laying N & 00 track, straights & curves.
**Trix Express** (Germany).
Continental Trix. Wide range of locos and rolling stock, track and accessories in N and HO gauges.
**Trux Scale Model Products,** Truxgarth, Kenn, Clevedon, Avon, BS21 6TS.
4 mm road vehicle and 0 gauge coach kits.
**Tyco** (USA).
Registered trade name for HO kits and ready-to-run models by Mantua Metal Products Co.

**Ultrascale.**
4 mm scale loco, coach and wagon wheels.

**Vau-pe** (Germany).
HO building kits and scenic equipment.
**Veeday Models,** PO Box 1, Wiveliscombe, Taunton, Somerset, TA4 2TT.
Plastic injection moulded lineside buildings.
**Vollmer (UK),** No 4 Factory Unit, Station Yard, Bala, N Wales.
N & HO building kits and accessories.
**Vulcan Model Engineering,** C.M. Arnott, 29 Pereira Rd, Harborne, Birmingham, B17 9JG.
0 gauge loco chassis kits.

**Wabash Valley Line** (USA).
HO & 0 freight car kits.
**Colin Waite,** 20 Berwick Road, London, N22 5QB.
Etched brass van kits and accessories.
**Walthers** (USA).
HO passenger and freight car kits.
**Weald Models,** 55 Farlington Avenue, Haywards Heath, Sussex, RH16 3E2.
009 and 00 cast metal loco kits.
**West Country Hobbies,** 26 East Hill, St Austell, Cornwall, PL25 4TR.
Electronic Controllers, Whistles, etc.
**Westdale Coaches,** The Old Granary, Bishops Waltham, Nr. Southampton.
00 and 0 coach body kits.
**Westside Model Co Inc.** (USA).
HO brass locomotives made in Japan.
**Westward Model Products,** Crow Meadow, Kingswood, Wotton-Under-Edge, Glos, GL12 8RX.
4 mm scale road vehicle kits and scenic accessories.
**W & H (Models) Ltd,** 14 New Cavendish St, London W1.
Manufacturers and wholesalers of model railway equipment and accessories, Romford wheels and motors. Importers of European equipment.
**Wiking** (Germany).
N and HO scale road vehicles.
**Wills Finecast,** Industrial Display Co Ltd, Lower Road, Forest Row, Sussex, RH18 5HE.
Wide range of cast metal loco and plastic building kits in 4 mm scale.
**Wooder Models,** 47 Berkeley Drive, Hornchurch, Essex, RM11 3PZ.
0-16 mm narrow gauge carriage kits.
**Woodland Scenics** (USA) (Distributed by Hammant & Morgan Ltd.) Tree kits and landscaping materials.
**G. & R. Wrenn Ltd,** Bowlers Croft, Basildon, Essex.
Manufacturer of ex-Hornby Dublo locos, coaches and wagons in 00 gauge.
**Wrightline Models,** 141 Portland Road, Bournemouth, Dorset, BH9 1NG.
Road vehicle kits previously issued by Westward, GS and Transport Replicas.
**WSM (Windlehurst Models),** 19 Prince Philip Ave, Wharley End, Cranfield, Beds.
Cast metal loco kits and etched metal valve gear sets.
**W & T Manufacturing (B'ham 7 Ltd),** 222 Warwick Rd, Greet, Birmingham, B11 1NB.
Road vehicle and rolling stock kits and accessories, electronic controllers.

**X-acto,** E. Keil & Co Ltd, Russell Gdns, Wick La, Wickford, Essex.
Craft knives and modelling tools.

**Zeuke** (East Germany).
TT and HON-3 locos and rolling stock.

# 4 Stockists

This guide to British railway stockists and model shops has been compiled from advertisements that have appeared in the main British model railway magazines over the past two-three years, on the assumption that any business prepared to take the trouble of advertising in the specialist model railway press is more likely to take the hobby seriously and therefore provide a satisfactory service to the modeller. Again, no responsibility can be accepted for the goods or services provided by these companies, nor can we guarantee up-to-date accuracy of all addresses.

## Avon

The Modellers Den Ltd, 2 Lower Borough Walls, **Bath,** BA1 1QR.
Bailey's Dailies Models, 48 Sandy Park Road, **Bristol.**
Beatties, 17/19 Penn Street, **Bristol,** BS1 3AW.
Model Highways, 85 Gloucester Road, **Bristol,** BS7 8AS.
Modeller's Den, 65 Fairfax Street, **Bristol,** BS1 3BG.
Max Williams, Model Centre, 5-9 Church Road, Lawrence Hill, **Bristol,** BS5 9JJ.
Bristol Models, 76 Station Road, Filton, **Bristol,** BS12 7JJ.
Terry's, 44 Station Road, Yate, **Bristol.**
Trapnells Model Shop, 82 Meadow Street, **Weston-Super-Mare.**
West Coast Kit Centre, 15 Oxford Street, **Weston-Super-Mare.**

## Bedfordshire

Bryan Scale Models, 74 Midland Road, **Bedford,** MK40 1QM.
V. Farrer, 18A, Cause End Road, Wootton, **Bedford.**
J & A Models, 6, Wendover Drive, **Bedford.**
Thameshead, 101, Harrowden Road, **Bedford.**
MK Models, 14-16, Church Street, **Dunstable.**
John Brandham, Tools & Model Railways, 14 Market Square, **Leighton Buzzard,** LU7 7EY.
Neal's, Hockliffe Street, **Leighton Buzzard.**
Aeromodels (Luton) Ltd, 20 Gordon Street, **Luton.**
Maple Models, 16 Maple Road, **Luton.**
Taylor & McKenna, 73 Arndale Centre, **Luton,** LU1 2TF.

## Berkshire

Jacksons Model Shop, 53 High Street, **Ascot.**
Mydons, 2, Bullbrook Shops, **Bracknell.**
Crownline Models Ltd, 60, Queen St, **Maidenhead.**
Trents, 25 Cheap Street, **Newbury.**
Eames (Reading) Ltd, 24 Tudor Road, **Reading,** RH1 1NH.
Reading Model Supplies, Chatham St Multi-Storey Car Park, **Reading,** RG1 7JF.
Trents, 51, Butts Centre, **Reading.**
Ritz Platform 2, Queensmere Centre, **Slough.**

## Buckinghamshire

Baker's Stores, 21, Buckingham St, **Aylesbury.**
Taylor & McKenna, 46 Friars Square, **Aylesbury,** HP20 2TA.
Wexham Model Railways, 42 High Street, **Chalfont St Peter.**
Keens, 28 The Arcade, **High Wycombe.**
Neal's, 73 Queensway, Bletchley, **Milton Keynes.**
Taylor & McKenna, 16 The Concourse, Brunel Centre, Bletchley, **Milton Keynes,** MK2 2ES.

## Cambridgeshire

Modelmania, 17, King St, **Cambridge.**
R&D Models, 18E, Chesterton Road, (Mitchams Corner), **Cambridge.**
Ren Models, 63 Fitzroy Street, **Cambridge,** CB1 1HF.
Townsends, 15 Burleigh St, **Cambridge.**
Leisuretime, 35 Chequers Court, **Huntingdon.**
The Signal Box Ltd, 77, High St, **Linton.**
The Model Shop, 717 Lincoln Road, **Peterborough,** PE1 3HD.
Orton Models, 1 Toll House Road, Orton, Longueville, **Peterborough,** PE2 0AG.

## Channel Islands

The Model Shop (Guernsey), No 1 Commercial Arcade, **Guernsey.**

## Cheshire

Waltons of Altrincham, 30 Stamford Street, **Altrincham.**
The Model Shop, 37 The Forum, **Chester.**
Eric N Carless Ltd, 234 Nantwich Road, **Crewe.**
J.L. Holbrook, 'Charnwood', Elmsway, **Hale Barns.**
Trevor Bailey, Mill Lane, **Macclesfield.**
Leisureland, 43 Chestergate, **Macclesfield.**
Premier Models, 46 Church Road, **Northwich.**
Merseyside Model Supplies, 41 Regent Street, **Runcorn.**
The Railway Age, 160 Cross Street, **Sale.**
The Railway Sidings, 27 St Petersgate, **Stockport.**

## Cleveland

'Houseproud', Orchard Shopping Centre, 6 Durham Lane, **Eaglescliffe.**
Cleveland Model Shop Ltd, 33 Parliament Road, **Middlesborough.**
High Level Models Ltd, 9 Norfolk Place, **Middlesborough.**
The Modellers Halt, 19 West Terrace, **Redcar.**
Leslie Brown, 95 High Street, **Stockton-on-Tees.**
The Modellers Halt, 17 High Street, **Stockton-on-Tees.**

## Cornwall

Bricknells, 35 Fore Street, **Bodmin.**
Atlantic Models Ltd, 9 Julia's Place, The Strand, **Bude.**
Railcraft, 103, Killigrew Street, **Falmouth.**
Toodees Models & Toys, Cliff Road, **Newquay.**
Railcraft, 7A Higher Market Street, **Penryn.**
The Model Shop, 35A, Causewayhead, **Penzance.**

## Cumbria

Keith O'Loughlin, 3 West Tower Street, **Carlisle.**
Merlin Models, 96 Yard (opp GPO), Stricklandgate, **Kendal.**
Minitrains, 50 Stramongate, **Kendal.**
Keith O'Loughlin, 44, Finkle Street, **Kendal.**

## Derbyshire

Edward Exley Ltd, The Ridge, Eaton Hill, **Baslow.**

Scaleways Ltd, 8, Field Close, **Breaston,** DE7 3AS.
Chesterfield Model Railway Centre, 132, Chatsworth Road, **Chesterfield.**
The Engine Drivers, 54 Saltergate, **Chesterfield.**
Sydnope Scale Models, 29A, The Common, **Crich.**
C & B Models, 103 Normanton Road, **Derby.**
Quality Models Ltd, 6 High Street, **Heanor.**
Matlock Bath Model Railway Museum & Exhibition, The Model Shop, Temple Road, **Matlock Bath,** DE4 3PG.

## Devonshire

Barnard—Rance Model Supplies, 22 Castle Street, **Barnstaple.**
North Devon's Model Kit Centre, 71 Boutport Street, **Barnstaple.**
The Model Shop, 9 City Arcade, Fore Street, **Exeter,** EX4 3JE.
The Old Train Shop, 2 Bartholomew Street West, **Exeter.**
Mansel's Models, 61 Palace Ave, **Paignton.**
Torbay Model Supplies, 59 Victoria Road, Ellacombe, **Torquay.**
Totnes Model Railway Centre, 103c High Street, **Totnes.**

## Dorset

Bournemouth Model Railway, 1 Orchard Street, **Bournemouth.**
Dudley Enterprises, 115 Charminster Road, **Bournemouth,** BH8 8UH.
G K Models, 390 Holdenhurst Road, **Bournemouth.**
Glenfern Models, 44 Glenferness Ave, **Bournemouth.**
The Model Shop, 18 Latimer Road, Winton, **Bournemouth.**
Railway Mart, 134 Seabourne Road, Southbourne, **Bournemouth.**
Wrightlines Models, 141, Portland Road, **Bournemouth,** BH9 1NG.
Geoff Barlow Models, 3/4, Towngate Place, **Poole.**
ECOS, 22 Britannia Road, Parkstone, **Poole,** BH14 8BB.
Mostly Models, 3 West Street, **Ringwood.**
Howleys, 5 Frederick Place, **Weymouth,** DT4 8HQ.
E.C. & P.J. Prowse, 147 Station Road, West Moors, **Wimborne,** BH22 0HT.
Roy Wood Models, 17 Merley Park Road, **Wimborne.**

## Co Durham

Davidson's, 7 Alhambra Terrace, **Fishburn,** Nr Sedgefield.

## Essex

Mike Norris Sports, 13 Radford Way, **Billericay.**
Osborns, Little Square, **Braintree.**
Arnolds Gift Centre, 4 High Street, **Brentwood.**
The Mailtrain Shop, 23 Hutton Road, Shenfield, **Brentwood.**
Tremains Canvey Ltd, 2 Craven Avenue, **Canvey Island.**
Anglia Scale Models Ltd, 48 Rosemary Road, **Clacton-on-sea.**
CCH Models, 5 Kings Ave, Holland-on-Sea, **Clacton-on-sea,** CO15 5EU.
Anglia Scale Models Ltd, 22 North Hill, **Colchester,** CO1 1EG.
Hancock & Smith, 55 High Street, **Epping.**
A.J. Blackwell, (Blackwells of Hawkwell), 200 Main Road, **Hawkwell,** SS5 4EH.
Don Thompson Models, 228 Hornchurch Road, **Hornchurch.**
Pages of Barkingside Ltd, 19 Broadway Market, Fencepiece Road, Barkingside, **Ilford,** IG6 1JR.
Ilford Hobby & Model Centre, 28 Ilford Lane, **Ilford.**
Ray Rippon & Sons, 1030 London Road, **Leigh-on-Sea.**
J&M Model Railways, 146A High Street, **Maldon.**
Continental Model Supply Co, 36 Grey Gardens, **Rainham,** RM13 7NH.
Beatties, 7/11 High Street, **Romford,** RM1 1JU.
Railway Roundabout, 8 Chase Cross Road, Collier Row, **Romford.**
Saffron Models Ltd, 1 Market Street, **Saffron Walden.**
The Tunbridge Wells Model Shop, 470A Southchurch Road, **Southend-on-Sea.**
Wrights of Tilbury Ltd, Montreal Road, **Tilbury.**
Wickford Model Exchange, St Peter's Terrace, London Road, **Wickford.**

## Gloucestershire

Cheltenham Model Centre, 127/129 Bath Road, **Cheltenham.**
The Modellers Den Ltd, 39 High Street, **Cheltenham,** GL50 1DY.
Langdons Model Railways, 82 Falkner Street, **Gloucester.**
The Train Shop, 161 Southgate Street, **Gloucester.**
The Model Shop, 22 High Street, **Stroud.**

## Hampshire

Concorde Models, Victoria Road, **Aldershot.**
Mainly Trains (David Cleal), 26 The Shopping Precinct, Winchester Road, **Chandlers Ford,** SO5 2GA.
Cowplain Models, Fernwood House, London Road, **Cowplain,** Nr Portsmouth.
Eastleigh Model Centre, 2E High Street, **Eastleigh.**
G.M.H. Bunce & Co Ltd, 206 West Street, **Fareham.**
Barlow's, 73/75 Lynchford Road, North Camp, **Farnborough,** GU14 6EJ.
Farnborough Models & Toys, 3 Firgrove Parade, Victoria Road, **Farnborough.**
Young World, 289/291 Fleet Road, **Fleet.**
Gosport Model Shop, 15 The Precinct, South Street, **Gosport.**
Young World, 4 Grand Parade, **Hook.**
Model Railways (New Milton), 99 Lymington Road, **New Milton.**
Fratton Bargain Shop, 165/173 Fratton Road, **Portsmouth,** PO1 5ET.
Beatties, 114 East Street, **Southampton,** SO1 1HD.
City Models & Woodcraft, 38 Northam Road, Six Dials, **Southampton.**
Hawkyards, 100 Shirley High Street, **Southampton,** SO1 4FB.
Winchester Model Railway Centre, 149 Alresford Road, **Winchester.**

## Hereford & Worcester

Evesham Models, 38–40 Port Street, **Evesham.**
DD Models, 23 Church Street, **Hereford.**
Young Activities, 16 High Street, **Pershore.**
85A Models, Newbold House, Bromyard Terrace, **Worcester.**

## Hertfordshire

Gamell, 5 Jackson Square, **Bishop's Stortford.**
Taylor & McKenna, 103 Marlowes, **Hemel Hempstead,** HP1 1BL.
Keiths Model Centre, 34 Tower Centre, **Hoddesdon,** EN11 8UD.

Emay Models, 45 London Road, **Sawbridgeworth.**
Cavaliers (Models & Hobbies), 28 Spicer Street, **St Albans.**
Sam's, 12 Hatfield Road, **St Albans.**
Beatties, 70 The Parade, High Street, **Watford,** WD1 1LN.
Railmail, 65 Vicarage Road, **Watford.**
Ritz Platform 2, 46 Fretherne Road, **Welwyn Garden City.**

## Humberside

Bobby's, 83 Promenade, **Bridlington.**
Loftis, Grimsby Road, **Cleethorpes.**
North Humberside, Model Railways, 22 Church Lane, Hedon, **Hull.**
Sutton Model Sales (Hull) Ltd, 137 Newland Avenue, **Hull.**

## Isle of Wight

Sandown Models, 88 Station Avenue, **Sandown.**

## Kent

Bexley Model Centre, 18 Bourne Road, **Bexley.**
The Model Shop, 83 Northgate, **Canterbury,** CT1 1BA.
Mayfair, 12 Belmont Parade, Green Lane, **Chislehurst.**
R.E. Williams Ltd, 34 Crayford High Street, **Crayford,** DA1 BR2.
ERG Models, 199 London Road, **Dover.**
Joytoys, 80 High Street, **Edenbridge.**
Harbour Models & Crafts, 38 Old High Street, **Folkestone.**
Baker's Model Shop, 14 Canterbury Street, **Gillingham.**
Leisuretime & Hobbies, 29 High Street, **Herne Bay.**
Hythe (Kent) Models, 153A High Street, **Hythe.**
The Model Shop, 19-23 Upper Stone Street, **Maidstone.**
Kingcraft Models, 136 High Street, **Ramsgate.**
The Model Shop, 70A Queen Street, **Ramsgate.**
Jezzard's, 16 King Street, **Sandwich,** CT13 9BT.
The Buffer Stop Shop, Kent & East Sussex Railway, Town Station, **Tenterden.**
E.M. Models, 42 Camden Road, **Tunbridge Wells.**
The Tunbridge Wells Model Shop, 96/98 Camden Road, **Tunbridge Wells,** TN1 2QL.
Hobbytime, 5-7 Ravenswood Crescent, **West Wickham,** BR4 0JH.

## Lancashire

Model Railway Centre, 66 Abbey Street, (Manchester Road), **Accrington.**
BETA Models (Blackburn) Ltd, 1 Nab Lane, **Blackburn.**
Beatties, 19 Houndshill Centre, Victoria Street, **Blackpool,** FY1 4HU.
Platform 3, Blackpool South Station, Waterloo Road, **Blackpool.**
Tower Models, 44 Cookson Street, **Blackpool,** FY1 3ED.
AD Model Supplies, 22 Plumbe Street, **Burnley.**
Mortons, 18 Moor Lane, **Clitheroe,** BB7 1BE.
North Western Models, Corner House, 22 Lowergate, **Clitheroe.**
Lancaster Model Shop, 8 China Street, **Lancaster,** LA1 1EX.
Barkers Motorail Accessories, 69-71 Chapel Street, **Leigh.**
Lowes, 28 Clifton Street, **Lytham.**
The Model Shop (Nelson) Ltd, 57 Railway Street, **Nelson.**
Hobbycrafts, 12 Tithebarne Street, **Poulton-Le-Fylde,** Nr Blackpool, FY6 7BX.
Preston Leisure Services, 57 Meadow Street, **Preston.**
Harry Welch Ltd, 85 Church Street, **Preston.**
Model & Miniature Railways, 120-122 Drake Street, **Rochdale.**
Lister's Model Supplies, 285 East Lancashire Road, **Swinton.**
Hart's Model Shop, 110 Buttermarket Street, **Warrington.**

## Leicestershire

Model Toys, 76 Front Street, **Birstall.**
Norcol Models Ltd, 30 Braunstone Gate, **Leicester.**
North's Models, 5 Melton Road, Melton Turn, **Leicester.**
Loughborough Model Shop, 64 Ashby Road, **Loughborough,** LE11 3BR.
Stanley Horsley & Son, 6 Park Road, **Melton Mowbray.**
Rutland Scale Model Centre, 11 Mill Street, **Oakham.**

## Lincolnshire

Model Railway Centre, 74 Austerby, **Bourne,** PE11 9JL.
Toy Cabins, 16 Watergate, **Grantham.**
Lincoln Model Shop, 19 Clasketgate, **Lincoln.**
Sports & Hobbies, 4 All Saints Street, **Stamford.**
Talland Models, 18a Scotgate, **Stamford,** PE9 2YQ.

## London

Hadleys Hobbies, 131 Middlesex Street, **Bishopsgate,** London, E1 7HY.
Henry S. Wood, 502 Roman Road, **Bow,** London, E3 5LU.
Wilro Models Ltd, 22 **Clarence Road,** London E5.
Arnold's Gift Centre, 132-4 **Hoe Street,** London E17.
Lea Model Co, 430 Hoe Street, **Walthamstow,** London E17 9AA.
Allan Brett Cannon Ltd, 32 Railway Approach, **London Bridge,** SE1.
Eltham Models, 54 **Wellhall Road,** London SE9.
Beatties, 210 Lewisham High Street, **Lewisham,** London, SE13 6JP.
Lewisham Model Centre, 45 Lee High Road, **Lewisham,** London SE13.
Model Road & Rail, 4 **Green Lane,** London SE20.
Patrick Models, 107-111 Lillie Road, **Fulham,** London SW6.
E.F. Russ, 101 **Battersea Rise,** London SW11.
Hobby Shop 2MR, 215, **Putney Bridge Road,** London, SW15 2NY.
Model Mania, Norbury Station Approach, London Road, **Norbury,** London SW16.
Bec Model Railways, 10 **Tooting Bec Road,** London SW17.
BMW (Models) Ltd, 327-329 Haydons Road, **Wimbledon,** London SW19.
Platform 2, 118 The Broadway, **Wimbledon,** London SW19 1RH.
Charles Covey (Models), 572 Kingston Road, **Raynes Park,** London SW20.
Model & Tool Supplies, 604 Kingston Road, **Raynes Park,** London SW20 8DN.
Beatties, 112 **High Holborn,** London, WC1V 6JS.
Hambling's (Models) Ltd, 29 Cecil Court, **Charing Cross Road,** London, WC2 N4EZ.
Mega Models, 26 **Rathbone Place,** London W1.
W&H (Models) Ltd, 14 **New Cavendish Street,** London W1.
Hobby Supplies, 540 High Road, **Chiswick,** London, W4 5RG.

Jones Bros Of Chiswick, 56 Turnham Green Terrace, **Chiswick,** London, W4 1QN.
Braley Models, 141 Little Ealing Lane, **Ealing,** London W5.
Allan Brett Cannon Ltd, 171 Railway Approach, **Shepherds Bush,** London W12.
H.A. Blunt & Sons Ltd, 133 The Broadway, **Mill Hill,** London, NW7 4RN.
Model Railway's, 14 York Way, **King's Cross,** London, N1 9AA.
Victor's, 166 Pentonville Road, **Islington,** London N1 9JL.
Hobbies & Models, 21/23 Ballards Lane, **Finchley,** London, N3.
Meks Models, 96 **Mackenzie Road,** London N7.
Muswell Hill Model Shop, 51 **Fortis Green Road,** London, N10 3HP.
Beatties, 10 The Broadway, **Southgate,** London, N14 6PN.
Chris Crawley Models, 121, Lordship Lane, **Tottenham,** London N17.
Beatties, 104-106 High Road, **Wood Green,** London, N22.

## Greater Manchester

Waltons of Altrincham, 30 Stamford Street, **Altrincham.**
Bolton Model Mart, 134 Bradshawgate, **Bolton,** BL2 1EH.
Scale Models & Kits, 551 Halliwell Road, **Bolton.**
Beatties, 4-6 Brown Street, Off Market Street, **Manchester,** M2 1EE.
Bradford Model Railway Centre Ltd, 4 Piccadilly Plaza, **Manchester.**
The Railway Clearing House, 210 Elliot Street, Tyldesley, **Manchester,** M29 8DS.
The Model Shop, 695 Ripponden Road, **Oldham.**
Norman Wisenden, 95 Chew Valley Road, Greenfield, **Oldham.**
Leighs Modelling Service, 52 Market Street, New Mills, Nr **Stockport,** SK12 4AA.
Model Traction Services, 95 Buxton Road, Furness Vale, Nr **Stockport.**
The Railway Sidings, 27 St Peters Gate, **Stockport.**
E&R Models, 281 Billinge Road, Pemberton, **Wigan.**
G. Foreshaw & Son, 58 Market Street, **Wigan.**

## Merseyside

Alec Green, 122 Oxton Road, **Birkenhead.**
Beatties, 36/37 Dawsons Way, St John's Centre, **Liverpool,** L1 1LJ.
City Models, 8 Elliot Street, **Liverpool** 2.
Hattons, 180 Smithdown Road, **Liverpool,** L15 3JS.
Lucas's Hobbies, 7-9 Tarleton Street, **Liverpool,** L1 1DS.
Vanguard Models, 102-104 Queens Drive, **Liverpool,** L13 0AR.
Hobby Shop (Southport) Ltd, 17-19 Bold Street, **Southport.**
KBC Models & Handicrafts, 3 Preston New Road, Churchtown, **Southport.**

## Middlesex

Jennings Ltd, 244-8 Hertford Road, **Enfield,** EN3 5BL.
EMA Model Supplies, 58-60, The Centre, **Feltham.**
Hobbies & Models, 217/219 Streatfield Road, Kenton, **Harrow.**
The Model Shop, 190-4, Station Road, **Harrow,** HA1 1JU.
Puffers, 134A Kenton Road, Kenton, **Harrow.**
Parker & Kirby, (Thameside Models & Hobbies), 12-14 Thames Street, **Sunbury-on-Thames.**
Teddington Model Supplies, 84/86 Broad Street, **Teddington.**
Hodgsons Toys & Models Ltd, 44/46 Hounslow Road, Whitton, **Twickenham,** TW2 7EX.

## West Midlands

Alton Models, 897 Walsall Road, Great Barr, **Birmingham.**
Beatties, 26 South Mall, Birmingham Shopping Centre, **Birmingham,** B2 4XD.
Bearwood Models, 45 Constitution Hill, **Birmingham** 19.
Bob's Models, 520-522 Coventry Road, Small Heath, **Birmingham** 10.
Midget Models, 20 Ashmead Rise, Rednal, **Birmingham,** B45 8AB.
Model Hobbies, 168 Highfield Road, Hall Green, **Birmingham.**
Powell's Model Centre, 765-769 Alum Rock Road, **Birmingham,** B8 3PX.
RB Model Railways, 10 Birmingham Road, Great Barr, **Birmingham,** B43 6NR.
The Road & Rail Shop, 330 Marsh Lane, Erdington, **Birmingham,** B23 6JD.
Roundhouse Models, 579 Bristol Road, Selly Oak, **Birmingham** 29.
The Selection Box, 15 Knights Road, Tyseley, **Birmingham,** B11 3QA.
Southerns Model Railways, 281 Vicarage Road, Kings Heath, **Birmingham** 14.
Wyatts Model Railway Ltd, 220-222 Warwick Road, Greet, **Birmingham,** B11 2NB.
Model Mecca, 5 Albion Parade, Wall Heath, **Brierley Hill.**
Models & Leisure (Railways), 101 Sewall Highway, **Coventry,** CV2 3DT.
The Train Shop, 18 Far Gosford Street, **Coventry.**
Tennent's Small Trains, 77 High Street, **Halesowen,** B63 3BQ.
Sutton Coldfield Model Railways, 6 Walmley Close, Walmley Road, **Sutton Coldfield.**
Modellers Mecca, 5 Albion Parade, **Wall Heath,** DY6 0NP.
Burtons of Walsall, 73 Bridge Street, **Walsall.**
Graingers of Walsall, 108 Caldmore Road, **Walsall.**
Geoff Parker Models, 123 Wolverhampton Street, **Walsall.**
The Train Shop, 130 Walstead Road, **Walsall.**
Bearwood Models, 8 Three Shires Oak Road, Smethwick 41, **Warley.**
Wolverhampton Models & Hobbies, 3 Bell Street, Manders Centre, **Wolverhampton.**

## Norfolk

The Train Shop, 9 Southdown Road, **Great Yarmouth,** NR31 0HU.
Galaxy Models, 88 Catton Grove Road, **Norwich.**
Langleys, Royal Arcade, **Norwich.**
The Train Shop, 37 Allens Avenue, Sprowston, **Norwich.**

## Northamptonshire

Cador Roberts, Bowen Square, **Daventry.**
Taylor & McKenna, 19-21 Gold Street, Newbrough Centre, **Kettering.**
CAB Models, 75 Kettering Road, **Northampton.**

The Model Shop, 230 Wellingborough Road, **Northampton.**
Taylor & McKenna, 41 & 43 Prince Walk, Grosvenor Centre, **Northampton,** NN1 2EL.
A. Watts & Sons Ltd, 80 Abington Street, **Northampton.**
Jessops Stores Ltd, Hobby Corner, 1 Market Street, **Wellingborough.**

## Nottinghamshire
C & C Models, 144, High Road, **Beeston.**
Robert Denny, 2 Wilsthorpe Road, Sawley, **Long Eaton.**
North Notts Scale Models, 11 High Street, Edwinstowe, Nr **Mansfield.**
Beatties, 3 Mount Street, **Nottingham,** NG1 6JW.
Gee Dee Models Ltd, 19/21 Heathcote Street, Off Goosegate, **Nottingham.**
J&R Models, 52 Station Road, **Sandiacre.**
Millholme Models, Lingwood Lane, **Woodborough,** NG14 7DX.

## Oxfordshire
Taylor & McKenna, 28 Bridge Street, The Cherwell Centre, **Banbury.**
Howes Model Shop, 9-10 Broad Street, **Oxford,** OX1 3AJ.
The Railway Book & Model Shop, 8 The Roundway, Headington, **Oxford,** OX3 8DH.
Railwayania, Ginge, Nr **Wantage,** OX12 8QS.

## Salop
G.A. Griffiths Model Railways, Sutton Farm PO, **Shrewsbury,** SY2 6HW.
The Hobby Shop, 1 Stafford Street, **Newport.**
Hobby Specialists (Shrewsbury) Ltd, 27 Wyle Cop, **Shrewsbury,** SY1 1XB.

## Somerset
Model Railway Centre, 58c High Street, **Burnham-on-Sea,** TA8 1PD.
Howell Dimmock Ltd, The Old School, Chantry, **Frome,** BA11 3LN.
Puff 'n' Stuff, 14 Norbins Road, **Glastonbury.**
Challis Models & Hobbies, 50B High Street, **Shepton Mallet.**
Hendford Halt, 43 West Coker Road, **Yeovil.**
Model Hobbies, Park Road, **Yeovil.**

## Staffordshire
J&N Models, 22 Derby Street, **Burton-on-Trent.**
Modellers World, 16 Smithfield Centre, **Leek.**
The Train Shop, 32 Bird Street, **Lichfield.**
Electropulse, 31 Westland Avenue, **Newcastle-under-Lyme.**
Mercian Model Rail, 105 Brereton Road, **Rugeley.**
John W. Bagnall Ltd, 18 Salter Street, **Stafford.**
Hobbyworld, 44 Eastgate Street, **Stafford.**
John W. Bagnall Ltd, 44 Piccadilly, Hanley, **Stoke-on-Trent.**
Hobbyworld, 181 London Road, **Stoke-on-Trent.**
Pleasure Treasures Ltd, 4 Swan Square, Burslem, **Stoke-on-Trent,** ST6 3EA.
Gillway, 14 The Precinct, **Tamworth.**

## Suffolk
Model Junction, 10 Whiting Street, **Bury St Edmunds.**
Rogers, 77A St Johns Road, **Bury St Edmunds.**
'Guards', 20, Tacket Street, **Ipswich.**
Railway City, Greyfriars, **Ipswich.**
Parrs, 252 London Road South, **Lowestoft.**
Alstons, North Street, **Sudbury.**
Chuffs Model Trains Peddlers Ltd, 86 Friars Street, **Sudbury.**

## Surrey
Addlestone Models Ltd, 63 Station Road, **Addlestone.**
The Loco Shed, 121 Station Road, **West Croydon.**
Dorking Model Centre, 13 West Street, **Dorking.**
Masters of Epsom, 29-31 Tattenham Crescent, Tattenham Corner, **Epsom Downs.**
Southern Model Railways, 13 Upper High Street, **Epsom.**
Farnham Models, 57A Downing Street, **Farnham.**
Witley Model Workshops, Petworth Road, Witley, **Godalming.**
The Model Shop, 23 Swan Lane, **Guildford.**
Grayshott Models, 5 Headley Road, **Hindhead.**
Beatties, 30/32 Eden Street, **Kingston-upon-Thames,** KT1 1EP.
Jack Kine Models, 10d St Marks Hill, **Surbiton.**
Whitewoods, 103 Brighton Road, **Surbiton,** KT6 5NH.
Thames Trains, 50 High Street, **Thames Ditton.**
RAE Models, 43 Church Street, **Weybridge.**

## Sussex
The Engine Shed, 8 Madeira Parade, Madeira Avenue, **Bognor Regis.**
Trains, 1A Lyon Street, **Bognor Regis.**
Kemp Models, 4 Queens Road Quadrant, **Brighton.**
John Taylor, 16 Spring Street, Off Western Road, **Brighton.**
Valelink Ltd, 53 Surrey Street, **Brighton.**
Heather Craft, 60 High Street, **Crawley.**
Langley Home Stores, 14 Langley Parade, Langley Green, **Crawley.**
Eastbourne Models & Hobbies Shop, 37 Seaside, **Eastbourne,** BN22 7NB.
Robert's Model Shop, 20 Winston Crescent, **Eastbourne.**
South Eastern Models, 5 The Parade, London Road, Felbridge, **East Grinstead.**
Robertson, 41 Vicarage Field, **Hailsham.**
Maintrack Models, 79 Queens Road, **Hastings,** TN34 1RL.
Autoroute, 16B Bishopric, **Horsham,** RH1Z 1QR.
J. Morris, 80 Manor Road, **North Lancing.**
Douglas J. Fryer (Lewes Model Centre), 10 Malling Street, **Lewes.**
Bonds O' Euston Road Ltd, Arundel House, Rumbolds Hill, **Midhurst,** GU29 9NE.
Adur Models, 16 John Street, **Shoreham,** BN4 5DN.
Hobby Horse Model, Railway Centre, 12 Littlehampton Road, **Worthing.**
Sussex Model Centre, 10 Teville Gate, **Worthing,** BN11 1TW.

## Tyne & Wear
Beatties, 43/47 Pilgrim Street, **Newcastle-upon-Tyne,** NE1 6QE.
The Model Shop, 18 Blenheim Street, **Newcastle-upon-Tyne.**
Northumbria Models, 53a Station Road, Forest Hall, **Newcastle-upon-Tyne.**

## Warwickshire

MJF Models, 6 Priory Road, **Kenilworth.**
The Train Shop, 31 St John's, **Warwick.**

## Wiltshire

Chippenham Model Craft Ltd, 65 New Road, **Chippenham.**
Amers (Model Land), 23 High Street, **Corsham,** SN13 0ES.
Cavalier Shop, 21 High Street, **Highworth,** Nr Swindon.
Railroad Models, 92-94 Fisherton Street, **Salisbury.**
Froude & Hext, 83 Victoria Road, **Swindon.**
Trents, 25 Bridge Street, **Swindon.**
C. Stroud Sims, 5 Silver Street, **Trowbridge.**

## Yorkshire

Frizinghall Model Railways, 202 Keighley Road, Frizinghall, **Bradford,** BD9 4JZ.
The Train Shop Supermarket, 4 Bertram Road, **Bradford,** BD8 7LN.
Dewsbury Model Railway Centre, 17 Union Street, **Dewsbury.**
Doncaster Model Railways Centre, 2 Nether Hall Road, East Laith Gate, **Doncaster,** DN1 2PW.
Highfield Models, Highfield House, Bishop Thornton, **Harrogate,** HG3 3JY.
J&J Noble, Holmfirth Road, New Mill, **Huddersfield.**
55G Railway Shop, 250B Wakefield Road, Moldgreen, **Huddersfield.**
Milburns, 90 Cavendish Street, **Keighley.**
Beatties, 16/18 King Charles Street, **Leeds,** LS1 6LT.
MRC, 10 St Annes Road, Headingley, **Leeds.**
Northern Model Railway Centre Ltd, 7 Empire Arcade, Briggate, **Leeds** 1.
RSB Models, 1 Grove Road, North Ormesby, **Middlesborough,** TS3 6EH.
Grovers, 216-217 High Street, **Northallerton.**
Beatties, 38 Pinstone Street, **Sheffield,** S1 2HN.
Hobbies (Sheffield), 248 Shalesmoor, **Sheffield.**
Marcway Ltd, 590 Attercliffe Road, **Sheffield** 9.
Rails, 25 Chesterfield Road, **Sheffield.**
M.G. Sharp Models, 712 Attercliffe Road, **Sheffield,** S9 3RP.
The Transport Scene, 86A Westgate, **Wakefield,** WF1 1EL.
Wakefield Model Railway Centre, 260 Dewsbury Road, **Wakefield.**
York Model Centre, 17 Davygate Centre, **York.**

## Ireland

Hobbies Ltd, 10 Grafton Arcade, Grafton Street, **Dublin** 2.
The Model Railway Shop, 18 Monck Place, Phibsboro, **Dublin** 7.
Model Railway Repair Centre, 109 Whitehall Road East, **Dublin** 12.

## Northern Ireland

McCullough's, 19 Bridge Street, **Bangor,** Co Down.

## Scotland

John S. McCracken, East Porte, **Burntisland,** Fifeshire.
John Mitchell, 141 King Street, **Castle Douglas,** Dumfries & Galloway.
Brackencraft, Lochee Shopping Centre, **Dundee,** Tay.
Scoonie Hobbies, 55 Perth Road, **Dundee,** Tay.
Railmart, 23 Guildhall Street, **Dunfermline,** Fife, KY12 7NR.
Edinburgh Wonderland, 116 Rose Street, **Edinburgh.**
Also at: 97 Lothian Road, **Edinburgh.**
Harburn Hobbies Ltd, 67 Elm Row, Leith Walk **Edinburgh,** EH7 4AQ.
J. Lawrie, 115-117 St Johns Road, Corstorphine, **Edinburgh.**
Scale Models Edinburgh, c/o R & W Forsythe, 30 Princes Street, **Edinburgh.**
Argyle Model Dockyard Ltd, 229-235 Argyle Street, **Glasgow,** G2 8DL.
Clyde Models, 44 Candleriggs, **Glasgow.**
Langside Models & Hobbies, 238 Battlefield Road, **Glasgow,** G42 9HU.
McMillan Models, 533 Cathcart Road, **Glasgow,** G42 8SG.
Railmail, 165A St Vincent Street, **Glasgow,** G1.
Scale Models (Scotland), PO Box 16, 87 Wellington Street, **Glasgow,** G2 6DQ.
Mackay Models, 44 Kirkton Park, Old Village, **East Kilbride.**
R&C Muirhead Ltd, Scotch Corner, 3&5 Bank Street, **Kilmarnock,** Strathclyde.
I&A Todd, 22 Central Avenue, **Kilmarnock,** Strathclyde.
Scoonie Hobbies, 91 St Clair Street, **Kirkcaldy,** Fife.
Mackay Models, 'The Old Booking Hall', 38 Old Sneddon Street, **Paisley,** S Clyde, PA3 2AL.
Peterhead Model Centre, 59 Broad Street, **Peterhead,** AB4 6JL.
Ian Kirk, 14 East Street, **St Monans,** Fife.

## Wales

Kivoli Centre, 1 Station Yard (Industrial Estate), **Bala.**
Noney's Model Shop, Station Road, **Barmouth.**
Cardiff Discount Centre, 28A Paget Street, **Cardiff.**
Garth Model Co, 109 Whitchurch Road, Heath, **Cardiff.**
James & Lendon, 192 Fidlas Road, Llanishen, **Cardiff,** CF4 5LZ.
Bud Morgan (Cardiff) Ltd, 24 Castle Arcade, **Cardiff,** CF1 2BW.
Number One Models, 5 Blue Street, **Carmarthen,** SA31 3LQ.
Colwyn Cycle and Model Centre, 451 Abergele Road, **Old Colwyn.**
Bay Models & Toys, 52 Conway Road, **Colwyn Bay.**
Kittle Hobby, 24 Pennard Road, **Kittle,** Gower, SA3 3JS.
Bay Models & Toys, 22 Madoc Street, **Llandudno.**
Towyn Hobbyshop, High Street, **Merioneth,** Gwynedd.
Ledom, 104 Lower Dock Street, **Newport,** Gwent NPT 2AG.
Make A Model, 123 Commercial Street, **Newport,** Gwent.
J.V. Models, 114, Chepstow Road, **Newport.**
Pembroke Models, 11 Lords Meadow View, Kingsbridge, **Pembroke,** Dyfed.
Doric Models, 7 Sardis Road, **Pontypridd.**
Festinog Model Railway Centre, Harbour Station, **Porthmadog,** Gwynedd, LL49 9NF.
Holt Model Railways, Orders & Correspondence: Holt House, Caswell Bay, **Swansea.** Retail Sales: 100, Bishopston Road, Bishopston, **Swansea,** West Glamorgan.
Talyllyn Railway Mail Order Dept, Wharf Station, **Tywyn,** Gwynedd, LL36 9EY.

# 5 Locomotive kits and models

The following list of British main-line company and British Railways locomotives, showing all known commercially produced ready-to-run models and construction kits, was correct at the time of going to press. Also included are some commercial models which were at one time readily available but have now been withdrawn. The supply situation of models and kits is not, and cannot be, static as manufacturers reserve the right to withdraw items from their range. Knowledge of withdrawn models is not without interest, however, as it is sometimes possible to come across samples in out-of-the-way places or to purchase them second-hand from retailers specialising in the sale of such equipment or perhaps by private sale. It is not unknown for manufacturers to re-introduce deleted items, so some models long since withdrawn and elevated to the status of collectors' items may once again appear on the retailers' shelves. I have, however, avoided including limited-run kits and models where it has been made known that the numbers to be produced are such that their availability cannot be guaranteed during the currency of this book. This applies in the main to a number of etched-brass kits and expensive hand-crafted models.

Models in 4 mm scale predominate, as one might expect, and the number of kits and models in the different gauges probably reflects the popularity of each gauge. For the sake of simplicity I have referred to all 4 mm scale kits as '00'. Most 00 gauge kits can be adapted to EM, Scalefour or Protofour standards but some kits, notably K's, can only be converted at the expense of discarding the wheels that come with the kit. Unless otherwise stated, all 00 kits are cast white metal but increasing use is being made of etched brass or nickel-silver frets, either for components such as chassis frames, coupling rods and valve gear, or for complete kits. CCW manufacture a number of 0 gauge cast white metal kits but most kits in this gauge are fairly basic, consisting of pre-cut sheet metal, rolled boilers and turned or cast metal fittings, requiring the constructor to find his own source of wheels and motor, and calling for a fair degree of skill for assembly and detailed finishing. At the opposite end of the scale, N gauge continues to attract a number of new ready-to-run models, thanks largely to Graham Farish whose chassis are also used by a number of other manufacturers producing cast white metal body-line kits for a wide range of British steam and modern motive power locomotives. Z gauge is now included for the first time following the announcement by Ellmar Products Co of their intention to produce models of British outline prototypes to fit Marklin Mini-Club chassis.

The range of currently available kits and ready-to-run models, particularly in 4 mm scale, is now truly remarkable. Whereas in the first edition of this book the check list of representative locomotive types considered to be worthy of modelling showed there to be nearly 60 classes not then covered by commercial manufacturers the number has now shrunk to less than 10. These are indicated by a dash —. Certainly there are no serious omissions and in many cases there is more than one kit and/or model of each locomotive class to choose from. The coverage provided by the trade deserves the fullest support from the model railway public.

In the following list (P) indicates that one or more examples of the class have been preserved or set aside for preservation.

**Great Western Railway classes**

| | | | | |
|---|---|---|---|---|
| 4-6-0 | 'King' Class | (P) | N | Lima ready-to-run model |
| | | | TT-3 | GEM kit |
| | | | 00 | Lima ready-to-run model |
| | | | 00 | Hornby Railways ready-to-run model |
| | | | 00 | Wills Finecast kit |
| | | | 00 | Jamieson kit |
| | | | 00 | Mr D.R. Taylor live-steam ready-to-run model |
| | | | 0 | Charles Covey 'Firmco' kit |
| " | 'Castle' Class | (P) | 00 | Airfix ready-to-run model |
| | | | 00 | Wrenn ready-to-run model |
| | | | 00 | Jamieson kit |
| | | | 00 | Wills Finecast kit |
| | | | 0 | Charles Covey 'Firmco' kit |
| " | 'Star' Class | (P) | 00 | Wills Finecast kit |
| " | 'Saint' Class | | N | P & D Marsh Monmouth Models cast metal body kit |
| | | | 00 | Wills Finecast kit |
| " | 'Hall' Class | (P) | N | Graham Farish ready-to-run model |

| | | | | |
|---|---|---|---|---|
| | | | 00 | Hornby Railways ready-to-run model |
| | | | 00 | Wills Finecast kit |
| | | | 0 | Leinster Models kit |
| ” | 'Grange' Class | | 00 | K's kit |
| ” | 'Manor' Class | (P) | 00 | Bristol Models kit |
| | | | 00 | Mainline Railways ready-to-run model |
| | | | 00 | Nu-Cast kit |
| | | | 00 | Models & Leisure (Railways) Premier Kits kit |
| ” | 'County' Class | | N | Langley Miniature Models cast metal body kit |
| | | | 00 | Bristol Models kit |
| | | | 00 | Nu-Cast kit |
| | | | 00 | Models & Leisure (Railways) Premier Kits kit |
| 2-8-0 | 28XX Class | (P) | N | GEM kit |
| | | | 00 | K's kit |
| ” | 47XX Class | | 00 | Nu-Cast kit |
| ” | ROD 30XX Class | | 00 | K's kit |
| 2-6-0 | 26XX 'Aberdare' Class | | 00 | Bristol Models kit |
| | | | 00 | K's kit |
| ” | 43XX Class | (P) | N | P & D Marsh cast metal body kit |
| | | | TT-3 | GEM kit |
| | | | 00 | Mainline Railways ready-to-run model |
| | | | 00 | K's kit |
| ” | 93XX Class | | N | P & D Marsh cast metal body kit |
| | | | 0 | CCW Kit |
| 4-4-2 | De Glehn Compound | | 00 | Wills Finecast kit |
| 4-4-0 | 'City' Class | (P) | 00 | Airfix Plastic kit |
| | | | 00 | Models & Leisure (Railways) Premier Kits kit |
| ” | 'Flower' Class | | 00 | Nu-Cast kit |
| ” | 'Bulldog' Class | | 00 | K's kit |
| | | | 0 | CCW kit |
| 4-4-0 | 'Duke' Class | | 00 | K's kit |
| | | | 00 | Mallard Models etched brass kit |
| | | | 0 | Mallard Models etched brass kit |
| ” | 'Dukedog' 32XX later 99xx Class | (P) | 00 | K's kit |
| ” | 'County' Class | | 00 | Hornby Railways ready-to-run model |
| | | | 00 | Wills Finecast kit |
| 2-4-0 | Barnum Class | | 00 | Mallard Models etched brass kit |
| ” | 1334 Class (MSWJR) | | 00 | Nu-Cast kit |
| 4-2-2 | 3031 'Achilles' Class | | 00 | Hornby Railways ready-to-run (limited production) |
| | | | 00 | K's Milestone Series kit |
| | | | 00 | Models & Leisure (Railways) Premier Kits kit |
| 2-2-2 | 'Firefly' Broad Gauge | | 4mm scale | Model railway Services kit |
| 0-6-0 | 322 'Beyer' Class | | 00 | K's kit |
| ” | 'Dean' 2301 Class | (P) | TT-3 | 3 mm Society kit |
| | | | 00 | Airfix ready-to-run model |
| | | | 00 | K's kit |
| ” | 'Dean' outside frame | | 00 | K's kit |
| ” | 2251 Class | (P) | N | Langley Miniature Models body kit |
| | | | TT-3 | ABS Models & Beaver Products kit |
| | | | 00 | Jaycraft moulded polyester resin body kit |
| | | | 00 | Mainline Railways ready-to-run model |
| | | | 00 | Wills Finecast kit |
| | | | 0 | CCW kit |
| | | | 0 | Charles Covey 'Firmco' kit |
| ” | 'Hercules' Broad Gauge | | 4 mm scale | Model Railway Services kit |
| 2-8-2T | 72XX Class | (P) | 00 | Nu-Cast kit |
| | | | 00 | K's kit |
| 2-8-0T | 42XX Class | (P) | 00 | Nu-Cast kit |
| | | | 00 | K's kit |
| 2-6-2T | 31XX Class | | N | Langley Miniature Models body kit |
| ” | 44XX Class | | 00 | K's kit |
| ” | 45XX Class | (P) | 00 | K's kit |
| | | | 0 | CCW kit |
| ” | 4575 Class | (P) | 00 | K's kit |
| | | | 00 | Lima ready-to-run model |
| | | | 0 | CCW kit |
| ” | 61XX Class | (P) | N | Graham Farish ready-to-run model |
| | | | 00 | Airfix ready-to-run model |
| | | | 00 | Airfix plastic kit |
| | | | 00 | Wills Finecast kit |
| 0-6-2T | 56XX Class | (P) | N | Langley Miniature Models body kit |
| | | | N | Beaver Products body kit |
| | | | TT-3 | GEM kit |
| | | | 00 | GEM kit |
| | | | 0 | Charles Covey 'Firmco' kit |
| ” | Rhymney Rly R Class | | 00 | Nu-Cast kit |
| ” | Taff Vale Rly UI Class | | 00 | Wills Finecast kit |

| | | | | |
|---|---|---|---|---|
| 0-6-2T | Taff Vale Rly A Class | | 00 | Nu-Cast kit |
| ” | Taff Vale Rly 04 Class | | — | |
| ” | Taff Vale Rly 01 Class | (P) | — | |
| 0-6-0T | 633 Class | | 00 | Models & Leisure (Railways) Premier Kits kit |
| 0-6-0ST | 850 Class | | 00 | Models & Leisure (Railways) Premier Kits kit |
| ” | 1706 Class (outside frame) | | 00 | Models & Leisure (Railways) Premier Kits kit |
| ” | 1804 | | 00 | Wills Finecast kit |
| 0-6-0PT | 1854 | | 00 | Wills Finecast kit |
| ” | 2021 Class (pannier tank) | | 00 | Nu-Cast kit |
| 0-6-0ST | 2021 Class (saddle tank) | | 00 | Nu-Cast kit |
| 0-6-0PT | 27XX Class | | 0 | CCW kit |
| ” | 2721 Class | | 00 | Hornby Railways ready-to-run model |
| 0-6-0ST | 1361 Class | (P) | 00 | K's kit |
| | | | 0 | Raven Scale Models kit or ready-to-run model |
| 0-6-0PT | 1366 Class | (P) | N | Beaver Products Co body kit |
| | | | 00 | DJH Kits Ltd kit |
| ” | 15XX Class | (P) | 00 | K's kit |
| ” | 16XX Class | (P) | 00 | Nu-Cast kit |
| ” | 54XX Class Auto | | 00 | Nu-Cast kit |
| ” | 57XX Class | (P) | TT-3 | GEM kit |
| | | | 00 | K's kit |
| | | | 00 | Jamieson kit |
| | | | 00 | Mainline Railways ready-to-run model |
| | | | 0 | Charles Covey 'Firmco' kit |
| ” | 64XX Class Auto | (P) | 00 | Nu-Cast kit |
| ” | 74XX Class | | 00 | Nu-Cast kit |
| ” | 8750 Class | (P) | N | Cav'N'dish body kit |
| | | | 00 | Hornby Railways ready-to-run model |
| | | | 00 | K's kit |
| ” | 97XX Class Condenser | | N | Cav'N'dish kit |
| | | | 00 | K's 'Bodyline' kit |
| ” | 94XX Class | (P) | N | Graham Farish ready-to-run model |
| | | | N | Lima ready-to-run model |
| | | | TT-3 | A.B.S. Models, Beaver Products Co. body kit |
| | | | 00 | Lima ready-to-run model |
| | | | 00 | Wills Finecast kit |
| 0-6-0T | Alexandra Docks Nos 666, 667 | | 00 | Centre Models kit |
| 2-4-2T | 36XX Class | | 00 | Craftsman kit |
| 0-4-2T | 48XX later 14XX Class | (P) | N | Langley Miniature Models kit (with Autocoach) |
| | | | 00 | K's kit |
| | | | 00 | Airfix ready-to-run model |
| | | | 0 | CCW kit |
| ” | 517 Class | | 00 | Mallard Models kit |
| | | | 00 | Models & Leisure (Railways) Premier Kits kit |
| 2-4-0T | 'Metro' tank | | 00 | Wills Finecast kit |
| ” | No 1196 (Cambrian Rlys) | | 00 | GEM kit |
| 0-4-0T | 1101 Class | | N | Cav'N'dish kit |
| ” | No 101 | | 00 | Hornby (Railways) ready-to-run model |
| 0-4-0ST | Taff Vale Rly 'S' Class | | 00 | K's kit |
| Diesel Railcar | | (P) | N | Langley Miniature Models kit |
| | | | 00 | Lima ready-to-run model |
| | | | 00 | Anbrico cast-metal kit |
| | | | 00 | K's kit |
| | | | 00 | MTK Ltd kit |
| Diesel Railcar 'Express Parcels' | | | N | Beaver Products kit |
| | | | 00 | Lima ready-to-run model |
| | | | 00 | MTK Ltd kit |
| Diesel Railcar (Twin) | | | N | Langley Miniature Models kit |
| | | | 00 | MTK Ltd kit |
| Steam Railmotor | | | 00 | Mallard Models etched brass kit |
| | | | 00 | Nui-Cast kit |
| | | | 0 | Mallard Models etched brass kit |
| A1A-A1A | Brown Boveri Gas Turbine No 1800 | | N | Langley Miniature Models body kit |
| | | | 00 | MTK Ltd kit |
| Co-Co Metrovick Gas Turbine No 18100 | | | 00 | Q Kits fibreglass body shell kit |

**London Midland & Scottish Railway classes**

| | | | | |
|---|---|---|---|---|
| 4-6-2 | 'Princess' Class | (P) | N | D & M body kit |
| | | | 00 | K's kit |
| | | | 00 | Bristol Models kit |
| ” | 'Coronation' Class | (P) | N | Langley Miniature Models body kit |
| | | | 00 | Wrenn ready-to-run model |
| | | | 00 | Hornby Railways ready-to-run model |
| ” | 'Coronation' Class Streamlined | | N | Langley Miniature Models body kit |
| | | | 00 | Hornby Railways ready-to-run model, no longer available |
| | | | 00 | K's kit |

| | | | | |
|---|---|---|---|---|
| | | | 00 | Jamieson kit |
| 4-6-2 | Turbomotive | | 00 | K's kit |
| 4-6-0 | 'Royal Scot' Class | | TT-3 | GEM kit |
| | | | HO/00 | Rivarossi ready-to-run model |
| | | | 00 | Mainline Railways ready-to-run model |
| | | | 00 | Wrenn ready-to-run model |
| | | | 00 | Wills Finecast kit |
| ,, | 'Royal Scot' Class Rebuilt | (P) | N | D & M body kit |
| | | | 00 | Airfix ready-to-run model |
| | | | 00 | Mainline Railways ready-to-run model |
| | | | 00 | McGowan Models kit |
| | | | 00 | Jamieson kit |
| | | | 00 | Bristol Models kit |
| ,, | 'Patriot' Class | | N | D & M body kit |
| | | | 00 | Hornby Railways ready-to-run model |
| | | | 00 | Millholme Models Ltd kit |
| | | | 0 | Leinster Models kit |
| ,, | 'Patriot' Class Rebuilt | | 00 | Mainline Railways ready-to-run model |
| ,, | 'Jubilee' Class | (P) | N | Peco ready-to-run model |
| | | | 00 | Bristol Models kit |
| | | | 00 | Jamieson kit |
| | | | 00 | K's kit |
| | | | 00 | Mainline Railways ready-to-run model |
| | | | 00 | Mr D.R. Taylor Live steam ready-to-run model |
| | | | 0 | CCW kit |
| ,, | 'Jubilee' Class Rebuilt | | N | D & M body kit |
| | | | 00 | McGowan Models kit |
| ,, | Class 5 | (P) | N | Graham Farish ready-to-run model |
| | | | 00 | Hornby Railways ready-to-run model |
| | | | 00 | K's kit |
| | | | 00 | Jamieson kit |
| | | | 0 | CCW kit |
| ,, | LNWR 'Claughton' | | 00 | Jidenco etched brass kit |
| ,, | LNWR 'Prince of Wales' | | 00 | GEM kit |
| ,, | LYR 'Dreadnought' | | 00 | Millholme Models Goldcast kit |
| ,, | CR 'Cardean' Class 903 | | 00 | GEM kit |
| ,, | CR Pickersgill Class 60 | | 00 | DJH Kits Ltd kit |
| ,, | CR Class 55 'Oban Bogie' | | 00 | DJH Kits Ltd kit |
| ,, | HR Jones Goods | (P) | 00 | DJH Kits Ltd kit |
| ,, | G&SWR Manson Class 381 | | 00 | DJH Kits Ltd kit |
| 2-8-0 | Stanier 8F | (P) | N | GEM kit |
| | | | 00 | K's kit |
| | | | 00 | Wrenn ready-to-run model |
| ,, | S&DJR | (P) | N | GEM kit |
| | | | 00 | Nu-Cast kit |
| | | | 00 | DJH Models Ltd kit |
| ,, | Fowler 7F | | N | GEM kit |
| | | | 00 | Nu-Cast kit |
| ,, | LNWR | (P) | 00 | GEM kit |
| ,, | LYR 7F | | 00 | Nu-Cast kit |
| 0-8-0 | LYR 6F (small boiler) | | 00 | Nu-Cast kit |
| 2-6-0 | Stanier | (P) | 00 | K's kit |
| | | | 00 | Millholme Models Ltd kit |
| ,, | Hughes/Fowler 'Crab' | (P) | 00 | Wills Finecast kit |
| | | | 00 | Lima ready-to-run model |
| ,, | Ivatt 2F | (P) | N | Hornby Minitrix ready-to-run model |
| | | | 00 | Hornby Railways ready-to-run model |
| ,, | Ivatt 4F | (P) | 00 | Millholme Models Ltd kit |
| ,, | CR Class 34 | | 00 | DJH Kits Ltd kit |
| 4-4-2 | LYR Aspinall | | 00 | Millholme Models Ltd kit |
| 4-4-0 | Compound 4P Fowler | | N | Graham Farish ready-to-run model |
| | | | 00 | Nu-Cast kit |
| | | | 0 | CCW kit |
| ,, | Compound 4P Johnson/Deeley | (P) | 00 | Hornby Railways ready-to-run model |
| | | | 00 | GEM kit |
| ,, | 3P MR Class 999 | | 00 | GEM kit |
| 4-4-0 | 2P | | TT-3 | ABS Models & Beaver Products Co (Ex BEC) kit |
| | | | 00 | Millholme Models Ltd kit |
| | | | 0 | CCW kit |
| ,, | 2P MR Deeley Rebuilt Fowler | | 00 | Maygib etched brass kit |
| ,, | LNWR 'George V' | | 00 | GEM kit |
| ,, | LNWR 'Precursor' | | 00 | GEM kit |
| ,, | CR Pickersgill | | 00 | Nu-Cast kit |
| ,, | CR Rebuilt '66' | | 00 | DJH Kits Ltd kit |
| ,, | CR '721' or 'Dunalastair 1' Class | | 00 | DJH Kits Ltd kit |
| ,, | HR 'Small Ben' | | 00 | Nu-Cast kit |
| ,, | HR 'Loch' Class | | 00 | DJH Kits Ltd kit |

| | | | | |
|---|---|---|---|---|
| 2-4-0 | LNWR 'Precedent' | (P) | 00 | GEM kit |
| ,, | MR Johnson | | 00 | Ratio Plastic Models Ltd plastic kit |
| 0-4-2 | Liverpool & Manchester Rly 'Lion' | (P) | 00 | K's Milestone Series kit |
| 0-6-0 | MR Kirtley 2F | | 00 | K's kit |
| ,, | MR Johnson 2F | | 00 | K's kit |
| ,, | LNWR 'Special' DX Goods | | 00 | Models & Leisure (Railways) Premier Kits kit |
| ,, | LNWR 17" Coal | | 00 | Models & Leisure (Railways) Premier Kits kit |
| ,, | LNWR 'Cauliflower' | | 00 | GEM kit |
| ,, | Fowler 4F | (P) | N | Lima ready-to-run model |
| | | | N | D & M body kit |
| | | | N | GEM body kit |
| | | | TT-3 | ABS Models & Beaver Products Co (Ex BEC) kit |
| | | | HO | Lima ready-to-run model no longer available |
| | | | 00 | Airfix ready-to-run model |
| | | | 00 | Jaycraft moulded polyester resin body kit |
| | | | 00 | Wills Finecast kit |
| | | | 0 | Lima ready-to-run model |
| | | | 0 | CCW kit |
| ,, | Johnson 3F | | 00 | Maygib etched brass kit |
| | | | 0 | CCW kit |
| ,, | LYR 3F | (P) | 00 | MPD etched brass kit |
| ,, | CR Drummond 'Jumbo' | | 00 | DJH Kits Ltd kit |
| ,, | CR McIntosh 812 Std MT Class | (P) | 00 | DJH Kits Ltd kit |
| ,, | HR 'Barney' Class | | 00 | DJH Kits Ltd kit |
| 4-2-2 | MR 'Single' | (P) | 00 | K's kit |
| ,, | CR 'Single' | (P) | 00 | Tri-ang/Hornby ready-to-run model—no longer available |
| 2-2-2 | LNWR 'Problem' Class | | 00 | K's Milestone Series kit |
| ,, | LNWR 'Cornwall' | (P) | 00 | Models & Leisure (Railways) Premier Kits kit |
| 2-6-6-2T | Garratt | | 00 | K's kit |
| 0-8-2T | LNWR | | 00 | Jidenco etched brass kit |
| 4-6-4T | LYR | | 00 | Millholme Models Ltd kit |
| ,, | Furness Railway | | 00 | Millholme Models Ltd kit |
| 4-6-2T | CR Pickersgill | | 00 | DJH Kits Ltd kit |
| ,, | LNWR Bowen-Cooke | | 00 | Millholme Models Ltd kit |
| 2-6-4T | Fowler | | N | GEM kit |
| | | | 00 | Hornby Railways ready-to-run model |
| | | | 00 | GEM kit |
| | | | 00 | McGowan Models kit |
| ,, | Stanier 2 cylinder | | 0 | CCW kit |
| ,, | Stanier 3 cylinder | (P) | 00 | Wills Finecast kit |
| ,, | Fairburn | (P) | — | |
| 2-6-2T | Fowler 3P | | 00 | K's kit |
| ,, | Stanier 3P | | 00 | Nu-Cast kit |
| ,, | Ivatt 2P | (P) | N | Hornby Minitrix ready-to-run model |
| | | | 00 | K's kit |
| 0-6-4T | MR 'Flatiron' | | N | Beaver Products body kit |
| | | | 00 | Wills Finecast kit |
| ,, | HR '39' Class | | N | Beaver Products body kit |
| | | | 00 | Nu-Cast kit |
| 0-6-2T | LNWR Webb 'Coal Tank' | (P) | 00 | K's kit |
| | | | 0 | CCW kit |
| ,, | LNWR 'Watford' Tank | | 00 | GEM kit |
| ,, | LYR Kitson Type 5' 1" | | 00 | Nu-Cast kit |
| ,, | FR 'Cleator' Class L2 | | 00 | McGowan Models kit |
| 0-6-0T | Johnson 3F | | 00 | K's Bodyline kit |
| | | | 00 | Craftsman kit |
| ,, | Fowler 3F 'Jinty' | (P) | N | GEM body kit |
| | | | 00 | Hornby Railways ready-to-run model |
| | | | 00 | Nu-Cast kit |
| | | | 0 | HB Models Live Steam kit and ready-to-run model |
| | | | 0 | Model & Miniature Railways Live Steam kit |
| ,, | CR 3F McIntosh | | 00 | Wills Finecast kit |
| 0-6-0ST | LYR 2F Aspinal | (P) | N | GEM body kit |
| | | | 00 | Nu-Cast kit |
| ,, | LNWR 'Special Tank' | | 00 | GEM kit |
| 0-6-0T | 2F Dock Tank | (P) | N | Hornby Minitrix ready-to-run model |
| | | | 00 | K's kit |
| ,, | NLR 2F | (P) | 00 | Mallard Models etched brass kit |
| | | | 00 | GEM kit |
| ,, | MR Johnson 1F | | 00 | MPD etched brass kit |
| | | | 0 | MPD etched brass kit |
| ,, | LYR 1F | (P) | 00 | Jidenco etched brass kit |
| 4-4-2T | LNWR 'Precursor' | | 00 | GEM kit |
| | | | 0 | CCW kit |
| ,, | LTSR | (P) | 00 | Nu-Cast kit |
| 2-4-2T | LNWR Webb 4' 6" | | 00 | GEM kit |

| | | | | |
|---|---|---|---|---|
| 2-4-2T | LNWR Webb 5′ 6″ | | 00 | Models & Leisure (Railways) Premier Kits kit |
| ” | LYR Aspinall 2P | (P) | 00 | Nu-Cast kit |
| ” | LYR Hughes 3P | | 00 | Nu-Cast kit |
| 0-4-4T | MR Johnson 1P | | 00 | Craftsman kit |
| ” | CR McIntosh Class 439 | (P) | 00 | DJH Kits Ltd kit |
| ” | Stanier | | 00 | Jamieson kit |
| 2-4-0T | LNWR Webb 'Chopper' | | 00 | GEM kit |
| 0-4-2ST | LNWR Dock Tank | | 00 | Models & Leisure (Railways) Premier Kits kit |
| 0-4-0ST | Stanier 0F | | 00 | Jidenco etched brass kit |
| ” | MR Johnson 0F | | 00 | K's kit |
| ” | LYR 'Pug' | (P) | 00 | Airfix plastic kit |
| | | | 0 | Sevenscal kit |
| ” | CR Drummond | | 00 | Hornby Railways ready-to-run model |
| Steam Railmotor LNWR | | | 00 | Mallard Models etched brass kit |
| Steam Railmotor LYR No 10600 | | | N | Langley Miniature Models kit |
| | | | 00 | Jidenco etched brass kit |
| Co-Co Diesel-electric 10000 | | | 00 | MTK Ltd kit |
| | | | 00 | Q Kits fibreglass body shell kit |
| 0-6-0 | Jackshaft diesel shunter | | 00 | MTK Ltd kit |
| **London & North Eastern Railway classes** | | | | |
| 4-6-2 | A1 Gresley | | 00 | Hornby Railways ready-to-run model |
| ” | A1 Peppercorn | | 00 | DJH Kits Ltd kit |
| ” | A2 Peppercorn | (P) | 00 | DJH Kits Ltd kit |
| | | | 00 | Wills Finecast kit |
| ” | A2/1 Thompson | | 00 | Nu-Cast kit |
| ” | A2/2 Thompson | | 00 | Nu-Cast kit |
| | | | 00 | Millholme Models Ltd kit |
| ” | A2/3 Thompson | (P) | 00 | Millholme Models Ltd kit |
| | | | 00 | Nu-Cast kit |
| ” | A3 | (P) | N | Langley Miniature Models kit |
| | | | 00 | Liliput ready-to-run model |
| | | | 00 | Hornby Railways ready-to-run model |
| | | | 00 | Mr D.R. Taylor live steam ready-to-run model |
| | | | 00 | Wills Finecast kit |
| | | | 00 | Jamieson kit |
| ” | A4 | (P) | Z | Ellmar Products Ltd ready-to-run model, proposed |
| | | | N | Hornby Minitrix ready-to-run model |
| | | | N | Langley Miniature Models kit |
| | | | TT-3 | GEM kit |
| | | | 00 | Liliput ready-to-run model |
| | | | 00 | Wrenn ready-to-run model |
| | | | 00 | Hornby Railways ready-to-run model |
| | | | 00 | Mr D.R. Taylor live steam ready-to-run model |
| | | | 00 | Wills Finecast kit |
| 2-6-2 | V2 | (P) | 00 | Jamieson kit |
| | | | 00 | Bristol models kit |
| | | | 00 | Nu-Cast kit |
| | | | 00 | Proposed Lima ready-to-run model |
| | | | 0 | Charles Covey 'Firmco' kit |
| ” | V4 "Bantam Cock" | | 00 | East Coast Joint Models kit |
| 4-6-0 | B1 | (P) | N | Langley Miniature Models body kit |
| | | | 00 | Jamieson kit |
| | | | 00 | Nu-Cast kit |
| | | | 00 | Bristol Models kit |
| | | | 0 | Leinster Models kit |
| ” | B2 GCR 'Sir Sam Fay' | | 00 | K's kit |
| ” | B4 GCR 'Immingham' | | 00 | McGowan Models kit |
| | | | 0 | Leinster Models kit |
| ” | B5 GCR | | 00 | Millholme Models Ltd kit |
| ” | B12/3 GER | (P) | 00 | Hornby Railways ready-to-run model |
| ” | B16/1, B16/3 | | 00 | DJH Kits Ltd kits |
| ” | B16/2, B16/3 | | 00 | Nu-Cast kits |
| ” | B17/1, B17/4 | | 00 | McGowan kits |
| ” | B17/4 'Football' Class | | 00 | Hornby Railways ready-to-run model |
| 2-6-0 | K1 Thompson | (P) | 00 | Jaycraft moulded polyester resin body kit |
| ” | K2 GNR | | 00 | Nu-Cast kit |
| ” | K3 | | 00 | Wills Finecast kit |
| ” | K4 | (P) | — | |
| 4-4-2 | C1 GNR | (P) | 00 | WSM kit |
| | | | 00 | K's kit |
| ” | C4/C5 GCR | | 00 | McGowan Models kit |
| | | | 0 | Leinster Models kit |
| ” | C7 NER | | 00 | DJH Kits Ltd kit |
| ” | C10 NBR | | 00 | GEM kit |
| 4-4-0 | D2 GNR | | 00 | Nu-Cast kit |
| | | | 00 | Models & Leisure (Railways) Premier Kits kit |
| ” | D3 GNR | | 00 | Models & Leisure (Railways) Premier Kits kit |

| | | | | |
|---|---|---|---|---|
| 4-4-0 | D6 GCR | | 00 | DJH Kits Ltd kit |
| ” | D10 GCR 'Director' | | 00 | Jaycraft moulded polyester resin body kit |
| ” | D11 GCR 'Director' | (P) | 00 | ABS Models & Beaver Products Co (Ex BEC) kit |
| ” | D16 GER | | 00 | Mallard Models etched brass kit |
| | | | 00 | Jaycraft moulded polyester resin body kit |
| | | | 0 | Mallard Models etched brass kit |
| ” | D20 NER | | 00 | DJH Kits Ltd kit |
| ” | D21 NER | | 00 | GEM kit |
| ” | D29 NBR 'Scott' Class | | 00 | GEM kit |
| ” | D34 NBR 'Glen' Class | (P) | 00 | GEM kit |
| ” | D40 GNSR | (P) | 00 | Nu-Cast kit |
| ” | D49 'Hunt/Shire' Class | (P) | 00 | Hornby Railways ready-to-run model |
| | | | 00 | McGowan Models kit |
| | | | 00 | DKJ Kits Ltd kit |
| 2-4-0 | E4 GER | (P) | 00 | Nu-Cast kit |
| 4-2-2 | GNR 'Single' | (P) | 00 | Millholme Models kit |
| 2-8-2 | P2 | | 00 | K's kit |
| 2-8-0 | 02 GNR | | 00 | Bristol Models kit |
| ” | 02/2, 02/3 | | 00 | Nu-Cast kits |
| ” | 04 GCR | (P) | 00 | K's kit |
| | | | 0 | Leinster Models kit |
| ” | 07 WD 'Austerity' | | N | McGowan Models kit |
| | | | 00 | McGowan Models kit |
| | | | 00 | Bristol Models kit |
| 0-8-0 | Q1 GNR 'Long Tom' | | 00 | Nu-Cast kit |
| ” | Q4 GCR | | 00 | Millholme Models Ltd kit |
| ” | Q6 NER | (P) | 00 | Nu-Cast kit |
| ” | 7 NER | (P) | 00 | DJH Kits Ltd kit |
| 0-6-0 | J3 GNR | | 00 | K's kit |
| ” | J6 GNR | | 00 | Nu-Cast kit |
| ” | J9/J10 GCR | | 00 | DJH Kits Ltd kit |
| ” | J11 GCR | | N | Langley Miniature Models body kit |
| | | | TT-3 | ABS Models & Beaver Products Co (Ex BEC) kit |
| | | | 00 | ABS Models & Beaver Products Co (Ex BEC) kit |
| ” | J15 GER | (P) | 00 | Nu-Cast kit |
| ” | J17 GER | (P) | 00 | ABS Models &M Beaver Products Co (Ex BEC) kit |
| ” | J19 GER | | 00 | Jaycraft moulded polyester resin body kit |
| ” | J21 NER | (P) | 00 | Nu-Cast kit |
| ” | J26/J27 NER | (P) | 00 | Nu-Cast kit |
| ” | J36 NBR | (P) | 00 | GEM kit |
| ” | J37 NBR | | 00 | Ian Kirk N B Models kit |
| ” | J39 | | N | D & M Castings body kit |
| | | | 00 | Wills Finecast kit |
| | | | 0 | Charles Covey 'Firmco' kit |
| 4-6-2T | A5 GCR | | 00 | Craftsman kit |
| | | | 00 | Nu-Cast kit |
| ” | A8 NER | | 00 | DJH Kits Ltd kit |
| 2-6-4T | L1 | | N | Beaver Products body kit |
| | | | 00 | East Coast Joint Models kit |
| ” | L3 GCR | | N | Beaver Products body kit |
| | | | N | Langley Miniature Models body kit |
| 2-6-2T | V1/V3 | | 00 | McGowan Models kit |
| 0-8-4T | S1 GCR | | 00 | Millholme Models Ltd kit |
| 0-8-0T | Q1 GCR | | 00 | Millholme Models Ltd kit |
| 0-6-2T | N1 GNR | | 00 | WSM kit |
| ” | N2 GNR | (P) | N | Langley Miniature Models body kit |
| | | | 00 | Wrenn ready-to-run model |
| | | | 00 | Airfix ready-to-run model |
| | | | 00 | Nu-Cast kit |
| ” | N4/N5 GCR | | 00 | Millholme Models Ltd kit |
| | | | 00 | McGowan Models kit |
| ” | N7 GER | (P) | N | Langley Miniature Models body kit |
| | | | 00 | Wills Finecast kit |
| ” | N8/9/10 NER | | 00 | Nu-Cast kit |
| ” | N15 NBR | | 00 | Ian Kirk N B Models kit |
| 4-4-4T | H1 NER | | 00 | DJH Kits Ltd kit |
| 4-4-2T | C12 GNR | | 00 | Craftsman kit |
| | | | 00 | Wills Finecast kit |
| ” | C13 GCR | | 00 | Nu-Cast kit |
| ” | C16 NBR | | 00 | Nu-Cast kit |
| 0-4-4T | G5 NER | | 00 | Nu-Cast kit |
| 2-4-2T | F1 GCR | | 00 | Nu-Cast kit |
| ” | F4/F5 GER | | 00 | Nu-Cast kit |
| ” | F8 GER | | 00 | Centre Models kit |
| 0-6-0T | J50 | | TT-3 | ABS Models & Beaver Products Co (Ex Bec) kit |
| | | | 00 | Lima ready-to-run model |
| | | | 00 | K's Bodyline kit |

| | | | | | |
|---|---|---|---|---|---|
| | | | | 0 | CCW kit |
| 0-6-0ST | J52 GNR | | (P) | N | Beaver Products body kit |
| | | | | N | D & M body kit |
| | | | | 00 | Hornby Railways ready-to-run model |
| 0-6-0T | J63 GER | | | N | Beaver Products body kit |
| " | J69 GER | | (P) | N | Graham Farish ready-to-run model |
| | | | | 00 | Wills Finecast kit |
| " | J70 GER Tram Engine | | | 00 | K's kit |
| " | J72 NER | | (P) | TT-3 | ABS Models & Beaver Products Co (Ex Bec) kit |
| | | | | 00 | Mainline ready-to-run model |
| | | | | 00 | K's kit |
| " | J83 NBR | | | 00 | GEM kit |
| | | | | 00 | Hornby Railways ready-to-run model withdrawn 1980 |
| " | J88 NBR | | | 00 | Ian Kirk N B Models kit |
| 0-6-0ST | J94 ex-MOS | | (P) | N | Fleetline kit |
| | | | | 00 | Centre Models kit |
| | | | | 00 | Airfix plastic kit |
| | | | | 00 | Ian Kirk N B Models kit |
| 0-4-0T | Y1/Y3 Sentinel | | (P) | 00 | Nu-Cast kit |
| 0-4-0ST | Y5 GER 'Coffeepot' | | (P) | 00 | Nu-Cast kit |
| 0-4-0T | Y7 NER | | (P) | 00 | Nu-Cast kit |
| " | Y8 NER | | | 00 | K's kit |
| " | Sentinel Cammell Steam Railcar | | | 00 | Nu-Cast kit |

**Southern Railway classes**

| | | | | | |
|---|---|---|---|---|---|
| 4-6-2 | 'Merchant Navy' Class | | | N | Graham Farish ready-to-run model |
| | | | | 00 | Millholme Models kit |
| " | 'Merchant Navy' Class rebuilt | | (P) | N | Langley Miniature Models kit |
| " | 'West Country'/ 'Battle of Britain' Classes | | (P) | N | Graham Farish ready-to-run model |
| | | | | 00 | Hornby Railways ready-to-run model |
| | | | | 00 | Mr D.R. Taylor live steam ready-to-run model |
| | | | | 00 | Airfix plastic kit |
| | | | | 00 | Bristol Models kit |
| | | | | 00 | Kemilway chassis kit |
| | | | | 00 | MTK Ltd kit |
| | | | | 00 | Ravenscale etched brass kit |
| " | 'West Country'/ 'Battle of Britain' Classes rebuilt | | (P) | 00 | Wrenn ready-to-run model |
| 4-6-0 | 'Lord Nelson' Class | | (P) | 00 | Craftsman Models kit |
| " | 'King Arthur' Class | | (P) | 00 | Wills Finecast kit |
| | | | | 00 | Hornby Railways ready-to-run model —withdrawn 1979 |
| | | | | 0 | Charles Covey 'Firmco' kit |
| " | N15X 'Remembrance' | | | 00 | Nu-Cast kit |
| " | H15 LSWR | | | 00 | DJH Kits Ltd kit |
| " | S15 | | (P) | N | Langley Miniature Models kit |
| | | | | 00 | DJH Kits Ltd kit |
| 2-6-0 | N, N1, U, U1 | N & U | (P) | 00 | Wills Finecast kit |
| " | K LBSCR | | | 00 | Mallard Models etched brass kit |
| | | | | 00 | K's kit |
| 4-4-0 | 'Schools' Class | | (P) | 00 | Airfix plastic kit |
| | | | | 00 | Hornby Railways ready-to-run model |
| | | | | 00 | Wills Finecast kit |
| | | | | 0 | Charles Covey 'Firmco' kit |
| " | L1 | | | 00 | Tri-ang ready-to-run model—no longer available |
| " | T9 LSWR | | (P) | 00 | Wills Finecast kit |
| | | | | 0 | Charles Covey 'Firmco' kit |
| " | T3 LSWR | | | 00 | Nu-Cast kit |
| " | K10/L11 LSWR | | | — | |
| " | D SE&CR | | (P) | 00 | Wills Finecast kit |
| " | D1/E1 SE&CR | | | 00 | DJH Kits Ltd kit |
| " | D15 LSWR | | | 00 | ABS Models & Beaver Products (Ex Bec) kit |
| " | G SE&CR | | | 00 | Nu-Cast kit |
| 2-4-0 | LSWR 'Falcon' Class | | | 00 | K's Milestone Series kit |
| 0-4-2 | A12 LSWR | | | 00 | Nu-Cast kit |
| " | B1 LB&SCR 'Gladstone' | | (P) | 00 | GEM kit |
| 0-6-0 | Q | | (P) | 00 | Wills Finecast kit |
| | | | | 00 | Jaycraft moulded polyester resin body kit |
| " | Q1 | | (P) | N | Langley Miniature Models body kit |
| | | | | TT-3 | ABS Models & Beaver Products (Ex Bec) kit |
| | | | | 00 | K's kit |

| | | | | |
|---|---|---|---|---|
| 0-6-0 | 700 LSWR | | 00 | ABS Models & Beaver Products (Ex Bec) kit |
| ” | 0395 LSWR | | 00 | DJH Kits Ltd kit withdrawn 1981 |
| ” | C SE&CR | (P) | 00 | Wills Finecast kit |
| ” | 01 SE&CR | (P) | — | |
| ” | C2X LB&SCR | | 00 | Nu-Cast kit |
| 4-6-4T | LB&SCR 'Remembrance' | | 00 | Langley Miniature Models kit |
| 4-4-2T | 13 LB&SCR | | 00 | Wills Finecast kit |
| ” | 0415 LSWR | (P) | 00 | K's kit |
| 0-8-0T | Z | | N | GEM kit |
| | | | 00 | Millholme Models Ltd kit |
| 0-6-2T | E4 LB&SCR | (P) | N | Langley Miniature Models body kit |
| | | | 00 | Weald Models kit |
| ” | E5 LB&SCR | | 00 | Wills Finecast kit |
| 0-6-0T | A1 LB&SCR 'Terrier' | (P) | 00 | K's kit |
| | | | 0 | Ravenscale etched brass kit |
| ” | E1 LB&SCR | (P) | 00 | Wills Finecast kit |
| ” | E2 LB&SCR | | N | Langley Miniature Models body kit |
| | | | TT-3 | ABS Models & Beaver Products Co (Ex Bec) kit |
| | | | 00 | Hornby Railways ready-to-run model |
| | | | 00 | Wills Finecast kit |
| ” | G6 LSWR | | TT-3 | ABS Models & Beaver Products Co (Ex Bec) kit |
| | | | 00 | Wills Finecast kit |
| | | | 0 | MSC Models brass body kit |
| ” | P SE&CR | (P) | 00 | Wills Finecast kit |
| ” | R1 SE&CR | | 00 | Wrenn ready-to-run model |
| ” | USA | (P) | HO | Hornby-Acho ready-to-run model—no longer available |
| 0-4-4T | H SE&CR | (P) | 00 | Wills Finecast kit |
| ” | M7 LSWR | (P) | 00 | Hornby Railways ready-to-run model—no longer available |
| | | | 00 | Wills Finecast kit |
| | | | 0 | CCW kit |
| ” | 02 LSWR | (P) | 00 | Wills Finecast kit |
| | | | 0 | MSC Models brass body kit |
| ” | T1 LSWR | | — | |
| 2-4-0T | 0298 LSWR | (P) | 00 | Proposed Weald Models kit |
| 0-4-2T | D1 LB&SCR | | 00 | Wills Finecast kit |
| 0-4-0T | B4 LSWR | (P) | N | Peco-Wills kit |
| | | | 00 | McGowan Models kit |
| | | | 0 | Vulcan Model Engineering etched brass kit |
| Co-Co CC1/CC2 Electric | | | 00 | MTK Ltd kit |
| Co-Co Diesel-electric Nos 10201/2/3 | | | 00 | MTK Ltd kit |
| 5-BEL | 'Brighton Belle' EMU | (P) | 00 | Wrenn ready-to-run model |
| **Miscellaneous Steam Locomotives** | | | | |
| 2-8-0 | USA Class S160 | (P) | — | |
| 0-6-2T | Metropolitan Rly 'F' Class | | 00 | GS Models kit |
| 4-4-0T | Metropolitan Rly Beyer Peacock | (P) | 00 | K's Milestone Series kit |
| 0-6-0T | Kerr Stuart 'Victory' | | 00 | Centre Models kit |
| 0-6-0ST | Hunslett Standard 16″ | | 00 | Centre Models kit |
| 0-4-0ST | Robert Stephenson & Hawthorns | | 00 | Centre Models kit |
| ” | Avonside | | 00 | Centre Models kit |
| **British Railways Standard classes** | | | | |
| **STEAM** | | | | |
| 4-6-2 | 'Britannia' | (P) | N | Hornby Minitrix ready-to-run model |
| | | | 00 | Hornby Railways ready-to-run model |
| ” | 'Clan' | | 00 | MTK Ltd kit |
| 4-6-0 | Class 5 | (P) | TT-3 | ABS Models & Beaver Products Co (Ex Bec) kit |
| | | | 00 | DJH Kits Ltd kit |
| ” | Class 4 | (P) | N | Langley Miniature Models body kit |
| | | | 00 | Mainline Railways ready-to-run model |
| 2-10-0 | Class 9 | (P) | N | Hornby Minitrix ready-to-run model |
| | | | 00 | Airfix plastic kit |
| | | | 00 | Hornby Railways ready-to-run model |
| 2-6-0 | Class 4 | (P) | 00 | Airfix plastic kit |
| ” | Class 3 | | — | |
| ” | Class 2 | (P) | N | Hornby Minitrix ready-to-run model |
| | | | 00 | Hornby Railways ready-to-run model |
| 2-6-4T | Class 4 | (P) | TT-3 | ABS Models & Beaver Products Co (Ex Bec) kit |
| | | | 00 | Wrenn ready-to-run model |
| 2-6-2T | Class 3 | | 00 | Tri-ang/Hornby ready-to-run model—no longer available |
| | | | 00 | MTK Ltd kit |
| | | | 00 | Kemilway kit |
| ” | Class 2 | (P) | N | Hornby Minitrix ready-to-run model |
| | | | 00 | K's kit |
| 2-10-0 | Austerity ex-MOS | (P) | N | McGowan Models kit |

| | | | | |
|---|---|---|---|---|
| | | | 00 | Bristol Models kit |
| 2-8-0 | Austerity ex-MOS | (P) | N | McGowan Models kit |
| | | | 00 | Bristol Models kit |
| | | | 00 | McGowan Models kit |
| 0-6-0T | Austerity ex-MOS | (P) | 00 | Airfix plastic kit—as for LNER J94 |
| **DIESEL** | | | | |
| Type 5 | 'Deltic' Class 55 | | Z | Ellmar Products Ltd ready-to-run model |
| | | | N | Lima ready-to-run model |
| | | | 00 | Lima ready-to-run model |
| | | | 00 | MTK Ltd kit |
| | | | 00 | Q Kits fibreglass body shell kit |
| " | Class 56 | | N | Langley Miniature Models body kit |
| | | | 00 | Q Kits fibreglass body shell kit |
| | | | 00 | MTK Ltd kit |
| Type 4 | English Electric Class 40 | | 00 | Jouef ready-to-run model |
| | | | 00 | MTK Ltd kit |
| | | | 00 | Q Kits fibreglass body shell kit |
| " | 'Peak' Classes 45/46 | | N | P&D Marsh, Monmouth Models kit |
| | | | 00 | Mainline Railways ready-to-run model |
| | | | 00 | MTK Ltd kit |
| | | | 00 | Q Kits fibreglass body shell kit |
| " | Brush Class 47 | | Z | Ellmar Products Ltd ready-to-run model |
| | | | N | Graham Farish ready-to-run model |
| | | | N | P&D Marsh kit |
| | | | TT-3 | ABS Models & Beaver Products Co (Ex Bec) kit |
| | | | 00 | Hornby Railways ready-to-run model |
| | | | 00 | MTK Ltd kit |
| " | English Electric Class 50 | | N | Anbrico kit |
| | | | 00 | Lima ready-to-run model |
| | | | 00 | MTK Ltd kit |
| | | | 00 | Jidenco etched-brass body kit |
| | | | 00 | Q Kits fibreglass body shell kit |
| " | 'Western' Class 52 | (P) | N | Lima ready-to-run model |
| | | | N | Beaver Products Co kit |
| | | | N | Fleetline body kit |
| | | | N | MTK Ltd kit |
| | | | 00 | Hornby Railways ready-to-run model |
| | | | 00 | Lima ready-to-run model |
| | | | 00 | Liliput ready-to-run model |
| | | | 00 | MTK Ltd kit |
| | | | 00 | Q Kits fibreglass body shell kit |
| " | 'Warship' Class 42 | (P) | N | Hornby Minitrix ready-to-run model |
| | | | HO | Fleischman ready-to-run model |
| | | | 00 | Lima ready-to-run model |
| | | | 00 | Mainline Railways ready-to-run model |
| | | | 00 | MTK Ltd kit |
| | | | 00 | Q Kits fibreglass body shell kit |
| " | A1A-A1A D600 North British 'Warship' | | 00 | MTK Ltd kit |
| " | D0260 'Lion' BRC&W Co/Sulzer | | 00 | Q Kits fibreglass body shell kit |
| " | D0280 'Falcon' Brush-Maybach | | 00 | Q Kits fibreglass body shell kit |
| " | DP2 English Electric | | 00 | Q Kits fibreglass body shell kit |
| " | HS 4000 'Kestrel' BrushıSulzer | | 00 | Q Kits fibreglass body shell kit |
| Type 3 | 'Hymek' Class 35 | (P) | N | Peco kit |
| | | | 00 | Hornby Railways ready-to-run model |
| | | | 0 | Novo Toys Ltd ready-to-run model |
| " | English Electric Class 37 | | N | Langley Miniature Models kit |
| | | | 00 | Hornby Railways ready-to-run model |
| " | Birmingham RC&W Class 33 | | 00 | Lima ready-to-run model |
| | | | 00 | MTK Ltd kit |
| | | | 0 | Lima ready-to-run model |
| Type 2 | North British Class 22 | | 00 | MTK Ltd kit |
| " | BR Derby Class 24 | (P) | 00 | MTK Ltd kit |
| " | BR Derby Class 25 | | N | Langley Miniature Models kit |
| | | | 00 | Hornby Railways ready-to-run model |
| | | | 00 | MTK Ltd kit |
| " | Birmingham RC&W Classes 26/27 | | N | Hornby Minitrix ready-to-run model |
| | | | 00 | MTK Ltd kit |
| " | North British Class 29 | | N | Langley Miniature Models kit |
| | | | 00 | Hornby Railways ready-to-run model |
| " | Brush A1A-A1A Class 31 | (P) | N | Lima ready-to-run model |
| | | | 00 | Hornby Railways ready-to-run model—withdrawn |
| | | | 00 | Airfix ready-to-run model |
| " | Metro-Vick Co-Bo | | 00 | Hornby Dublo ready-to-run model—no longer available |
| Type 1 | Clayton Class 17 | | 00 | MTK Ltd kit |

| | | | | |
|---|---|---|---|---|
| Type 1 | English Electric Class 20 | | 00 | Wrenn ready-to-run model |
| | | | 00 | MTK Ltd kit |
| Shunter | 350 hp Class 08 | | N | Graham Farish ready-to-run model |
| | | | 00 | Wrenn ready-to-run model |
| | | | 00 | MTK Ltd kit |
| ,, | 350 hp Class 09 | | 00 | Lima ready-to-run model |
| | | | 00 | MTK Ltd kit |
| ,, | Ruston & Hornsby Class 07 | | 00 | MTK Ltd kit |
| ,, | North British 040/060 | | 00 | MTK Ltd kit |
| ,, | 204 hp Drewry Class 03 and 04 | (P) | N | Beaver Products body kit |
| | | | 00 | Airfix plastic kit—no longer available |
| | | | 00 | MTK Ltd kit |
| DMU | Class 117/2 Pressed Steel Co. | | 00 | Lima ready-to-run model |
| ,, | Class 124 Trans-Pennine 6-car | | 00 | Liliput ready-to-run model |
| ,, | Class 253/254 HS 1 High Speed Train | | Z | Ellmar Products Ltd ready-to-run model |
| | | | N | ECM Kit (power car) |
| | | | N | MTK Ltd kit |
| | | | 00 | Hornby Railways ready-to-run model |
| 4-wheel Railcar AC Cars Ltd | | (P) | 00 | Anbrico kit |
| **ELECTRIC** | | | | |
| EM2 | Co-Co | | 00 | Tri-ang/Hornby ready-to-run model—no longer available |
| Class 81 | Bo-Bo | | N | Lima ready-to-run model |
| Class 83 | Bo-Bo | | 00 | Liliput ready-to-run model |
| Class 85 | Bo-Bo | | 00 | MTK Ltd kit |
| Class 86 | Bo-Bo | | 00 | Hornby Railways ready-to-run model |
| | | | 00 | MTK Ltd kit |
| Class 87 | Bo-Bo | | Z | Ellmar Products Ltd ready-to-run model |
| | | | 00 | Lima ready-to-run model |
| Class 71 | Bo-Bo | (P) | 00 | MTK Ltd kit |
| Classes 73 & 74 Electro-diesel | | | 00 | MTK Ltd kit |
| Class 370 | APT Advanced Passenger Train | | 00 | Hornby Railways ready-to-run model |

# Index